SEA CHARTS of the EARLY EXPLORERS
13th to 17th Century

Michel Mollat du Jourdin and Monique de La Roncière
with
Marie-Madeleine Azard, Isabelle Raynaud-Nguyen
and
Marie-Antoinette Vannereau

Translated by L. le R. Dethan

THAMES AND HUDSON

This book has been written by a team of experts:

The Introduction is by Michel Mollat du Jourdin, member of the Institute and the Académie de Marine, emeritus professor at the Sorbonne.

The Notes on the Plates have been compiled by
Monique de La Roncière, honorary curator at the Bibliothèque Nationale (1, 13–14, 20–26, 28–38, 41, 45–46, 52–55, 59, 63, 70, 72–73, 75, 77, 79, 81–82, 85–87, 90, 93–96, 98–100);
Marie-Madeleine Azard, PhD (39–40, 42–44, 47–51, 58, 60–61, 67, 69, 71, 78, 80, 84, 92, 97);
Isabelle Raynaud-Nguyen, agrégée (2–12, 15–19, 27, 56–57, 62, 64–66, 68, 74, 76, 83, 89);
Marie-Antoinette Vannereau, honorary curator at the Bibliothèque Nationale (88, 91).

Isabelle Raynaud-Nguyen wrote the glossary.

Translated from the French
Les Portulans: Cartes marines du XIIIe *au XVII*^{e} *siècle*

© 1984 Office du Livre S.A., Fribourg
English translation © 1984 Office du Livre S.A., Fribourg
First published in the USA in 1984 by Thames and Hudson Inc.,
500 Fifth Avenue, New York, New York 10110

Library of Congress Catalog Card Number 84-50006

All Rights Reserved. No part of this publication may be reproduced or transmitted in any form or by any means, electronic or mechanical, including photocopy, recording or any other information storage and retrieval system, without permission in writing from the publisher.

Printed and bound in Switzerland

Contents

Introduction		7
The Image of the World Before the Portolan Charts		8
A New Image of the World: The Portolan Chart		11
The Ptolemaic 'Shock-Wave' and the Cartography of the Age of Discovery		20
Precedence of Mediterranean Cartographic Schools		23
The Western Schools		27
The Portolan Chart and Its Public		33
Plates		37
Commentaries		197
No. 1	*'Carte pisane'* (end of the 13th century)	198
No. 2–4	*Atlas* by Petrus Vesconte (1313)	198
No. 5–6	*Atlas* by Petrus Vesconte (ca. 1321)	199
No. 7	*From the Baltic Sea to the Red Sea* by Angelino Dulcert (1339)	201
No. 8	*Catalan Atlas* (ca. 1375)	202
No. 9	*Mediterranean Sea* by Guillelmus Soleri (ca. 1385)	202
No. 10	*Venetian Atlas* (end of the 14th century)	203
No. 11	*The Mediterranean Sea and the Black Sea* by Albertino de Virga (1409)	204
No. 12	*From the Baltic Sea to the Niger* by Mecia de Viladestes (1413)	205
No. 13–14	*'Liber insularum Archipelagi'* by Cristoforo Buondelmonte (1420)	206
No. 15	*The Mediterranean* by Jacobus de Giroldis (1422)	206
No. 16	*The Mediterranean Sea and the Black Sea* by Gabriel de Vallsecha (1447)	207
No. 17	*Atlantic Ocean, Mediterranean Sea, Black Sea* by Petrus Roselli (1462)	208
No. 18–19	*Atlas* by Grazioso Benincasa (1467)	209
No. 20	*Globe* by Martin Behaim (1492 [1847])	210
No. 21	*'Christopher Columbus Chart'* (1492?)	211
No. 22	*Mappa Mundi* by Juan de la Cosa (1500)	212
No. 23	*Coast of Greece* (16th century)	213
No. 24	*Aegean Sea* (16th century)	214
No. 25	*The 'Cantino' Planisphere* (1502)	214
No. 26	*Planisphere* by Nicolaus de Caverio (ca. 1505)	216
No. 27	*The Dijon Portolan Chart* (ca. 1510)	217
No. 28	*Atlantic Chart* by Piri Re'īs (1513)	218
No. 29–34	*Miller Atlas* (ca. 1519)	219
No. 35–36	*'Kitab-i-bahriye'* by Piri Re'īs (1525–1526)	222
No. 37	*Planisphere* by Diogo Ribeiro (1529)	223
No. 38	*Atlantic Chart* by Gaspar Viegas (1534)	224
No. 39–40	*'Boke of Idrography'* by Jean Rotz (1542)	226
No. 41	*Mappa Mundi* by Battista Agnese (1543)	227
No. 42	*Planisphere* by Guillaume Brouscon (1543)	228
No. 43–44	*Pilot's Manual for the Use of Breton Sailors* by Guillaume Brouscon (1548)	228
No. 45	*Atlantic Chart* (after 1549)	230
No. 46	*Atlantic Ocean Chart* by Diego Gutierrez (1550)	231
No. 47	*Planisphere* by Pierre Desceliers (1550)	232
No. 48–51	*'Universal Cosmography'* by Guillaume Le Testu (1556)	232
No. 52–54	*Atlas* by Diogo Homem (1559)	234

No.	55	*Universa ac navigabilis totius terrarum orbis descriptio . . .* by Andreas Homem (1559)	235
No.	56	*Atlantic and Mediterranean* by Giacomo de Maggiolo (1563)	236
No.	57	*Mediterranean Basin* by Georgio Sideri, called Calapoda (1565)	237
No.	58	*Planisphere* by Nicolas Desliens (1566)	238
No.	59	*Atlas* by Fernão Vaz Dourado (1571)	239
No.	60	*Brazil* by Jacques de Vau de Claye (1579)	240
No.	61	*Rio de Janeiro Bay* by Jacques de Vau de Claye (1579)	240
No.	62	*Atlas* by Joan Martines (1583)	241
No.	63	*Portuguese Planisphere* (ca. 1585)	242
No.	64–65	*Atlas* by Joan Martines (1587)	242
No.	66	*The Mediterranean* by Nicolaos Vourdopolos (early 17th century)	244
No.	67	*Atlantic Ocean* by Guillaume Levasseur (1601)	244
No.	68	*Atlantic, Mediterranean Sea, Black Sea* by Francesco Oliva (1603)	246
No.	69	*Description of New France* by Sieur de Champlain (1607)	247
No.	70	*Atlantic Ocean (N.E.), Mediterranean Sea and Western Black Sea* by Harmen and Marten Jansz (ca. 1610)	248
No.	71	*Atlantic Ocean* by Pierre de Vaulx (1613)	249
No.	72	*Japanese Chart of the Indian Ocean* (ca. 1613)	249
No.	73	*Atlantic Chart* by Domingos Sanches (1618)	250
No.	74	*Atlas of the Mediterranean* by Charlat Ambrosin (1620)	251
No.	75	*The Pacific* by Hessel Gerritsz (1622)	252
No.	76	*Aegean Sea* by Alvise Gramolin (1624)	253
No.	77	*Japanese Chart of the Nipponese Archipelago* (ca. 1625)	254
No.	78	*Hydrographic Description of France* by Jean Guérard (1627)	254
No.	79	*Atlantic Ocean (North)* by Hessel Gerritsz (ca. 1628)	255
No.	80	*Northern Ocean* by Jean Guérard (1628)	256
No.	81–82	*The 'Duchess de Berry' Atlas* (ca. 1628)	257
No.	83	*Provençal Atlas of the Mediterranean* by Augustin Roussin (1633)	258
No.	84	*Universal Hydrographic Chart* by Jean Guérard (1634)	259
No.	85	*Indian Ocean* by João Teixeira Albernas I (1649)	259
No.	86	*Pacific Ocean* by João Teixeira Albernas I (1649)	260
No.	87	*Indian Ocean* by Pieter Goos (1660)	261
No.	88	*Macassar Roadstead* by Fred Woldemar (1660)	262
No.	89	*Mediterranean* by François Ollive (1662)	263
No.	90	*Indian Ocean* by John Burston (1665)	264
No.	91	*North Atlantic* by Denis de Rotis (1674)	265
No.	92	*Isle of Bréhat* by Pierre Collin (1666)	266
No.	93	*Hudson Strait and Davis Strait* (before 1677)	267
No.	94	*Empire of Monomotapa* by João Teixeira Albernas II (1677)	268
No.	95	*Mocha* by Augustine Fitzhugh (1683)	268
No.	96	*Northwest Coast of Java* by Joan Blaeu (1688)	269
No.	97	*Chart of the Isle of Newfoundland* by Pierre Detcheverry (1689)	270
No.	98	*The Banda Islands* (end of the 17th century)	270
No.	99	*Persian Gulf* by John Thornton (1699)	271
No.	100	*Amoy Bay* by John Thornton (1699)	272

Appendices 275
  Glossary 276
  Genealogy of the Hydrographic Schools 279
  Classification of the Portolan Charts by Hydrographic Schools 279
  Acknowledgments 280
  Bibliography 281
  Photo Credits 290
  Index of Proper Names 291
  Geographic Index 294

Introduction

The invention of the sea charts known as portolan charts in the late thirteenth century came about in a period of dramatic change in western man's perception of his world. The word portolan derives from the Italian *portolano* which referred to written descriptions of coasts and their landmarks. Portolan charts were realistic depictions of coastlines and their ports, drawn by navigators from their own experience and for their own guidance. The empirical and practical nature of the portolan charts was in marked contrast with the religious purpose of mediaeval mappae mundi, which had been based on theological beliefs more than on scientific observation.

The Image of the World Before the Portolan Charts

The mediaeval way of investigating the physical world, up to the close of the thirteenth century, was to speculate on the role of the habitable surface of the earth—the *oikoumenê*— within God's scheme for the universe. Mediaeval 'geography' reduced the more objective findings of the Graeco-Roman heritage, transmitted by the compilers of late antiquity such as Strabo, Pomponius Mela, Macrobius and Orosius, to a mainly bookish tradition. The notion of the sphericity of the earth known to Anaximander (sixth century B.C.), a pupil of Thales, and the calculation of its circumference by Eratosthenes (end of the third, beginning of the second century) seem to have been forgotten. On the other hand, Herodotus' concept of the existence of a peripheral ocean around the terrestrial disc persisted for a long time. Unlike the Muslim geographers, until the fifteenth century the West was only acquainted with a part of the works of Ptolemy; and of the geographical information derived from the expedition of Alexander the Great and the Asiatic and African contacts of the Hellenic world there remained only a tangle of legends, which confused genuine observations. With a few exceptions, the attention of the Church Fathers and early mediaeval authors was directed more towards natural phenomena than towards objective geographical description. Credit is due to Isidore of Seville in the seventh century for codifying the knowledge of his day, and in England to the Venerable Bede in the eighth century for his careful observation. Later, at the end of the eleventh century, Adam canon under Archbishop Adalbert of Bremen, contributed first-hand information on northern Europe.

The essence of what could be called the 'backcloth' of mediaeval geography before the thirteenth century dated from the reorganization of the Roman Empire under Diocletian (284-305). The clerical mind explained the Creator's organization of the world by giving a Christian interpretation to the learning of antiquity, complemented by biblical elements. If, for example, they wished to depict the world as created by God and maintained by His providence, then the image would naturally assume the perfect and infinite form of a circle, a reflection of divine eternity and perfection *(Terrarum Orbis)*, whence the designation of this type of universal map by its initials 'T. O'. Within the circle formed by the letter O, the T expresses the tripartition of the world, which corresponds to the Trinity as well as to the ancient division of the *oikoumenê* (Europe, Asia and Africa) and to the population of the earth by the descendents of the three sons of Noah: Shem, Ham and Japheth, described in Genesis (IX:19). The eschatalogical harmony of this synthesis is completed by the assimilation of the T to the *tau* of the redemptive cross of Christ and by the arrangement of the inhabited world around a theological centre (Jerusalem), chosen as such from the eleventh century. Predestined to be the site of the spreading of the Gospel, the Mediterranean serves as the axis of the whole structure. Everything stems from there, in a convergence of the knowledge of antiquity and biblical traditions: the Garden of Eden was sited

Mappa Mundi of the Beatus Type
Paris, B.N.

This is without doubt the best of the ten mappae mundi deriving from the archetype by the Spanish monk Beatus de Liébana (eighth century); it was executed at the Abbey of Saint-Sever in the middle of the eleventh century. Visible here is a part of the T.O. chart: half the circular Ocean, the vertical stem and start of the western part of the T. At the top, a cartouche in the east (*Oriens*) depicts Adam and Eve near the Tree of the Knowledge of Good and Evil; a temple with six columns marks Jerusalem.

on the borders of Asia, with its central fountain, source of the four rivers (Nile, Euphrates, Tigris and Ganges); and far away in Asia, the accursed tribes of Gog and Magog, pushed back by Alexander towards the frozen north, awaited the end of the world to cross their confining wall and launch an apocalyptic invasion.

This theocentric, anthropocentric and geocentric schema inspired western Christian cartography from the eighth century to the middle of the thirteenth. Its archetype was to be the work of the Spanish monk Beatus de Liébana, whose name is used to designate this kind of theological mappa mundi, and it was not by accident that this model was used in the eleventh century by another monk, from Saint-Sever in Gascony, to illustrate the theological view of human destiny contained in the Apocalypse of Saint John. This T.O. type of map, reworked and enriched over five centuries, found its most perfect and meaningful form in the mappa mundi of Ebstorf (near Lüneburg) in the middle of the thirteenth century, about fifty years before the decisive change in cartography which took place around 1300. This map, made up of 30 vellum leaves and almost square (358 x 356 cm), was the largest mediaeval mappa mundi. Kept in Hanover, it was unfortunately destroyed there during an air raid in 1943; fortuitously, it had been minutely studied and photographed. Without going into a detailed analysis, we should note a few of its major features. A quintessence of theological cartography, the terrestrial orb is depicted as subject to the kingship of Christ, just as Pope Innocent III had defined it some decades earlier. The Saviour's head appears in the east, at the top of the map; in the north and south, His hands

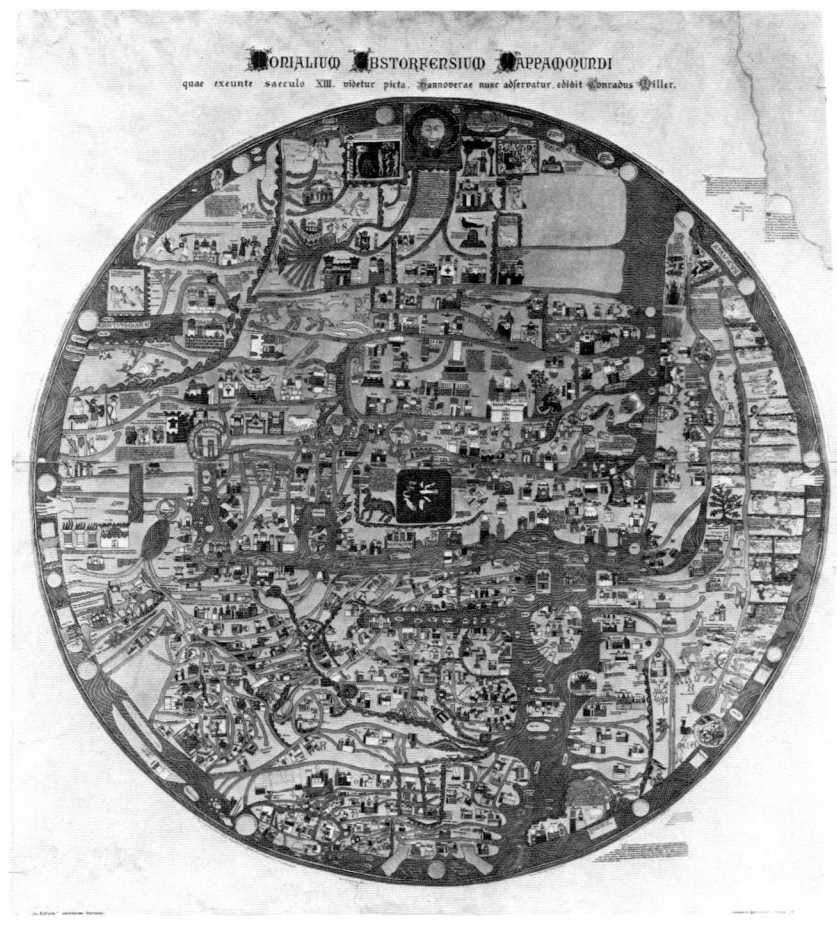

Ebstorf Mappa Mundi
Paris, B.N.

This is the most perfect example of a mediaeval theological chart. Particularly noteworthy are the abundant vignettes representing places, topographical features, fauna, flora and nomenclature.

support the world, which rests on His feet in the west. The author has proceeded in the style of the chroniclers, whose accounts went back to the Flood, if not to the Garden of Eden: the map shows Mount Ararat and places Adam and Eve in Asia. However, the substance of this narrative was becoming diluted in monastery and parish annals; the cartographer, having started with the intention of portraying the world, finally contents himself, as a German monk, with giving detailed images of places in the Holy Roman Empire. A traditional approach perhaps, but the attention to local detail is not solely a reflection of the parochialism of limited horizons; in it can be detected an attempt, in embryo, at regional observation and description.

This attitude of mind and this kind of cartography, at once universal and parochial, were not confined to the Christian West. From the ninth and tenth centuries the geographers of the Muslim world shared the same concepts. Their share of the Ptolemaic legacy was more complete, and the extension of Islam from Morocco to the Indus, and then to the East Indies, provided them with a wider panorama. But the zone of holy places on the Jerusalem-Medina-Mecca axis constituted the centre of their world perspective at least as much as it did for the Christians. However, the Indian Ocean region (at that time visited only by their coreligionists) benefited, thanks to them, from a description in which reality was not totally replaced by the fabulous. An analogous conceptual approach can be discerned in Chinese cartography of the same period, in which the Middle Kingdom justified its name by its situation at the heart of the universe.

The Ebstorf mappa mundi dates from around 1240. Traditional in concept, yet clearly influenced by its own period, it poses the contradictory problems of the persistence of the old conceptual schism and the awakening of curiosity for concrete detail. Only a few years after the Ebstorf mappa mundi, around 1246, Gossuin de Metz produced a compilation in

6,600 French verses, entitled *Image du monde*, of the information summarized a century and a half earlier by Honorius of Autun in his *Imago mundi* and given cartographic form (also around 1100) by Canon Henry of Mainz under the evocative title of *Imago mundi de dispositione orbis*, a work dedicated to the Empress Matilda. The notion of an empirical image of the world was in the air; it obsessed twelfth-century intellectual circles, dissatisfied with the knowledge drawn from the ancient, patristic and mediaeval *auctoritates*. Lambert de Saint Omer, in his *Liber Floridus*, describes and illustrates the marvels of nature in a mappa mundi in order to edify the reader and turn him towards God. Lambert died in 1125. His contemporary Guillaume de Conches (1080-1154) drew two maps with the same intention, but as a result of them the scholars of the Chartres school, contemplating the 'mighty fabric of the world', deemed that man as the artisan *(faber)* of the *aedificium Dei* should penetrate its secrets and disclose the workings of its mechanism. The stimulus given by the Chartrains to the understanding of the world promoted the observation and analysis of nature. This orientation towards the concrete, or even the practically useful, shows itself, for example, when Roger de Hoveden, speaking of Richard the Lion Heart's crusade, describes in detail the roads and coasts from Marseilles to Acre, probably using books of navigation and information gathered in the Kingdom of Sicily, and possibly inherited from Idrīsī. In his turn, the cartographer-monk of Ebstorf offered his information to travellers seeking a geographical guide.

Thus, however conceptual cartographic tradition may have been, by the thirteenth century its products had practical aims. Some earlier known examples include various regional maps of northern Europe such as the Anglo-Saxon 'Cottonian' map at the British Library in London, which dates back to the end of the tenth century. But it is to the thirteenth century and again to England that we must turn for fairly accurate regional maps, although they are still of the non-scientific stock of traditional cartography, such as the maps illustrating Matthew Paris's Chronicles (circa 1250) and the Hereford Cathedral mappa mundi (circa 1290). Circumstances and psychological attitudes conspired at this time to suggest a new type of map, based upon observed data, and serving as a foundation for calculations with practical applications.

A New Image of the World: The Portolan Chart

The regional map, whose maritime use began towards the end of the thirteenth century, contrasts in almost every respect with the traditional T.O. mappa mundi. Empiricism and experience prevail where formerly the conceptual dominated. To understand this it is only necessary to examine the oldest portolan charts in existence (which are the first to be described in this book): the famous 'Carte pisane' (No. 1) and the charts of Petrus Vesconte (Nos. 2-6) and Angelino Dulcert (No. 7). Despite its poor state of preservation, the 'Carte pisane', and especially the works that follow it, reveal the extent to which the cartographer's observation has changed its focus, aim and method. The material used is a sheepskin or calfskin, and the animal's neck, recognizable by its shape, is often placed on the left. At first sight, the framework of the drawing, with its crisscross pattern, on the 'Carte pisane' of red and green lines for example, somewhat resembles a spider's web; but a closer look reveals the organization of this network. Some of these lines (the sixteen 'rhumb-lines') radiate regularly within tangential circumferences, forming compass roses where their points of intersection with the circumference create 16 'nodal points', and marking off 16 compass-point divisions, each of 22° 30′. Other lines, joining these nodal points together, make up a series of parallelograms, squares and rectangles. The vertical lines seem to act as meridians, the horizontal lines as parallels; however, they are only reference lines, for despite their regular arrangement, they do not form a system of graduated coordinates. The latter only appear in the sixteenth century, under the influence of the rediscovered *Geography* of Ptolemy. This skeleton-map showing the compass points served as a framework for the plotting of coastlines: its original name—naturally in Italian since the technique originated on the peninsula—was *marteloio* (one suggested etymology is *mar-teloio*, or 'sea backcloth', another *martelogio* [*martelogium* in mediaeval Latin]).

The delineation of coastlines on the chart and the location of ports were made by triangulation, according to the direction of the winds, whose names (quarter by quarter)

Marteloio without Geographical Outline · Lyons, Bibliothèque de la Ville, ms 175, fol. 2

This framework by Petrus Vesconte illustrates the new technique of cartographic construction, in use from the end of the thirteenth century, consisting of a series of circles and squares based on nodal points.

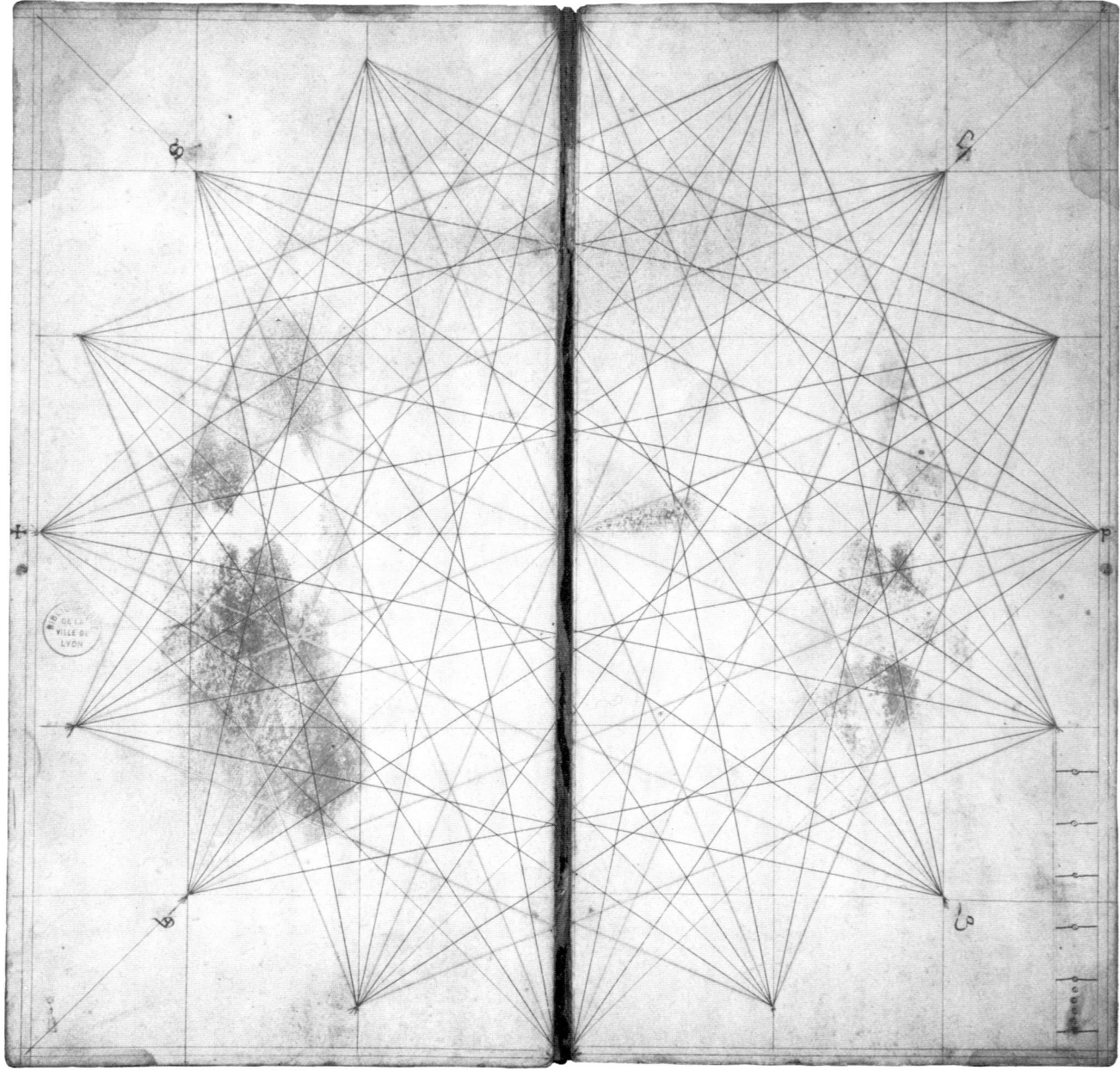

are mentioned on the 'roses' in dialect (at first in Italian). This detail demonstrates the experimental and practical ancestry of the portolan chart. The execution of this form of cartography obviously required the ability to take bearings and estimate distances, and thus to determine the distance to be covered and the course to be followed. This could only be done with the aid of calculating instruments and careful observation. Navigators and cartographers could avail themselves of *portolani* ('portolan-books') which gave written descriptions of coasts, listing ports in succession and their distances from each other. Whether or not these *portolani*—ancestors of our modern Sailing Directions—descended from the explorations of antiquity is disputed. In any case, as we shall see, the oldest *portolano* in existence is almost contemporary with the 'Carte pisane'.

The compass points were used to determine the angle of the course followed in sailing from one point to another. The possession of this data presupposed the existence of a corpus of knowledge and calculations of vital importance to mariners and cartographers. First the locations of places had to be determined. In order to do this, reference works, then newly available, contained an updating of ancient calculations: even the Tables of Toledo and Marseilles of the twelfth century had been replaced in the thirteenth by those of King Alfonso the Wise (1221-84). The introduction of the compass was even more of an innovation; however, certain writers (H. Wagner, E. Nordenskiöld) have minimized its influence on the origins of the nautical chart. In any case it was used to plot and maintain the ship's course, that is, to preserve the invariability of the angle between its direction and the orientation of the magnetic needle. The invention of its receptacle *(bossola)* predated the 'Carte pisane' by only a few decades; likewise the *Compasso da navigare*, which will be discussed later, is its contemporary.

The preceding observations combine to explain other features of the nautical chart from its very beginnings. In the top right-hand portion of the 'Carte pisane' are two distance scales. To calculate these, both in time and distance, the use of the hour-glass had long been known. Away from the coast and in areas where the direction and speed of the winds were well known, Mediterranean navigators had always calculated by days of sailing. Off-shore, however, the location of points indicated by the portolan-books permitted more precise calculations. Navigation had fathered the portolans (both books and charts); now portolans, in their turn, showed the way to navigators.

When mariners and cartographers wished to extend the use of the portolan chart to the ocean in estimating distances, they encountered the problem of defining a basic unit of calculation. Since the mile was used in the Mediterranean and the league in the Atlantic, the difference between the two units led to an imbalance in proportions, for only like should be compared with like. Using the Roman mile, the constructor of the 'Carte pisane' rectified, at the first attempt and with a surprising accuracy, the longitudinal extent of the Mediterranean to within 1° of its true measurement. Ptolemy had lengthened it to 62°, or more than half again the real figure, and Arab estimations had varied from 42° to 52°.

By implication, even magnetic variation was not unknown to late mediaeval cartographers, if we examine their works closely (Y.K. Fall). When a ship lost sight of the coast it was necessary to correct for drift, as, for example, in the open sea to the west of Corsica and Sardinia. Furthermore, historical research into variations has revealed strong magnetic anomalies between the Syrtes of Africa and Sicily around 1500. It is probably difficult to find a mention of the directional difference between geographic north and magnetic north before the beginning of the sixteenth century and Alonso de Santa Cruz (1502); nevertheless, on a mappa mundi by Vesconte (Vatican, Cod. Pal. Lat. 1362 A) dating from around 1320 or 1321, a slight displacement of the Pole-Star to the east can be observed. An exception perhaps, but still significant. In any case, unlike traditional mediaeval mappae mundi, the new sea charts henceforth place the north at the top.

Self-portrait of the Cartographer Petrus Vesconte · Venice, Biblioteca del Civico Museo Correr, ms 28, fol. 2

On the leaf corresponding to the Sea of Marmara and the Black Sea in his atlas of 1318, Vesconte has depicted himself seated at a desk, constructing his chart. At the top, an inscription reads: *Petrus Vesconte de Janua fecit istam [tabulam] in Venecia anno Dñi [= Domini] M CCCXVIII [1318]*, followed by his signature. This is a rare example of a portrait of a mediaeval cartographer at work.

A problem often given scant examination is the absence of projection in the construction of portolan charts. To start with, the expression 'projectionless chart' contains an internal contradiction. Any drawing that aims at delineating a portion of the earth's surface must involve a certain connection between that portion and the points of the chart, that is to say, a certain type of projection, even if the connection is not made explicit (F. Russo). This is so true that, even in the case of portolan charts from the beginning of the fourteenth century, it has been possible to speak of a kind of implicit Mercator's projection: the north-south direction lines are obviously not geographic meridians, but rather magnetic ones, as has been established for a chart of 1325 by Angelino Dulcert (Florence, Bibl. Corsini). The lines drawn from port to port along a constant angle between the ship's course and the orientation of the magnetic needle foreshadow loxodromic constant-course navigation.

To sum up, the portolan chart was born of experience and intended for practical use. This explains its semiological features: the colours given to the lines forming the web of the skeleton-map (green and red in the case of the 'Carte pisane'), the heavier lines used for the coastlines, particularly those of islands and where estuaries are shown. The wish to make the chart easier to read also governed the arrangement of coastal nomenclature. Thus, on the 'Carte pisane', names of ports are written in black, with the most important shown in red. The names are all placed inland along the coast, perpendicular to the sea and in such a way that it is sufficient to turn the chart to read them off in sequence. Thus, right from the beginning, mnemonic techniques were adopted, in a sort of cartographer's language.

Portolan nomenclature and semiology evolved, increased and diversified over the years, providing us with a number of ways of identifying and authenticating unsigned and undated maps. They also help us to identify the schools to which maps belong, as we shall see later. However, there are other indicators for dating, at least approximately. One of these is the differing value, both in space and time, of magnetic variation. Another is provided by the delineation of shores and reefs and the names they are given. Thus a comparison of charts of various periods throughout the fourteenth century provides the example of some rocks lying at the centre of the Mediterranean, between Sicily and Tunisia, northwest of Cape Bon. They are indicated by a sign (often a cross) and with a succession of names; nowadays shown as 'Skerki Bank' on English nautical charts, they may correspond to the *Arae* where, in his *Aeneid,* Virgil locates the wreckage of three Trojan ships. The realities of nature are continuous, but man subjects them to his own interpretations.

The portolan chart does not possess, therefore, the conceptual finality of a theological mappa mundi, which transcended its ignorance of geographic details. The portolan chart is a tool of the sea trade; without being a true navigational chart, it provides a 'catalogue of directions to follow between notable points' (L. Denoix). Thus the portolan chart is a reflection of an observed reality and a witness to a period in western civilization, summoned to widen its horizons to the furthest reaches of the earth. In place of the T.O. ideogram, enclosed in its conventional frame, there is substituted the possibility of infinite representations of reality, based on the calculation of the positions of places and the distances separating them, and the construction of a system of compass roses proliferating from one to another.

Historical circumstances combine with the practical experience of navigators to explain the appearance of this new type of chart in the second half of the thirteenth century. It is unnecessary to postulate, like Nordenskïold, the hypothesis of an original 'normal portolano' the source of a whole generation. It is even less necessary to imagine, like Hapgood, an amalgam of cartographic fragments inherited from ages as remote as protohistory. The extremely varied sizes of the portolan charts cannot be reduced to those of a single prototype, and why deny thirteenth-century men a capacity for inventiveness? Their scientific and technical background was adequate, and the usefulness of a chart for navigation provided an active stimulus. In this context we may recall, like Condorcet, that a discovery results less from a need than from links with already known truths and the possibility of bridging the gap separating them from this progress.

This is apparent from a combination of circumstances. The invention of the portolan chart came at a peak period in the astronomical and mathematical researches of Arab and western science. It is contemporary with Roger Bacon's plea in favour of the primacy of practical experiment and the observation of phenomena. It corresponds to the maritime expansion of the Venetians and Genoese, whose ships, at the end of the thirteenth century, sailed through the Straits of Gibraltar and up the coasts of western Europe as far as Bruges, founding merchant colonies on their way at Bordeaux, La Rochelle, Nantes, Rouen, Southampton and London. Therefore, it was entirely logical that the portolan charts should originate in the Mediterranean area, and in Italy first of all. Besides, the chronology is convincing: the first indisputable dating (1311) refers to a chart of the Genoese Petrus Vesconte, but the 'Carte pisane' cannot be later than 1291, as it still bears the name of Acre, under the Christian flag until that year, nor can it be earlier than 1275, since it appears scarcely less ancient than its natural partner the *portolano* known as the *Compasso da navigare* (preserved in Berlin), which can be dated to between 1248 and 1256, that is to say after the foundation of Aigues-Mortes by Saint Louis, which it does mention, and before the foundation of Manfredonia by Manfred of Savoy, which it does not. The coastal toponymy, usually more abundant in the description of the *Compasso* (1,177 names) than in the nomenclature of the 'Carte pisane' (927 names), adds a linguistic similarity, probably resulting from a common Tyrrhenian origin, to the practical complementarity of these navigational tools. The two documents must have effectively served navigators for centuries. They may have belonged to the military and maritime Order of San Stefano before leaving Pisa simultaneously in 1830, according to Motzo, for their two separate destinies.

In any case, the nautical role of the *Compasso* and the 'Carte pisane' is unequivocally confirmed by several texts. The most remarkable of these concerns a definitely established event in 1270, when Saint Louis was making his way to Tunis. Off Sardinia he wished to know the position of his ship. 'The king', says Guillaume de Nangis in his chronicle, 'asked the sailors how far they were from the port of Castel Castre and how near they were to the shore. The sailors ... sent for a chart and showed the king the location of the port of Castel Castre and how near they were to the shore.' Thus the recourse to a portolan chart and the calculation of distances are indicated with a clarity rendering any commentary superfluous. More open to dispute is a passage from Ramón Llull's *Arbor scientiae* (circa 1295), concerning sailors, whose Latin terms have been translated in various ways. The author wrote: '*Habent chartam, compassum, acum et stellam maris.*' *Acum* can mean the magnetic needle of the compass; *stellam maris* refers to the compass rose as well as to the Pole-Star; *compassum* refers either to a compass, or perhaps to the *Compasso da navigare*, that is, the *portolano*. Thus some interpretations have put words into the author's mouth. In any case, the references to the nautical chart and the *portolano* are highly credible and, furthermore, they are corroborated by a Sicilian inventory of the same period, published by Charles de La Roncière.

In fact the introduction of the use of the portolan chart and the *portolano* marks an important stage in the development of western interest in the physical world. Without overstressing the point, J. Vernet has raised the possibility of Chinese cartographic influences. Zhu Siben (around 1311-1320) employed a system of squaring to represent distances, without using any type of projection; such influences might have travelled in the wake of the first western voyages to the Far East. The news brought back by the Franciscan William of Rubruek in the middle of the thirteenth century was almost immediately in the possession of Vincent de Beauvais and Roger Bacon. Information may have passed through Mongol Persia, from where Bar Sauma came to Italy and France at the beginning of the reign of Philip the Fair. Above all, we should not forget that it was in 1298 in a prison in Genoa that Marco Polo, recently returned from his travels, dictated his *Description of the World*. At the time when the portolan charts and the *portolani* were born, this interest in distant worlds manifested itself in more concrete forms than fabulous tales. Missionaries accompanied or preceded the merchants, and for the use of both there appeared a new literary form, the glossary, such as the trilingual *Codex cumaniancus* (circa 1300) intended for travellers to Asia. Not less significant is the date, almost contemporary with the 'Carte pisane', of the expedition by the Vivaldi brothers to the ocean west of Gibraltar. They did not return from it, but all these coincidences are signs of the times: at the moment when, in the papal bull *Unam sanctam* (1300), the Church was affirming its universal vocation with a renewed clarity, the West was inventing and experimenting with the instrument for an annexation of space, which would be put into effect at a later date. The rose, as fashionable in the *Roman de la Rose* that bears its name as in sculpture where it was used profusely, would extend, step by step, the spider's web of its rhumb-lines over the known and coveted world—a civilization always finds expression in its maps.

Despite the progress in accumulating real facts, fiction was deeply entrenched and for a long time was intermingled with the facts reported by travellers. Reliable information often came from fishermen who regularly visited the same areas. The charts of Dulcert (1339, No. 7), Soleri (1385, No. 9) and Viladestes (1413, No. 12) bear witness to this. The same can be said of the geographical information brought to Catalonia and Majorca from the Maghreb in the fourteenth century. Likewise, cartographers were able to utilize the observations gathered by the Dominican Guillaume Adam, who had sailed the Indian Ocean around 1320 and even stayed on the little-known island of Socotra. The Catalan Atlas, as we shall see (No. 8), is full of pieces of information borrowed from Marco Polo. But nowhere, before the sixteenth century, does reality show through more vividly than on the great mappa mundi constructed in Venice in the middle of the fifteenth century by the Camaldolese Fra Mauro for the king of Portugal, a copy of which is preserved in the Biblioteca Marciana; the author even declares that he did not have enough room to inscribe all the information received from travellers.

On the other hand, many improbabilities and a large number of oddities fill the emptiness of the vast oceans and the blank spaces of continental *terrae incognitae*. It is often difficult to distinguish among a belief in fables, tradition, humour or pure imagination. From certain fables going back to pagan and biblical antiquity can be traced the origins of the depiction of legendary islands or frightening sea monsters, borrowed from ancient folklore or the Apocalypse; likewise the location of ferocious beasts in Egypt is connected with the memory of the ordeals of the Theban hermits. This survival of legends in portolan cartography is not surprising: it is akin to the enduring confusion between astrology and astronomy; books on both these subjects would have been found on the shelves of cartographers' workshops.

The mappa mundi was a sort of fictional novel and, as Baltrusaitis has observed, a synoptic image of all the peculiarities of every continent. Fantastic beings, the cynocephali,

Monsters Adorning Hartman Schedel's *Liber Chronicarum* (1493)
Paris, B.N., Réserve imprimés, G 504, fol. 12ᵛ

Despite the advances in cartography, fantasy and the fantastic continued to populate geographic works with monsters until well into the Renaissance period. Michael Wolgemuth, the author of the woodcut charts for Schedel's work, was Albrecht Dürer's teacher and introduced him to the art of geography.

▷

Humorous Cartography of the Fourteenth Century
Vatican, Biblioteca Apostolica Vaticana, ms lat. 6435, fol. 77ʳ

Despite being dumb and paralysed in his right arm, Opicinus de Canistris, a clerk from Pavia, expressed his fantasies in a chart that may have been constructed on a portolan-chart framework at Avignon around 1337. Latin inscriptions criticize the state of Christian society, for the author—born on 24 December, Christmas Eve (*dies ante Christum*)—took himself for the Antechrist.

cyclopes, sciapods and dragons of the twelfth century reappear in the fourteenth on, for example, the mappa mundi of Ranulph Higden (1363). Nor is fantasy lacking in the Catalan Atlas, where it is used to illustrate the gaps that later cartography was content to fill with a laconic 'terra incognita'. At Avignon, also in the fourteenth century, Opicinus de Canistris was reworking the fanciful elements used by Honorius of Autun in the twelfth century. When the latter portrayed towns in the guise of wild animals he was possibly expressing an anti-urban bias: Rome was given the appearance of a lion. Opicinus employed humour in a 'geographical game': Europe, represented by a female head, and Africa, by a male head, face each other from either side of Gibraltar like Adam and Eve at the moment of their fall; the Mediterranean, 'the diabolical sea' *(diabolicum mare)*, is a sort of octopus, grasping the European peninsulas with its tentacles; and through the Straits, the inland sea receives all the evil borne by the ocean. Nevertheless this imaginary map is a contemporary (1335–1341) of the pragmatism displayed by the portolan charts. The reader has even more cause for astonishment when he observes fantastic beings still inhabiting Le

Testu's maps (Nos. 48-51) in the sixteenth century. Europe, of course, is free of them, and America was too recently discovered to have acquired the store of legends with which Africa and Asia are burdened: men with lips hanging down to their chest, with a single eye in the middle of their forehead or eyes in their chests, standing on a single leg, with a foot large enough to serve as a parasol when they lie down on the ground, or pygmies barely 6 inches tall. But the frontiers of this fantasy world retreated in step with the shrinking of unexplored areas. If the *oikoumenê*, in its traditional sense, was still represented as the realm of normality, it was because—centred around the Mediterranean—its mission was to be the heartland of civilization, as opposed to its, as yet, inchoate surroundings.

As the storehouse of the cartographic traditions of antiquity, in Islam as well as in Christendom, the Mediterranean area retained, right up to the age of the great maritime discoveries, if not the central position it had occupied in the conceptual mappae mundi, at least a major role. This was due less to Ptolemaic calculations than to the very concept of the role of the *mare nostrum*. Sea of seas, the Greek *thalassa* had lost its universal significance and had been annexed by Rome. At first geography concerned itself with the fragmentation of the Mediterranean into regional sectors that we have retained *(mare Tirrenum, Ligusticum, Balearicum, Siculum, sinus Adriaticus)*. An orographical examination of its mountainous surroundings only came to the fore in the early centuries of the Middle Ages, for example with Isidore of Seville, and the expression *Mediterraneum mare* appears in the twelfth century from the pen of Bernard Silvestris. The portolan chart originated, therefore, in an enclosed central space before its expansion beyond the inland sea. The great Arab scholar Ibn Khaldūn remarked on this subject: 'The countries bordering on the Mediterranean are noted on a *sakifa* [i.e., a portolan chart], which gives their positions on the coast and information concerning them. ... It is with this that navigators guide themselves. Nothing similar exists for the ocean'. The situation described was that of the fourteenth century; it illustrates the precedence of the Mediterranean cartographic schools over their Atlantic successors. It also illuminates the achievement of their cartographic initiatives: the awakening of a closed society to the awareness of a wider universe.

The Ptolemaic 'Shock-Wave' and the Cartography of the Age of Discovery

As we have said, one of the principal merits of the portolan chart, right from the beginning, was to have corrected the traditional exaggeration of the longitudinal extent of the Mediterranean. Late-mediaeval cartographers did not totally part company with Ptolemy, however. A century later the rediscovery of his *Geography* provoked a sort of shock-wave, whose contradictory effects provided both a stimulus and a brake on progress in the representation and understanding of the world.

Chronologically the first of the great western discoveries, as G. Gursdorf has described it, was the rediscovery of Ptolemy's *Geography*, which was above all an event in the history of Humanism. It occurred in Florence, where the Byzantine Emmanuel Chrysoloras had come to teach at the beginning of the fifteenth century, bringing with him a Greek manuscript of the *Geography*. One of his Tuscan pupils, Jacopo Angiolo, made a Latin translation of it, which he offered to Pope Alexander VI in 1409. The work immediately attracted attention in scholarly circles: Pierre d'Ailly was then finishing his *Imago mundi* (1410); his colleague at the Sacred College, Guillaume Fillastre, had a copy of the *Geography* dedicated to him in 1427, which already contained a revision of the Alexandrian's work. It was

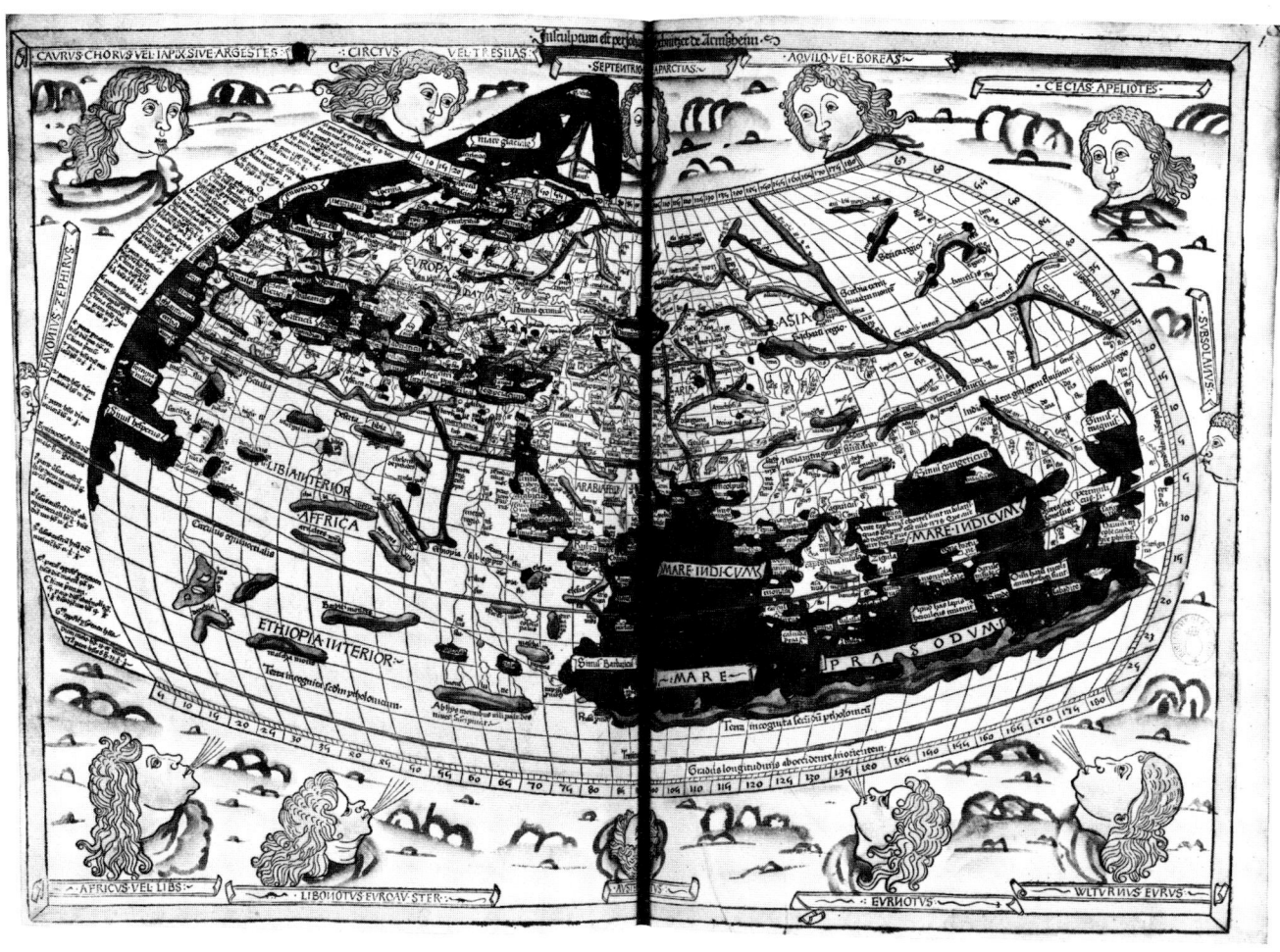

Vision of the World according to Ptolemy · Paris, B.N.: *Cosmographie* by Ptolemy (Ulm edition), 1482

Among the various fifteenth-century editions of Ptolemy, this one rivals the artistry of the illuminated manuscript. The area of Eurasia is exaggerated and the African land-mass is joined to the *Terra incognita secundum Ptholomeum*, a mysterious Antarctic continent taking the place of the peripheral ocean on the T.O. charts. Around the terrestrial circumference, curly-headed angels symbolize the winds, which are named here according to Mediterranean terminology.

particularly ardently discussed in the group which, meeting at the Convent of the Angels between 1410 and 1440, combined the most prestigious names in Florentine Humanism: Strozzi, Bruni, Vespucci (an uncle of Amerigo), Toscanelli, Niccoli, Piccolomini (in the person of Enea Silvio, the future Pope Pius II). The *Geography*, the subject in over half a century of some fifty known manuscripts, became with the Bible one of the first printed books, particularly in Italy—Vicenza (1475), Bologna (1477) and Rome (1478), Florence (1482)—then in the Holy Roman Empire—Ulm (1482), Strasbourg, Basle. The *Geography* was reprinted seven times between 1475 and 1500; however, the homeland of Fillastre and d'Ailly had to wait until 1535 before Michel Servet produced the first French translation of the *Geography*, which was printed at Lyons. Thus, until around 1540, at the height of the Age of Discovery, Ptolemaic thought enjoyed a popularity that did not abate until some forty years later, with Mercator. This paradox may perhaps be explained by the need for a choice, or at least a compromise, between abstract mathematical geographical ideas and the concrete demands of cartography. Stimulated at first to a certain extent by the influence of Ptolemy, in their turn the voyages of discovery won acceptance for realism. Learned Ptolemaic cartography was, however, not in conflict with the pragmatic cartography of the portolan chart.

Nancy Globe (or Sion Cup)
Nancy, Musée historique lorrain

At the beginning of the sixteenth century, the passion for geography displayed itself in the making of drinking vessels which, together with their lids, formed a terrestrial globe. This one, in silver gilt, is one of the earliest of its type and seemingly inspired by the mappa mundi of Oronce Finé (1531). It is surmounted by an armillary sphere and supported by a statuette of Atlas.

The Ptolemaic invasion, both on the eve of and during the Age of Discovery, played a paradoxical role as both stimulus and brake on cartographic technique. The return to Ptolemaic concepts involved regression as far as the calculation of terrestrial measurements was concerned, whereas the portolan chart had, at its very first attempt, corrected the 20° excess in longitude which the science of antiquity had attributed to the Mediterranean. As a result of this inheritance, the southern part of Africa was depicted askew, curving eastwards, and a peninsula, the 'Golden Chersonesus', completed the enclosure of the Indian Ocean. The oceans did not connect with each other. As for the exaggerated dimensions attributed to the Eurasian *oikoumenê*, it misled several generations of explorers, including

Christopher Columbus himself, convinced as they were of the relative proximity in the west of Europe and the Far East. 'I do not believe everything Ptolemy says'. This sentence was written by Fra Mauro on his great mappa mundi, itself rich in observed reality, at a date about halfway between the rediscovery of the *Geography* and the naming of the 'New World', dedicated to Amerigo Vespucci.

Ptolemaic cartography was progressively updated, complemented, revised, criticized, but not rejected. Thus, as early as 1427, Nicolas Clavus enriched his copy of the *Geography* with a map of the Scandinavian regions unknown to Ptolemy. In his turn, Nicolas Germanus bestowed a mathematical precision on the maps of the first scientific edition of the *Geography* (Bologna, 1478) by plotting on them a network of meridians and parallels. Therefore, the return to Ptolemy brought with it the principle of a method of calculating a 'point', which is indispensable in the construction of an accurate map and was to stimulate the search for a mathematical system of projection. Not at all at variance with the technique of the portolan chart, these methods were, on the contrary, a stimulus, fruitful at least in time. In Venice in 1511, Bernardus Sylvanus tried, with inadequate data, to correct the Ptolemaic maps with the aid of portolan charts. This attempt at reconciling the two cartographies was most significant.

The principal benefit of the Ptolemaic revival, however, was the affirmation of the sphericity of the earth. This compensated for 'errors' in outline and dimensions in Ptolemaic cartographic delineation, which would be corrected in the future. While this advance in knowledge stimulated geographic discovery and the search for solutions, it presented cartographers with the difficult problem of finding a projection suited to the needs of the chart's users. Being intended for nautical use, the portolan chart could not adopt just any projection; it had to enable the navigator to plot his course.

On another point, the Ptolemaic global view of the terrestrial world coincided with the concept of the portolan chart, which, through its capacity for extending its compass roses step by step, lent itself, as we have seen, to an indefinite representation of the surface of the earth; the Ptolemaic geographical view considered the universe as a whole. As a prelude to their research into adequate systems of projecting a spherical surface on a plane, scholars of around 1500 such as Martin Behaim (No. 20), Hieronymus Münzer and Johann Schöner sought in the globe a shape corresponding to that of the sphere. A representation of the world as a whole (globes, mappae mundi, planispheres) characterizes the cartography of the Age of Discovery; it is accompanied by treatises (*Sommes, Cosmographies*, etc.) describing the known regions, or the coasts where newly discovered regions were concerned. This approach, at once descriptive and figurative, recalls the parallel use of *portolano* and *compasso*, portolan chart and rutter, chart and nautical instructions. The problem retains a dual aspect: calculation and image. Cartography cannot do without either one, although it could give priority to one or the other. Thus mathematical geography flourished particularly well in the Holy Roman Empire, and practical cartography in the maritime countries where, with time, various schools developed, whose originality deserves to be emphasized.

Precedence of Mediterranean Cartographic Schools

Both the history of western maritime navigation and the existing documentation lead one to attribute to the Mediterranean peoples, and more particularly the Italians of the Tuscan and Ligurian coasts, the authorship of the first surviving portolan charts. The Pisan school would seem to have instructed first the Genoese and Catalan-Majorcan schools and then the Venetian school. Then, if we accept the genealogical table drawn up by R. Hervé (see p. 279), all the other cartographic schools would have derived from these three. There is nothing unusual about these relationships when one bears in mind the preponderance exerted in the western Mediterranean in the fourteenth and fifteenth centuries by the crown of Aragon which, at the time of the Catalan school, for example, was contending with the Genoese and the Venetians for the domination of the eastern Mediterranean.

The fundamental kinship between the various procedures for constructing a network of compass roses does not prevent the observation of certain distinguishing features. The 'Carte pisane' is very bare; the planisphere of Giovanni da Carignano (circa 1306) is rudimentary, despite the flow of information brought back from Asia and Africa by merchants, and transmitted from Venice to Genoa. The initial dependence of the first of these cities on the second shows up clearly in the maps—the first ones to be signed—of Petrus Vesconte (Nos. 2-6), made at the request of Marino Sanudo, to illustrate his plan of campaign for a crusade *(Liber secretorum fidelium crucis)*. The effort to keep pace with recent information is apparent, expressing itself in the nomenclature, where the Arabic origin sometimes shows through.

Saharan Africa as Seen by Catalan Cartography in the Middle of the Fifteenth Century · Modena, Biblioteca Estense, C.G. A 5d

A fragment of an anonymous mappa mundi attributed to the Majorcan school and dating from the middle of the fifteenth century, when the Genoese Malfante was in the Touat. Some noteworthy features are the outline of the Saharan Atlas, the Red Sea, the Nile-Niger confluence, the portrayal of 'kingdoms' by castles and sovereigns under tents decked with flags, which fill the desert void together with the inscriptions.

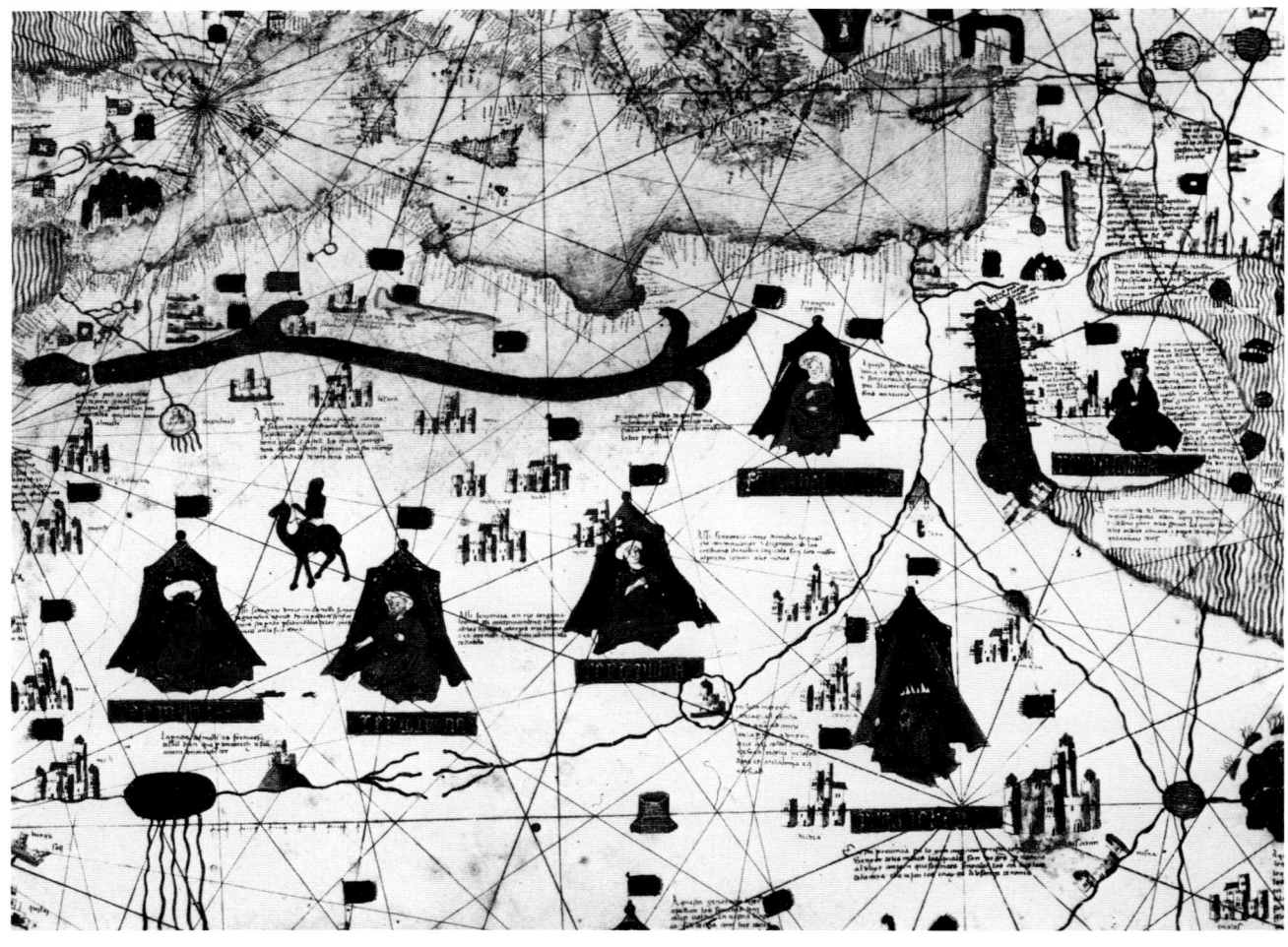

The Majorcan school originated at almost the same time as the Pisan school and, in any case, earlier than one would expect from one of its most prestigious products, the chart by Angelino Dulcert of 1339 (No. 7). The unique character of this school seems to be implied in R. Llull's allusions to it; and the presence in Palma of a scholarly Jewish and Arab society, which had remained in touch with the Maghreb, determined its personality. Of course the Catalan and Majorcan cartographers had contacts with their Italian colleagues and were influenced by them; nevertheless, Majorca became a centre for the manufacture of sea charts and for instruction in this skill that was even capable of attracting cartographers from Italy.

The market for charts was expanding proportionally to the development of navigation and the progress in the use of portolans. In 1354, the king of Aragon forbade the master of any ship to set sail without possessing at least two charts. This explains the existence of cartographic workshops not only in Majorca, but also in Barcelona and, in the fifteenth century, in Valencia. The Catalan cartographers had their habits, which remained constant. The arrangement of their charts, on a roughly dressed skin, conforms to the model observed in the 'Carte pisane'. A vertical distance scale is often placed on the part of the chart corresponding to the neck of the animal. The wind directions are indicated by four medallions, whose colours, red and yellow, sometimes betray their Aragonese origin. The nautical charts consist mainly of indications of natural features: rivers and their mouths, capes, bays, towns and ports surrounded by their walls and surmounted by armorial banners, and including the delineation of relief by festoons of mountain ridges. Inland seas are represented by lines of waves; the Red Sea consists of an elongated blob of the same colour with a strip left blank to mark the passage of the Israelites. Islands are gilded on Dulcert's chart, and the nomenclature is in the vernacular. In addition to this common element in Catalan charts, certain decorative features enable the specialist to recognize the various workshops: for example, the Virgin and Child, Christ on the Cross, or Saint Christopher. The Majorcan production demonstrated both a great technical mastery of contemporary marine cartography and a delicate artistic sense; it is scarcely necessary to recall that the Catalan Atlas (No. 8) is rightly regarded as the masterpiece of Majorcan cartography. Occasionally works of art, these charts were also intended for scholars, and above all for merchants and navigators, in whose interests the cartographers kept themselves up to date with the most recent information gathered, as we have seen in the case of Dulcert, from navigators and fishermen who had sailed the African coasts of the Atlantic.

From the fourteenth century onwards, the Catalans, with their very small percentage of errors (about 1%) and their wealth of information, gained a lead over the Italians that the latter were unable to regain until the following century. Italian charts were often limited to the representation of the Mediterranean and its adjacent areas and were content to indicate the coasts; Carignano, the Medici Atlas of 1351 and Pizigano are examples of this. When they attempted a wider approach, they caught up with the Catalan model again, to the point of vying with it in quality. But the Tyrrhenian ports lost their initial superiority, handing over the lead to the products of Venice from the end of the fourteenth century. However two types of document continued to flourish in Italy: the traditional *portolano* and the *isolario*. In the case of the former, it is only necessary to stress the enrichment of its data and the precision of its nautical observations. The latter developed from the fifteenth century onwards: the *Liber insularum Archipelagi* of Cristoforo Buondelmonte was, in 1420, the prototype of this genre, taking the form of a tourist guide for the area from the Ionian Sea to Anatolia, illustrated, according to manuscript sources, with more than a hundred maps and plans, and dedicated to Cardinal Orsini (Nos. 13, 14). The *isolario* of Bartolomeo Sonetti (1485) and that of Benedetto Bordone (1528) simply followed this pattern.

Passing by stages from Venice to Genoa and Messina, cartographic science spread naturally through the Greek islands and the Ottoman Empire and carried with it Portuguese influences. Of the earliest of these we have selected two examples (Nos. 57, 66), whose commentaries illustrate the role of Crete as a meeting-place of influences. But the name of Piri Re'īs deserves a special place; the diversity of his linguistic skills and information blends Arab sources with Catalan, Venetian and Portuguese influences. Some two hundred plans and charts of the *Kitab-i-bahriye* (1525), now published, and the charts preserved at the Topkapi Sarayi museum show affinities to the work of Fra Mauro, the Catalan Atlas and a chart by Columbus (1498), now lost, of which the chart of Piri Re'īs (1513) remains the only reminder (Nos. 28, 35, 36).

Although some of their most remarkable charts date from the sixteenth century, the Mediterranean schools also produced interesting works in the seventeenth century, among which those of the Marseilles cartographers Oliva (No. 68), Ambrosin (No. 74), Roussin (No. 83) and Ollive (No. 89) deserve mention. The third of these, by dedicating an atlas of the Mediterranean to Cardinal Richelieu in 1633, testified in his way to the efforts then being made by France to assert its influence, a policy inaugurated by Francis I when he negotiated the famous Capitulations with the Porte.

The Western Schools

The history of marine cartography is closely linked to the general world situation. Thus the torch was passed successively to those countries with access to the recently discovered ocean horizons: Spain, Portugal, France, England and Holland.

According to some writers, the practice of state secrecy *(sigillo)* may be the main reason for the rarity of existing Portuguese charts prior to the sixteenth century. We must not conclude from this that Portuguese cartography did not exist before this period, as this would be to ignore major events, such as the expedition of Dom Pedro, brother of Henry the Navigator, who scoured Italy in search of maps. In 1428, in particular, he is said to have brought back from Venice a mappa mundi whose Ptolemaic extension of the Far East constituted an invitation to discovery. It was only to be expected that the Infante called the 'Navigator' would collect cartographic documentation at Sagres, since it was in his lifetime that the court of Evora placed the well-known order with Fra Mauro. Later on, Portuguese influence can be detected in a certain number of Catalan and Italian charts and vice versa. The very beautiful, and too little-known, Dijon portolan chart (circa 1510), is an example of a mixture of influences (No. 27).

The contributions of Portuguese and Spanish cartography naturally led to an enrichment of the techniques that had originated in the Mediterranean from the teachings of nautical experience and from geographical data obtained on distant voyages. The formula dear to Duarte Pacheco Pereira, 'experience, mother of all things', is directly applicable here. Cartography became an official service, to which the kings in Portugal and Castile sought to attract foreign scholars. Jafuda Cresques, son of Abraham Cresques, the presumed author of the Catalan Atlas, possibly worked at Sagres with the Infante. Martin Behaim was invited by John II to Lisbon, where the *Casa da India* (as did the *Casa de Contratación* in Seville soon afterwards) gathered information that would be of use in the revision of the official prototypes of sea charts (*padrão real* and *padrón real*) and in the instruction in their use of pilots commissioned by the king. The direction of these offices was entrusted to cartographers of renown: in Lisbon, to Lopo Homem, 'cosmographer to the king

The Use of the Cross-Staff · Paris, B.N., ms français 150, fº 16

The *Premières Euvres de Jacques de Vaulx, pillote en la marine* (1583) is a treatise on nautical science from Le Havre, in which the author shows himself to be as skilled a cartographer and miniaturist as he was an experienced navigator. On the same page, on a vast expanse of sea on which four ships (two of which are galleons) are sailing, he describes and depicts the manner in which a sailor took sightings with a graduated cross-staff (or Jacob's staff) to determine the altitude of a star.

(Manuel)', and to Pedro Reinel, 'master of navigational charts' to King John III. Cartographers passed easily from the service of one prince to another, as did for example the two Reinels, Pedro and his son Jorge, and Diogo Ribeiro. In Seville, the *piloto mayor* supervised the hydrographic bureau charged with attending to the making of charts and their authentication; this duty was performed by Amerigo Vespucci, Juan Díaz de Solís, Sebastian Cabot and Diogo Ribeiro, among others, and their names were a guarantee of quality.

Not least of the merits of the Iberian geographers was that of having recognized, thanks to their experience, the errors in plane charts, which did not take into account the curvature of the earth and the convergence of the meridians. Diogo Ribeiro was thus the first to correct the east-west axis of the Mediterranean. On a nautical chart of his (1529), the 36th parallel passes correctly through Gibraltar and Cyprus (No. 37). As for Pedro Reinel, he was one of the very first to solve, with a satisfactory approximation, the problem of the location of the latitude and longitude of places and regions in both the northern and the tropical zones. He employed a polar projection, and from his time onwards, some cartographers, taking the magnetic variation into account, delineated in the Newfoundland area an auxiliary-latitude scale inclined by 22½° (Nos. 45, 46). Despite the opposition of Sebastian Cabot to the double graduation of latitudes, this scale remained in use and can be found at the end of the seventeenth century among Basque cartographers (Nos. 92, 97), who had borrowed it from the Portuguese.

Dieppe, Bird's-eye View in 1625
Paris, B.N., Cartes et Plans, S.H. Archives No. 10

This cartouche was placed at the top of a chart by Jean Guérard (dated 1625) and provides an accurate plan of this Channel-coast town on a curve of the estuary of the Arques; on the right bank lies the suburb of Le Pollet (No. 78).

It is in the years 1520 to 1525 that Portuguese cartography seems to achieve full mastery of its technique, for example in the admirable Miller Atlas (Nos. 29-34) and in a very beautiful chart by Pedro Reinel, preserved at the Topkapi Sarayi and considered by Marcel Destombes to be a 'vital document' in the history of the great discoveries and their cartographic representation. Indeed it is, for it depicts the knowledge of the world as it was at the time of Magellan.

The chief service performed by the Iberian cartographers—and especially the Portuguese— was thus to give an image of the recently discovered regions as geographically accurate and as scientifically exact as possible. State secrecy, even if it was official policy, was in any case poorly kept. In the years 1520 to 1550, Portuguese charts were a prize much coveted by corsairs. Governments in search of overseas opportunities, enlightened minds thirsting for knowledge, both sought to obtain charts and, even more, the services of cartographers and pilots. The Ottoman sultans were able to acquire charts (Nos. 35, 36), and some of the best. The Reinels were not the only ones to desert the banks of the Tagus. Venice attracted the exiled Lopo Homem and Battista Agnese (No. 41), who popularized Spanish prototypes there over a long period (1536-1564). Before the latter, in the first years of the century, the nautical planisphere (1504-1506) of the Genoese Nicolaus de Caverio had already been inspired by the Portuguese discoveries (No. 26). Verrazano, on his second and third voyages (1526-1528), used Portuguese charts, and the English were not slow in employing them either. It is significant that Sebastian Cabot should have gone to Seville to practise his art: the Portuguese map was in favour and setting a standard.

Portuguese influence on the French cartographers of the sixteenth century is undeniable, without masking the originality apparent in the middle of the century in the Breton and Norman schools. At Le Conquet, Guillaume Brouscon is the first name in a long line of constructors of hydrographic instruments, charts, nautical calendars and tide tables, whose scientific data is made accessible to poorly educated sailors by an iconographic technique

▷

Planisphere by Nicolas Desliens: Atlantic Section (1541) · Paris, B.N.: Cartes et Plans, G.E. DD 935

A facsimile of a mappa mundi, destroyed at Dresden, this is the first dated chart of the Dieppe school. The cartographer is well acquainted with the recent discoveries of Jacques Cartier. The presence at the top of the chart of a ship with its prow pointing westwards illustrates the obsession with the search for a Northwest Passage. The chart is constructed on rhumb-lines; the central rose visible on the photograph is over Guinea. The unknown southern continent covers most of the foot of the chart.

similar to that of cartoons (Nos. 42-44). Their content is very like the observations of Pierre Garcie (alias Ferrande) in his *Grant Routier;* it is also related to the experience of another Portuguese of renown, a naturalized Frenchman then living in France, Jean Fonteneau, called Alfonse de Saintonge, author of the *Voyages aventureux* and a qualified pilot. He changed his place of residence from La Rochelle to Honfleur and deployed his talents in the service of Jean Ango. Far from being limited to confrontations at sea, Franco-Portuguese contacts frequently took the form of the presence of Portuguese pilots on French ships. Francis I courted them, and through them information and influences were transmitted. Dieppe, where a learned Humanist circle flourished, made the Portuguese pilots very welcome, and a hydrographic school grew up there, where a priest from Arques, Pierre Desceliers, a mathematician and cartographer (No. 47), gave pilots a scientific training. Norman cartography is very close to Portuguese in this respect. It preserves, however, the traditional features of the Ptolemaic influence and even—in the rich iconography of Le Testu—a recollection of the fables of antiquity (Nos. 48-51).

Norman cartographic production was prolific: more than two hundred charts between 1534 and 1587, to which must be added the far from negligible works of later generations, like those of Guillaume Levasseur (No. 67), Pierre de Vaulx (No. 71) and Jean Guérard (No. 84). The most brilliant period of the Norman school covers some forty years between about 1540 and 1580, from Nicolas Desliens and the Harleian mappa mundi (named after its eighteenth-century owner, Lord Harley) to Jacques de Vau de Claye (Nos. 60, 61), and including Jean Rotz or Roze (Nos. 39, 40), Vallard, Desceliers himself, Le Testu and Jean Cossin.

Dieppe cartography followed the stages of discovery as closely as Portuguese cartography did, and sometimes overtook it in the originality of its delineations. Two examples bear witness to this; the first concerns America. Informed by the explorations of Giovanni da Verrazano and Jacques Cartier, the Dieppois gave more and more faithful representations of the northern regions. From being an archipelago, Newfoundland assumes its true insular identity, and there is no question of a hypothetical Northwest Passage. Likewise, the Brazilian coast is treated with an accuracy akin to that of the Portuguese, but enriched with individual and original information. The second example concerns the famous 'Java Major', sketched by Jean Rotz, and developed by his successors with features that seem to outline the coast of northern Australia. Norman cartographic production thus displays the fortunes of the maritime ambitions of France at the time of Francis I, Coligny, Henry IV and Richelieu. Apart from the Normans, we should not forget that Champlain became a cartographer (No. 69) and that, at the end of the reign of Louis XIII, Père Georges Fournier synthesized in his *Hydrographie* the nautical knowledge then current in France.

Not long ago Abbé Anthiaume and, more recently Roger Hervé and Helen Wallis, have demonstrated that the Normans kept abreast of scientific advances. Astronomical navigation was practised from the beginning of the sixteenth century, for example by de Gonneville on his voyage to Brazil (1504). Jean Rotz introduced two latitude scales on his charts, with a differential of 4°; other cartographers constructed plane charts whose compass roses were drawn in after the completion of the delineation and the inscription of the nomenclature. Generally speaking, the Normans employed the systems of projection then current. Le Testu, for his part, employed original and curious ones, such as a star projection on four gores, which is of more geometrical than truly geographical interest. Such ingenuity knows no bounds; in the footsteps of Le Testu, Jean Cossin may have invented a sinusoidal projection, which was not to be rediscovered before the middle and late seventeenth century by Nicolas Sanson and John Flamsteed. Projection with crescent-shaped latitudes—inspired by Mercator—characterizes the work, first of Guillaume Levasseur (1601, No. 67), then of Jean Guérard (No. 84) some thirty years later. According to Père Fournier, it was from the French that the Dutch learned the use of reduced-scale charts. Indeed, between the western cartographic schools, as well as between those of the Mediterranean, can be perceived at least influences and inheritances, if not direct links.

Commercial crossroads, centres of learning and focal points for the dissemination of news of discoveries exerted a decisive influence on the cartographic workshops. Perhaps the awakening of English cartography should be attributed to the period when a Frenchman from Dieppe, Jean Rotz, served under Henry VIII, although N. Broc has pointed out 'how remarkable the prototype [of English cartography, the Gough Map] is for its period', the fourteenth century. Likewise, on the morrow of John Cabot's first voyage to Newfoundland (1497), John Day sent a sketch of the Isles of the Seven Cities from Bristol to the *almirante mayor* (Christopher Columbus), in place of the chart he had drawn, with which he was dissatisfied. And the chart on which Thomas More disguised the few geographical facts that he had gathered in Antwerp under a whimsical nomenclature can hardly be considered to add to the sum total of scientific geography. Thus, half a century was to elapse before George Lily, an Englishman living in exile in Rome, constructed—in 1546—the first British chart to free itself from the Ptolemaic tradition.

Between 1574 and 1579, no doubt in response to the administrative needs of the government of Elizabeth I, Christopher Saxon devoted himself to constructing thirty-six charts of the counties of England and Scotland, but he gave only the barest details on their maritime activities. He had had to have recourse to Flemish engravers, and the precision of the topographical surveys and the elegance of the drawing prepared the way for the *Speculum Britanniae* project, initiated in 1593 by John Norden. In 1607, Norden would illustrate a new edition of William Camden's *Britannia* (Camden was head of the royal school at Westminster) and share in its successful publication; however, the first English atlas (1611) is the work of John Speed.

British cartography did not confine itself to national geography alone; it widened its horizons to include the high seas and the flowering of maritime expansion. In cartographic history this initiative is symbolized by the exceptional work of Richard Hakluyt. With his encyclopaedic knowledge he could not restrict himself to the compilation of a particularly rich assortment of travel tales, but also produced many maps. After 1582, the date of publication of his *Divers Voyages Touching the Discovery of America and the Islands Adjacent*, the influence of his work stimulated the development of British cartography. In the same year Michael Lok produced a representation of the northern hemisphere containing the data acquired in that century, and John Dee constructed for Sir Humphrey Gilbert a chart of the circumpolar regions centred on the North Pole. The continuing search for a Northwest Passage encouraged cartographers to provide explorers with charts, and on their return, the explorers brought back further details with which the mapmakers could attempt to enhance the accuracy of their delineations. In his turn in 1585, John White, a shipmate of Sir Walter Raleigh, did not hesitate to locate the passage in the same place already indicated by Verrazano. Less than twenty years after the *Divers Voyages*, in 1598-1600, Hakluyt was able to add two volumes to the second edition of his *Principal Navigations* (the first edition in one volume had been published in 1589). We find in it, for example, a very interesting planisphere (1599) by Emeric Molineaux and Edward Wright. The trigonometrical tables drawn up by the latter for the determination of coordinates enabled Mercator's projection to be used to greater advantage and made charts constructed by this technique easier for navigators to use.

Around 1590, in response to demand from seafarers, London cartographers installed their workshops on the banks of the Thames near the Tower and, in order to obtain a legal status, affiliated themselves to the powerful Drapers' Company. As we shall see later, this was the origin of the Thames school of cartography, which was destined to develop individual characteristics during the seventeenth century, on which we shall have occasion to comment (Nos. 90, 93, 99 in particular).

Thus certain features of English cartography emerge: a close relationship with maritime discovery in the period around 1600, and a fundamentally practical nature. This is also displayed in other English charts of the beginning of the seventeenth century: those by Henry Hudson (1612), John Smith (1614), Samuel Purchas (1625), John Mason (1635) and Thomas James (1631), who concentrated on North America and the Northwest Passage, while Gabriel Tatton and Wright extended their cartographic horizons towards South America and the Pacific (1600).

Thus, around 1630, English cartography held an honourable position among its emulators and occasional rivals on the Continent, in particular the Dutch, whose cartography was then in full flower.

On the Continent the leading role in cartography recently played by the Dieppe school in France had passed first to Antwerp and then on to Amsterdam, in a way comparable to the activity displayed not long before by Seville and Lisbon. Antwerp, thanks to Christopher Plantin a centre of printing, copied and redistributed portolan charts of any origin. The king of Spain supported this drive, which benefited from the bounty of international patrons: merchants, ship-owners, bankers and scholars. It was in Antwerp in 1559 that Andreas Homem signed the largest Portuguese planisphere of the age (No. 55). It was there also that the universal map appeared—drawn by Ortelius, official geographer to Philip II, and one of the most honoured figures in the city. But the brilliance of the Antwerp school was not to survive the misfortunes of the age: the sack of the city by the 'Spanish fury' (1576) and the closure of the Scheldt by the Dutch.

Amsterdam took up the torch from Antwerp. The foundation in 1593 of the cartographic workshop of Jodocus Hondius was one of the first symptoms of the rise of the Dutch school, which benefited from the knowledge acquired from the schools that had preceded it. In response to the positive mentality and needs of a nation of traders, which it had to satisfy, Dutch cartography was to turn towards the concrete, that is, the service of the great maritime trading companies: the Northern Company, the East India Company, known by its initials V.O.C. (*Vereenigde Oost Indische Compagnie*) and the West India Company (W.I.C., *West Indische Compagnie*).

From their creation, the companies immediately organized hydrographic services intended to provide their shipping with the charts that the war prevented them from acquiring in the realm of Philip II, or for which they were reluctant to ask. Cartographic workshops operated at Edam, Warder and Enckhuysen, where in 1584 Wagenaer published a collection of sea charts of western Europe. The first Dutch charts often copied Portuguese originals. Thus the Iansz brothers published the first nautical chart of distant seas in 1592, after an original attributed to Pedro de Lemos. Shortly afterwards (1595), Van Linschoten published a collection of rutters bearing the title *Itinerarium in orientalem Indiam*, which was to become a manual for Dutch navigators; he had lived in the Indies for six years and participated in Barentsz's voyage to polar waters. The first contributions of Dutch cartography related to the Arctic seas—the work of Hessel Gerritsz for example (No. 79)—but at the same time other Dutch contributors revealed and accurately delineated the shores of the southern and Far Eastern seas. The Dutch gift for organization provided their companies with hydrographic services vying with those of the *Casa da India* or the *Casa de Contratación*. 'Writer of charts' ranked as a profession under the command of the cartographer-in-chief of one of the great companies. In 1633, the succession to Gerritsz in this office passed for seventy-two years to three successive generations of the Blaeu family, under whose name a great number of charts and atlases were published throughout the seventeenth century (No. 96).

The Amsterdam hydrographic office first revised and then completed, with the aid of ships' logs and merchants' journals, the sketches made in the Indies themselves by South Seas pilots. Later on, the cartographer-in-chief of the Batavia hydrographic office was allowed a wider initiative in the production of charts and their distribution among ships' captains. Towards the end of the seventeenth century, six to ten mapmakers were employed at the Batavia workshop, whose inventory then numbered more than a thousand charts; therefore, we should not underestimate the importance of Dutch cartographic production either in Batavia or Amsterdam. The day-to-day use of nautical charts is confirmed by the pencil marks indicating the routes followed. Above all this cartography reflects, step by step, the increase in geographical knowledge. Thus it reveals the progressive discovery of the Australian and Tasmanian coasts; it also contributes information on Japan, a country hardly open to westerners (No. 87).

As we know, the Dutch were neither the first nor the only Europeans to make contact with the Land of the Rising Sun; the Portuguese had preceded them there as early as the sixteenth century. Thus our world survey of the expansion of the art of the portolan chart and the cartography that derived from it finishes with some Japanese versions of the Portuguese portolan chart of the first half of the seventeenth century (Nos. 72, 77) for which the Dutch are not responsible. Moreover, an interesting cultural exchange can be observed: the Japanese cartographers have assimilated western cartographic technique with great speed, and, for their part, the westerners have benefited from new astronomical data.

The Portolan Chart and Its Public

From its beginnings around 1300 until the Age of Enlightenment, the geographical revolution brought about by the invention of the portolan chart continued to bear fruit, producing a growth and diversification in cartographic production and a widening of its clientele, which was in itself a civilizing influence, as important in the social and intellectual spheres as in the technical domain.

The era of great maritime discoveries, together with the spread of printing, led to a change of direction in the creation of portolan charts. From the fourteenth century, the portolan chart, like the manuscript book, had a dual purpose as an item of daily use and as a luxury product, both of them expensive, although not to the same degree. Of the former, naturally intended for navigators, few examples remain; but these are recognizable by the courses plotted on them, by the annotations, resembling commentaries, and by their distorted shape from having been rolled up. The obligation imposed on all Aragonese ships' masters in the middle of the fourteenth century to have two charts on board implies that charts for current use were available, although this could hardly be called mass production: cartographers everywhere seem to have worked to order, until the end of the sixteenth century.

Orders for working copies of charts came from business circles as well as from navigators; charts appear in merchants' stock lists and in their correspondence. Thus, in 1400, Simon d'Andrea Bellandi, factor to the great Tuscan merchant Francesco di Marco Datini, ordered four mappae mundi from a Genoese *mestre de cartes de navegar*, Francesco Becha or Becaria in Barcelona. The contract listed the nature of the illustrations for the charts: 165 people and animals, 25 ships, 100 fish, 140 trees and—a detail typical of Catalan cartography—340 banners of cities and castles. This example displays an enduring feature of cartographic work, the way it adapts itself to demand by marrying luxury and utilitarian

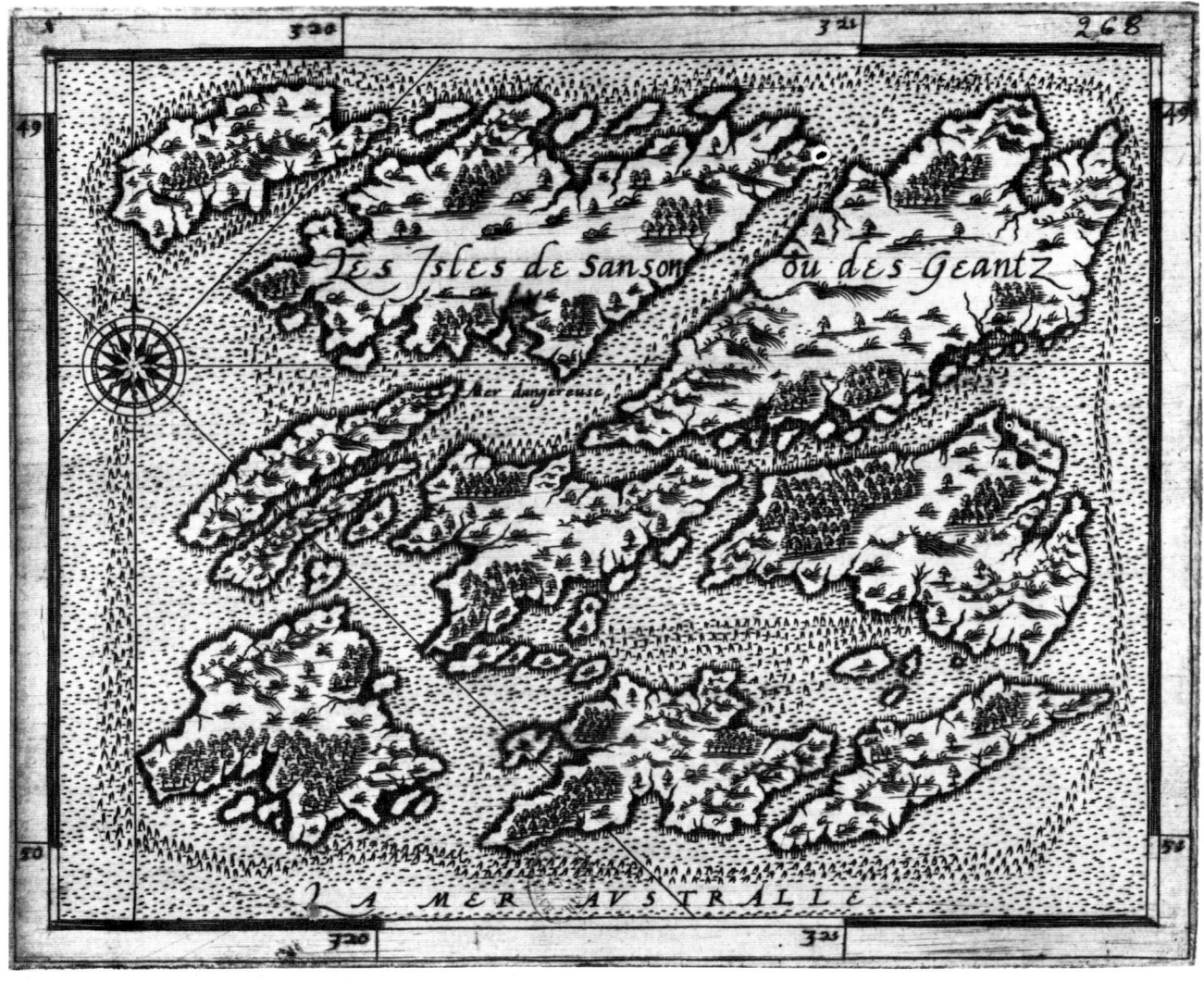

'The Islands of Samson', or 'of the Giants' · Paris, B.N., ms français 15452, fol. 269

In his *Grand Insulaire*, André Thevet, gives a description of this chart, showing the fairly accurate information already available in 1586 on the archipelago now known as the Falkland or Malvinas Islands.

production. Logically, in both cases, an identical outline is drawn by the geographer, then the illuminator in charge of decoration intervenes: this was the same method used in the production of manuscripts.

The mappae mundi ordered by Francesco Datini's factor were intended for the kings of Aragon, Navarre and England, which reminds us of the Catalan Atlas offered twenty-five years earlier to King Charles V of France. Princely inventories often list maps among the precious furnishings, because great mural mappae mundi often took the place of tapestries and hangings on the walls of palaces and castles.

For a long time the major market in sea charts belonged to the states of the crown of Aragon, from Barcelona and Palma to Messina. It then passed to the cities of the Italian peninsula, which retained this role until the middle of the sixteenth century, when market conditions altered and the leadership passed to France and Holland. Printing arrived at an opportune time for sea charts, as it had in every other sphere, providing a more numerous public of sailors and scholars with less expensive charts than the carefully illuminated portolan charts. Printing did not yet lend itself to colour reproduction; printed cartography therefore parallels developments in engraving.

Among the first sea charts printed in France, we should mention those of Nicolas de Nicolaï in his *Navigations et pérégrinations orientales* (1567), preceded by an adaptation of the *Arte de navegar* of Pedro de Medina (1553), which was destined to serve as a navigational manual until the beginning of the seventeenth century. This was shortly after the first printed nautical charts, which dealt with the Mediterranean (1539 and 1541), were published by Giovanni Andrea di Vavassore. In fact, a prior claim—heralding a lasting preeminence—should be attributed to the Dutch for the printing of a chart of the Baltic Sea by Cornelis Anthonisz in 1543. By the end of the sixteenth century and the beginning of the next, Amsterdam had become the centre of cartographic printing, and it was there that it turned into an industry. The public had grown, especially in the maritime sphere, and was demanding, in addition to large-sheet maps, collections of maps that could be more easily handled either by navigators or students who used these albums as manuals: thus was the atlas born. No doubt it had earlier origins if we accept (in agreement with Mireille Pastoureau) that any book containing more maps than text is an atlas. F. de Dainville, for his part, contends that the first true French atlas does not in fact call itself an atlas: it is the *Théâtre françoys* (1594) by Maurice Bouguereau. It was a contemporary of the first Dutch productions of this genre, and its printer (Gabriel Tavernier) was in close contact with his colleagues in Amsterdam. Throughout Europe the words *théâtre, theatrum, miroir, Spiegel* or 'mirror' preceded the word atlas. England had its *Mariner's Mirror* published in 1585, and around 1590 the Drapers' Company organized a sort of cartographic workshop in London, although its technical standards did not equal those of Dutch or French cartography.

In fact, after being a distribution centre for Dutch maps, Paris did not long delay in declaring its independence, thanks to Nicolas Sanson and his sons. Cartography thus mirrored Franco-Dutch rivalry at the time of Richelieu and then Colbert. France (which had not published any collections of charts specifically designed for navigation since the *Grant Routier* of Garcie, alias Ferrande) was to take its revenge at the end of the seventeenth century. A ship's master from Le Havre published sixty-four maps in *Le Petit Flambeau de la Mer* (1684), at the same time as the Académie des Sciences in Paris was undertaking a systematic survey of the coasts of Europe, from which emerged the twenty-nine charts of the first *Neptune françois* (1693). It was an important event: the Dutch were reduced to pirating the Paris edition, and whereas France founded the first hydrographic service for its Royal Navy in 1720, England had to wait until 1795 for its own. Thus eighteenth-century cartography was able to exploit the scientific potential of the portolan chart already discernible in embryo in the fourteenth century.

1 'Carte pisane', ca. 1290

2 Petrus Vesconte, 1313

3　Petrus Vesconte, 1313

4   Petrus Vesconte, 1313

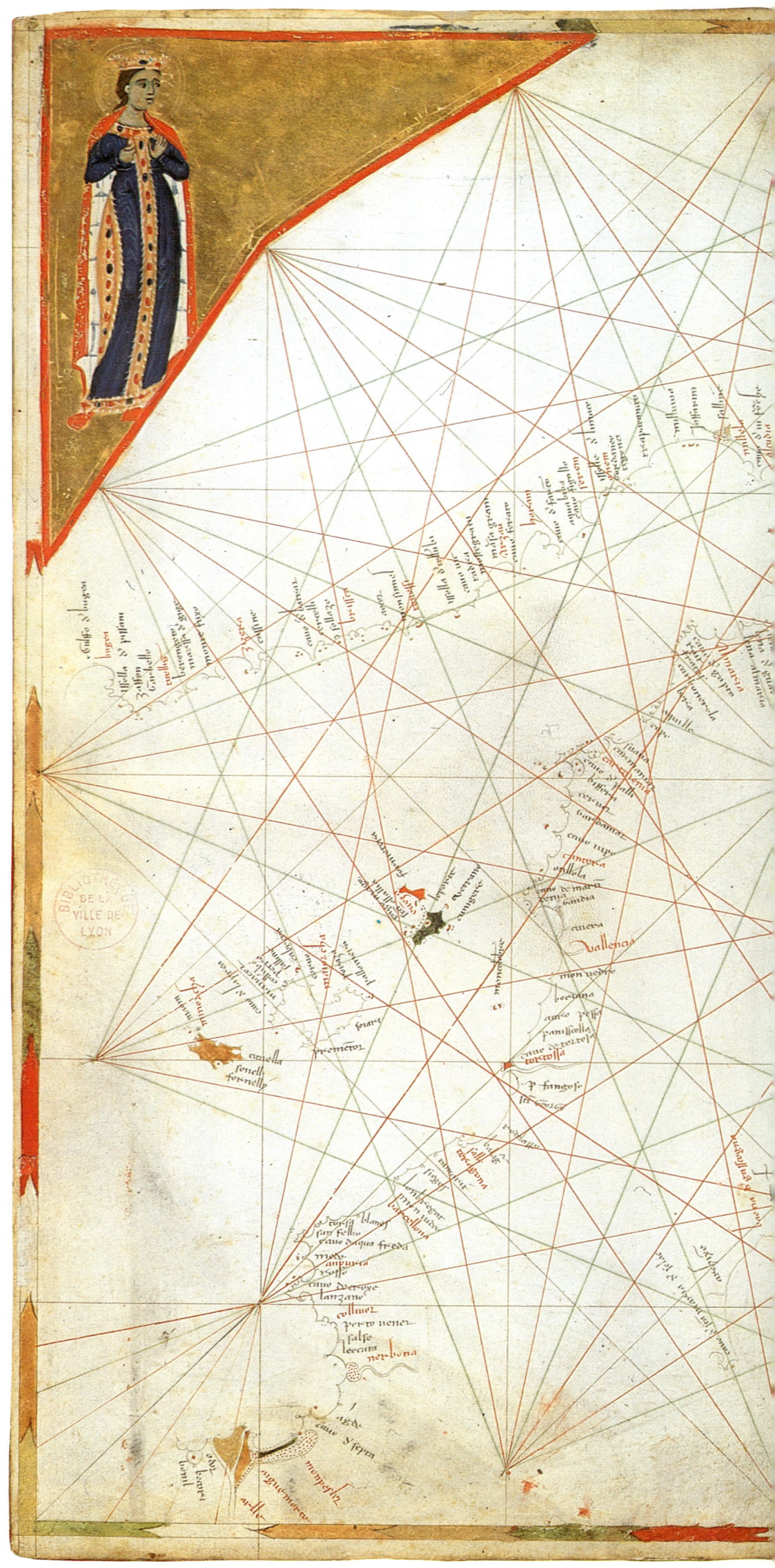

5   Petrus Vesconte, ca. 1321

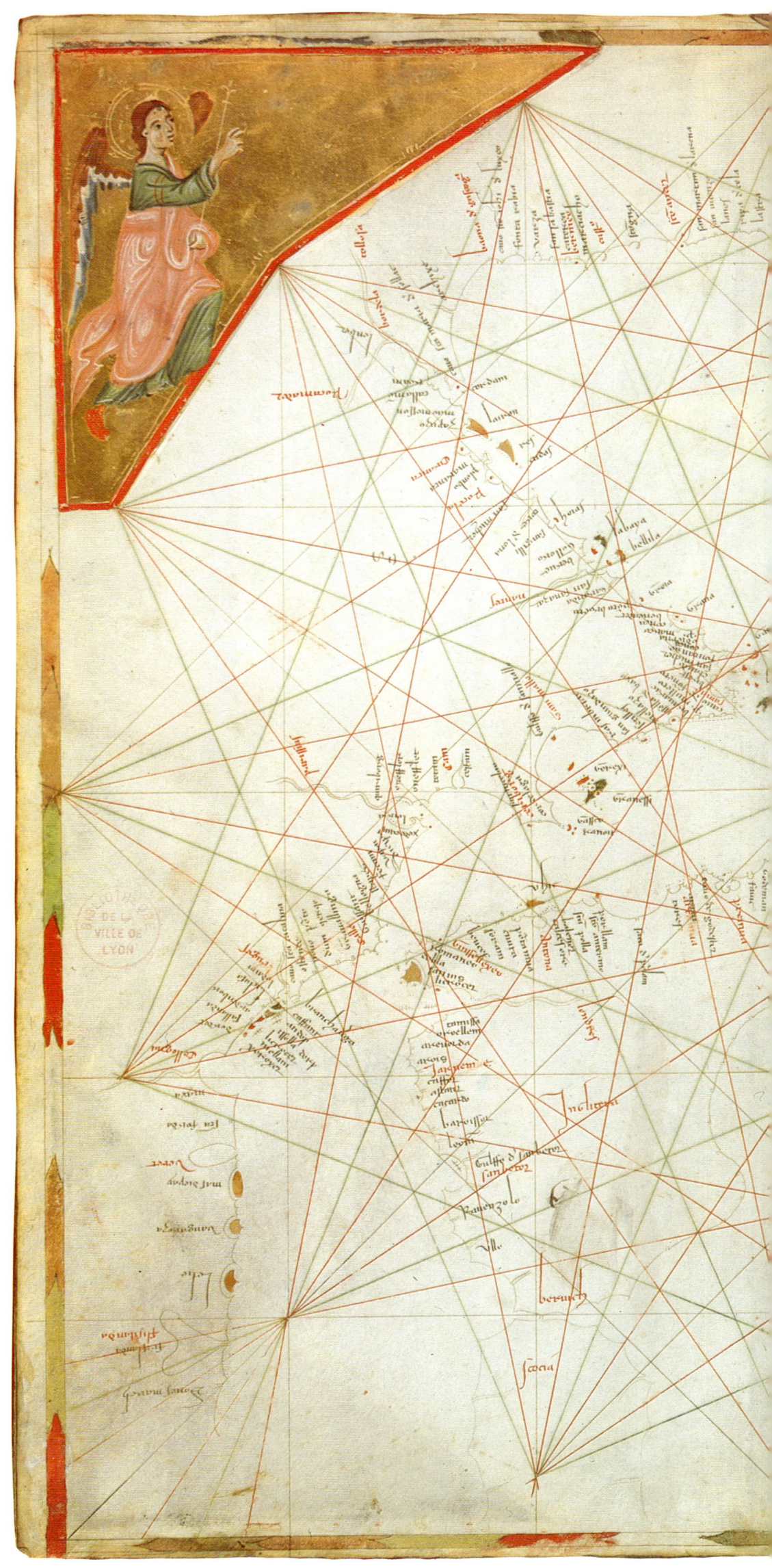

6 Petrus Vesconte, ca. 1321

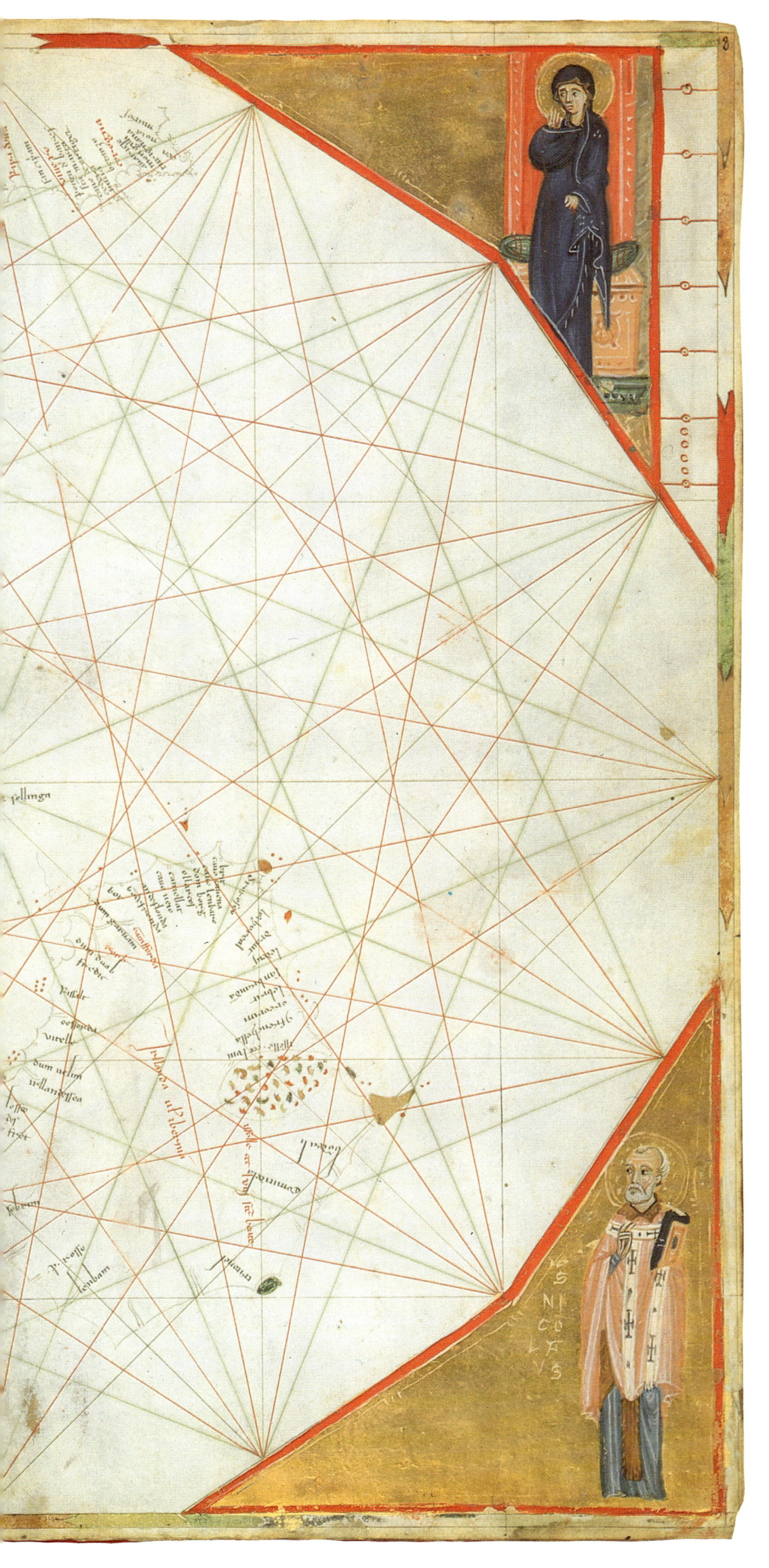

7 Angelino Dulcert, 1339

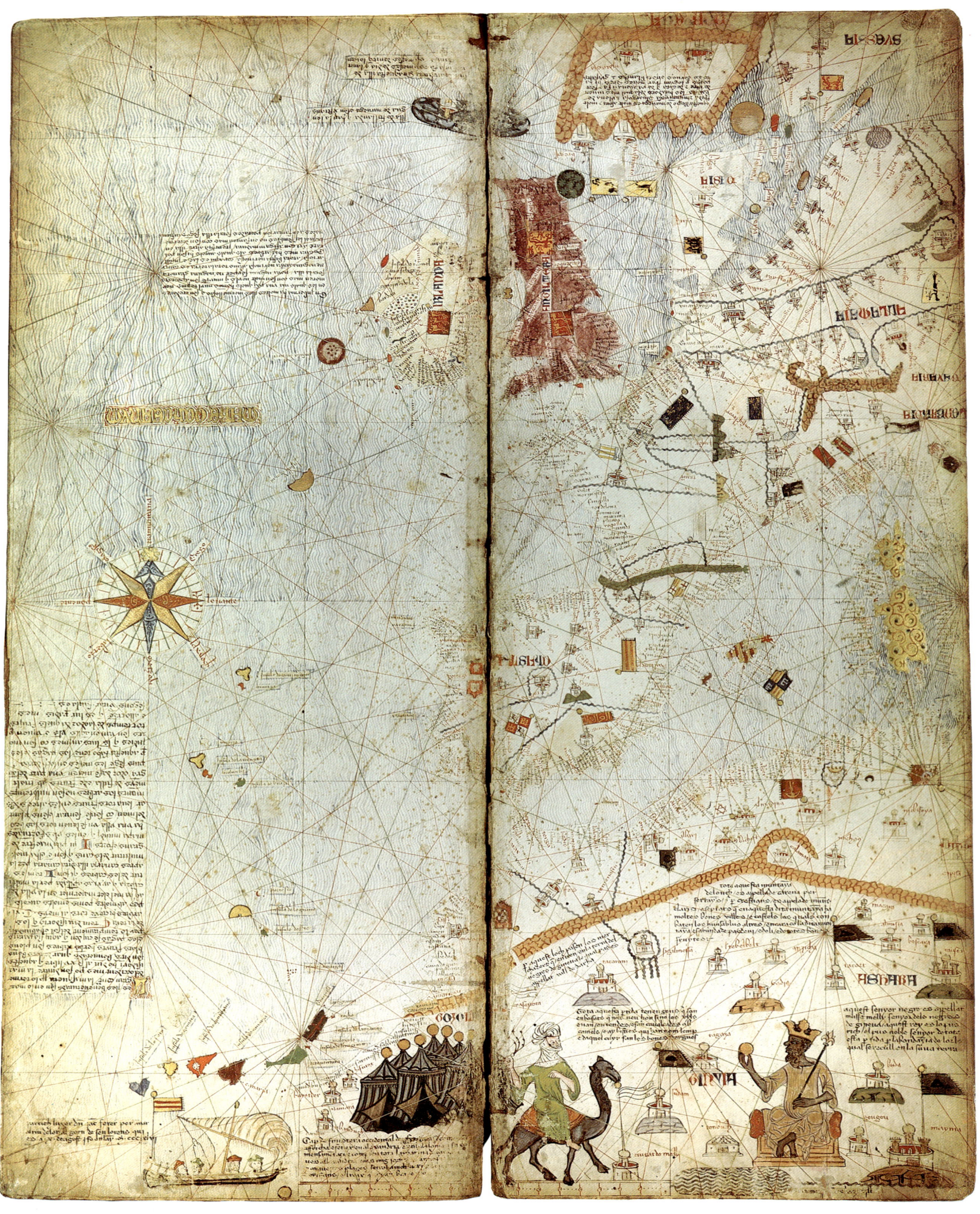

8 Catalan Atlas, ca. 1375

9   Guillelmus Soleri, ca. 1385

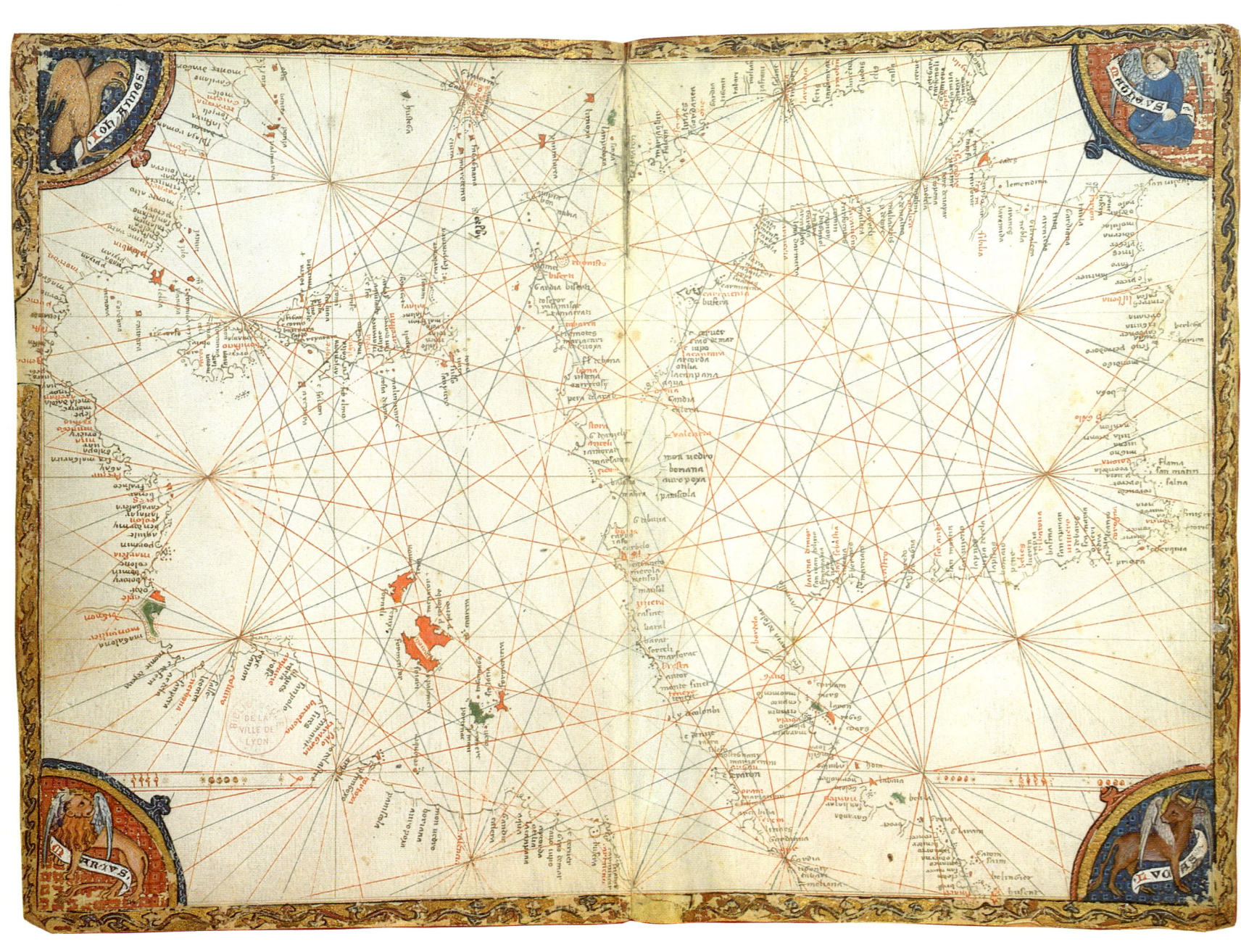

11 Albertin de Virga, 1409

12 Mecia de Viladestes, 1413

13   Cristoforo Buondelmonte, 1420

14 Cristoforo Buondelmonte, 1420

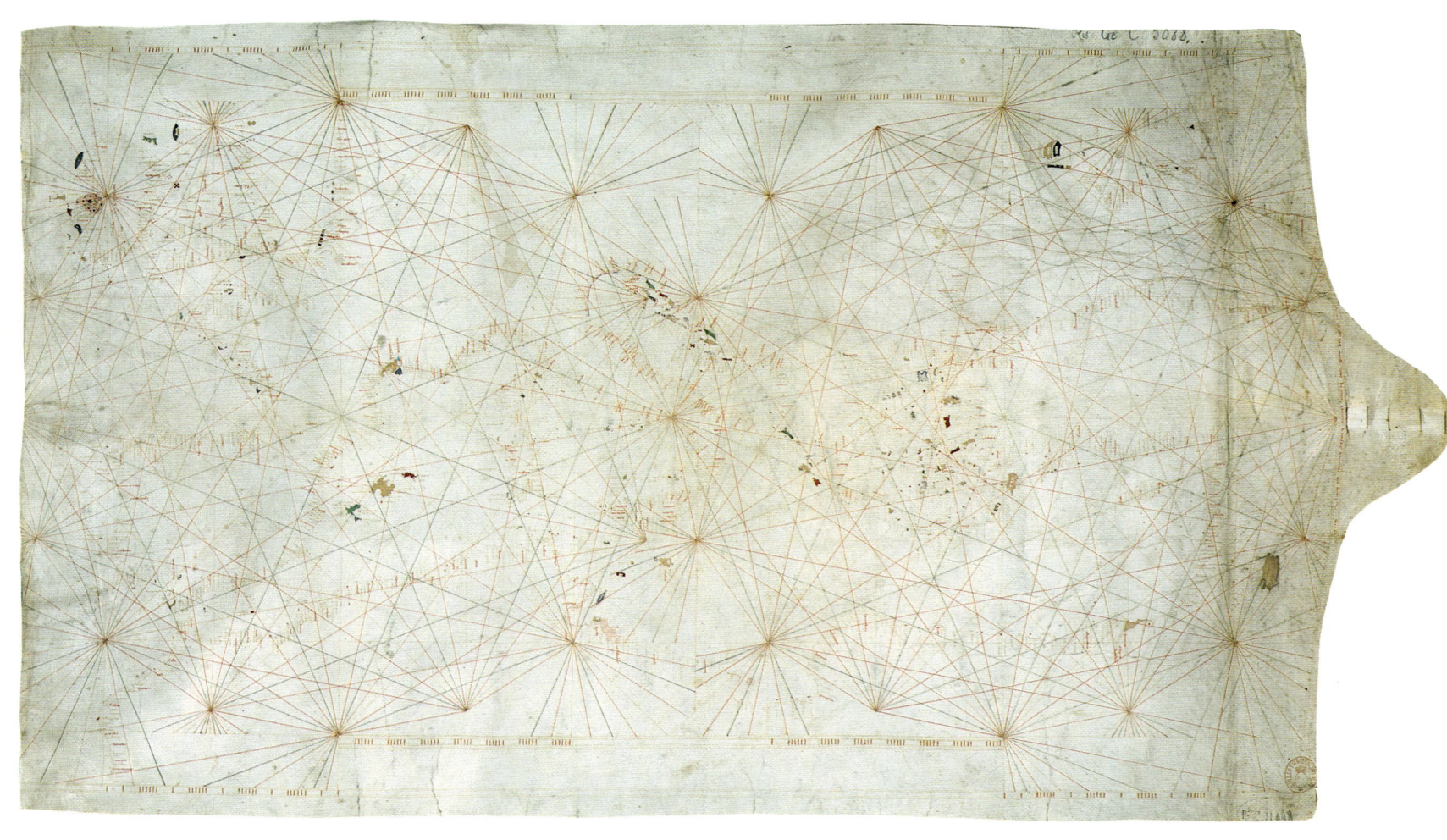

15 Jacobus de Giroldis, 1422

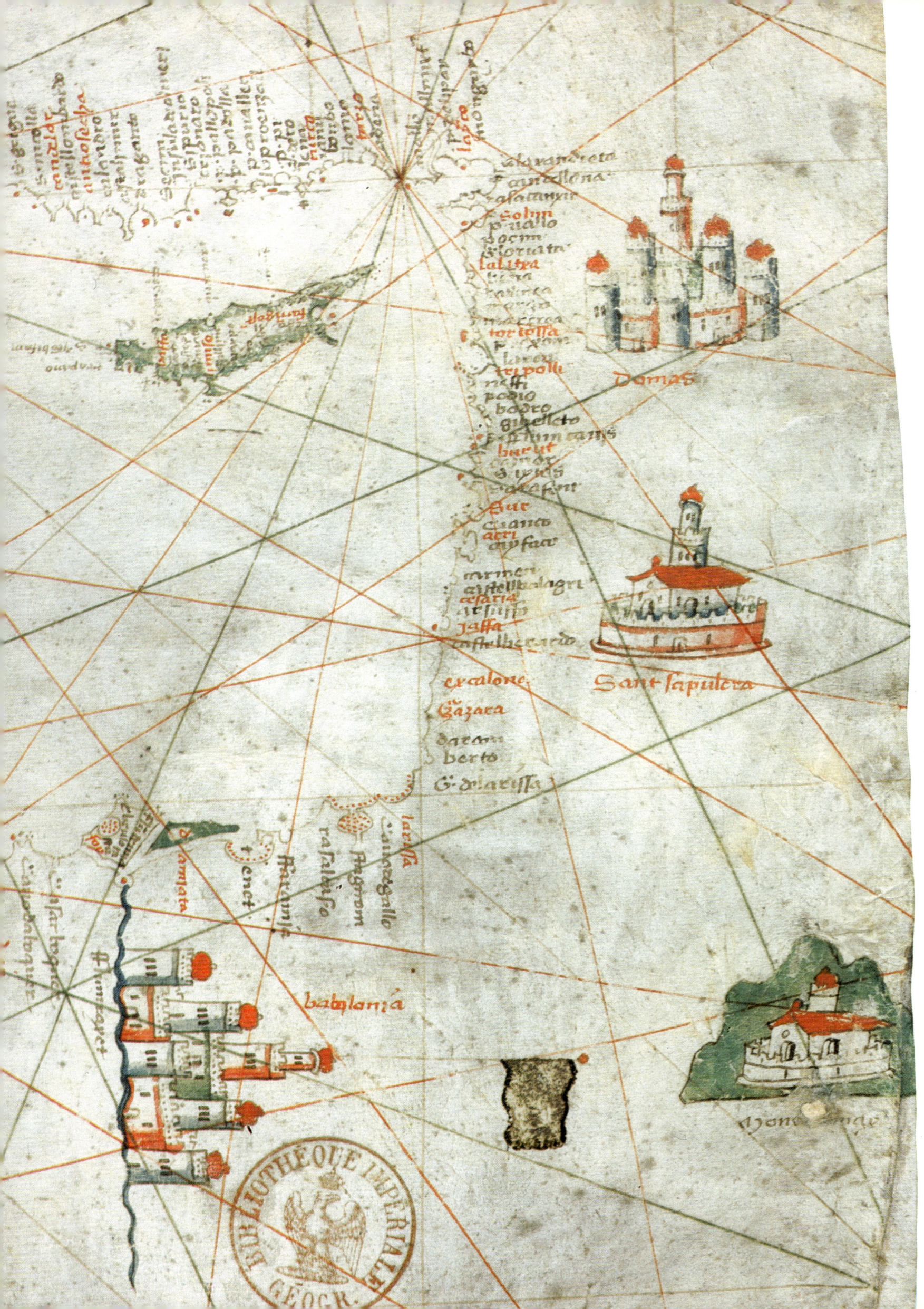

17 Petrus Roselli, 1462

18 Grazioso Benincasa, 1467

19 Grazioso Benincasa, 1467

20 Martin Behaim, 1492 (1847)

21 anon., 1492?

22 Juan de la Cosa, 1500

23 anon., ca. 1500?

24 anon., ca. 1500?

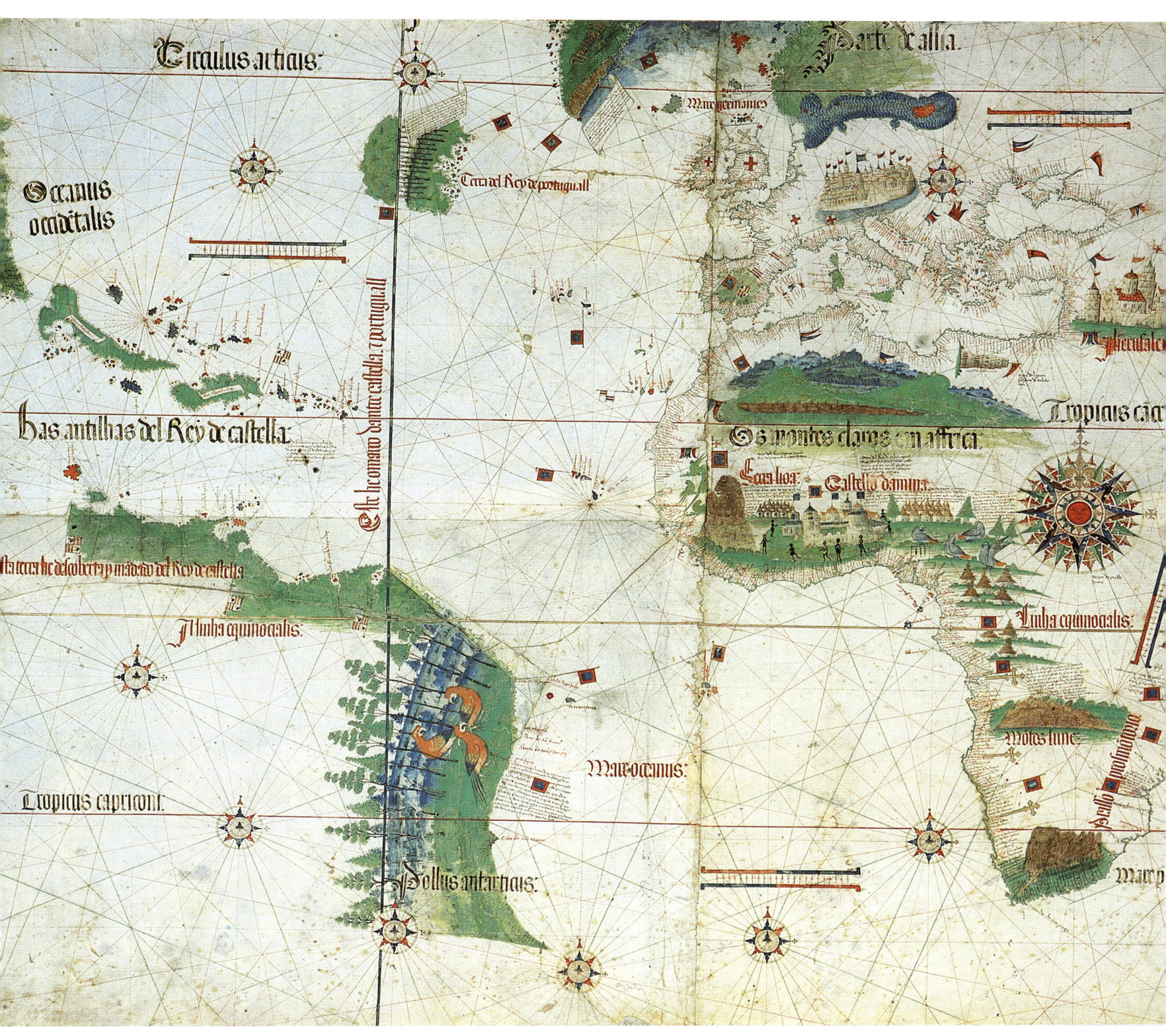

26   Nicolaus de Caverio, ca. 1505

27 anon., ca. 1510

28 Piri Re'is, 1513

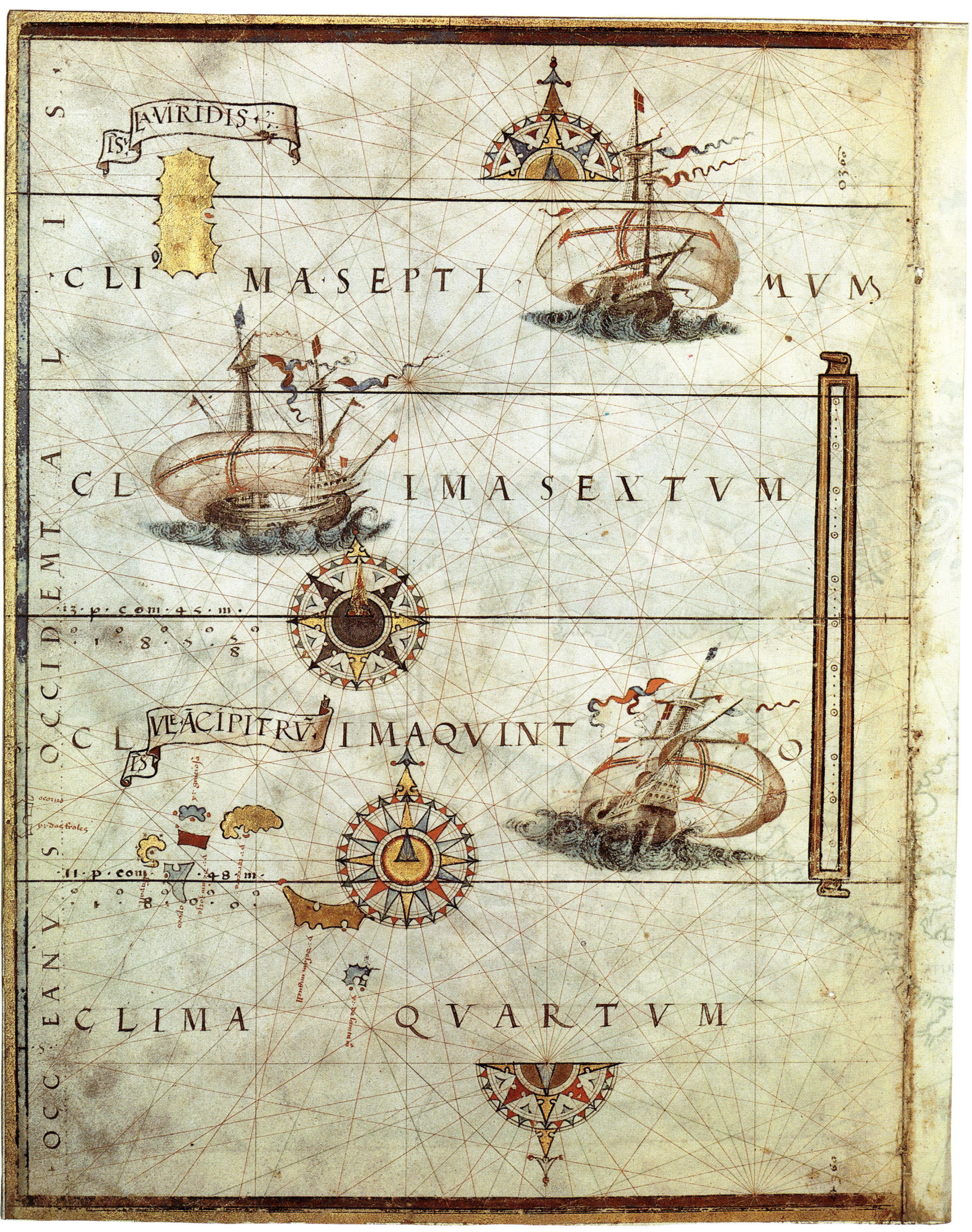

Miller Atlas, ca. 1519

31 Miller Atlas, ca. 1519

33　Miller Atlas, ca. 1519

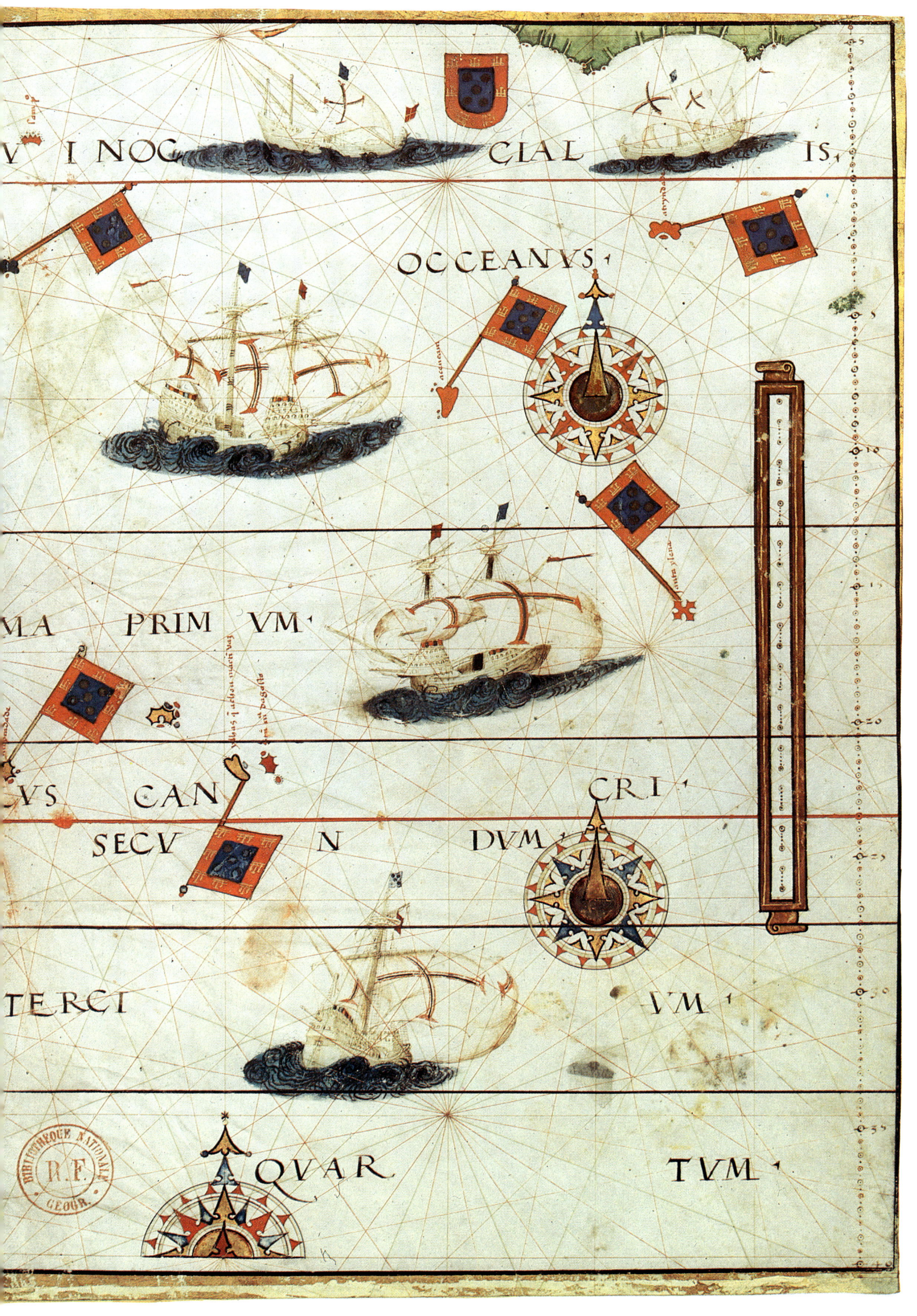

34 Miller Atlas, ca. 1519

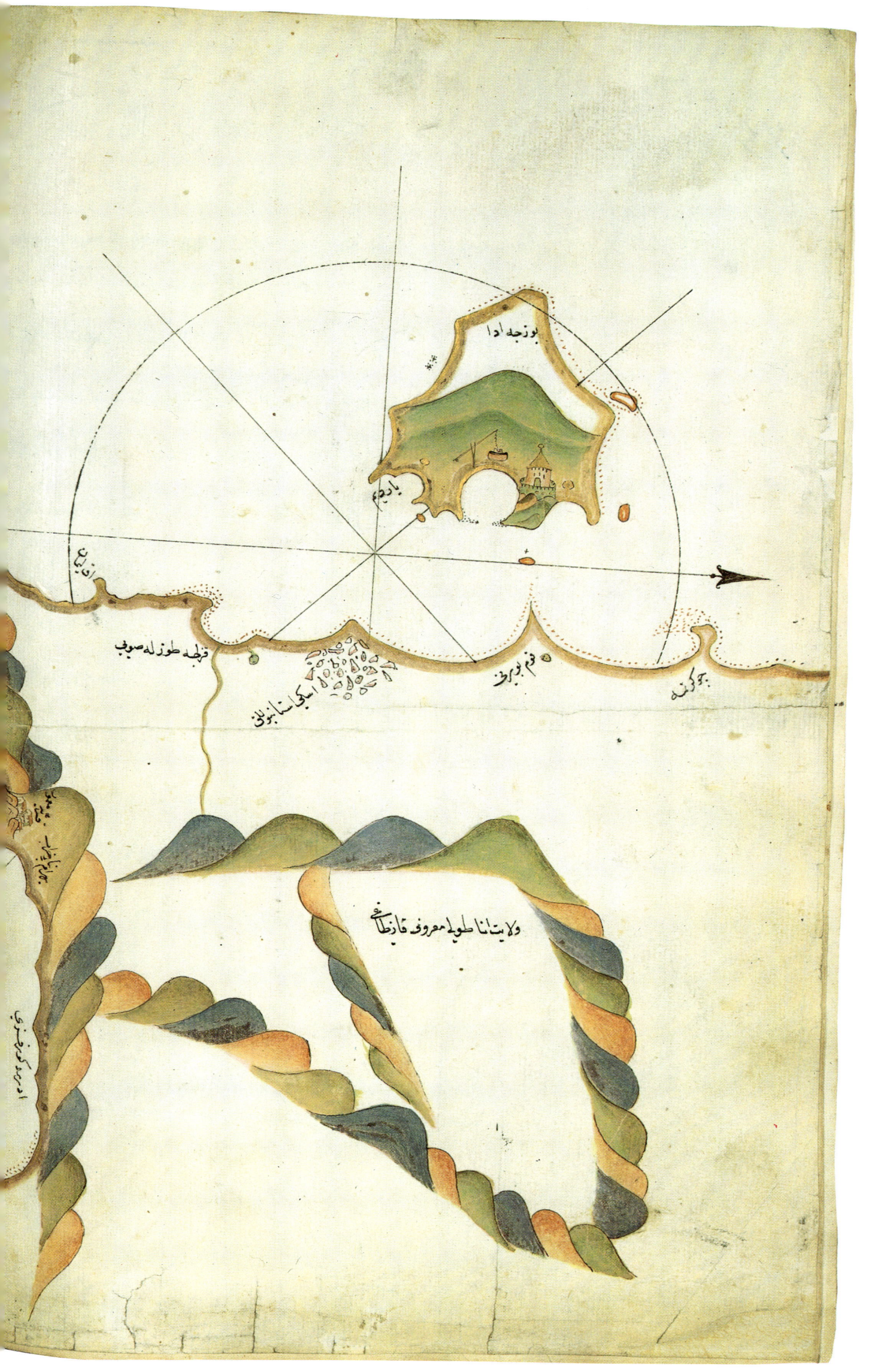

36 Piri Re'is, 1525-1526

37   Diogo Ribeiro, 1529

39 Jean Rotz, 1542

40 Jean Rotz, 1542

41 Battista Agnese, 1543

42   Guillaume Brouscon, 1543

43 Guillaume Brouscon, 1548

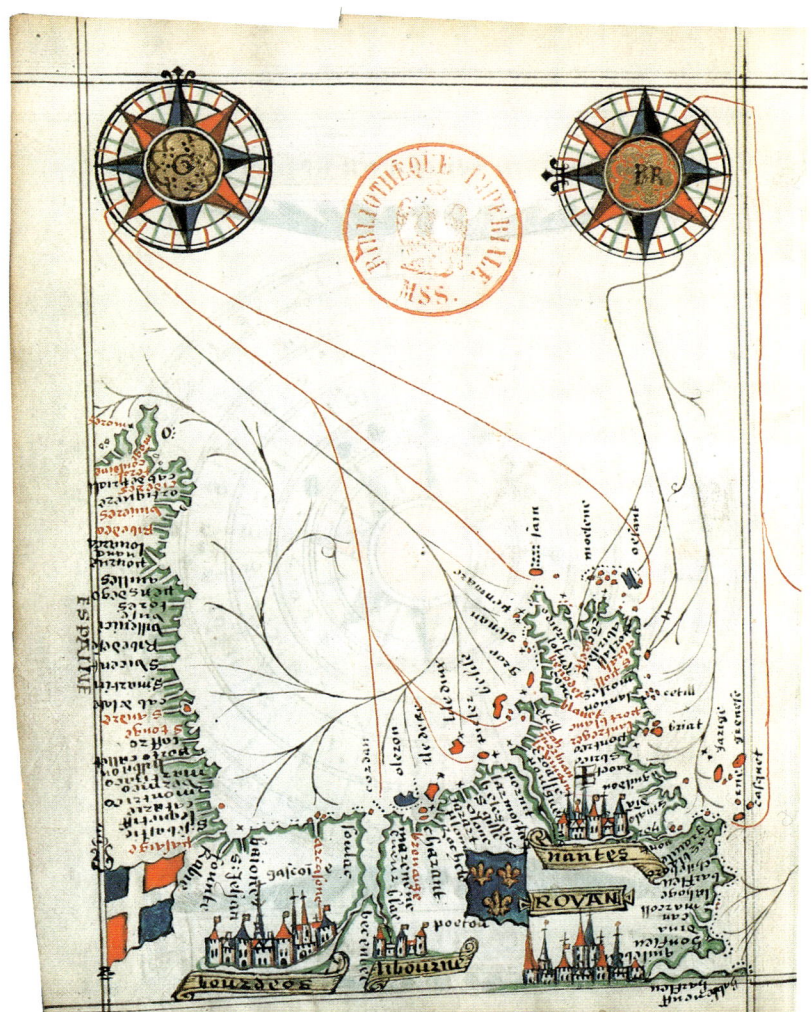

44   Guillaume Brouscon, 1548

45 anon., ca. 1550

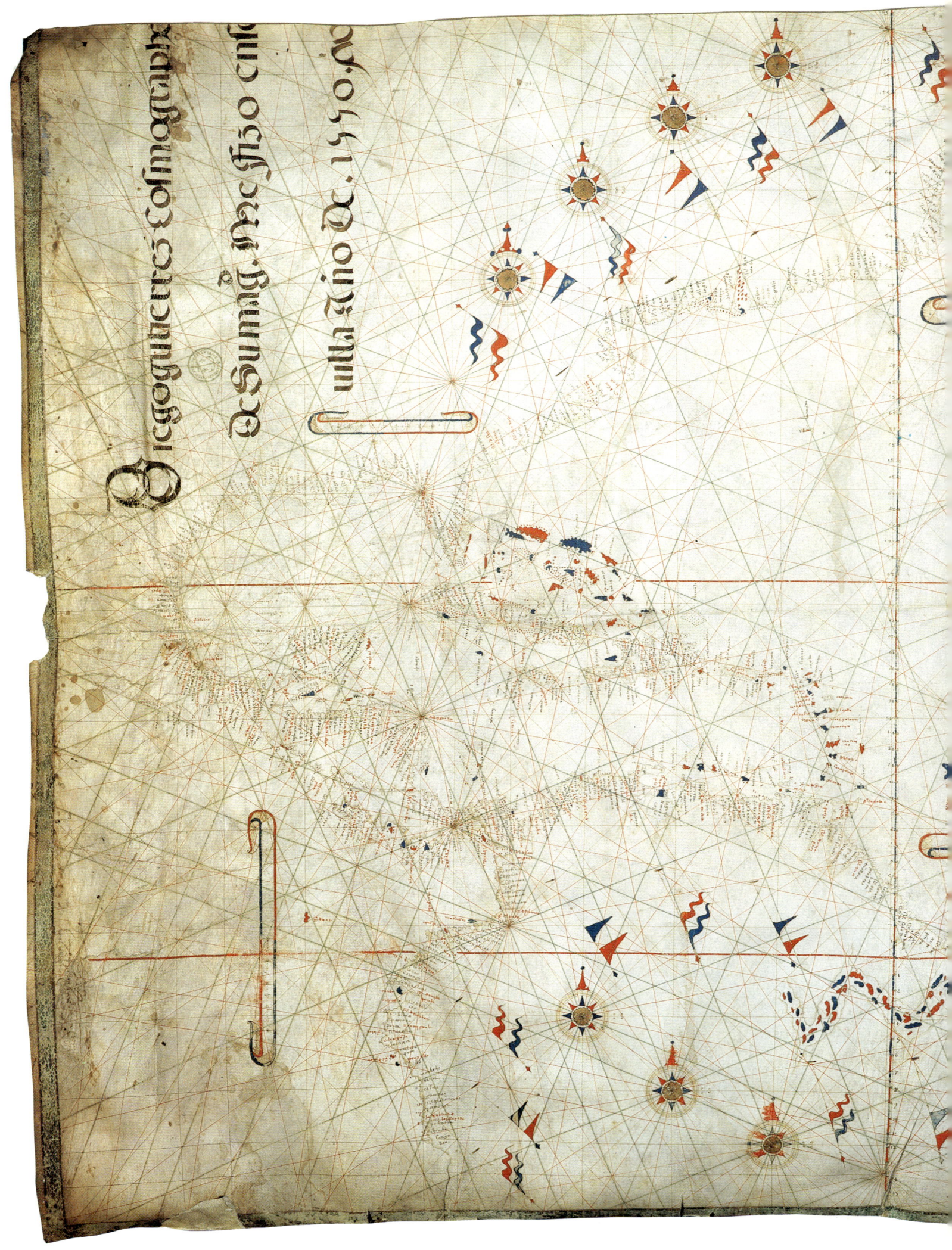

46   Diego Gutierrez, 1550

47 Pierre Desceliers, 1550

48   Guillaume Le Testu, 1556

49 Guillaume Le Testu, 1556

50 Guillaume Le Testu, 1556

51 Guillaume Le Testu, 1556

53   Diogo Homem, 1559

54 Diogo Homem, 1559

55 Andreas Homem, 1559

56 Giacomo de Maggiolo, 1563

57 Georgio Sideri, 1565

58 Nicolas Desliens, 1566

59 Fernão Vaz Dourado, 1571

60 Jacques de Vau de Claye, 1579

61 Jacques de Vau de Claye, 1579

64 Joan Martines, 1587

66 Nicolaos Vourdopolos, ca. 1600-1610

68 Francesco Oliva, 1603

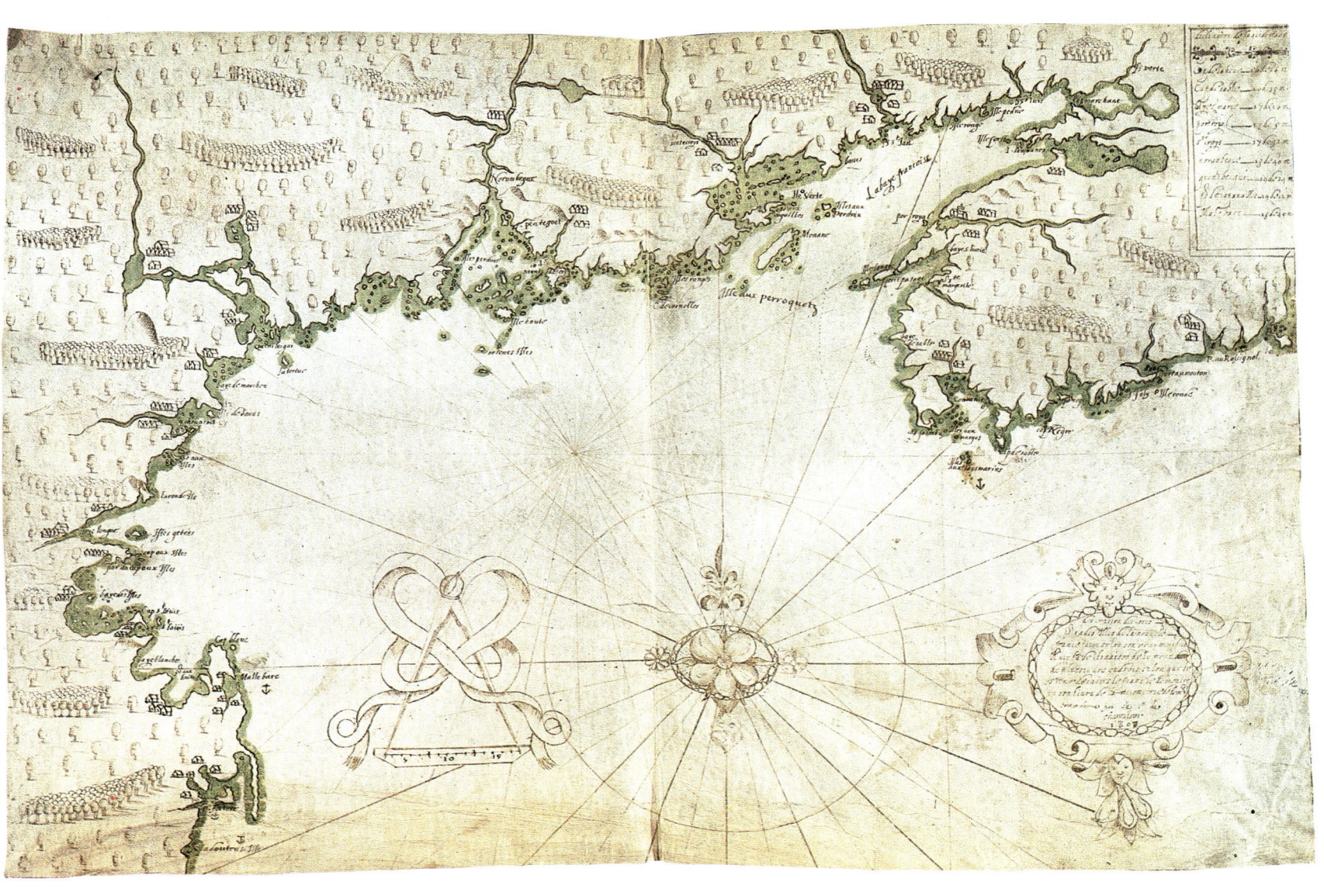

69 Samuel de Champlain, 1607

71 Pierre de Vaulx, 1613

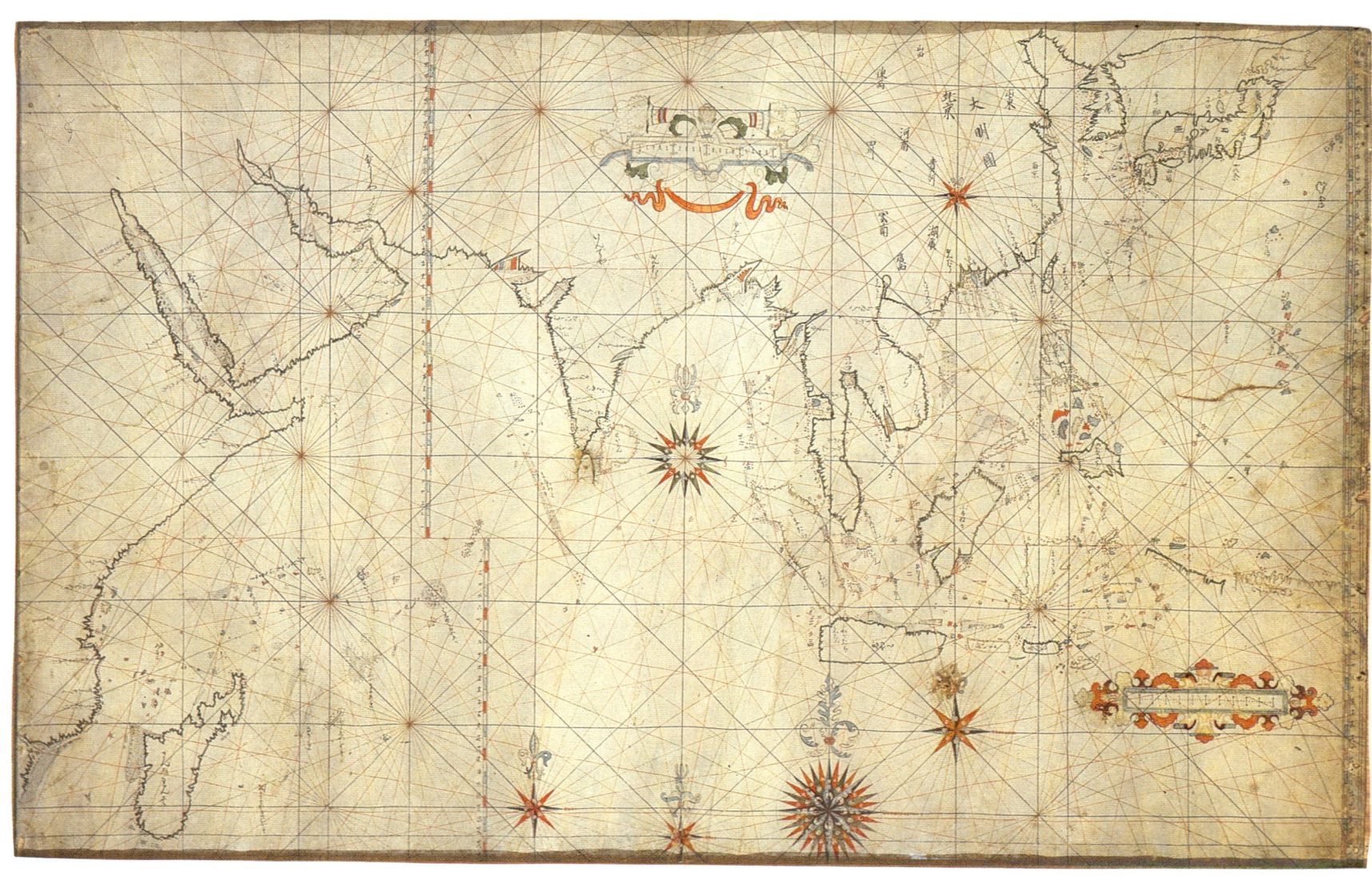

74 Charlat Ambrosin, 1620

75 Hessel Gerritsz, 1622

76 Alvise Gramolin, 1624

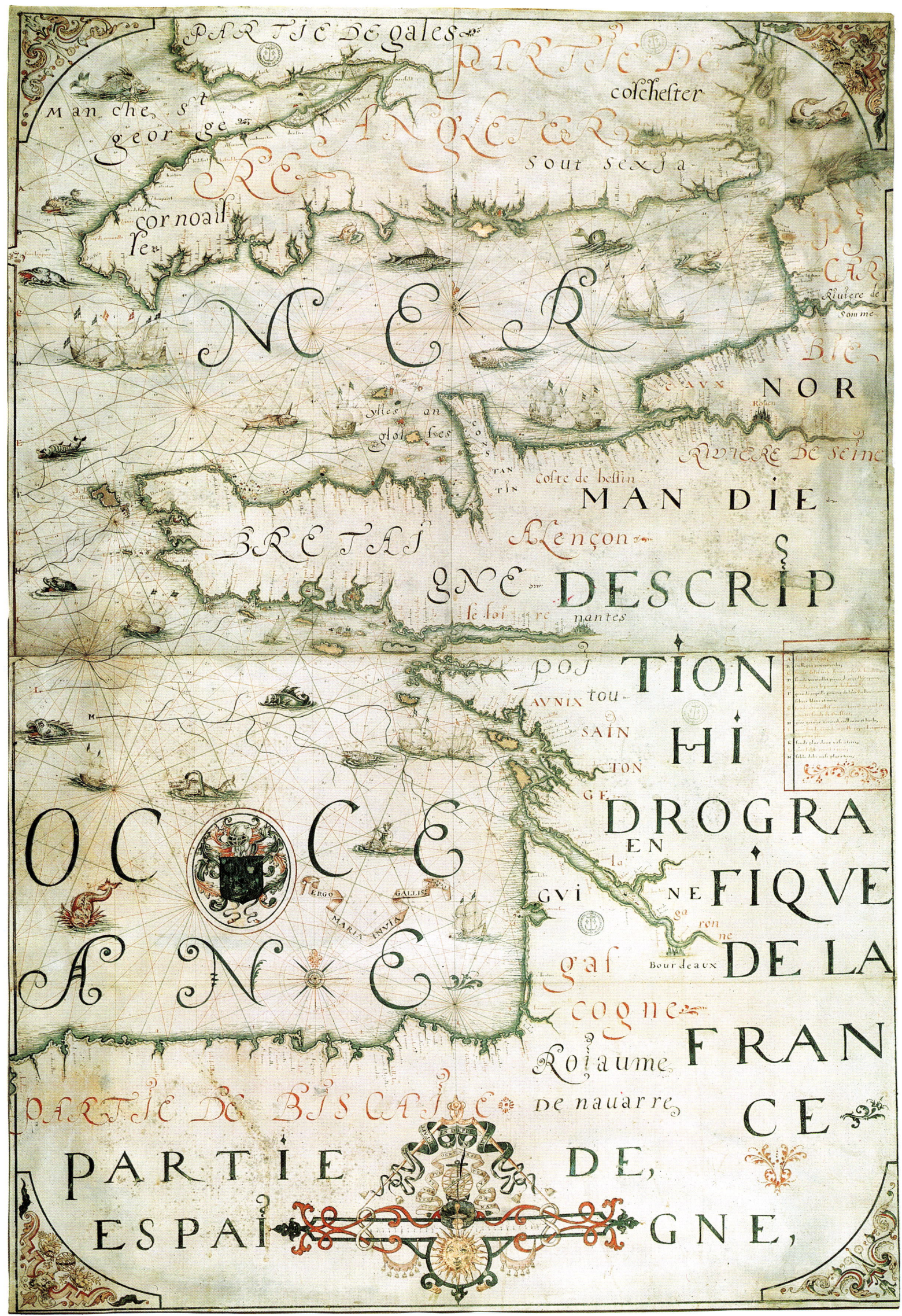

78 Jean Guérard, 1627

79 Hessel Gerritsz, ca. 1628

80 Jean Guérard, 1628

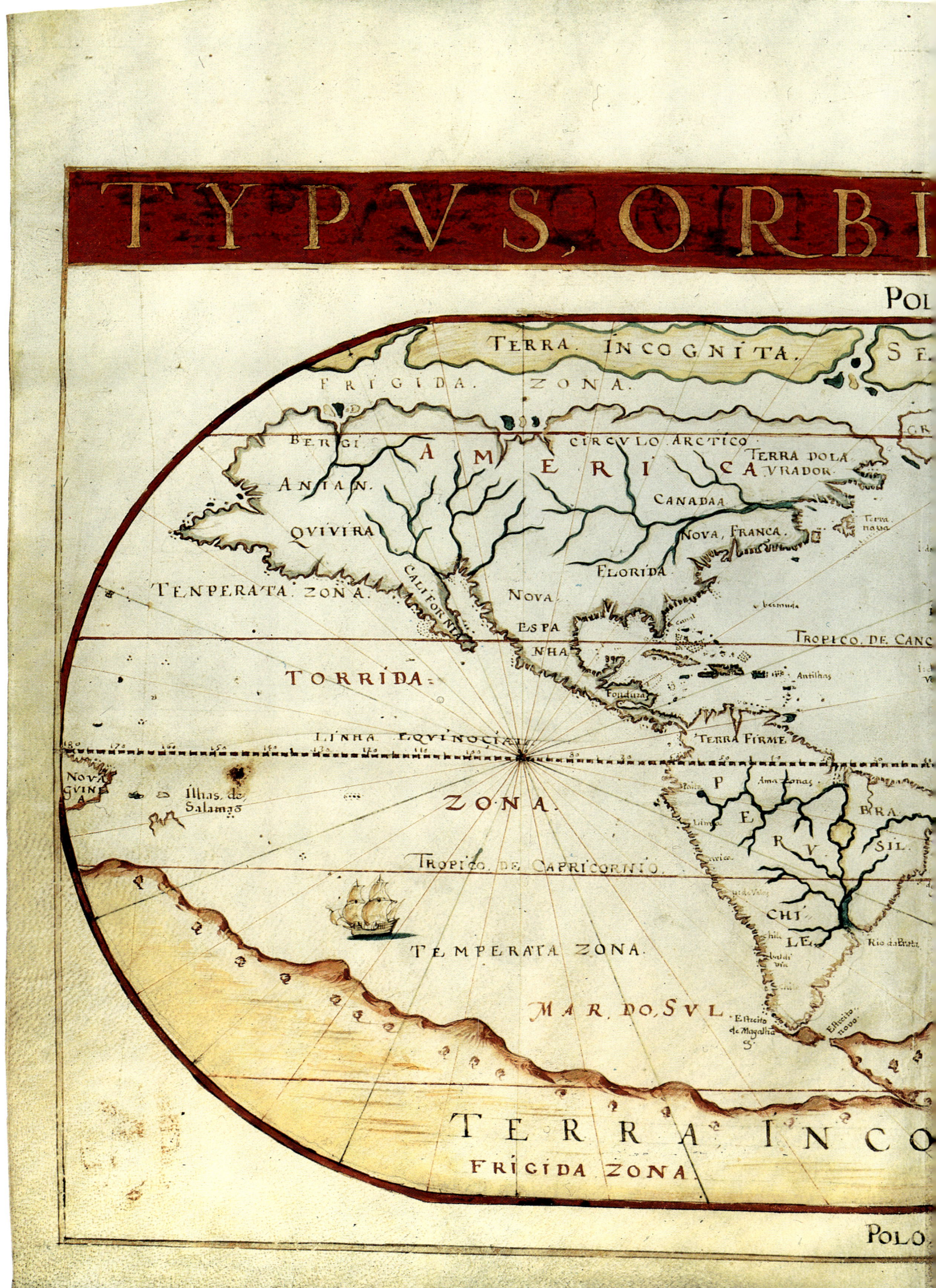
81 anon., ca. 1628

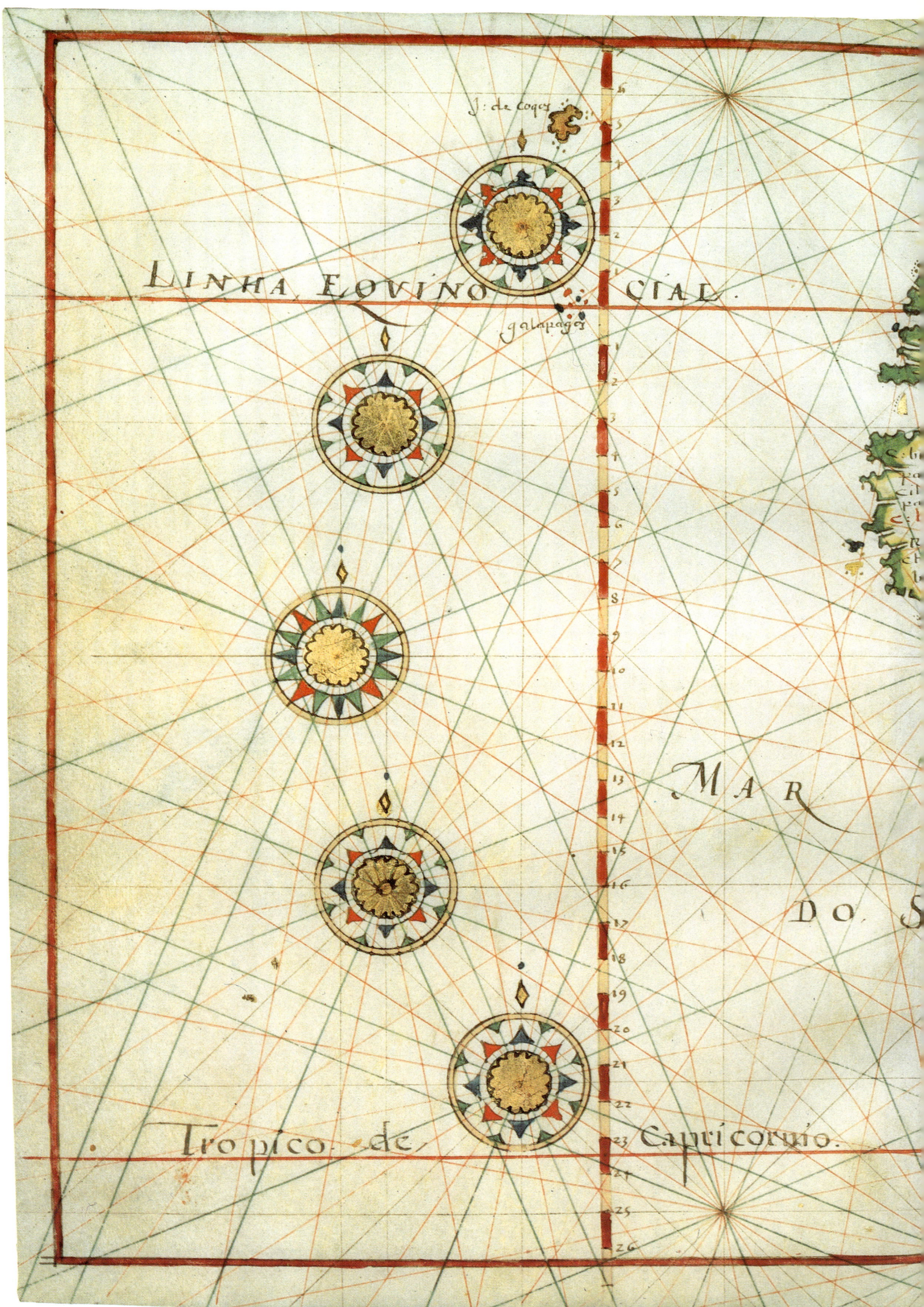

82 anon., ca. 1628

83 Augustin Roussin, 1633

84 Jean Guérard, 1634

85 João Teixeira Albernas I, 1649

87 Pieter Goos, 1660

88 Fred Woldemar, 1660

89 François Ollive, 1662

90 John Burston, 1665

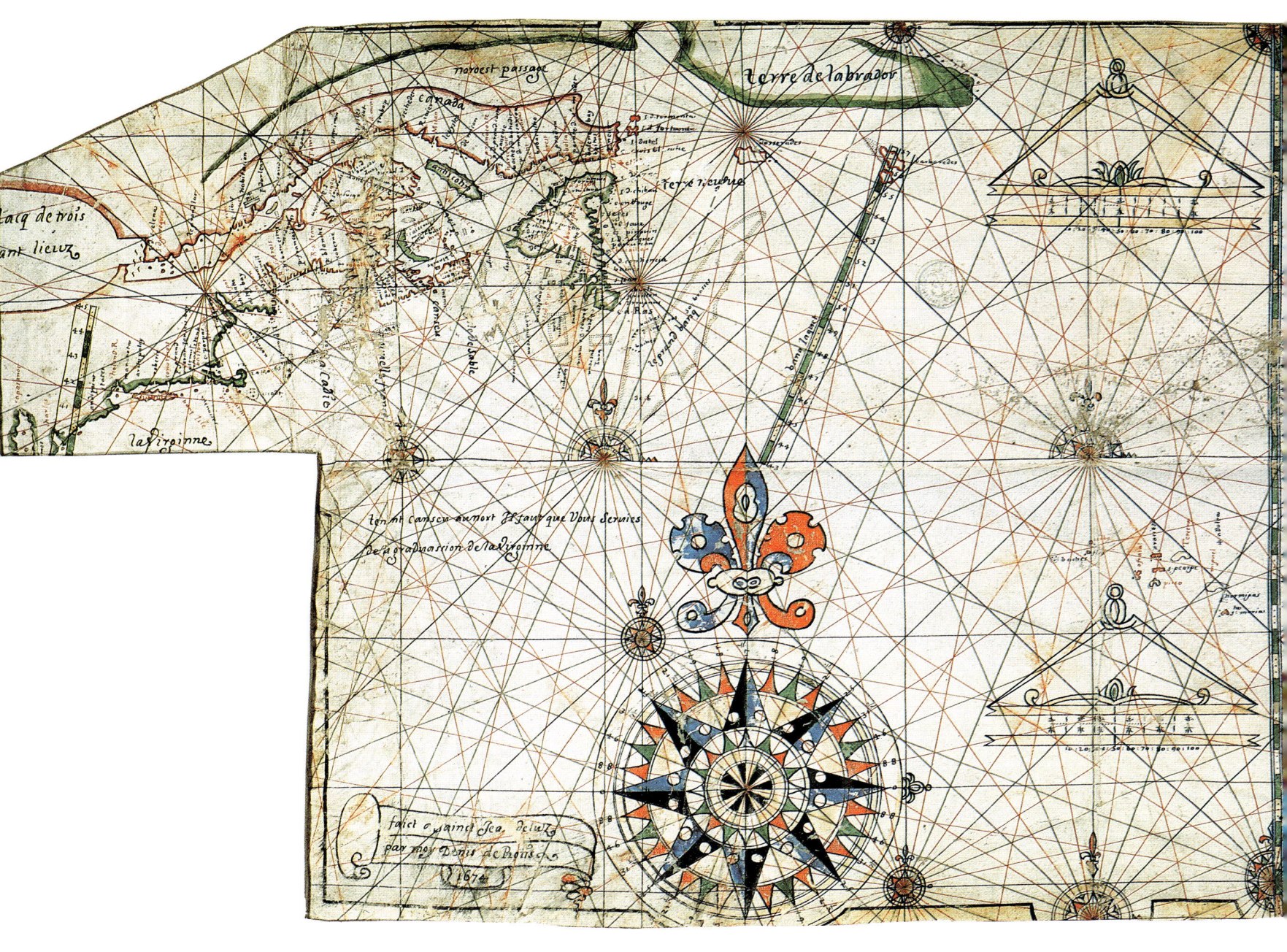

91 Denis de Rotis, 1674

92 Pierre Collin, 1666

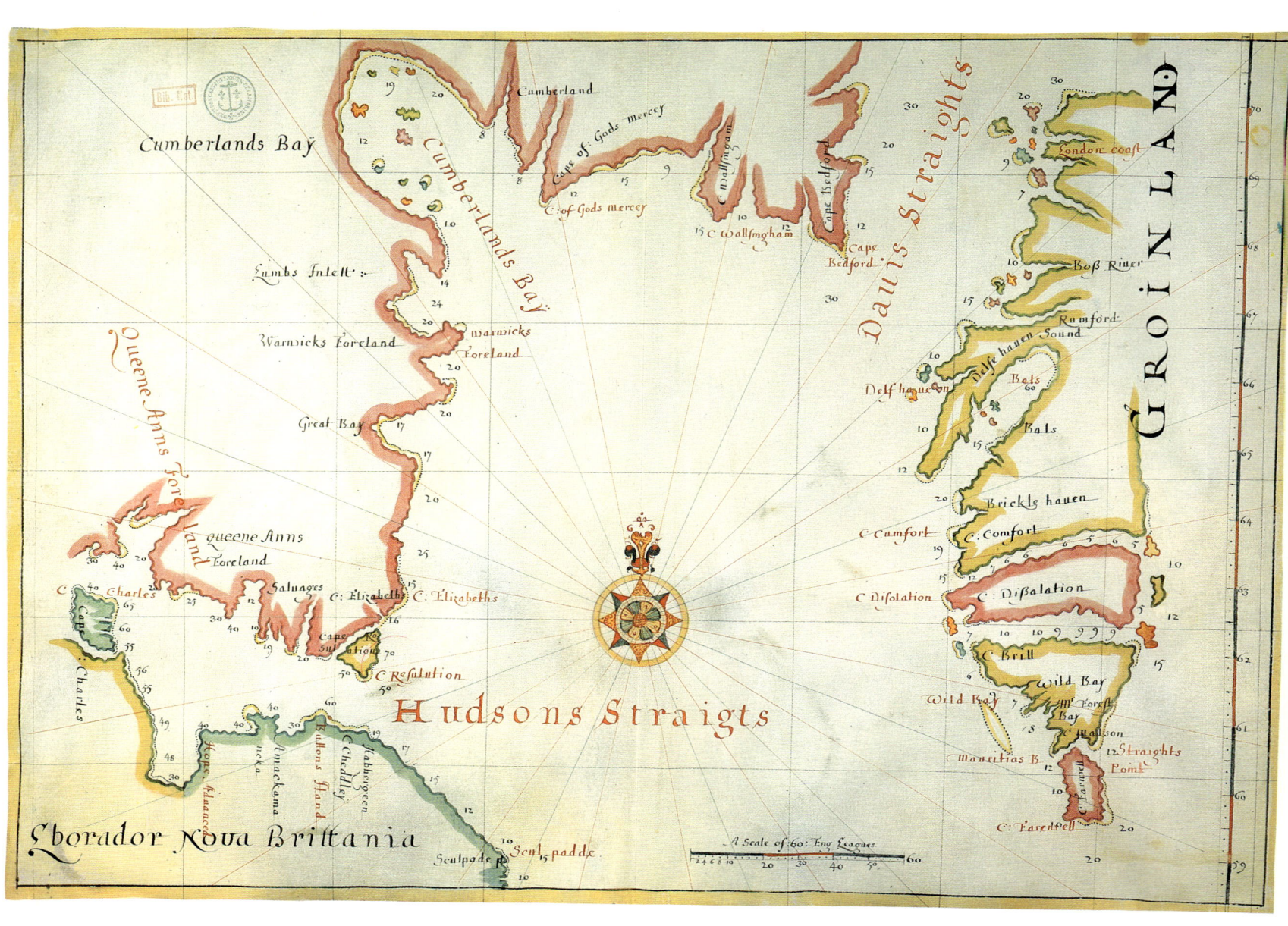

In This forme apereth the

A Table of the moste Remarckable and principall places About
Moha
A | Is a Peninsula wheareon Standeth an old Gally and a Fun
B | Is a Smalle Groue or heape of trees
C | Is a Tree Standing alone by it Selfe
D | Is a Pagoth or moOrish Church
E | Is a Castle
F | and H are two Small Steples
G | is the hieft Steple and Chefeft musquit or Church and Stande
  | A wry leaning to the Norwards
I | Is a Key or Mould wheare all Goods is landed and Shipped
K | Is a Pagouth or morish Church
L | Is a Whight house
M | Is a Black house on the poynt of the Land

95 Augustine Fitzhugh, 1683

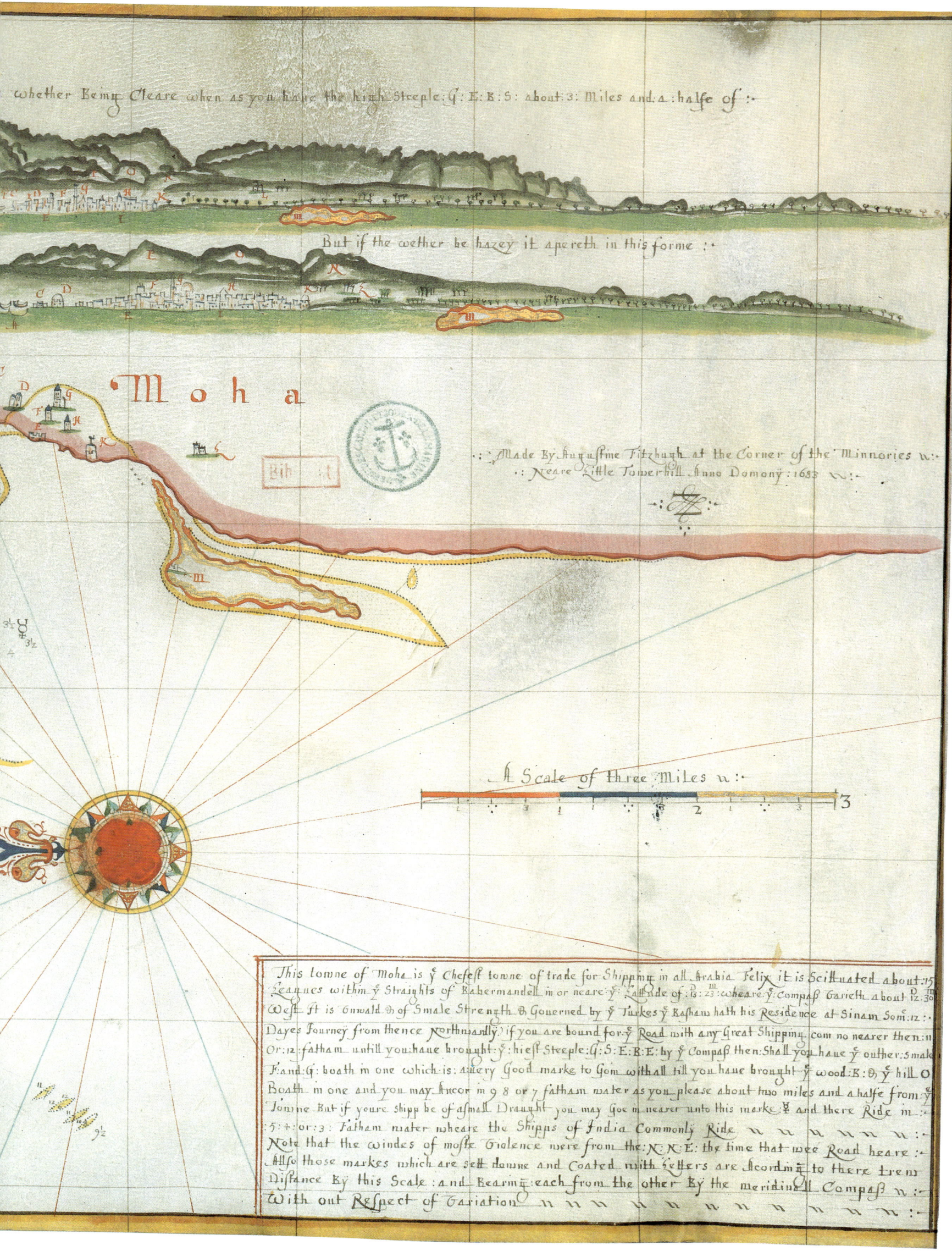

96 Joan Blaeu, 1688

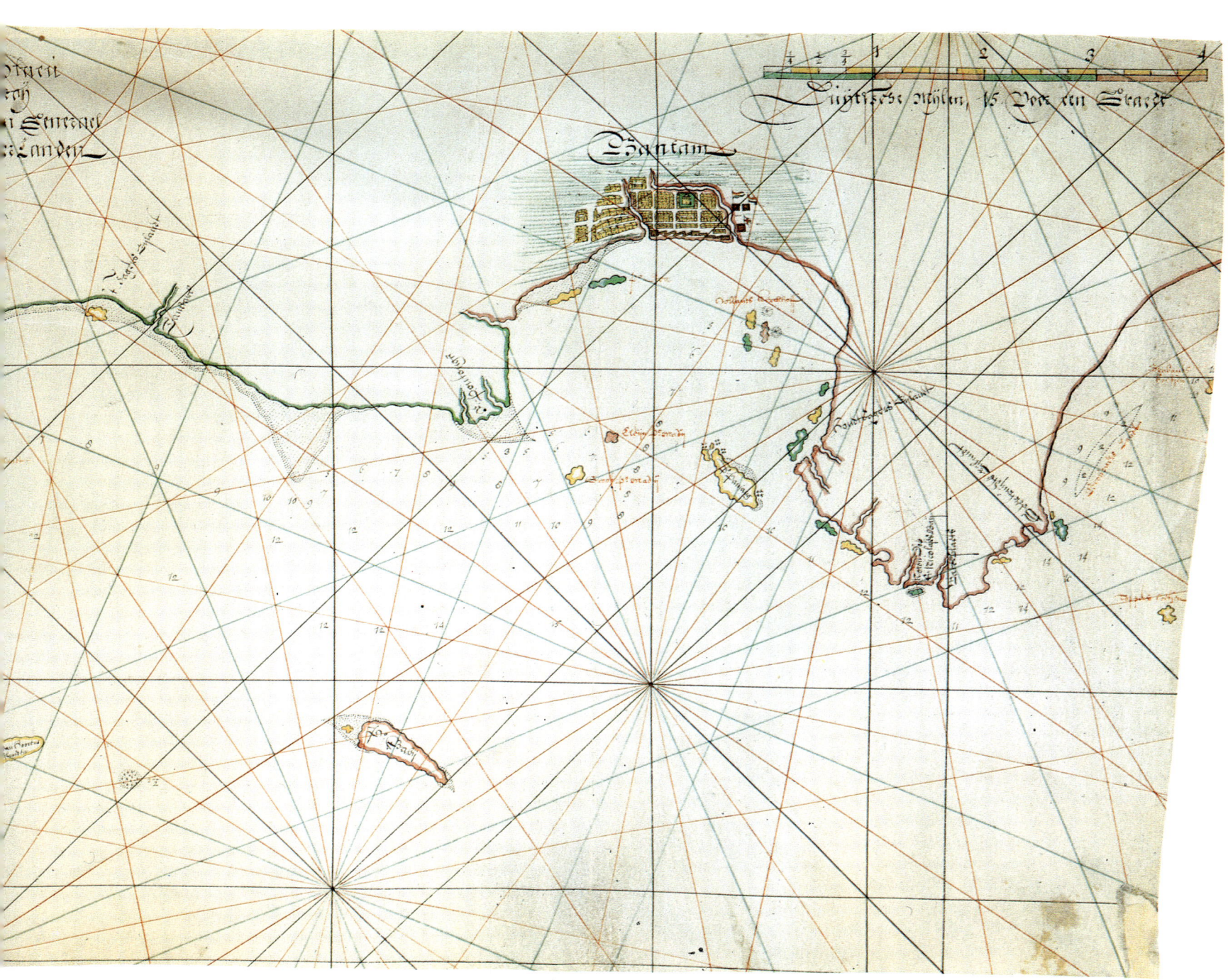

97 Pierre Detcheverry, 1689

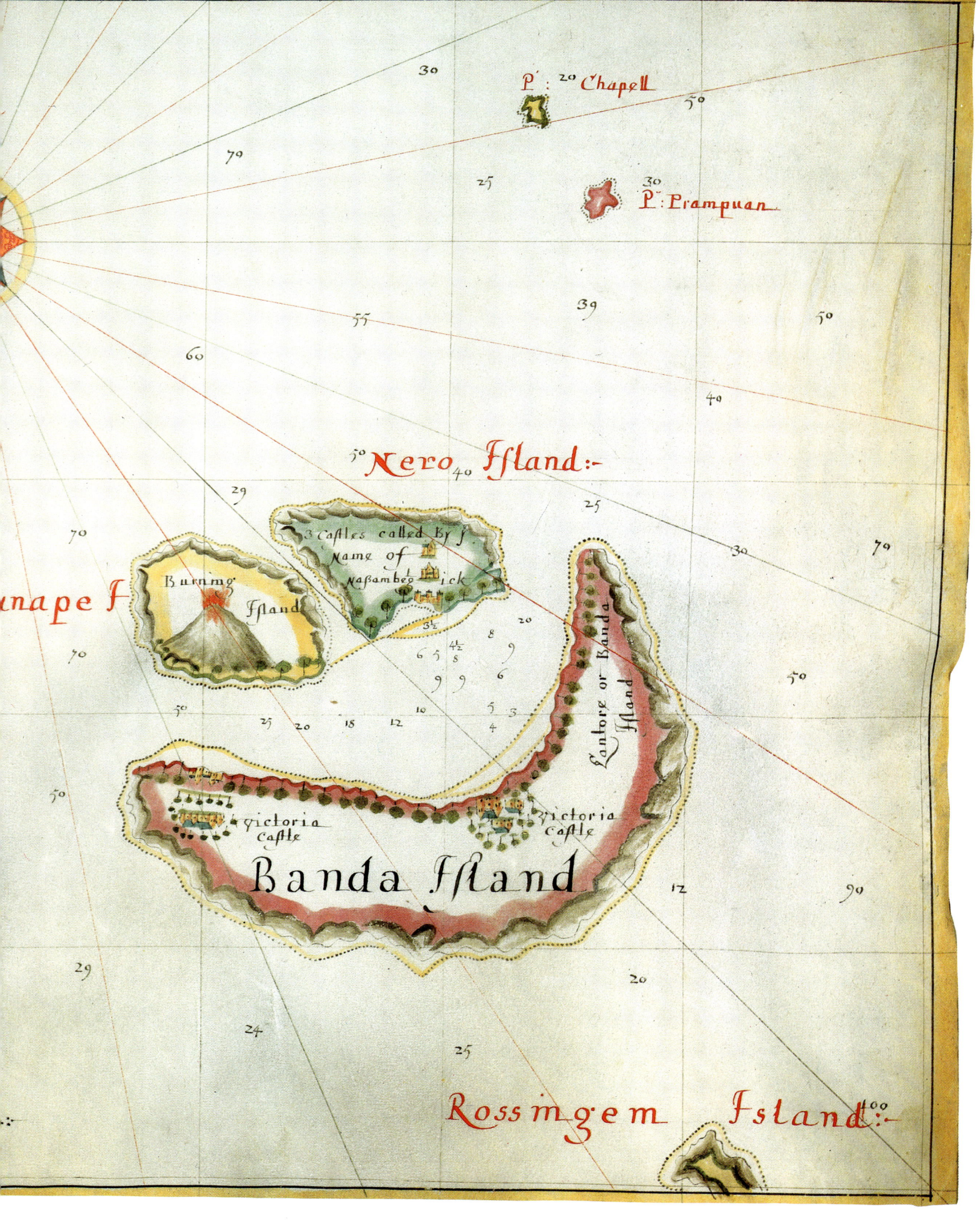

99 John Thornton, 1699

A

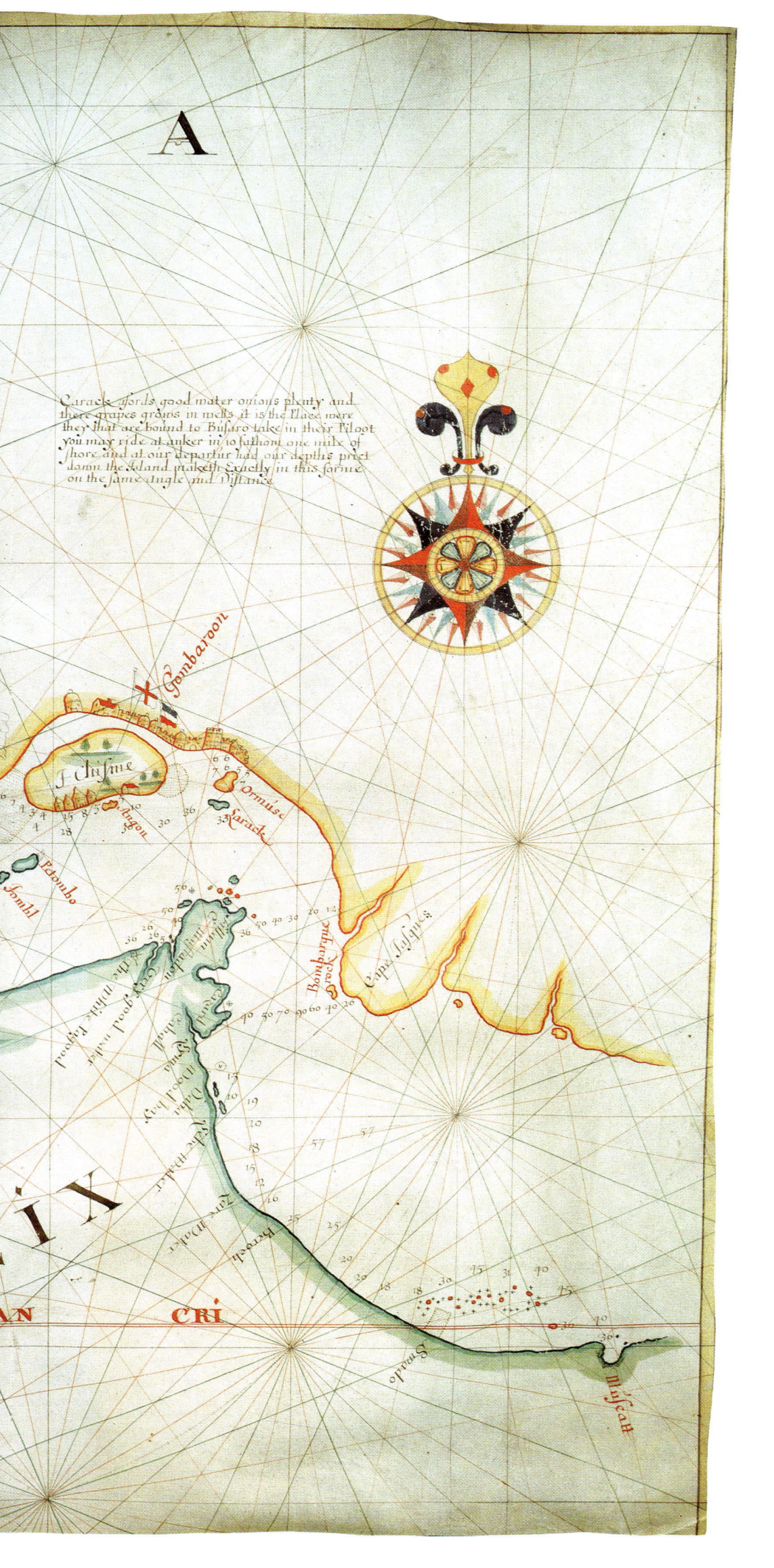

Carack afords good water onions plenty and there grapes growis in wells it is the Place were they that are bound to Bussaro take in their Piloot you may ride at anker in 10 fathom one mile of shore and at our departur had our depths prict down the Iland maketh exactly in this forme on the same angle and Distance

100 John Thornton, 1699

Commentaries

Abbreviations

B.N. Bibliothèque Nationale, Paris
fol. folio
ms manuscript
r recto
v verso

Names taken directly from the portolan charts are in italics.

1

'CARTE PISANE'
(End of the thirteenth century)
1 vellum leaf ms, 500 × 1050 mm
Paris, B.N.: Cartes et Plans, Rés. Ge B 1118

The Bibliothèque Nationale in Paris has the good fortune to possess the oldest known western sea chart. It dates from the end of the thirteenth century and is unsigned. Purchased from an old Pisan family during the nineteenth century, it is known as the 'Carte pisane', although its script appears to be Genoese. Moreover, the first mention of the existence on board of a 'portolan chart' was made on the Genoese ship that carried Saint Louis from Aigues-Mortes to Tunis in 1270.

This first sea chart, drawn with a pen on a sheet of vellum, succeeds in delineating the coasts and islands of the Mediterranean basin with great precision of scale. It has suffered the ravages of time: damp stains and numerous tears make the nomenclature of the Black Sea illegible; the Atlantic coast beyond the Straits of Gibraltar and as far as the city of Bruges remains imprecise and schematic. The south of England, only sketched in, is barely recognizable. As on all documents of this nature, the names of the ports are inscribed perpendicularly along the coasts: some in black; others, considered more important, in red. No geographical details appear inland. On the right, in the narrowest part of the vellum, originally the animal's neck, there is a circle containing the distance scale.

Apart from a Maltese cross on Saint John of Acre (*Acry*), which did not fall into Saracen hands until 1291, no decoration exists to distract the eye, and the austere structure of the chart gives us an inkling of its method of construction—something which no contemporary account has revealed. With no apparent projection or geographical coordinates, the delineation of the outline appears to have been drawn on a geometrical framework, whose red squares with green diagonals are visible in several places, one side of a square being equal to two divisions on the scale. Our attention is also drawn by a sheaf of radiating lines that intersect within two juxtaposed circles, one of which covers the western basin, the other the eastern basin of the Mediterranean. These lines, known as 'rhumb-lines' fan out from the four cardinal points (*Tramontana*: north; *Levante*: east; *Mexjorno*: south; *Ponente*: west) and some intermediary centres and correspond to the directions on a compass rose. They form a sort of web commonly known as the *marteloio*, which remains a trademark of the sea chart for more than four centuries.

This new chart, oriented towards magnetic north, is closely linked to the use of the compass. Henceforth a sailor could set a course, plan a route (to sail from one point to another he would follow a particular rhumb-line) and calculate the distance to be travelled. In addition, he would have a sea book, a sort of guide originating in the voyages of antiquity. The oldest of these in existence, the *Compasso da navigare*, is held in the Berlin Municipal Library (Ms Hamilton 397). For the sailor of those days, it was the equivalent of the books of sailing directions used by today's navigators. Dated January 1296, it is a contemporary of the 'Carte pisane' and would, according to Professor Motzo, have had the 'Carte pisane' itself, or a similar chart, attached to it.

Although complementary to each other, the fortunes of the guide and the chart were to be dissimilar; early examples of the sea book are even rarer today than those of the sea chart, of which over a hundred specimens dating from the fourteenth and fifteenth centuries still exist.

2-4

ATLAS
by Petrus Vesconte (1313)
6 vellum leaves, illuminated ms, 480 × 400 mm
2 Leaf 2: *Black Sea*
3 Leaf 5: *Central Mediterranean*
4 Leaf 4: *Aegean Sea and Crete*
Paris, B.N.: Cartes et Plans, Rés. Ge DD 687

Although the Genoese origin of the 'Carte pisane' is not absolutely certain, there is no doubt at all about the origin of the works by Petrus Vesconte signed *de Janua* ('of Genoa') and dated between 1311 and 1327.

This cartographer's work deserves consideration on account of both its very high quality and the number of items still extant, most of which are atlases. The 1313 atlas is not only the earliest he drew, but also the first of the genre to have come down to us. Nowadays kept flat and in a modern cloth binding, the six vellum leaves that form the atlas were originally fixed between wooden boards, which the leaves of the atlas held together, but the boards were smaller than the leaves by half. This method of mounting the vellum (also found in other atlases by Vesconte) explains the damage it has suffered, particularly at the former 'joints'. It also explains the expression *istas tabulas* used in the signature, whereas the author writes *ista carta* when referring to an individual map.

Petrus Vesconte de Janua fecit istas tabulas anno dni M CCC XIII is written in red ink on the first leaf of the atlas. After a circular calendar, the atlas contains charts of the Black Sea, the Aegean Sea and the various basins of the Mediterranean from east to west in that order. The Atlantic Ocean and the Adriatic Sea are grouped together on the last leaf.

The technique employed is obviously akin to that of the 'Carte pisane' (No. 1), but there are slight variations. For instance, the outer circle of the *marteloio*, previously drawn in red ink, is now just assumed—as was almost always to be the case in future. The names of the eight chief winds now appear in the form of initials; only the east wind (*Levante*) is represented symbolically by a cross that constantly reappears in later cartography. In three cases the graphic scale is still inscribed within a double red circle, but elsewhere it is embodied horizontally or vertically in the frame.

The orientation of the charts, some facing north (Black Sea, Aegean Sea), others east (central Mediterranean), and their individual proportions—the Aegean Sea, for example, is on a scale twice as big as the others—suggest that they have a certain autonomy from each other. The impression given is that the cartographer has reassembled a collection of partial surveys without completely harmonizing them. His principal concern in this operation seems to have been to preserve the unity of the maritime basins, leading him to subject peninsulas and coastlines to arbitrary divisions. There are, however, several manuscript notes indicating to the user the areas covered by each chart and specifying their limits.

The accuracy of the delineation and the improvements in nomenclature (when compared with a chart dated 1311 preserved in the State Archives of Florence), together with a comparison with other sources for Genoese maritime history, all bear witness to the fact that this chart's cartographer was aware of contemporary realities. For example, if we take the Black Sea, where the Genoese, who had been solidly entrenched there since 1261, controlled the supply ports for the eastern trade routes and procured supplies of local products, Vesconte specifies in the top right-hand corner of the chart: '*Hoc est mare tanna* [Tana was the most important Genoese trading post, at the far end of the Sea of Azov, at the mouth of the River Don] *cum mare Maiore usque ad bucha daneo cum Costantinopoli*' ('Sea of Tana and Major Sea as far as the mouth of the Danube and Constantinople'). On these shores, where the estuaries of the Dnieper and the Danube are highlighted with gold on a red, green and violet background, he has indicated a certain number of localities in red ink: *Puntarachia, Sinope, Simisso, Vatiza, Trapezonda, Flaxio*, etc., whose commercial importance is also known to us from their frequent mentions in Genoese notarized documents of the end of the thirteenth century.

As for the maritime route that led from Genoa to these trading posts, we know about it from, among other sources, the journals and logs that carefully recorded the stages of the journey. On a trip ships spent 60 per cent of their time in ports of call, some of which were major ports, compulsory stopping places where Genoa had a consul and a *fondouk*, or quarter, reserved for its merchants. Genoese galleys called in there for commercial transactions, stores, maintenance and fresh crews. On the Tyrrhenian coast of Italy and as far as the Otranto canal, these ports (clearly visible on No. 3) were Gaeta, Naples, Salerno, Messina and Crotone, all indicated in red. But there were also 'emergency' moorings, which might be needed in bad weather, when there was risk of pirates or simply at night fall, since sailors avoided sailing at night near coasts or in shallow waters unless it was absolutely necessary. Hence the profusion of place-names indicating possible shelter: we note the bay of Portovenere, where a Genoese citadel had been built long before, the bay of Terracina (*teracina*), at the foot of Monte Circeo, and Ugento, protected by Cape Santa Maria di Leuca (*cavo di Lece*).

Beyond the Otranto canal navigation was possible as far as Romania by going from island to island, the most important of which were carefully illuminated by Vesconte. Thus in No. 4 we see Euboea (*Nigpōt* = Negroponte), Crete (*Candea*), Rhodes (*Roda*), Chios (*Scio*) and Mytilene (*Metelini*). Even the smaller islands are not forgotten: Velopoula (*Velopola*) and Gerakounia (*Farchenire*) for example, mile-stones on the Monemvasia-Milos crossing, and all the others that offered refuge to Genoese galleys in places corresponding to the pace of their navigation. They are all in flat tint, and their names are distinguished from the coastal place-names by being inscribed in the opposite direction to them.

Thus, responding to clearly defined needs, the portolan chart provided an appropriate solution to the problems encountered daily by sailors in the Mediterranean Sea and the Black Sea. Nor is it surprising that the portolan chart should have been perfected in Genoa in the decades spanning two centuries (from 1275 to 1325), for the city of Saint George was experiencing a privileged moment of prosperity and a period of astonishing creativity in the fields of maritime and commercial techniques.

5-6

ATLAS
by Petrus Vesconte (ca. 1321)
9 parchment leaves pasted on 8 wooden boards and the inner faces of the binder's boards, 143 × 292 mm

5 Leaf 7: *Coast of Spain*
6 Leaf 8: *Coast of France, England and Ireland*
Lyons, Bibliothèque de la Ville, Ms. 175

In the extant work of Vesconte, there is a gap for the years between 1313 and 1318. From the latter date onwards, however, there are many charts, all of which were executed in Venice. Vesconte collaborated there with Marino Sanudo Torsello, illustrating his *Liber secretorum fidelium crucis*, a work of propaganda advocating a revival of the Crusades. The mainly geopolitical and economic nature of the argument of the *Liber* benefited from being supported by maps; and although most of them are anonymous, Vesconte's handiwork is clearly recognizable.

Whether Vesconte went to Venice at the request of Torsello or for some other reason, the decorative element of a number of his works took on a pronounced Venetian character there, especially this atlas preserved in the Bibliothèque de la Ville in Lyons. Still in its original format, it is mounted on eight small boards and on the inner faces of a fine binding of wooden mosaic, encrusted with ivory. The signature, written in red ink at the top right of the third leaf, is partly illegible: 'Petrus Vesconte de... fecit istam tabulam In Venecia....' In addition to a dragon (the symbol of Saint George and of Genoa) just underneath the signature, the corners of the charts are adorned with the figures of saints particularly venerated in Venice, like Saint Nicolas and Saint Lucy. Around the perpetual calendar at the beginning of the work are the four Evangelists represented symbolically. There is also a charming Annunciation. Venetian sensitivity is most apparent, however, in the style of these miniatures in which the passing from a lingering Byzantine-influenced style to a freer, more Gothic manner can be observed, as it can be in the *mariegole* (the registers in which religious and professional brotherhoods recorded their statutes of the same period). This change is expressed in the sketching of the figures' gestures and in their more relaxed postures.

To preserve the unity of the work while avoiding monotony, its composition was carefully planned: the number of illuminations and their arrangement vary from page to page but still relate to each other by a system of symmetrical inversions that provide the cartographer with the space he needs. The graphic scale (either horizontal or, more often, vertical) is placed in different positions on the margins so as to integrate itself into the whole. It is obvious that the Lyons atlas is primarily a work of art, a collector's piece.

Although he was an artist, Vesconte was nevertheless a cartographer, anxious for his work to be up-to-date and accurately plotted. In such a sumptuous work, the austerity of the second leaf of the atlas comes as a surprise: it consists of a simple *marteloio*, without illumination or geographical delineation, whereby the author indicates the southerly orientation of all the charts that follow and their scale, which is the same for all. This insistence on the rhumb-line network can be seen again in another Vesconte atlas preserved in the Biblioteca del Civico Museo Correr in Venice, which is very similar to the Lyons atlas in form and content. Above his signature, Vesconte has drawn himself, seated at his desk, both hands on the *marteloio* he is completing (see p. 14). No doubt he wished to draw attention to the originality of a technique he had not invented himself, but which he had greatly helped to perfect and make known.

He mastered this skill sufficiently well to be able to map the regions beyond the Mediterranean successfully, and we can evaluate here the progress made in the knowledge of the coasts of Europe in just a few decades. Where the 'Carte pisane' has a straight SW-NE line drawn between Lisbon and Denmark, the two relevant charts of the Lyons atlas show the changes in direction of these coasts, making them perfectly recognizable if not always totally accurate. Thus the French coast (No. 6), for example, despite being foreshortened between Bayonne (*Baona de Gascogna*) and the Pointe de Grave (*Cavo Sta Maria de Sollac*), too compressed in Brittany and curiously elongated at the base of the Cotentin, nevertheless achieves its familiar arrowhead shape with the addition of the coastline of Flanders. It would seem that the cartographer based his delineation on certain navigational key points in the Atlantic, whose relative locations are well sited (Cape Saint Vincent, Cape Finisterre, Land's End), but which he has joined together by sections of unevenly surveyed coastline. Judging by the density of the nomenclature between Saint Nazaire (*San Sanazar*) and Saint-Malo (*San Mallo*), he is familiar with Brittany as well as the French and Flemish coasts from Caen (*Cam*) as far as Dordrecht (*Dordrec*). Likewise he knows England on its southern and eastern flanks as far as Hull (*Ullo*), and southern Ireland from Lough Corrib (the island of 358 saints—*isole ccclviij Sce Beate*) to north of Dublin (*Dum Velim*). Elsewhere the contours are uncertain and the nomenclature hesitant, particularly in northern Ireland, the west coast of England, Scotland and the shores of the North Sea beyond the Rhine.

This relative accuracy in the configuration of Atlantic Europe is connected with the fairly long-standing activities in these areas of Mediterranean mariners. In the second half of the thirteenth century, several of Vesconte's compatriots had taken service with European sovereigns (Bonifacio in England, the Pessagnos in Spain, Benedetto Zaccaria in France) in order to organize their navies. No doubt the campaigns in which they took part allowed them to collect information on the spot. But, above all, Genoese merchants, already established at Almeria (*Almaria*) and Seville (*Sibilla*) since 1147, and in Portugal in 1251, were trading by sea with Flanders and England by the end of the thirteenth century. Judging by the contracts for chartering ships, these maritime contacts rapidly became regular. After putting in at several ports in the western Mediterranean (*Aigue morte, Maiorcha*), and on the Spanish and Maroccan coasts (Ceuta—*Septa*, Casablanca—*Niffe*), the galleys went either to Sluis (*Laclusa*), twin port to Bruges, or to Sandwich (*Sanuis*), Southampton (*Antona*) or London (*Londres*).

Other nations soon joined the Genoese, in particular the Venetians, whose first fleet in Flemish waters is recorded in 1318. The charts drawn by Vesconte may have helped to encourage these voyages which, in return, provided cartographers with new and enriched information. Ireland does not appear on the Biblioteca del Civico Museo Correr atlas of 1318. It is present, although very clumsily drawn and without nomenclature, in the Vatican museum atlas of 1320. Therefore we may reasonably postulate that the Lyons atlas, which has lost its date, is later than both of them.

7

FROM THE BALTIC SEA TO THE RED SEA
by Angelino Dulcert (1339)
2 vellum leaves, illuminated ms assembled into a chart, 750 × 1020 mm
Paris, B.N.: Cartes et Plans, Rés. Ge B 696

In the history of cartography, the Majorcans were not left behind by the Genoese. The first chart demonstrably produced in Majorca is by Angelino Dulcert and dated 1339. It is signed in Latin on its eastern margin, at the feet of the *Usbech* emperor: *Hoc opus fecit Angelino Dulcert ano M CCC XXX VIIII de mense Augusti in civitate maioricharum*.

This chart is constructed on two tangential systems of rhumbs placed exactly in the centre of the chart, which divide the horizon into thirty-two compass points, and the delineation of the Atlantic coasts has been further improved. Three of the Canary Islands are recorded for the first time; on one of them is mentioned the name of the Genoese who had taken command there on behalf of Portugal between 1320 and 1330: *Insula de Lanzarotus Marocellus*. An improvement can also be observed in the nomenclature of the British Isles, both in the Bristol Channel (where Cornwall has a far more accurate outline) and on the east coast of Scotland as far as the River Tay (*Latara*).

But what really distinguishes this chart from the preceding ones is the presence, inland, of an abundant toponymy, accompanied by symbolic signs: maroon ribbons for the principal mountain chains, blue loops for rivers and lakes, vignettes identifying towns and banners indicating sovereignty. Moreover, the geographical space covered in this work extends a great deal beyond the areas normally found on nautical charts. In Africa, south of the Atlas mountains (*mons athlans*), it reaches the 'land of Negroes' (*terra nigrorum*) and the kingdom of Mali. In Europe it maps Norway and the northern shores of the Baltic Sea; in Asia it not only delineates the Caspian Sea (*mare de Bacu sive Caspium*) into which the Volga flows, but also shows Mesopotamia and Persia.

In these outer zones on the perimeter of the areas visited by Mediterranean shipping, the network of rhumb-lines has been simplified; on the other hand there are an impressive number of inscriptions (about thirty) illustrated with delicate miniatures, providing information on the commerce, resources and customs of the inhabitants, or relating biblical or classical traditions.

The chart in question is therefore not only the first dated and signed Majorcan portolan chart, but also a work with a totally individual concept, whose author is trying to establish a cartographic synthesis of the known world that recalls, in certain respects, the traditional mappa mundi but is based this time on the portolan chart and composed in accordance with its methods.

A long controversy has divided the learned world as to the 'nationality' of this cartographer, who may well be the same person as Angelino Dalorto, the (Genoese?) author of a chart of a very similar nature constructed in 1330.

In actual fact, even if a Genoese influence is entirely plausible in Majorca, where the Genoese had been established since the twelfth century, we cannot fail to take into consideration the obvious affinities between Dulcert's chart and the environment in which it was produced. The Kingdom of Aragon, which annexed Majorca in 1229, had created an enormous maritime empire for itself in the thirteenth and fourteenth centuries, developing commercial relations with the whole Mediterranean, penetrating into Barbary as far as the Tafilalet, maintaining a permanent embassy at the court of the Khan of Persia and preceding, and probably guiding, the Genoese on the route to Flanders and England. Besides, other indicators suggest that on this island, which had benefited from years of contact with Arab and Jewish scholarship, nautical cartography had very early reached a level that rendered it comparable, in the eyes of its contemporaries, with Genoese cartography. In 1335, Opicinus de Canistris, an apostolic penitentiary working in Avignon, was using nautical charts from both Genoese and Majorcan sources. Moreover, it is in a text by the Majorcan Ramón Llull, that the first indication can be found of a possible use at sea of a *marteloio*.

In short, there is no doubt that Dulcert's chart is an expression of authentically Majorcan knowledge, which sprang from several sources and whose originality lay precisely in a readiness to synthesize that resulted in a recognizable, individual style, which was perpetuated for three centuries by the cartographers of the Majorcan school.

8

CATALAN ATLAS
(ca. 1375)
12 parchment leaves, illuminated ms pasted on 5 wooden boards and on the inner faces of the binder's boards, 640 × 250 mm
Leaves 5ᵛ and 6: *Atlantic and western Mediterranean*
Paris, B.N., Ms espagnol 30

The Catalan Atlas is very well known to the discerning public; it has been published several times and shown at major exhibitions. It is neither dated nor signed and cannot be definitely attributed to Abraham Cresques, despite some efforts to do so. In fact that attribution relies on the conflation of two chronologically irreconcilable documentary traditions. The first, and probably the most dependable of these, is based on the successive inventories of the Bibliothèque Royale, later the Bibliothèque Nationale in Paris, where the atlas is still preserved. If these inventories are to be believed, the map apparently entered the collections of Charles V between 1375 (the probable date of its production, furnished by the perpetual calendar which accompanies the charts) and November 1380, when a stock check declares that: *il y est* ('it is there'). If this is really the case, it could not possibly be the map of 'Cresques the Jew' which the heir to the throne of Aragon, the future Juan I, said he wished to offer to the king of France in a letter of November *1381*.

Whether or not it is by the hand of that renowned artist who was protected by the king of Aragon and his appointed purveyor, the atlas of Charles V is in any case one of the finest examples of Catalan cartography of the fourteenth century. The language of its legends, its graphic design and the style of the illuminations all point to its belonging to the Catalan school, a fact that is also apparent in the very concept of the work—a portolan chart extending as far as Asia. The leaf of the atlas that maps the archipelagos of the Atlantic is a good example of the cartographer's desire to synthesize information obtained from different sources. Anxious to include the most recent data, he has depicted a ship off the African coast and recalls, with two lines of commentary, the departure of Jacme Ferrer for *le riu de lor* (Senegal) in 1346. The Canary Islands, all of which had been visited by 1341 and several times since, are now complete. Further north, the cartographer seems still in doubt: faced with the dilemma of choosing between facts of meagre substance and well-attested theories, he draws a group of islands that may be the Azores and Madeira archipelagos, but which he describes in a long inscription as fabulous and paradisiac islands, 'the Fortunate Isles', on which subject he quotes Isidore and Pliny.

This is a unique document of an exceptional size. The method of assembly, whatever it was originally—some think, in accordance with inventory descriptions from before the sixteenth century, that it consisted initially of 'six large wooden leaves'—prevented it from being examined as a whole. It was necessary, therefore, to find a means of indicating the orientation in a more compact way than by inscribing the names of the winds on the edge of the *marteloio*. The form chosen was a compass rose, like those painted on the backgrounds of compasses; restrained in style and yet richly decorated, it is annotated in blue, red and gold with the Catalan names of the eight principal winds: *Tramuntana, Grego, Levante, Lexaloch, Metzodi, Labetzo, Ponente, Magistro*. Two compass points are particularly emphasized: the east of the classical mappae mundi, adorned with a trefoil, and compass north, with the seven stars of the Little Dipper.

A century later, the Little Dipper gave way to the fleur-de-lis of the House of Anjou. The illuminated compass rose, of which we have here the first example, was to become a classical element of the portolan chart.

9

MEDITERRANEAN SEA
by Guillelmus Soleri (ca. 1385)
1 leaf illuminated ms, 1020 × 650 mm
Paris, B.N.: Cartes et Plans, Rés. GB 1131

Having been notched while it was rolled up, this chart suffers from deep indentations in several places; nevertheless, it is still extremely beautiful, owing to the typically Catalan decorative elements, painstakingly executed by the author, in particular the discs arranged around the margin on which the names of the winds are inscribed.

Three of these have had their names placed in magnificently illuminated discs: they are *Tramuntana* (north), a gold star on a blue background, *Levant* (east), a red sun ablaze with gold and *Metzodi* (south), a crescent moon with a human face. Nearby, three inscriptions in vermilion ink, each reading in a different direction, concern respectively Europe, Asia and Africa. Of each continent it is said that it represents a third of the world (*es la ters part del mondo*), and the text specifies the religion of the inhabitants. The cartographer has placed his signature (in Latin) beside the inscription relating to Europe, 'where the Christians live': '*Gujllelmus Soleri civjs maioricha[rum] me fecit.*' This preoccupation with religion and this biblical view of the world— that of the tripartite mappae mundi—also appear in Arabia and Syria, where the vignettes, more voluminous than elsewhere, and inscriptions recall the places of pilgrimage: the Holy Sepulchre (*Santo Sepulcro*), the monastery of Saint Catherine, perched on Mount Sinai, and Mecca, 'where the prophet Mahomet is buried' (*Mecha enesta ciutat es la sepiutura de M...t profeta*).

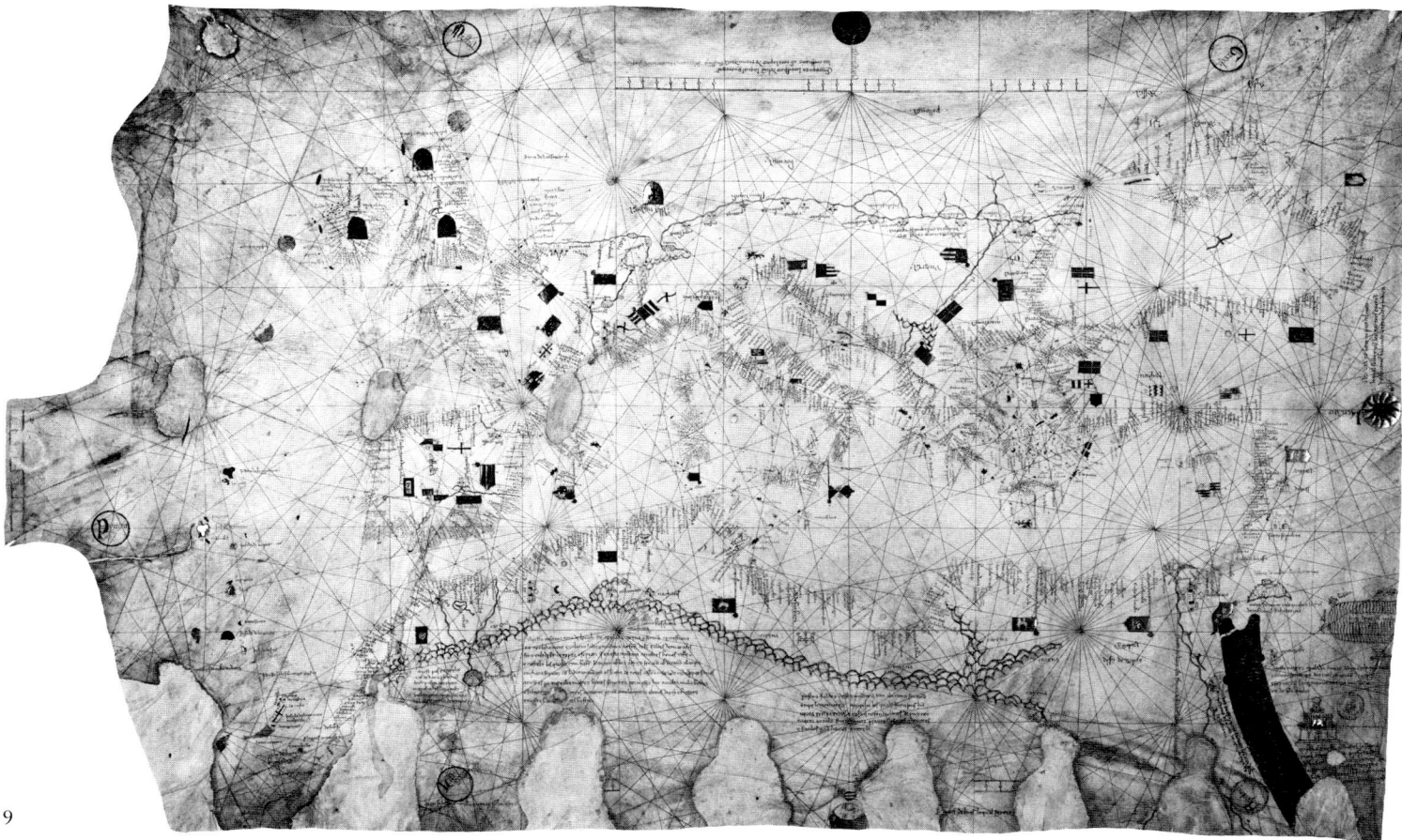

9

Such emphasis is all the more striking because this chart is more strictly a nautical chart than other Catalan works. It covers little more ground than the 'normal portolano', except in Africa, and the nomenclature of the interior is minimal, although that of the coasts is very rich. In the Atlantic, to the north of the Canary Islands, the cartographer has taken pains over the delineation of archipelagos which, despite being too near the continent and in an incorrect N–S orientation, nevertheless certainly represent Madeira and the Azores. Their Italian toponymy bears this out, and the Portuguese who 'discovered' them in 1431 were, in several cases, simply content to translate their Italian names. Thus the *Insula de Legname* later became Madeira. More accurate than the Catalan Atlas (No. 8)—there are two additional islands: *Lovo* (the Formigas Rocks) and *Capraria* (Santa Maria)—this chart by Guillelmus Soleri is less well informed than the one he signed in 1385 and which is kept in Florence today. Therefore this undated document is usually attributed to the period 1375 to 1385; however, a close analysis of its toponymic content by T. Campbell suggests a later date.

Whether the discoverers of these islands were Genoese in the service of Portugal, Catalans (*Salvatge* comes from their language) or Norwegians using birds to locate landmarks (an hypothesis based on the place-name *Corvi Marinis*), this newly navigated area is present on nautical charts from the second half of the fourteenth century. It was in this vast expanse of more than two million square kilometres 'from the westernmost of the Azores to the easternmost of the Canary Islands (*Chaunu*)', that Western mariners were to practise 'off-shore traffic on the high seas' for a century before launching themselves on the ocean, towards Africa and America.

10

VENETIAN ATLAS
(End of the fourteenth century)
8 parchment leaves, illuminated ms pasted on 3 small wooden boards and on the inner faces of the binder's boards, 235 × 155 mm
Leaves 5 and 6: *Western Basin of the Mediterranean, Atlantic Coasts of Portugal, Spain and France*
Lyons, Bibliothèque de la Ville, Ms 179

This is a little-known and highly unusual atlas, unfortunately anonymous. An indication of its origin is given by the binding, which is made of wood, engraved and painted with the arms of the Cornaros, an illustrious Venetian family that provided the Republic of Venice with a doge from 1365 to 1368. Above the shield, a female silhouette—no doubt representing the crest of a helmet—wears a garment dating from the very end of the fourteenth century. A study of the nomenclature confirms this identification: the lisped or abbreviated place-names (*Zenoa* for Genoa, *Frezur* for Fréjus, *Vignon* for Avignon) are in Venetian dialect.

The corners of the four plates making up the atlas are adorned with blue or red grids on which monsters writhe, with human heads that are sometimes crowned. On No. 10 finely drawn symbols of the Evangelists can be found, winged figurines bearing on scrolls the four names: *Iohannes, Matheus, Lucas, Marcus*. The golden frame with red and blue foliated scrolls is interrupted when necessary to leave room for the cartographer's outline.

Visibly cramped by the parchment available to him, the latter has contrived, on two of the leaves of the atlas, to arrange on a single network, outlines constructed on different scales (the Black Sea is twice as small as the Aegean Sea) or differently oriented. Thus the western basin of the Mediterranean is depicted on the left of the *marteloio* with an easterly orientation; whereas on the right, the Iberian peninsula and the French coast face south. To ensure the transition from one group to another, the Iberian coast between *Valencia* and Cartagena (*Cartaiena*) and the African coast from *Marzaqbir* (Mers el Kebir) and *Meliana* (Moulouya) are repeated.

This technique involved a curious bringing together of geographically remote coastlines: those of the Maghreb can be seen quite close and running parallel to those of France between the Gironde and Ushant (*Husent*). But for the pilot of the Flanders *Mude* (a convoy organized by the Serenissima) who put in at Valencia or Almeria before sailing out on to the ocean, the cartographer has inserted the most important items: the directions thanks to which the pilot could set a course and the relative distances from one shore to another of the same maritime basin.

11

THE MEDITERRANEAN SEA AND
THE BLACK SEA
by Albertino de Virga (1409)
1 vellum leaf, coloured ms, 680 × 430 mm
Paris, B.N.: Cartes et Plans, Rés. Ge D 7900

On this fairly small chart, the coastal names are indicated in an elegant but minute script. The author has signed in an even finer hand, at a slant, in the neck of the vellum, trimmed to the shape of a gable: '*1409. Alber... Virga me fezit in Vinexia.*'

The cartographer has framed his subject with precision within this small space, by executing an initial dry-point sketch, which the final outline does not always follow. The Irish and Moroccan coasts are cut off by the edge of the vellum in such a way that there is no room for any archipelagos in the Atlantic, apart from the British Isles. On the opposite side, the Black Sea, which in its normal position would have been beyond the margin, has been reduced in scale and moved to the northwest where it is curiously placed above the Aegean Sea. On the northeast margin of the parchment a special scale indicates: *Questi mig[lia] sie di questo mar maior* ('these miles are those of the Major Sea'). Virga probably had recourse to these methods, already employed by the anonymous author of the Lyons atlas (No. 10), for the same reasons: either a lack of parchment, or the client's wish to have a portable chart.

Apart from the Black Sea, the 'miles' on the chart are given on three other scales, but the appearance of the Atlantic coastlines, foreshortened in a north-south direction, demonstrates that—unknown to the cartographer—the unit employed to measure them is not the same as the one used for the Mediterranean basin. This inconsistency of scale between the Atlantic and the Mediterranean is a feature of the portolan charts right from the beginning. It combines with the northwest torsion suffered by the outlines, owing to magnetic variation, to place certain eastern Mediterranean localities at too high a relative latitude: here Venice is on the same east-west parallel as Boulogne-sur-Mer (*Bologna*).

It is primarily the coasts that the Flanders convoy did not go near which are too short; like the Genoese ships, the Venetian galleys often steered a straight course from Seville and were unfamiliar with the Portuguese and French coasts. On the other hand, the cartographer has given more precise measurements for the English coasts and the approaches to the Scheldt, which the Flanders convoy regularly visited after the interruptions imposed by the Black Death and the Hundred Years War.

However, the cartographer's attention is directed above all towards the east. It is here that he has drawn an elaborate rhumb network centred on Greece; elsewhere on the chart the *marteloio* has been simplified. The rare decorative features are in the east: discreet clover leaves on eight of the points of the *marteloio* and floral motifs in arabesques in the neck and corners. Moreover, it is toward the east that the document must be turned, in order to appreciate its symmetrical arrangement. Finally it should be noted that the author emphasizes the mapping of certain regions. Thus the place-names of the Italian peninsula, Sicily and the Dalmatian coast are all inscribed in red ink. As for the city of Venice, not only is it shown with its lagoon closed off by a cordon of islets scattered from Aquileia to Ravenna, but it is also linked to dry land by a cruciform network of rivers (the Piave, Brenta and Adige?), which connects it with Treviso (*Triviso*), Padua (*Padoa*) and Ferrara (*Firara*), the first two of which had just been conquered by the Serenissima in the years prior to the construction of the chart (1404–1406). Similarly, the branches of the Nile are reunited at Cairo (alias Babylon), one of the most prosperous anchorages of Venetian commerce.

Such awareness of current events is not surprising on the part of a cartographer capable of producing his one other known work: a mappa mundi in which he demonstrates his knowledge of the most recent information on still poorly explored regions of Asia, northern Europe and Africa. To the latter, in particular, this cartographer attributes a configuration close to reality, several years before its circumnavigation by the Portuguese.

12

FROM THE BALTIC SEA TO THE NIGER
by Mecia de Viladestes (1413)
1 vellum leaf, illuminated ms, 850 × 1150 mm
Paris, B.N.: Cartes et Plans, Rés. Ge AA 566

Discovered by Joaquín Lorenzo Vilanueva in the archives of the Charterhouse of Val de Cristo, near Segorbe, this large chart was described by him for the first time in 1806 in his *Viage literario a las iglesias de España*. It is a brightly coloured document, richly illuminated, on which are depicted Africa's solemn sovereigns: the sultan of Egypt (*LO SOLDA*), the king of Kanem (*REX ORGANA*), the king of Nubia (*REX ONUBIA*) and Prester John (*PESTRE IOHA*), the legendary Christian sovereign whose alliance was sought by the West in order to attack Islam from the rear; also *REX MUSAMELI*, the Mandingo emperor, master of the gold of the Sudan, as well as *REX BUBEDER*, a nomad chief mounted on a camel and bearing a royal title but lacking the insignia of office. The artist also turns his gaze toward the ocean (*MAR HOCCEANI*), where two ships are sailing: off the African coast the ship of Jacme Ferrer flying the Aragonese flag; on the opposite side in the direction of Iceland, a cog at anchor near a 'great fish' (*grans peses*) serves as base for two sailors in a fishing-boat, who are busily whaling. The boat also recalls the marvellous voyage of Saint Brendan by the presence on board of a bishop. If the legend is to be believed, Saint Brendan mistook one of the cetaceans for an island and landed on it.

The chart is oriented towards the west, where, on what had been the animal's neck, appears its only reference point: a blue disc with a gold cross (*Poñat*). It is here that the signature is placed in gold letters on a network of arabesques: '*Mecia de Viladestes me fecit in ano M CCCC XIII*'. No country of origin is indicated, but it is quite apparent: the area is the same as that covered by Dulcert (No. 7), the style of the paintings recalls the Charles V atlas (No. 8) and the forty-odd inscriptions are in Catalan. The author (by whom only one other work is known) can surely be identified as the 'convert' Macian de Viladestes, authorized by a Majorcan licence to land in Sicily in January 1401. He must therefore have been one of those Majorcan Jews (usually protected by the kings of Aragon, although sometimes forced to submit to baptism) among whom grew up the most illustrious figures in Catalan cartography.

The cartographer's probable origins in Majorcan Jewish circles explains his interest, similar to that of his predecessors in the same school, in the representation of the routes of trans-Saharan commerce. From one edge to the other of the great desert, these routes connected the gold-producing empires of the Sudan with the sultanates of the Maghreb and with the western mariners who came in search of the precious metal. The author obviously knows some of these routes, which he has dotted with towns. The most visible one here (though not the most used at the time Viladestes was drawing) was the direct track that started at the water-encircled town of Sidjilmassa (*Segelmese*) and reached Timbuktu (*Tenbuch*) on the Niger via Tabelbalat (*Tabelbet*) and the oases of the Touat–Tamentit (*Tamantet*) and Bouda (*ciutat de Buda*). Shorter than other tracks but more rugged as it crossed a redoubtable *tanezrouft*, it had the advantage of a halt at *Tegaza*, where the caravaneers could obtain the salt that they would exchange further south against its weight in gold in the rituals of silent barter still witnessed in the nineteenth century.

The cartographer's accurate knowledge of these trails may be explained by the existence, in all the towns north of the Sahara, of Jewish communities linked by manifold commercial contracts with those of Barcelona and Majorca. It was through these Jewish communities of the northern Sahara, helped by those of Barbary, especially the community of Tlemcen (*Telimsen*)—which merchants reached by crossing the Atlas mountains through the valley of the Draa (*Val de Sus*)—that the Majorcan cartographers obtained their information on the Sudan gold routes.

As for the gold-producing regions, kept carefully hidden from the caravan traders, Viladestes, who provides them with long inscriptions, knew about them from Arab sources. It is from the Arabs that he has borrowed the *Ued Nil* (the Nile), alias *riu de lor*, which combines the Nile, the Niger and the Senegal in a single river. He interrupts it with a gold-spangled lake, fed by five tributaries descending from the *montanies dellor* and an *Insula de Broneb*, 'where gold is collected in the river'. Already represented in this way by Idrisi in the twelfth century, these would appear to be the gold-panning zones of the upper Niger and upper Senegal, respectively near the gold mines of the Bouré and the Bambouk.

The Sahara, however, is considerably foreshortened in latitude; obviously the cartographer has only a hypothetical knowledge of its oceanic fringe beyond

Cape Bojador (*cap de Buyeter*). He has therefore worked hard at enriching it, adding manuscript notes in this region, and he does know of a more westerly trail starting at Ofran (*Uferen*) more and more used by caravans in the fifteenth century.

Gold from the Sudan was the indispensable basis of Mediterranean trade at this time. It was the aim of the Catalans—as the ship of Jacme Ferrer reminds us—and after them the Portuguese, to bypass their Muslim intermediaries and reach the Sudan directly from the Atlantic. But when caravels replaced caravans on the gold route, cartography gradually lost the knowledge it had acquired of the interior of the continent.

13-14

'LIBER INSULARUM ARCHIPELAGI'
by Cristoforo Buondelmonte (1420)
44 paper leaves, coloured ms, 295 × 205 mm
13   Leaf 2^v: *Corfu*
14   Leaf 32: *Chios*
Paris, B.N.: Cartes et Plans, Rés. Ge FF 9351

These two large-scale gouache drawings of the islands of Corfu and Chios are borrowed from the *Liber insularum Archipelagi* by Cristoforo Buondelmonte, which began to circulate in western Europe in the year 1420. The author, a highly cultured scion of a great Florentine family, set sail in the first years of the fifteenth century for the island of Rhodes, where he is believed to have resided for eight consecutive years. Thereafter, he travelled the islands of the archipelago for another six years in search of ancient Hellenic manuscripts that he feared might fall into the hands of the Turks. Either out of modesty or playfulness, the author hides behind an acrostic that, expanded, reveals his identity and that of the Humanist to whom the work is dedicated, the Roman prelate Cardinal Giordano Orsini. The initial letters of the eighty-two chapters of the book spell out: *Cristoforus Bondelmonti de Florencia. Presbiter, nunc misit Cardinal Iordano de Ursinio. MCCCCXX.*

In his book Buondelmonte shows himself to be an innovator; he brings back from his long voyage not a compendium of nautical instructions, but a sort of tourist guide to the Cyclades and the Ionian Islands, illustrated with individual maps, whose number varies according to the manuscript from seventy-nine to more than ninety. In a brief introduction, Buondelmonte explains to Cardinal Orsini the aim he has set himself: 'You will find here briefly narrated numerous tales concerning the men of Antiquity.... You will also see verdant mountains white with snow, springs, pastureland... plains... ports, with neighbouring capes and shoals, fortified towns and stretches of sea.' The author is careful to specify, for each of the islands visited, the perimeter of its coastline (given in nautical miles) and to describe its natural beauties, archaeological sites, economic resources and fortified cities.

Speaking of Corfu (No. 13), he praises its southern mountains covered with oaks from whose acorns tannin was extracted. On a high mountain, which he calls *Amphipolis*, he draws the Castle of Saint Angelo, constructed in the previous century by Angelo Comneno, 'which sailors can see from afar'. Facing the coast of Epirus stands the old citadel of *Corfu*, commanding from its promontory the access to the port. Occasionally errors slip into the orientation of the delineation—thus the island of Corfu is shown with north at the bottom, which suggests a possible borrowing from some appropriately enlarged sea chart.

Details on the island of Chios (No. 14), which the author knows particularly well, are even more numerous: 'The northern part of the island bristles with high mountains, planted with a multitude of pines and plane-trees, from these mountains gush springs of cold drinking water. Here and there fortified towns appear, some on mountains, others on plains. The town of Chios (*Chyos*), restored by the Genoese, is provided with a very safe harbour.' On the miniature, two lighthouses guard the entry to the harbour, and the wall of the Kastro (still admired today) is located with precision. In the southwest section of the island, a long inscription indicates the valley of Mastikhochoria where, to this day, grow the mastic-trees whose resin is used to flavour alcohol and the sweets of which the Greeks are so fond.

These cartographic sketches, drawn roughly to scale like those in our tourist guides, appear quite archaic today, with their imprecise contours, and yet at the beginning of the fifteenth century they were considered a great novelty. Buondelmonte's book was one of the bestsellers of its time, frequently copied and several times translated into Greek and Italian. Its charts remain the prototypes of those in the *isolari* printed later. As early as 1485, Bartolomeo Turco (alias Bartolomeo dalli Sonetti) drew inspiration from them, sometimes even copying them shamelessly. Buondelmonte had opened up a new road that would be followed until the end of the seventeenth century: his book, thanks to its sketches, marks a new stage in the history of maritime cartography.

15

THE MEDITERRANEAN
by Jacobus de Giroldis (1422)
1 vellum leaf, coloured ms, 880 × 510 mm
Paris, B.N.: Cartes et Plans, Rés. Ge C 5088

The works of Giroldis, which span the period from 1422 to 1446, are another example of the Venetian style and even more austere than those of Virga

(No. 11). Nothing is shown that is not strictly geographical, and the scales incorporated in the double frame are the only decoration. The signature is inscribed there also, in continuous script, at the base of the neck of the parchment: *'MCCCCXXII mensse junij die primo Jachobus de Ziroldis de Venecijs me fecit in ys.'*

The most striking feature of this chart, whose black ink has faded a great deal, are the 'conventional signs' of mediaeval hydrography, painted in beautiful colours that have lasted better: red dots for shallows or sandbanks (Chersonesus, Syrtes Major [Gulf of Sidra], Syrtes Minor [Gulf of Gabes], Lough Corrib), blue dashes for chains of coastal islets, small crosses indicating promontories or reefs, gold and blue illumination for deltas (here only those of the Dnieper, the Nile and the Rhone are shown) and flat tints for the archipelagos that serve as landmarks along the trade routes.

In Venice, these routes belonged to the state convoys, and their every stage was strictly laid down in the contracts between the Republic and the shipowners. In 1422 the *da mercato* galleys sailed to Romania and reached Tana and Trebizond. There was also an important trade with Alexandria and the ports of the Syrian coast, where the nomenclature is particularly dense. The Aigues-Mortes convoy had been doubled since the previous year, and all its ports of call are shown here. Finally, there is the Flanders route that headed for England and the Low Countries; on the chart we can see the chequer-board of the Zeeland islands and the broad elbow-shaped outline of the western Scheldt with *Anguersa* (Antwerp) and *Mallines* (Mechlin) inland, which traders reached via the Dyle and the Rupel. Naturally all these convoys first sailed down the Adriatic, setting their course by the Dalmatian archipelago, of which Giroldis has detailed knowledge (forty place-names).

If some mishap at sea caused a mariner to stray from his course on any of these routes, he could easily find it again thanks to the *marteloio*, as long as he also had navigational tables. The latter, known as *toleta de marteloio* ('*marteloio* tables'), must surely have been used in conjunction with portolan charts from the end of the thirteenth century, but the first confirmed example is found in a Venetian atlas contemporary with this one. Making use of simple trigonometrical calculations, these tables indicate, in front of the names of the eight principal winds, the distance strayed from the desired course (*alargar*), the distance to be covered in order to return to it (*retorno*), as well as the theoretical paths of the initially planned course in relation to those actually followed (*avançar* and *avanço*).

Mathematical navigation allied to the use of the chart and the compass, enabled the Venetian fleets to continue sailing in the Mediterranean during several winter months, thereby doubling their convoys, particularly to Egypt, and likewise multiplying the quantity of merchandise transported.

16

THE MEDITERRANEAN SEA AND THE BLACK SEA
by Gabriel de Vallsecha (1447)
1 vellum leaf, illuminated ms, 580 × 930 mm
Paris, B.N.: Cartes et Plans, Rés. Ge C 4607

A glance at the neck of the parchment reveals both the author and the recipient of the chart. The signature is in Catalan, in black ink, in a dense and elaborate script: *Gabriel Devallsecha la affeta en mallorcha an M CCCC XXXX VII* The cartographer is known to have been in Majorca from 1439, when he executed his finest work, the one over which the French author George Sand, on her travels, unfortunately spilled an ink-well. As for the purchaser, he must surely have been a councillor of Alfonso V (*Franciscus de Sancto Severino, Comes Laurie, Dux Terre Scalae*), who is mentioned several times in the Aragonese archives between 1442 and 1448, for the escutcheon ('argent with three azure bends') surmounted by a ducal coronet is that of the Laurias, a family of famous mariners in the service of the Aragonese monarchy since the thirteenth century.

This is a true navigational chart, something of a rarity in what remains today of Catalan cartography: nearly all inland nomenclature has been banished, and the chart confines itself to a description of the coasts of the Black Sea and the Mediterranean. Although the torsions associated with magnetic variation are still very plain, it is apparent that the proportions of the whole basin are much more accurate than on previous charts, thanks in particular to relative shortening of its longitudinal axis. The coastal toponymy, especially abundant in the western Mediterranean, is clearer when red ink is used; the script in black ink is thicker and often illegible.

Curiously, the cartographer has positioned an isolated rhumb focus in Spain, but the main network is arranged around a small and very sober compass rose, in the style of the Charles V atlas (No. 8). However, on the periphery of the *marteloio*—except in the east, north and south—the initials of the winds are indicated in superb pink discs encircled in green.

The artist has used the same colours to depict *in situ* some bird's-eye views of the great Mediterranean trading cities. Those selected were to be found henceforth almost without variation on later charts: drawn the same way round as the inscriptions of place-names on the chart and following the order of the *compasso da navigare*, they are Tlemcen (*Trimse*), the great commercial centre of the 'Abdalwādids; Cairo (*Babilonia*), the city of the Mameluke sultans; Jerusalem, symbolically represented by the Holy Sepulchre (*Santo Sepulcro*); Damascus, also a Mameluke city; Vicina (*Visinia*) on the Danube, which belonged to the Prince of Moldavia and was used as a stage on the road joining the Black Sea to Venice and Poland; Venice (*Venesia*) in its lagoon; Genoa (*Genova*) with its mole; Avignon (*Avinyo*) lying beside the Rhone and finally *Granada*, last Muslim bastion in Spain, perched on what is meant to represent the Sierra Nevada. Over these cities and others float the banners of their sovereigns: the keys of Saint Peter over Avignon, for example, and over Constantinople—for a few more years—the standard of the Palaeologi, stamped with the four B's of Byzantium. Instead of a flag, the Aragonese islands are marked with a shield or striped red and gold.

Following a royal ordinance of 1354, all Aragonese boats were expected to have on board two *cartes de marear* ('sea charts'). It is unlikely that they were all as ornate as this one, which probably saw no practical employment; however, this specimen enables us to measure the difference in execution between hydrographic works of the Catalan school, with its fondness for illumination, and the austerity of those of the Italian school.

17

ATLANTIC OCEAN, MEDITERRANEAN SEA, BLACK SEA
by Petrus Roselli (1462)

1 vellum leaf, coloured ms, 530 × 830 mm
Paris, B.N.: Cartes et Plans, Rés. Ge C 5090

Although it is smaller in size, different in colouring and deals with the shores of the Atlantic, this chart is very similar in style to the preceding one. It has the same combination of discs and compass roses, identical banners and the same bird's-eye views of towns. However Genoa and Granada have disappeared—possibly for lack of space—whereas Mount Sinai and Saint Catherine Monastery are now inserted. In the areas bathed by the Atlantic and the North Sea, the cartographer has chosen to depict Marrakech (*Marochs*), the ancient Almohade capital and point of arrival of a gold route, Santiago de Compostela (*St Jacobus Galicia*) and Cologne (*Colunya*), the great Hanseatic city.

This Catalan style is not surprising in a work executed in Majorca, as indicated by the Latin signature on the left-hand side: *Petrus Roselli composuit hanc cartam in civitate Maioricarum anno Domini M CCCC LXII*. For a long time, the author was erroneously thought to be an Italian, because of his name and because he pays homage in one of his charts to the Genoese Battista Becharius. In fact, Roselli was one of the most prolific Majorcan cartographers of the fifteenth century, with a production extending over a

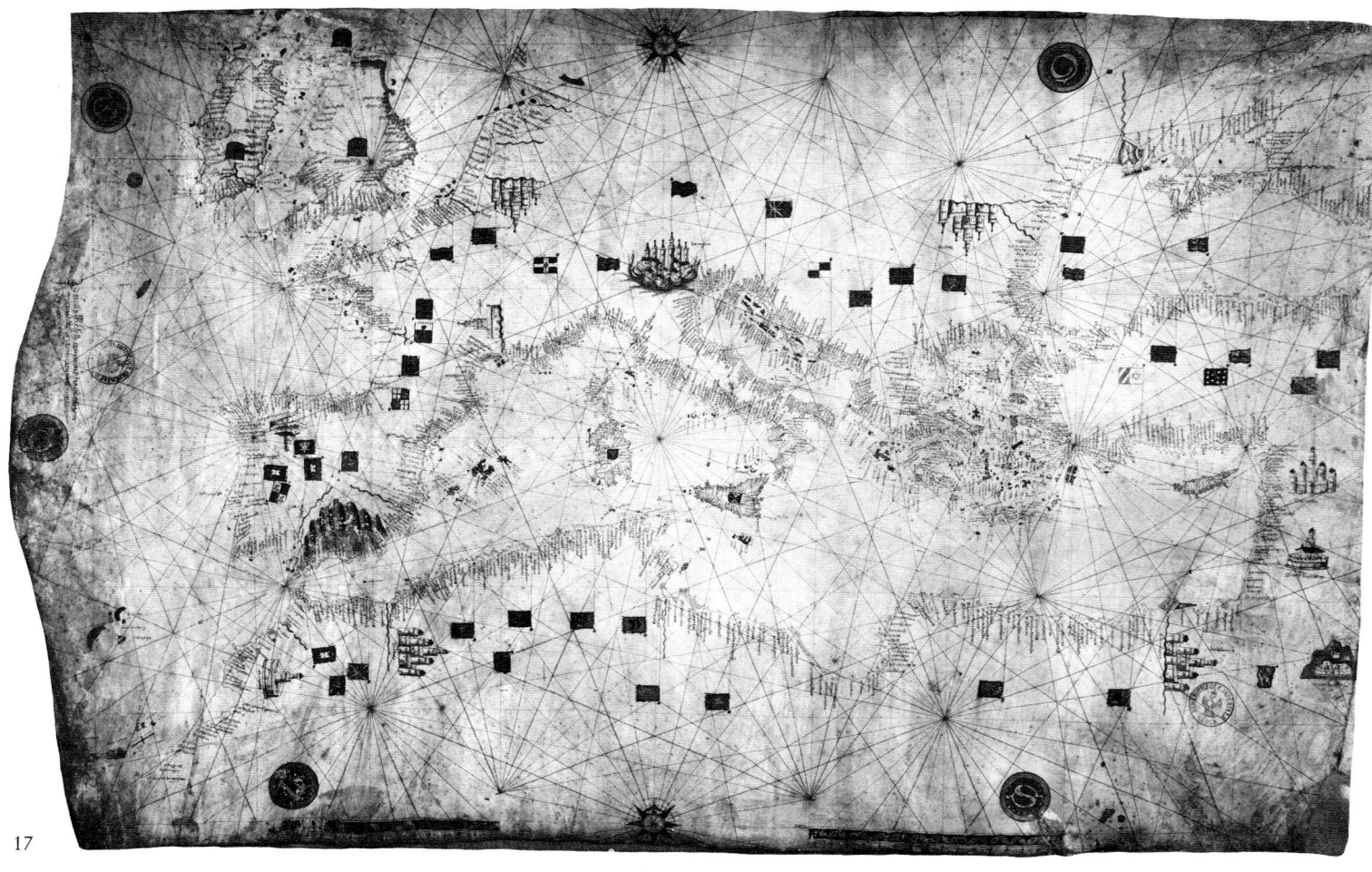

17

score of years between 1447 and 1468. Six of his charts survive today, all produced in Majorca, where the name Roselli is known in Jewish convert circles from the twelfth century.

Although the 1462 chart is not particularly remarkable for its style, it is remarkable for its content. The first thing we notice is the effort made to harmonize the proportions of the Atlantic and the Mediterranean. Even if certain stretches of oceanic coastline are obviously less well known—as the spacing of the nomenclature reveals, for example, on the Portuguese coast between *Lisbona* and *Portoportogall*, or the French coast from Fuenterrabía to the Pointe de Grave—the north-south outlines have been noticeably extended, which may be the debt Roselli owes to 'the art of Battista Becharius' (*de arte Baptista Becharius*), who possibly passed on to him the teachings of an eponymous Genoese Francesco Becharius. The latter declared, on a chart of 1403, that he had increased the length of the coasts of the ocean 'by a certain number of miles, or leagues', especially the coasts of Portugal, Biscay, Brittany and England, having learnt about them from the mouths of 'many sailors, captains and pilots who have sailed there often and for a long period of time'.

No doubt it was this teaching based on experience that Roselli followed when he modified the delineation of northwestern Europe. The coast beyond the Rhine and Cologne, instead of darting straight to the tip of Denmark (as had been the case on nautical charts since Vesconte) now cleaves for the first time to the WSW-ENE outline of the Dutch and German shores, with their fringe of Frisian Islands. Thus the coast runs from the Marsdiep (*Masdiepa*) to the Elbe (*Eleva*), then follows a SE-NW course revealing Heligoland Bay. On the poorly orientated Jutland peninsula, Cape Skagen is named (*Scagunt*). The low lands of Brabant (*Brabāt*) and Holland (*Olanda*) are treated as an island, and into the stretch of sea surrounding them flows the Rhine (*Rim*) and probably the IJssel. The author has thus given concrete expression to the maritime route used since the twelfth century, which provided a passage via the Lek, the IJssel and the Vecht from the great Zeeland delta to the Zuider Zee and into the North Sea.

Notable improvements are also apparent in the configuration of the British Isles: Ireland, although too narrow and elongated, is close to its true shape. In England, the Thames estuary has broadened, but the north of the country is elongated; whereas Scotland, on the contary, is foreshortened. The nomenclature has become much richer, especially in northern Ireland and on the west coast of England, where certain place-names first appear beyond Milford Haven (*Micsforda*): Cardigan (*Cardegom*), Liverpool (*Lecripoli*), Lancaster (*Lancastell*). All these details revealing a greater familiarity with these regions may have been borrowed from contemporary nautical charts drawn by Dutchmen or Hanseatics, which have now disappeared.

Roselli, however, far from persevering with this cartography based on experience, turned back after 1464 to the prototypes that he had previously abandoned, and in this he was imitated by most cartographers. This more accurate view of northwest Europe, created in 1462, only survived in a few rare portolan charts and in an edition of Ptolemy's *Geography* published in Venice in 1511 by Bernardus Sylvanus, in which all the recent place-names have disappeared and been replaced by the Ptolemaic set of names. Thus knowledge gained from experience succumbed to the strength of imitation and tradition.

18-19

ATLAS
by Grazioso Benincasa (1467)
5 vellum leaves, illuminated ms pasted back-to-back on cardboard leaves in a stamped binding mounted on wooden boards, 346 × 442 mm
18   Leaf 1: *Atlantic, from Spain to Cape Verde*
19   Leaf 2: *Atlantic, from Denmark to Malaga*
Paris, B.N.: Cartes et Plans, Rés. Ge DD 1988

Born in Ancona, Benincasa spent his youth sailing the Mediterranean and the Black Sea as a trader. A set of nautical observations in his hand, made day by day on his voyages between 1435 and 1445, still survives. Having lost his ship to Genoese pirates off Tunis in 1460, he set himself up as a cartographer and proved to be very productive. Twenty-two of his signed works remain (seventeen of them atlases), executed between 1461 and 1482. He worked mostly in Venice, except for a short stay in Rome during 1467 and, at the end of his life, when he returned to Ancona.

It was in Rome that Benincasa signed this atlas, which is still conserved today in a finely tooled leather binding. At the top of the third leaf, over the Adriatic, after a fine decorative initial, is written: *Gratiosus Benincasa Anchonitatus composuit Rome anno domini MCCCCLXVII*. The first and second leaves deal with the shores of the Atlantic. Curiously enough, this former sailor did not follow the example of Roselli's 1462 chart (No. 17) as regards northern Europe. On the contrary, he greatly contributed to spreading the prototype to which Roselli later reverted and which dated back to Vesconte in its main features, though it was slightly improved by the Catalans: *Irelanda* or *Ibernia* protrudes to the west, with an exaggerated Achill Head (*Adoim*); Lough Corrib, dotted with islands, is called the Fortunate Lake (*Lacus Fortunatus ubi sunt insule que dicuntur y Sc̄e beate CCCLXVII*). Only the east coast of England is well known. Scotland is bounded in the south by two rivers (the Solway Firth and the Humber), fed by the circular sources of mediaeval tradition. As for the Dutch and Danish coasts, they have once more become a straight line heading due north and do not go beyond Ribe (*Ripis*).

On the other hand, Benincasa has recent, first-hand information on the African coastline. In 1434 Gil Eanes finally sailed past Cape Bojador (*cavo de Buçedor*), the southern boundary of mediaeval navigation in the Atlantic. Portuguese expeditions multiplied with the encouragement of Prince Henry the Navigator, and in twelve short years Cape Verde (*Cavo Verde*) and Cape Roxo (*Cavo Rosso*) were reached. Benincasa's chart, which repeats the one drawn by the Venetian Andrea Bianco (1448), with a few lacunae, allows us to follow this descent of the coast of Africa step by step, just as the Portuguese chroniclers relate it. Apart from those having a geographical meaning (*terra alta* or *piagge bassa*), the toponyms recall important events on the voyages of exploration. *Porto Cavalier* indicates the spot where Antão Gonçalves was dubbed knight; *Terra de Gallo* the rock resembling a galley where Afonso Gonzales Baldeia was forced to turn back in 1436. The outlines strongly emphasize the projections and inlets of the coast, whose length is grossly overestimated in places—Cape Blanc for example—no doubt in proportion to the difficulties inherent in exploratory navigation.

The following year, Benincasa, back in Venice, was perfecting the mapping of the African coast still further, taking into account this time the information brought back by Cadamosto, especially as regards the Cape Verde archipelago. As we have seen, Venetian hydrography played a major role in recording the Portuguese discoveries; through the intermediary of Andrea Bianco it spread the news of them as far as England. Since for still unexplained reasons, no contemporary Portuguese chart has survived, Venetian hydrography still remains our major source of information.

20

GLOBE
by Martin Behaim (1492 [1847])
Vellum gores, painted and illuminated ms on a globe, 507 mm in diameter
Paris, B.N.: Cartes et Plans, Rés. Ge A 276

This German terrestrial globe, constructed in 1492 under the direction of Martin Behaim, is considered to be the oldest western terrestrial sphere known today. Intended for the Municipal Council of Nuremberg, it is now the property of that town's Nationalmuseum and one of its most treasured possessions. The photographic reproduction given here has been taken from a manuscript copy of the original globe made in 1847 for the Bibliothèque Nationale in Paris.

Made by Glockengiesser and Kalperger, it has vellum gores on which Georg Holzschuher drew the outline of a map of the world, inspired by the great mappa mundi of Henricus Martellus Germanus, which was rediscovered in Austria and recently acquired by Yale University Library.

The decoration of Behaim's globe is sumptuous, the colours very vivid; nevertheless, it is not the decoration that holds our attention as much as the arrangement of land and sea, which portrays to perfection the world as it was conceived by the Florentine cosmographer Paolo Toscanelli and by the Genoese navigator Christopher Columbus. This view of the world decided the latter in favour of a westerly route to reach the Indies, which he imagined would be faster than going around the south of Africa. Completely won over, like Toscanelli, by the cosmographical ideas of Cardinal d'Ailly, Christopher Columbus was totally convinced of the sphericity of the earth, thirty years before it was demonstrated by Magellan's circumnavigation (1519–1521). The same sea, he believed, bordered on the Pillars of Hercules (Gibraltar) and on Cathay (China). He overestimated the west-east extent of the Eurasian continent, which, according to him, covered 230 degrees of the earth's surface, making the Atlantic into a great interior sea, 130 degrees in longitude. In this view of the world, the American continent and the still undiscovered Pacific are totally displaced by the immense bulge of the continental land-mass of Europe and Asia. On leaving the Canary Islands on his first voyage, Columbus headed due west, expecting to reach the coast of China (Cathay and Mangi), which he situated roughly in the area occupied in reality by the coasts of Virginia and Florida. Two landfalls were expected on the way: the mythical island of Antillia (at 85 degrees west of Lisbon) and the island of Cipangu, or Japan, of whose golden roofs and fabulous wealth Marco Polo had heard.

The distance to China was thought to be relatively small. Columbus had adopted the value for a degree laid down by the Arab astronomer Alfragan; but, making an error in his favour when he calculated the equivalence between the Arab mile and the Italian nautical mile, Columbus thought he would find Cipangu at only 750 leagues from the Canary Islands—no distance at all, with a fair wind.

The representation of the Atlantic on Martin Behaim's globe translates Columbus's ideas so faithfully that we are justified in wondering whether the Nuremberg businessman, who was admitted to the circle of scholars surrounding the king during his stay in Lisbon (1485 and following years), may not have held in his hands the dossier Columbus submitted to John II the previous year in support of his audacious scheme.

Although this globe is not a maritime document, it seemed necessary at this turning-point in world history to encapsulate in this illustration the sudden awareness in Europe of the fact, that the world was round, which was to lead to the discovery of America and to present nautical cartography with many new problems (the calculation of longitude at sea, magnetic variation and loxodromics) that had not yet come to light in the confines of the flat, circular world of the Mediterranean basin.

21

'CHRISTOPHER COLUMBUS CHART'
(1492?)
1 vellum leaf, illuminated ms, 700 × 1100 mm
Paris, B.N.: Cartes et Plans, Rés. Ge AA 562

This illuminated sheet of vellum is a curious document: two seemingly unrelated maps are juxtaposed and separated by a line set off in gold. On the right there is a classical portolan chart of the Atlantic and the Mediterranean; on the left, a small world map surrounded by the celestical spheres symbolizes the geocentric view of the universe held in the last quarter of the fifteenth century. The only thing the two maps seem to have in common is a large quantity of Latin inscriptions.

The portolan chart represents the coast of the Atlantic from the south of Norway to the mouth of the Congo, the river baptized the *rio Poderoso* in 1484 by Diogo Cão, on account of its strength. To the east, the chart does not go further than the eastern extremities of the Black Sea and the Red Sea. Out to sea, from Iceland to the Gulf of Guinea, is a series of real and imaginary islands. In the northwest part of the ocean, *Frixlandia* and *Brasil* are present, and beneath the compass rose, here in its tripartite and almost imperceptible form, the Isles of the Seven Cities. Many fables remain attached to those legendary islands. Was it not said that the Isles of the Seven Cities (often called Antillia) had given refuge to seven Portuguese bishops expelled with their flocks by the Muslim invader? It was also said that sailors had brought back from there gold picked up from the sand. These fabulous tales inflamed the imagination of navigators who all dreamt of reaching those mysterious isles.

Inland, some thirty vignettes, drawn with a pen in red and black ink, indicate the most important cities: Cologne, Paris, Genoa, Venice, etc. In Spain, apart from Santiago de Compostela and Seville, Granada is recognizable and, nearby, what must be Santa Fe, where Ferdinand of Aragon and Isabella of Castile entrenched themselves in order to follow the vicissitudes of the siege of Granada from close at hand. The Spanish banner over the drawing of the city inclines us to believe that the chart is later than its capture (2 January 1492).

In Africa, the cartographer is perfectly aware of the Portuguese discoveries. The coastal nomenclature is very abundant, and the Portuguese flag flies over Ceuta, Arguin, Elmina, the Azores, Madeira, the Cape Verde Islands and Principe. On the African continent itself, each region's export articles are indicated: ostrich feathers from the Sahara, ivory and civet from Senegambia, malaguetta or pepper from Guinea, parrots from Benin. In West Africa, two black archers harmoniously fill a geographic void.

The chart is sprinkled with long inscriptions; near Iceland is a Latin one stating that that country is called *Thile*. Then follows information on 'the length of the days and nights there, on the food of the inhabitants (who live entirely on frozen fish) and on their trade relations with England. A land of uncouth and primitive people, the English say, who remain enclosed for six months in underground dwellings so severely does the sea freeze'. These details, and the drawing of the two cathedrals of Holar and Skalholt, suggest that the cartographer was well informed.

Beside the Cape Verde Islands, the author is careful to recall that 'these islands were discovered by a Genoese, Antonio de Noli...' and adds that 'they produce the best sugar and some cotton; but, on the other hand, their wheat is ravaged by locusts'. Finally, near the Red Sea, an inscription stresses its length 'which requires six months of navigation'; and 'from there', says the cartographer, 'it takes a whole year to reach India'.

On the left, occupying the narrower part of the parchment, a disc-shaped mappa mundi is surrounded by nine circles or spheres: the spheres of the Moon, Mercury, Venus, the Sun, Mars, Jupiter and Saturn; the eighth circle bears the signs of the zodiac; the ninth is empty. In its centre, the small mappa mundi has a representation of the ancient world, but Africa is also shown as far as the Cape of Good Hope, whose discovery by Bartolomeu Dias was known in Europe in 1488. The delineation of the eastern part of the world is borrowed from Ptolemy's map. To the north of the northernmost coast a whole series of islands is drawn in reference to the legend of Saint Brendan, an Irish monk of the sixth century, who set out in a wickerwork coracle with sixty companions on a voyage of discovery of the northern seas. Off *Cathay* (Marco Polo's China) the 'Earthly Paradise' is situated within a ring of mountains. On either side of the mappa mundi are inscribed two very long astrological inscriptions containing this vitally important observation: 'that the mappa mundi, although drawn on a plane, should be considered to be spherical'.

Thanks to the inscriptions, we may be able to trace the mysterious cartographer. The great majority of them are borrowed from Cardinal d'Ailly's cosmographic treatise, *Imago Mundi*, printed at Louvain in 1483; it would seem that they were taken from Christopher Columbus's personal copy of that book, still preserved in the Biblioteca Colombina in Seville. The explorer had copiously annotated the margins of his book with *postillae*, several of which are reproduced on the chart at the Bibliothèque Nationale. Better still, in the inscription that flanks the Red Sea on the portolan chart, there is an error that also appears in the margins of the book in the Biblioteca Colombina. Therefore, it is not surprising that the Paris chart contains such solid, apparently verbatim, economic information, for Columbus called in at the Cape Verde Islands while on his way to the castle of Elmina in 1482. As for the information concerning Iceland, Columbus's biographers (his son Ferdinand and Father Bartolomeo de Las Casas) both agree that he sailed 100 leagues (= 300 nautical miles) beyond Thule (Iceland) in February 1477. Thus a host of coincidences seem to indicate a famous authorship for this chart. Besides, when Columbus and his brother Bartolomeo were in Lisbon before 1485, the two of them also made a living from their cartographic production. Moreover, in a note in his copy of the *Imago Mundi*, Christopher Columbus refers the reader to his 'four charts on paper, all of which also contain a sphere'—an unusual thing at the time.

The chart in the Bibliothèque Nationale showing a 'reconquered' Iberian peninsula, but not yet giving the outline of the West Indies, must have been completed just after the capture of Granada at the beginning of 1492. Although the attribution of this document to the discoverer of America is plausible in many respects, decisive proof is still awaited. A technical study of the internal dimensions, or cartology, remains to be made. This might enable us to reach a definitive conclusion.

22

MAPPA MUNDI
by Juan de la Cosa (1500)
Several vellum leaves, illuminated ms assembled in a chart, 955 × 1770 mm
Madrid, Naval Museum

This mappa mundi by Juan de la Cosa gives the earliest representation of the West Indies. Its author, whose signature can be seen under the effigy of Saint Christopher, drew it at the end of 1500 in the little port of Santa Maria, situated near Cadiz at the mouth of the Guadalete. A pilot and cosmographer, the Spanish Basque Juan de la Cosa was the owner of the ship the 'Santa Maria'; he accompanied Christopher Columbus on his first two voyages (1492-1494) before continuing with the reconnaissance of the American coast on successive voyages until 1504.

The document as a whole consists of two panels that seem to face each other: on one side is a representation of the Old World, showing the most recently discovered part of it—the Cape of Good Hope (1488); on the other side are the lands of the New World, sighted by the Spaniards between the years 1492 and 1500 and painted on a larger scale than the rest of the chart.

The mappa mundi is constructed in the style of the old portolan charts, with rhumb-lines, compass roses and a distance scale. The absence of a latitude scale shows that the Spaniards, guided only by the magnetic needle, still practised navigation exclusively by dead reckoning. The tropic of Cancer and the equator are shown, but without graduation. The tropic even appears to the south of *La Española* (Haiti), instead of passing to the north of Cuba, as it should. This mistake may perhaps have been caused by trying to make two cartographic sections constructed to different scales co-exist within one chart.

The decoration is sober but highly evocative. To the north of the West Indies and at the foot of the document, two heads wearing sailor's caps of the period represent the sometimes very violent winds in these parts of the world where frequent cyclones rage. To the left, in the narrowest part of the parchment, the figure of Saint Christopher symbolizes Christopher Columbus's role as a bearer of Christianity and as the glorious Admiral of the Ocean Sea. The Nativity scene painted in the centre of the large compass rose may represent the fortress of 'Navidad' built on the north coast of Haiti the day after the shipwreck of the 'Santa Maria' (Christmas Day, 1492). Having lost a ship, Columbus had to leave some thirty men there with provisions for a year; on his return the following year he would not find a single survivor.

The eye is particularly drawn to the uninterrupted outline of a green continental land-mass, which encircles the arc of the West Indies. This outline has given rise to a variety of interpretations. Was the cartographer already aware (and how could he have been) of another world stretching from Greenland to the Brazilian coast? Or did he intend to depict the furthest eastern extremities of the continent of Asia that the first explorers (Columbus, Cabot) thought they had reached? The answer will never be known.

To the north, four English banners and the inscription (*Mar descubierta por los Ingleses*) recall the voyages of the Venetian John Cabot (1496-1498), carried out on behalf of King Henry VII of England. Although he did not return from his third exploration, a famous series of letters about his second voyage (by John Day, Raimondo de Soncino) relates that in 1497, having sailed from Bristol on the 'Matthew', Master 'Zoane Caboto . . . rounded Ireland and after sailing for some time further west, found dry land, hoisted the royal flag there and took possession of it in the name of the King . . . the 24th of June, he landed in a wooded region, near his first landing-place, then sailed along the coast for a month without landing again. . . .' It would seem that Cosa was aware of these voyages.

Above the equator, the cartographer takes note of the first three voyages (1492-1500) of Christopher Columbus, the chart being earlier than his fourth voyage (1502-1504). Spanish flags indicate the archipelago of the *Guanahani*, where the first landing was made on

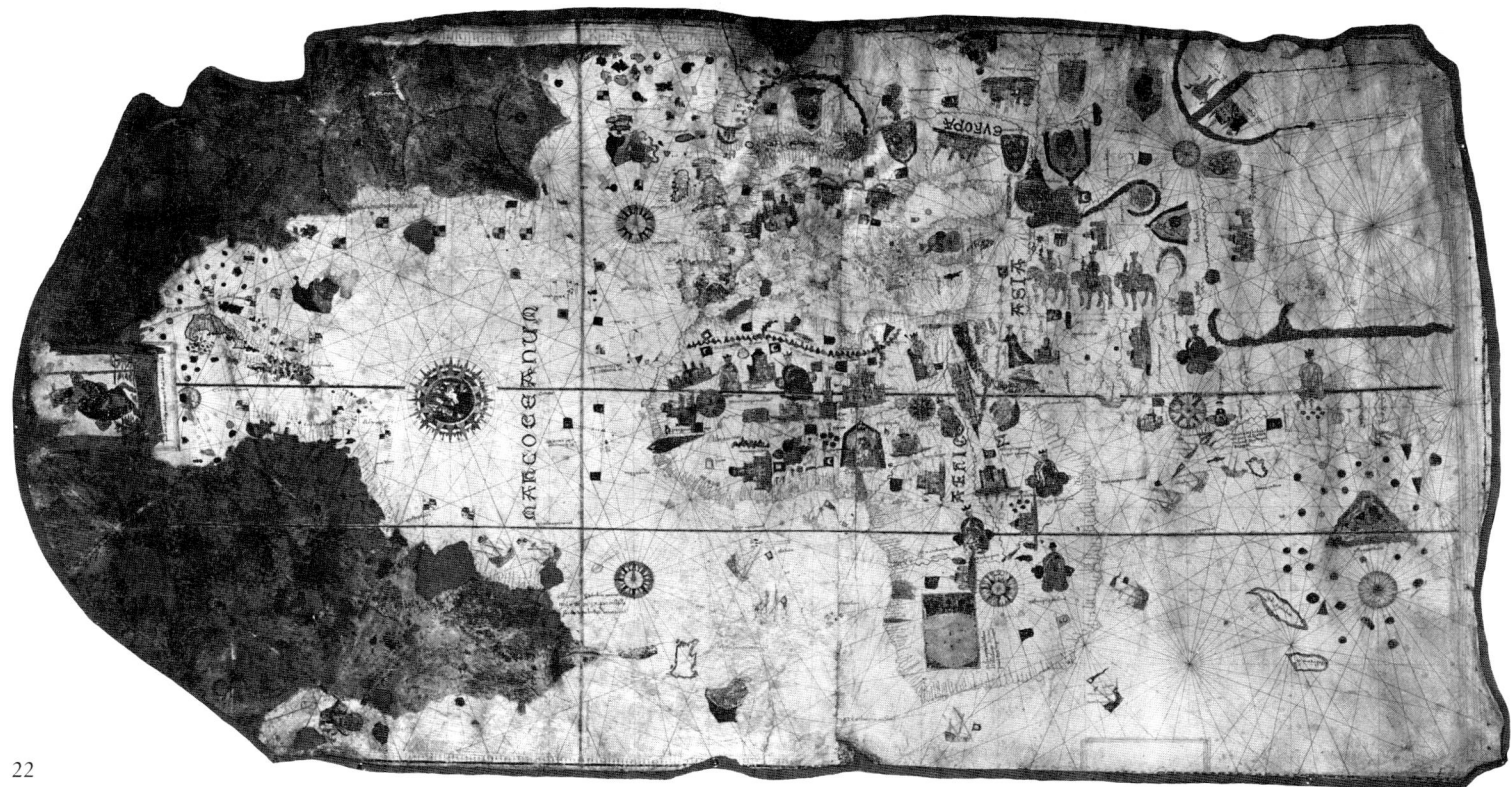

22

12 October 1492. Then the islands of *Cuba* and *La Española* (Haiti) are drawn in their correct place, if not with their true configuration, contrary to the opinion of Columbus who saw them only as a peninsula of Asia. On the latter island, the cartographer is careful to indicate the site of *Isabella*, the first town founded in America by Europeans (1494), which soon declined owing to a lack of adequate food and qualified workmen. Then the smaller of the West Indies are shown (Martinique, Guadeloupe, etc.) as the *Cannibal Islands*, where at the end of 1493 Columbus and his companions endured the spectacle of Caribs eating human flesh. Lower down we gain an inkling of the fact that South America might really be a continent. Its coasts had been sighted by Castilians following in the footsteps of Columbus. The Pearl Coast, stretching from the Gulf of Paria to the Bay of Maracaibo, had been discovered by Captain Hojeda who, together with Juan de la Cosa and Amerigo Vespucci, had made a broad reconnaissance of the coasts of Guyana and Venezuela from May 1499 to June 1500. On the coast of Brazil at the approximate latitude 8° South, an inscription stating 'this cape was discovered in the year 1499 by Vicente' recalls the landing of the expedition led by Vicente Yáñez Pinzón, who came ashore at the point which the Portuguese named Cape Saint Roch one year later.

Ships bearing the arms of Aragon and Castile on the sea and numerous flags on the coast illustrate these voyages. The greatest dead-reckoning navigator of all time, Christopher Columbus had opened the road to the west that many others were to follow, expanding the known world enormously in the space of only a few years. The chart by Juan de la Cosa (rediscovered in Madrid in the nineteenth century by Alexander von Humboldt) remains one of the first graphic witnesses of this expansion. Certain inaccuracies in the nomenclature have led to the suggestion that it might only be a copy of an original that has now disappeared.

23

COAST OF GREECE
(Sixteenth century)
1 vellum leaf, coloured ms, 600 × 410 mm
Paris, B.N.: Cartes et Plans, Rés. Ge D 7898

This charming cartographic sketch, with the colouring of a Japanese print, is anonymous. Its nomenclature and sober style suggest that it is the work of an Italian artist of the sixteenth century. It represents the coast of peninsular Greece from *Volona* in Albania to the Gulf of Volos in Thessaly. On the sea lanes among the Ionian Islands, Corfu, Cephalonia and Zante are recognizable. South of the Peloponnese, *Cerigo* (Kythera) and *Cerigotto* (Antikythera) are shown. In the Aegean Sea, the coast is charted as far as Euboea by way of the western Cyclades from *Millos* (Melos) to *Cia* (Kea). The scales in miles are inscribed at the top and bottom of the chart. The delineation of the coasts is still schematic, and the orientation of the islands sometimes inaccurate. The mountainous landscape that characterizes this

213

whole region is painted as seen from the sea: a series of hills in half-shades, drawn in perspective. The towns and villages are depicted in bird's-eye view as mediaeval castles or simple red-roofed houses.

The main interest of this document lies in the fact that it is a cartographic work that has not reached the final stages of its construction. There are no rhumb-lines on the chart, but the clear presence of a double squaring allows one to guess at how it was composed. The first squaring, made up of 'undisclosed' parallels and meridians (since there is no mention of latitude) is closely linked to the delineation of the coasts; the second squaring, arranged diagonally, lays the foundations for a network of rhumb-lines whose centre is indicated south of the Gulf of Corinth and whose circle is partly sketched in. Today we can only make tentative assumptions about the techniques used in ancient marine cartography, and a document such as this (like the 'Carte pisane' [No. 1] two and a half centuries earlier) lifts the corner of a veil from the secrets of its construction.

24

AEGEAN SEA
(Sixteenth century)
1 vellum leaf, illuminated ms, 730 × 404 mm
Paris, B.N.: Cartes et Plans, Rés. Ge AA 567

The workmanship is the same as on the preceding chart but more complete. Doubtless it is by the same hand. This chart depicts the shores of the 'Archipelago': in Europe from *Modon* (Methoni) in the southwest of the Peloponnese as far as Constantinople, and in Asia from *Scutari* (Üsküdar) on the Bosphorus to Rhodes. The slightly oblique slant of southern Crete, whose configuration is otherwise almost perfect, shows that the whole chart is not oriented to the north but to north-northwest, as the orientation of the Peloponnese and of the Chalcidice also indicate. No doubt this stemmed from a wish to express an awareness of magnetic north.

The distance scales are inscribed on the left-hand and right-hand margins of the document. The outlines remain schematic: the coasts, picked out in bistre, have a hemmed appearance, recalling the style of some *isolari* of the end of the fifteenth century. The islands are coloured like stained glass: blue, green, violet, red and gold, thus making it easier for the mariner to distinguish them. As on the previous chart, landscapes and houses are seen in perspective.

On the sea, with its jagged shores and innumerable islands, the cartographer has decided to increase the number of rhumb-line networks. Thus four are juxtaposed: two intended to facilitate navigation along the coasts of Greece, the other two to assist in steering a course along the coasts of Asia Minor. A reasonable assumption is that this unknown cartographer, who painted what could be seen from a boat and who was so acutely aware of the pitfalls of navigation in the Aegean, was probably a sailor himself, with personal knowledge of the dangers of coastal sailing on a sea littered with traps for the unwary.

25

THE 'CANTINO' PLANISPHERE
(1502)
3 vellum leaves, illuminated ms assembled in a chart, 220 × 1050 mm
Modena, Biblioteca Estense

The 'Cantino' chart is one of the oldest examples of Portuguese nautical cartography. Its history is also one of the best known: an inscription in the top left-hand corner indicates that 'this sea chart of the islands recently discovered in the regions of the Indies has been presented to the Duke of Ferrara, Ercole d'Este, by Alberto Cantino'. The latter, a diplomatic agent of the Italian prince living in Lisbon, had obtained it clandestinely from a cartographer whose name is not revealed. It can be dated with certainty (summer 1502), as the correspondence concerning the transaction still exists, and it is definitely known that the Duke of Este received it in November 1502. Today it is still among the treasures of the library of the princes of Este in Modena.

Of considerable size, the Cantino planisphere, which represents the known world at the time, was doubtless copied from the *padrão real*—the standard cartographic prototype that was constantly kept up to date and whose secrets were not to be divulged on pain of death—which indicates the particular interest of this prestigious document of noble provenance. On this chart is the first mention in marine cartography of the line of demarcation fixed by the Treaty of Tordesillas, which Castile and Portugal signed in June 1494; the treaty appointed an ideal meridian, 370 leagues west of the Cape Verde archipelago, which divided the world into two zones of influence: Spanish in the west, Portuguese in the east. As this planisphere indicates, Newfoundland and Brazil were allocated to Portugal, the rest of America was given to Spain.

The beauty of the illumination is impressive, for both its purity of line and richness of colour. It would be hard to remain indifferent to the elegance of the broad panorama of the city of Venice, the bird's-eye view of the Atlas Mountains, the painting of the superb fortress of São Jorge da Mina in Guinea (Elmina in Ghana) or the precision involved in depicting the attitude and colouring of the parrots of the Brazilian coast, which had fascinated the first explorers. The style of

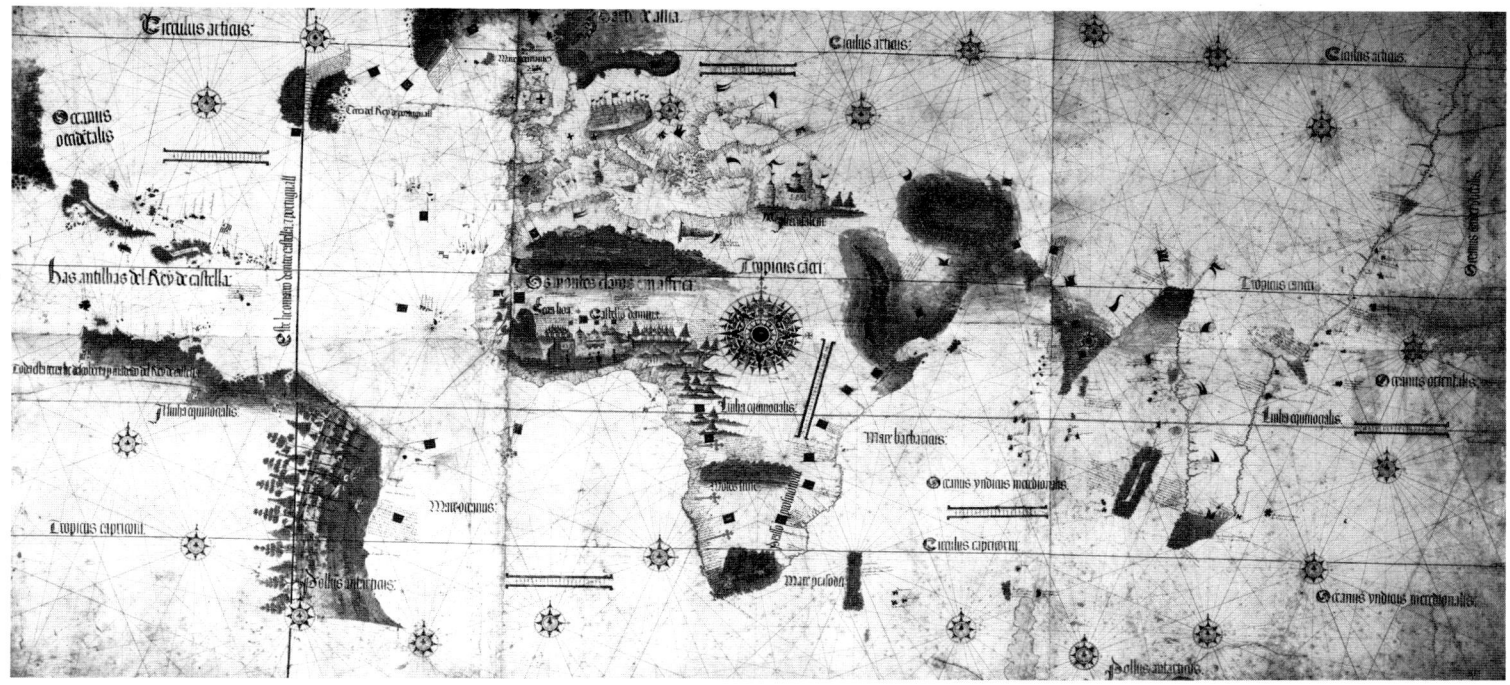

the draughtsmanship and decoration can be attributed to the influence of the Flemish miniaturists Alexandre Bening and Guillaume Vrelant who had found scope for an astonishing output in the Iberian peninsula at the beginning of the sixteenth century.

The chart is completely up to date concerning Portuguese discoveries made before the summer of 1502. Naturally, knowledge of the American coastline remains fragmentary. In the northwest, Greenland is indicated by a Portuguese flag and an inscription which confirms that 'the Portuguese have reached it, but according to the cosmographers it is called the point of Asia. Those who saw it, did not land there, but saw only serried mountain ranges'. Further west, a row of majestic trees recalls the description that the Corte Reals had given of the east coast of Newfoundland on their return to Lisbon in October 1501: 'they saw tall trees in abundance and pines of such size in height and width that they could not be used to build masts for even the biggest ship on the sea', as Pietro Pasqualigo reported to the Signoria of Venice (18 October 1501). In the West Indies (*Antilhas*), an inscription in Gothic script warns that 'these are the West Indies of the king of Castile, discovered by Columbus... Admiral of these islands... at the command of the most high and mighty King don Fernando....'

To the northwest of the island of Cuba (*Issabella*) a land that is a subject of controversy is drawn: to whom do we owe this outline of Florida, which was not officially discovered until eleven years later (1513)? Possibly to a semi-official Spanish voyage (1497) in which Amerigo Vespucci may have taken part, unless it was brought back by some Portuguese pilot (perhaps Corte Real or Duarte Pacheco Pereira) who entered Spanish waters clandestinely in 1497-1498.

To the south, Brazil takes shape in a totally north-south direction. On the coast mention is made of *Porto Seguro* with a flag; there Cabral touched land on 22 April 1500. An inscription recalls his visit and names the place for the first time: 'Vera Cruz, given this name... by Pedro Álvares Cabral... he discovered it when he went as captain-major of fourteen ships, which the king of Portugal sent to Calicut; diverted from his way, he came upon this firm land which he took for a continent'. The author of the planisphere was apparently unaware that the Spanish pilot Vicente Pinzón had already landed on the same territory a short while before (1499), but at a more northerly latitude.

In North Africa, where the Atlas chain appears as the 'Bright Mountains', we can read: 'Land of the King of Nubia, who is continually at war with Prester John, and whose king is a Moor and a great enemy of Christians'. Then in Sierra Leone, near a great lion standing on its hind legs, 'there is much gold in Sierra Leone, of the most precious [sort] there is; it is sent to Portugal together with many slaves... and many fine carpets and cotton cloth'. In Guinea, beneath the castle of Elmina founded by the Portuguese in 1484, is mentioned: 'From here is carried every year, to the Prince dom Manoel, King of Portugal, twelve caravels full of gold, each caravel carrying 25,000 pesos in gold... as well as many slaves, pepper and other things of excellent profit.'

Juan de la Cosa sang the praises of Spanish navigators in the year 1500. Two years later, in Lisbon, this sumptuous portolan chart, drawn and painted for Ercole d'Este, celebrated with its accurate delineation, iconography and inscriptions, the great Portuguese explorations in east and west between the years 1484 and 1502, under the command of those illustrious pilots Diogo Cão, Bartolomeu Dias, the Corte Reals, Vasco da Gama and Cabral.

26

PLANISPHERE
by Nicolaus de Caverio (ca. 1505)
10 vellum leaves, illuminated ms assembled in a chart, 1150 × 2250 mm
Paris, B.N.: Cartes et Plans, S.H. Archives no. 1

This great nautical planisphere of the beginning of the sixteenth century, the work of a Genoese cartographer, Nicolaus de Caverio, is preserved in the collections of the Service hydrographique de la Marine in Paris. In the bottom left-hand corner of the chart, the author has placed his signature in a scroll inscribed: *Opus Nicolay de Caverio Iannensis* ('the work of Nicolaus de Caverio, Genoese'). The resemblance between this planisphere and the 'Cantino' planisphere (No. 25) is striking, and there is no doubt that they had very similar origins. The fact that Caverio must surely have had access to a Portuguese prototype is borne out by the entirely Portuguese nomenclature of this document, which can be dated to circa 1505, since no discovery made after 1504 is mentioned.

At the top and bottom of the chart, large ribbons contain the distance scales. The centre of the network of rhumb-lines is in Africa and represented by a mappa mundi surrounded by the celestial spheres whose contours are emphasized by the eighteen compass roses, each bearing a cross in the east. Henceforth on all the great Renaissance planispheres, the compass roses, which served as both a navigational aid and a decoration, are multiple. Here, however, on the right and left of the chart, they are replaced by a sun and a crescent moon symbolizing east and west, a last echo of the symbolism introduced two centuries before by the Majorcan school. Finally, on the left-hand margin of the document, an absolutely new cartographic element appears: the latitude scale graduated from 55°S to 70°N. This is a vital innovation that does not appear on any sea chart before the sixteenth century, and marks the point of departure of a fundamental revolution in navigation as well as in cartography. As long as mariners limited themselves to sailing timidly along the coast, they had been content to navigate by dead-reckoning. But now they were venturing on to the high seas and were obliged to have recourse to astronomical observations in order to determine the position of their ship. The king of Portugal's pilots had instructions to complement observations made at sea with surveys of latitudes carried out on land so as to produce an exact hydrographic survey of newly discovered coasts, with the maximum possible accuracy.

The effects of this great innovation on Caverio's planisphere can be seen in the remarkable outline of the coasts of Africa, along which is inscribed a rich toponymy indicating ports of call on the way to the Indies. These had been surveyed from 1484 to 1499 during the successive explorations of Diogo Cão, Bartolomeu Dias and Vasco da Gama. Moreover stone columns, or *padrãos*, appear on the chart; engraved with the arms of Portugal and surmounted by a cross, they were carried from Lisbon in the ship's hold and erected every time a landing was made on new territory. These columns stud the coastline from Cape Lopez to *Melinde* (Malindi). In the Indian Ocean, *Madagascar*—discovered by a companion of Cabral's (1500)—is correctly located and still bears its original name, before it became the Isle of Saint Lawrence a few years later.

The Red Sea and the Persian Gulf, where the Portuguese had not yet penetrated, are still depicted fancifully. India, on the other hand, has taken shape. On the Coromandel coast *Cambaye* (Bombay), *Cananor* (Cannanore), *Calicut* and *Cochin*, which Vasco da Gama had visited (1498), all appear in the right place. The inscriptions often provide economic information of an amazing accuracy: near Bombay we read 'here, there is lacquer, fine materials... dried figs, raisins, incense, musk, amber... all of this comes from the interior'. In Calicut 'benzoins grow.... Pepper as well many other commodities come from many different places: cinnamon, ginger, cloves, incense, sandalwood and all sorts of spices... pearls of great value....' The island of Ceylon is not named, but its outline is accompanied by a note: 'Here grows cinnamon and many other spices, and pearls are fished. The inhabitants of this island... trade with Calicut.' Finally, near Sumatra, we read: 'This island called *Taporbana* is the largest island found in the world, the richest in gold, silver, precious stones, pearls, rubies and silk.... the people here trade with foreigners, exporting the goods which they have and importing those which they do not have.'

The originality of this planisphere lies in the strange shape of the eastern peninsula, at whose extremity *Malacca* and *Singapur* are already indicated, although the Portuguese had not yet been there. Doubtless the outline of the whole Far East was based on information gathered from Muslims, and the same applies to the island in the top right-hand corner named *Cingirina*, probably already a reference to Japan. Nearby, an inscription explains, 'this island is very rich; porcelain leaves here for Malacca. Benzoin, aloes and musk are found here'.

We shall not linger over the incomplete outlines of the New World that reproduce more or less those of the 'Cantino' planisphere (No. 25). Only the Brazilian coast is richer in nomenclature than that noble chart. These place-names are definitely the result of two expeditions made on behalf of the king of Portugal. The first, from 7 August 1501 to 7 September 1502, in which Amerigo Vespucci took part, reconnoitred the whole coast of Brazil as far as the region of the tropic of Capricorn. The second (1503–1504) was under the patronage of Fernando de Noronha who, sailing with 'new Christians', planned to found a fortress and trading-post, probably in Rio de Janeiro Bay. The influence of these expeditions on Caverio's planisphere permit it to be dated circa 1505.

The decoration is sober. Only a few vignettes depict the ports of Venice, Genoa, Granada and Lisbon in Europe, the Portuguese trading-posts of Arguin and Elmina in Africa and the religious cities of Jerusalem and Mecca in Asia. Only one sovereign is portrayed: the Great Khan, seated under his tent in Central Asia. Three great wild beasts (a lion, a girafe and an elephant) fill the geographic void of the interior of the African continent. As on the 'Cantino' chart (No. 25), there are drawings of coloured parrots in Brazil. More than fifty banners indicate trading-posts or zones of political and commercial influence: twenty-one are Portuguese; twenty, with a crescent, Muslim; eight Spanish and two Genoese.

Caverio's portolan chart had a very great influence on Renaissance cartography. His outlines and particularly his nomenclature can be found again in the works of the Saint-Dié geographer Waldseemüller, who inserted a first *carta marina* ('sea chart') in his 1513 edition of Ptolemy's *Geography*. Caverio's influence is even more noticeable, however, in the great planisphere in twelve leaves, entitled 'Carta Marina Navigatoria Portugallen Navigationes', which Waldseemüller published in 1516 and which seems to be directly derived from Caverio's planisphere. Research up to the present has failed to produce a solution to the mystery of how the cartographer from Lorraine came to hear of the work of the Genoese cartographer.

27

THE DIJON PORTOLAN CHART
(ca. 1510)
1 parchment leaf, (an irregular trapezium), maximum dimensions: 995 × 665 mm
Dijon, Bibliothèque publique, Ms 550

This large portolan chart, the only one of its kind in Dijon's Archives Municipales, was discovered serving as a binding and transferred in 1852 to Dijon's Bibliothèque publique, where it is still preserved. Despite a few blunders—the rhumbs, for example, are divided into two in several places—it is drawn in a harmonious medley of red and green on an untrimmed parchment, whose border of black ink follows the shape of the animal skin. Some tears, especially to the east of the Red Sea, must have caused the loss of the colophon: the document is now anonymous and undated; and its attribution, further complicated by erasures and over-writing, has been highly controversial and is still a problem.

Consulted on this subject in 1851, the Portuguese historian and collector Viscount de Santarem had already noticed 'the Spanish royal standard' flying over Granada, reconquered by Ferdinand the Catholic in 1492. 'It follows', he wrote, 'that the chart is later than that date'. Several indicators suggest that it is quite a few years later. If we consider, for example, the geographical outlines, the Baltic does not appear in this form until the turn of the century; likewise certain external characteristics: the writing of the toponyms *EVROPA* and *AFRICA*, and above all the style of the compass roses—the symbol for north is no longer placed inside the circle of the rose but immediately above it, which is not known to occur before 1502.

More precise chronological clues are perhaps provided by the unusual presence of crosses in the form of swords drawn in red ink on several parts of the Maghreb coast. In Morocco they appear next to the fortress of Ceuta (*Cepta*) and to the west of *huxemas* (Alhucemas); then at *Oram* (Oran), where the place-name has been superimposed in larger script on another, which has been deliberately effaced and of which only the initial *ma* (Mers El Kebir?) remains. A few miles to the east, a third sword indicates *Monte Sines*, near Ténès. The last sword is close to the fortress of Bougie at the entrance to the gulf of the same name (*G. de Bugea*). This could be a symbolic representation of the points on the North African coast conquered by Spain in the aftermath of the siege of Granada, between 1497 and 1510. However, if instead of simply representing the Spanish possessions in Africa, these sword-crosses are meant to denote the resounding campaigns Pedro Navarro won for Spain (surprise occupation of Peñón de Velez in 1508, capture of Oran in 1509, victorious operation at Bougie, January 1510), the absence of sword-crosses at Tripoli, which did not fall until July 1510, provides the *terminus ad quem* that was missing up to now. In that case, the chart would have been constructed between January and July 1510.

This hypothesis would explain another singularity of this chart: the duplication of nearly all the banners of non-Muslim towns, from Ceuta to Venice, by a 'banner of Christianity' (either red with a white cross, or vice versa), which matches the Islamic crescent floating from Africa to Anatolia. Indeed, one of the features of the African *conquista* was that it was regarded as a 'crusade'. Spurred on by religious passions inflamed by the Morisco revolt of 1501, the African campaign was also given financial and moral support by the Papacy from 1493 onwards and encouraged by the Spanish clergy, notably by Cardinal Ximénez. At the same time, in the part of Morocco reserved for them by the Pope's arbitration of 1494, the Portuguese were installing their garrisons from Alcácer Ceguer to

Safi (occupied in 1508). While doing so, they occasionally came upon Spanish intruders who, coming from the Canary Islands, had landed at Santa Cruz de Mar Pequeña (*marpequeno*), now Agadir.

At such a late date, the undoubted Catalan character of some features in the decoration, rightly emphasized by Viscount de Santarem—the Red Sea coloured red, the tents in Africa, the vignettes of towns—does not indicate the nationality of the author: Catalan prototypes had been copied from the beginning of the fifteenth century, notably in Genoa and Venice. As for the nomenclature, it borrows from all the languages of Mediterranean cartography.

However, the presence of Portuguese toponyms on the western part of the chart in unexpected places (*Bela Ilha* for Belle Ile in France, or *Terra Vermelha* in England in the region of Yarmouth), together with the characteristics of the compass roses (eight-pointed stars with the fleurs-de-lis, or chess pawns, in the north are typical of Portuguese cartography) point to a Portuguese origin. Furthermore, in outline, nomenclature and decoration, this chart is the twin sister to an anonymous fragment also executed in Portugal and preserved at the Arquivo Nacional da Torre do Tombo; the resemblance is such that it is tempting to think they are by the same hand.

The author, who has taken great care over the depiction of the port of Genoa, may have been Genoese—there were many in the service of Portugal—but the author's interests are Iberian. Behind the façade of a Christian world united against Islam, the Dijon portolan chart, with its detailed knowledge of the Portuguese coast and its obvious interest in the demarcation of the respective domains of Portugal and Spain, seems to illustrate an aspect of the Luso-Castilian rivalry that was shaking the foundations of the world at that time.

28

ATLANTIC CHART
by Piri Re'īs (1513)
1 vellum leaf, painted and illuminated ms,
900 × 650 mm
Istanbul, Topkapi Sarayi Museum

Born in Gallipoli on the shores of the Dardanelles around 1470, the author of this Turkish chart was the nephew of Admiral Kemal Re'īs who, after many years spent as a pirate, took supreme command of the Ottoman naval forces at the end of the fifteenth century. Piri Re'īs was passionately fond of the sea; at the age of twelve he joined his uncle's crew and took part in all sorts of naval actions in the Mediterranean in the following years. Only a few episodes of his long maritime career are known; he too began in piracy and ended as admiral of the Ottoman fleet in the Southern Seas—the Indian Ocean, Red Sea and Persian Gulf. Piri Re'īs is known to have taken part in several campaigns waged by the Turks against Venice (1499-1502) and Egypt (1516-1517), and to have participated in the campaign of 1523 which subjected Rhodes to the dominion of the Sublime Porte. Although his biography remains fragmentary, his works speak for him. Re'īs was a cultured man, who besides his native language also knew Greek, Italian, Spanish, Portuguese and Arabic and took a very keen interest in the science of navigation. He left posterity several charts and a sea book, the *Kitab-i-bahriye* (Nos. 35–36), which has a unique place in Mediterranean cartography of the sixteenth century.

The Atlantic chart reproduced here was rediscovered in Istanbul in 1929 when the Topkapi Museum was established. As indicated by the incomplete network of rhumb-lines that would originally have extended much further eastwards, this is only the western part of a great planisphere that has now disappeared; it represents the eastern shores of the New World and the western coasts of the Iberian peninsula and Africa. The Azores, Madeira, the Canary Islands and the Cape Verde Islands are all in place. The West Indies are shown, but with an archaic and completely inaccurate outline. The island of Haiti is facing in a north-south direction, and its shape recalls that of the island of Cipangu or of Antillia on Martin Behaim's globe (No. 20). With its three compass roses, two large distance scales and no latitude scale, the Turkish chart is still based solely on directions and distances. It is coloured, and—contrary to Islamic cartographic tradition—it is copiously illustrated. The kingdoms of Portugal, Marrakech and Guinea are indicated by their sovereigns. In America (especially in Brazil), the cartographer draws, alongside fantastic people and animals, a very genuine llama and puma, and parrots are perched on the islands. In the North Atlantic, a whale, on whose back two castaways seem to be living, obviously refers to the legendary adventure of Saint Brendan and his companions who, in the early Middle Ages, had mistaken a whale for an island! To the south, the immense continent closing off the Atlantic is an adaptation of the Ptolemaic concept of the world, still widespread in the first quarter of the sixteenth century. Dhows and caravels sail on the sea.

When they are deciphered, the numerous inscriptions support the assertion that the chart drawn in 1513 by Piri Re'īs and based in part on Portuguese and Arab sources, was also copied (especially the newly discovered region called 'Antilya Coast') from a chart made by Columbus himself. In one of the inscriptions the author refers to a Spanish slave of his uncle Kemal Re'īs, who claimed to have accompanied Columbus three times to America and told marvellous anecdotes on the subject. It must be presumed that a chart by Columbus was found on a Spanish vessel captured by the Turks in the Mediterranean around 1501.

Not the least of the merits of this chart by Piri Re'īs is that it is possibly the only echo we have today of a chart which Christopher Columbus may have drawn in 1498.

29-34

MILLER ATLAS
(ca. 1519)
4 vellum leaves, ms illuminated recto and verso, 415 × 590 mm
29 Leaf 1ᵛ: *The Azores*
30 Leaf 2ᵛ: *Madagascar*
31 Leaf 2ʳ: *Arabia, India*
32 Leaf 3ᵛ: *East Indies, the Moluccas*
33 Leaf 4ʳ: *Brazil*
34 Vellum leaf, ms illuminated recto and verso, 610 × 1180 mm: *The Atlantic*
Paris, B. N.: Cartes et Plans, Rés. Ge DD 683 and Rés. Ge AA 640

These prestigious charts are part of a Portuguese atlas of circa 1519, known as the Miller Atlas, after the name of its last owner before it entered the collections of the Bibliothèque Nationale at the end of the nineteenth century. Unfortunately incomplete—its African charts have been lost without trace—this atlas originally contained charts of the whole of the known world before Magellan's circumnavigation.

Its decoration is sumptuous: twenty-seven illuminated compass roses, each with thirty-two branches, shine like jewels; forty-seven Portuguese, Muslim and Chinese ships of the high seas plough the oceans with all sails set, and Portuguese or Spanish emblems indicate trading-posts or new discoveries. The towns are depicted in artistic, if not always accurate, bird's-eye views, and the names of regions are often inscribed in gold capitals on purple scrolls. Landscapes and scenes of native life appear in miniature paintings, while multicoloured birds and quadrupeds of various species conjure up visions of exotic fauna.

Everything seems to indicate that this atlas was intended for a noble patron. It was found on the French market; perhaps it was originally made for Francis I, whose passion for the arts was common knowledge. Or it might have been intended for the king of Portugal, Manoel the Fortunate. No archival material has been found to solve this enigma. It is possible that a rather schematic mappa mundi, signed by Lopo Homem and dated 1519, which was acquired by the Bibliothèque Nationale (Rés. Ge D 26179) from Marcel Destombes in 1976, may once have appeared at the beginning of this atlas, but the other charts in it do not seem to be by this cartographer. Although Lopo Homem held the post of 'Master of Sea Charts' in Lisbon from 1517, he was still young and inexperienced and, according to A. Cortesão and Teixeira da Mota, it is highly likely that he called upon his former master Pedro Reinel and Reinel's son Jorge for assistance, and that they were charged with this royal commission. The illumination, which is by the same hand on all the charts, may have been entrusted to the painter Gregorio Lopes.

This magnificent atlas still shows signs of several borrowings from Ptolemy's *Geography*. The great Alexandrian's influence can be detected in the representation in black of the seven 'climates', the outline of the imaginary *Sinus Magnus* in the Far East and, on a chart of the Mediterranean, a timid attempt at a longitude scale graduated from a Prime Meridian that Ptolemy located west of the Canary Islands. However, the work as a whole remains essentially nautical: each chart except for the one of the Atlantic has a network of rhumb-lines 420 millimetres in diameter, with sixteen secondary centres; there are an abundance of place-names perpendicular to the coastlines, usually a distance scale inscribed in a frame bordered with black and gold, a latitude scale on the right-hand margin of the leaf, and the equator and the tropics indicated in red. In short it is an elaborate nautical atlas, whose importance cannot be overemphasized. The cartographer has drawn the overall outlines of the arc of the West Indies and the Brazilian land-mass with great accuracy, and he has defined the contours of the western Indian Ocean, given Madagascar its definitive shape, established the location of the main archipelagos, improved the outline of Arabia and the Persian Gulf, executed the first satisfactory drawing of the Bay of Bengal, given Sumatra an appearance approaching reality and supplied the first cartographic survey of the Moluccas group. The Miller Atlas is too often thought of simply as a work of art, but its scientific value, which is of the first order, should not be underestimated.

Except for the leaf concerning the Azores, all the charts reproduced here show territory discovered within thirty years or less of the atlas's construction in the course of voyages to both east and west, from Christopher Columbus (1492) to Magellan (1519).

29 *The Azores*

The portolan chart of the Azores (No. 29) is beautifully arranged: three Portuguese ships of the high seas are sailing in the Atlantic, with the cross of the Order of Christ on their sails. This order had been founded by the king of Portugal in 1317 to inherit the property of the Order of Knights Templars after its suppression. In the fifteenth century, Prince Henry the Navigator was the administrator of the Order of Christ, which then had its own ships. Between the two complete compass roses the title *[Ins]Vle Acipitru* floats in a scroll over the islands of this archipelago, explored and colonized by Portugal since 1432: *Samta M.* (Santa Maria),

Sam Miguell (São Miguel), *Terceria, Sam Zorge* (São Jorge), *Opyco* (Pico), *Graciosa, Y. dos Froles* (Flores), *Fayall* (Faial) and *Ocomo* (Corvo). In the top left-hand corner, on the latitude of Ireland, a mysterious island, *IsuLa Viridis*, illuminated in gold, gleams on the parchment. Its presence is doubtless an allusion to the 'green island', or Greenland, where Corte Real's expedition perished with all hands, after setting out in 1504 to find a Northwest Passage to Cathay. The incompleteness of the rhumb-line network shows that the chart continues to the east, for the Azores portolan chart is the first panel of a great chart of the Mediterranean, which is not shown here, but into which it merges perfectly.

30 Madagascar

This (No. 30) appears to be the oldest nautical chart of Madagascar: it was drawn after Tristan de Cunha and Alfonso d'Albuquerque circumnavigated the island in December 1506 and January 1507. The island is called the Isle of Saint Lawrence, after the Christian name of its discoverer, Lourenço Ravasco, a member of Cabral's expedition, who discovered it in the year 1500. The presence of Antongil Bay (*Baia d'Antonio Gonsalvez*) on the east coast and of the *rio de Bamara* (today the port of Vohemar) further to the north, suggests that the cartographer was also aware of the exploration of Pedreanes, known as Le Français, who went to found a trading-post on the island in 1514-1515.

A Portuguese flag flies over Cape Ambre, others indicate the Comoro Islands (*Ylhas de Cornoro*) and the Agalega Islands (*Abroal.o*). To the north and east the Seychelles, Mauritius and Réunion (*Samta Apelonya*) are sketched in. An inscription at the bottom declares that Madagascar 'is considered to be the biggest of all the islands in the sea; it is inhabited by Mohammedans who are subject to no king of any sort. . . .' The conversion to Islam of the East African coast and then of Madagascar was the work of Bantu sailors, whose explorations date from the eighth century. When the Portuguese arrived at the end of the fifteenth century, the chief trading settlements on this large island were completely dominated by converts to Islam. In the upper left-hand corner of the chart on the East African coast is a vignette showing the town of *Mogadoxo* (Mogadishu), one of the most thriving ports on the coast in the Middle Ages. Portuguese caravels and Arab dhows sail on the ocean illustrating the intensive trade and the ensuing rivalries which were only just beginning.

The incomplete rhumb-line network proves that the Madagascar portolan chart was originally joined to a cartographic representation of southern Africa that has now disappeared.

31 Arabia, India

This chart of Arabia and India (No. 31), drawn shortly after the first Portuguese maritime reconnaissances (Vasco da Gama, Cabral, Juan Coelho, Albuquerque, 1489-1515), is quite exceptional; the orientation of the outlines and the overall proportions are remarkable, and the—implicit—longitude between Cape Gardafui and Malacca is almost correct.

The already abundant nomenclature in Arabia and along the west coast of India bears witness to visits by explorers. *Aden* is shown, with an evident attention to geographical precision, as a mountain crest surmounted by fortifications. The coast of Oman, visited by Albuquerque, has real place-names in the right order for the first time, among which is Muscat (*Mazaquete*). In the Persian Gulf, we can recognize the island of Bahrein (*Baharem*) and the town of Hormuz (*Aramuz*), which is represented by a great citadel. On the Malabar coast, all the places discovered within the last twenty years or less are shown: *Diu, Goa, Cananor, Calecut,* Cochin (*Couchim*). Beyond Cape Comorin, on the other hand, the Coromandel coast is devoid of place-names. In the Bay of Bengal the cartographer knows of the Ganges delta and, roughly speaking, the orientation of the Burmese coast. Ceylon and the north of Sumatra (*Traporbana*) are in the correct place. To the southwest of the Indian peninsula, a group of fantastic, multiform and multicoloured islands seems to foreshadow the Laccadive and Maldive Islands: near them an inscription states: 'Here the stone of Hercules [the magnet] is produced. On account of this ships with iron nails are halted'. Valentim Fernandes had already indicated the importance of magnetism in these regions in 1502.

The hinterland, devoid of geographical data, is stocked with charming miniatures illustrating the people, fauna and flora of these distant lands. In Arabia, a caravan is crossing the desert; scanty palms indicate the presence of oases, and in Mecca (*Mecha*), a miniature depicts the Kaaba, built in the seventh century and still standing today in the centre of the sacred mosque. In southern Arabia a superb Yemeni warrior shows off his sabre and shield. In northern India, near some mountains shown as seen from above, wild animals are dotted over the parchment: a lion, a rhinoceros and two elephants are visible. The forests are indicated by illustrations of various trees, both palm trees and deciduous trees. On the Deccan plateau, two Hindu warriors, sword in one hand and shield in the other, seem to be threatening each other. Finally, on the Indian Ocean, a dozen Portuguese, Chinese and Muslim ships recall the diversity of the merchant fleets in the area, although the Portuguese flag predominates.

32 East Indies, Moluccas

This is the oldest European chart to provide an approximate location for the east coast of Sumatra in relation to the west coast of Malaysia from which the Gulf of Siam is still absent. The pot-bellied shape of the Malay peninsula is very inaccurate; however, the most important trade centre in Southeast Asia, *Malaqua*, the port where all the spice trade was concentrated and which had been conquered by Albuquerque in 1511, is shown; in fact it appears twice. It is also rather remarkable that the port of *Singapura* should appear in the correct place, at latitude 2°5' North. Then we see an incipient Saigon River (*Sobanus F.*) and a sort of foreshortened Vietnam, drawn as far as a great gulf (probably the Gulf of Tonkin) beyond which begins the famous *Sinus Magnus* borrowed from Ptolemy, which is pure invention. To the left along the margin, an inscription informs us that: 'Before and after *Taprobana* [Sumatra] there is a multitude of islands... 1,378 in all.' They gleam on this chart (No. 32) like many-hued enamels, and among them we can recognize, to the east of Sumatra and parallel to it, the islands of Java (*Java Major*), possibly Bali (*Java Minor*) and the Sunda Islands (*Candin Insula*).

On the right-hand panel in the present latitude of Celebes, the Moluccas (*Maluc Insvle*) appear for the first time in western cartography: Ceram (*Seilam*), Amboina (*Amboriyo*) and Banda (*y: debamda*). On the island of Ceram, the chart even shows the port of *Guli-Guli*, where Abreu cast anchor at the beginning of 1512. Above this archipelago an inscription curiously entitled 'Islands of China' (*Chinarum Insule*) explains that 'in these islands much gold and silver is extracted, and moreover there is a great abundance of corn and other fruits, pepper, cinnamon, nuts [spikes] of clove, sandalwood and nutmeg; all kinds of spices grow there and the kings govern their subjects with firmness'. On the other hand, no reference is made yet to Ternate, although Abreu's companions had lived there for over seven years.

There are many vessels sailing on the ocean, and Portuguese flags are sprinkled here and there, including along the imaginary coast of *Sinus Magnus*, which forms the right-hand margin of this fine chart.

33 Brazil

It was less than twenty years since Cabral, thanks to a contrary wind, had touched land and officially discovered what was to be known as Brazil (22 April 1500), and yet the coast of *Terra Brasilis* (No. 33) is already drawn on this chart in the greatest detail, from the mouths of the Amazon to beyond the mouth of the Plate (35° South). The presence of the arms of Portugal at 37° South even suggests that, before Juan de Solís, on behalf of the king of Castile, made the official discovery of the great southern estuary in 1516, the entrance to the vast River Plate had been visited by some Portuguese navigator—possibly João de Lisboa and Estevan Froes during their expedition in 1511-1512. An Indian squatting on his heels with his arms stretched out seems to watch over the entrance to that great river. On the ocean, the Portuguese flag also flies over the islands of Fernando de Noronha, Trinidad and Martin Vaz as well as—further east—over Ascension and Saint Helena.

In the top left-hand corner, a long inscription relates the Europeans' impressions of this strange new land: 'The inhabitants are dark-skinned, primitive and very cruel: they eat human flesh. They are also very skilled in the handling of bows and arrows. In this country live multicoloured parrots, innumerable birds and monstrous wild beasts.... It is here that the tree called brazil, used to dye cloth purple, grows in enormous quantities.'

Some fine miniatures in the interior of the continent are even more evocative. In the heart of the forest we can see Indians wearing clothes and head-dresses made of feathers: they are hunters, as the bows and arrows that they carry indicate. Lower down, other Indians, completely naked this time, are collecting brazil-wood, which one of them is chopping up with an axe. To fell these trees, the Indians burnt the foot of the trees, then stripped the bark off the trunks with hatchets and cut it into pieces 1 or 2 metres long that were carried to the nearest river. On the chart there is a clearing in which several felled tree trunks are lying. The forest is alive with pink, blue and red parrots, monkeys and even a fabulous hydra, while the immensity of the Atlantic is dotted with numerous caravels sailing under the cross of Christ and harmoniously balancing the composition of the picture.

34 The Atlantic

This chart of the Atlantic, whose dominant feature is its illumination, is painted on a parchment nearly 80 square decimetres in area, on the verso of a representation of the Mediterranean. It was originally an integral part of the Miller Atlas, in the form of a loose plate that could be folded to the format of the rest of the atlas. Despite its sumptuous decoration, the chart itself seems unfinished, since it has no rhumb-lines. Their absence doubtless testifies to the uncertainty of mariners, baffled by the unsteadiness of their compass needle and still ignorant of the relative locations of places in the Old and New Worlds. It is a fact that, in this atlas, the cartography of the East Indies is almost perfect in its overall proportions, whereas that of the West Indies still shows certain weaknesses: the distance between Newfoundland and northern Europe is too small; the Gulf of Mexico is not long enough in the north-south axis, and the size of Florida is exaggerated.

Nevertheless, it is apparent that the cartographer has devoted all his efforts to the representation of the coastline of the New World, as the title *Mundus Novvs*, inscribed in black capitals at the foot of the document seems to imply. Indeed in the east, the coasts of Europe and Africa are only sketched in, and no place-names are given; the various countries and islands are only identified by armorial shields. In Africa, a wooded landscape is depicted, in which extremely lifelike monkeys and parrots roam freely. In the west, on the contrary, the newly discovered lands are drawn with a real attention to accuracy. The American coast is delineated from Newfoundland to the region at the mouth of the Amazon, albeit in fragmented sections interspersed with blank spaces for the still unknown areas.

In the northwest, under the red border of the trompe-l'oeil frame, is a country called *Terra Corte Regalis* marked with Portuguese arms, followed by another, even further west, termed *Terra Frigida*. They represent the east coast of Newfoundland and part of the coast of Nova Scotia, along which the Corte Reals had sailed during their successive voyages from 1500 to 1504. Pilots to the king of Portugal, the Corte Reals were searching those frozen northern regions for a passage to China and were eventually to perish there. A charming miniature in the middle of the chart shows a forest scene with a herd of big deer. Above, a long inscription in a broad scroll recalls that: 'Corte Real, travelling in this region, first discovered and named it for himself; he found wild men there, the same colour as us. . . . As for the terrain, it is almost all rough and mountainous; there are goats, stags and bucks there and other animals of the same kind. Many bears and other ferocious beasts live there. There are many great rivers, at whose mouths navigators can find inlets that assist them in penetrating further into the interior of the country.' Newfoundland is not yet shown separate from the continent.

Further to the southwest, a precursor of Florida, here called *Terra Bimene*, is located in the correct latitude, but drawn without place-names. In the cartographer's mind it was an island that not only had the reputation of being rich in gold and precious stones but also of concealing a spring, a sort of Fountain of Youth with the power of rejuvenating anyone who drank from it or bathed in it. The Spanish navigator, Ponce de León, left Puerto Rico on 1 March 1512 in search of this island paradise and its Fountain of Youth. It is shown here in a skilfully painted watercolour: against a background of mountains, pure water flows from a shady rock surrounded by tall trees. Bears, stags and a fox live on good terms with each other in this peaceful landscape, its silence broken only by the flight of innumerable birds. To the right of the painting an inscription informs us that: 'this country, called by the geographers *Mvndvs Novvs* and situated in the west, is vast; its boundaries are the country of Brazil, the land of Corte Real and also Norway; it is very fertile in gold and other commodities'. It is certain that since Vespucci published his tract *Mundus Novus* in 1503 the idea of the existence of another continent had begun to take root. Henceforth it would be accepted that a 'New World' separated Europe from China and Japan, although it was not long since Christopher Columbus writing to Pope Alexander VI had boasted of having occupied 1,400 islands and 333 leagues of Asian soil (February 1502). It is quite apparent that the cartographer of the Miller Atlas has been won over by Vespucci's argument.

Lower down, we can only marvel at the remarkable outline of the chain of greater and lesser Antilles (*Anteyllas*). The configuration of each of the islands and their location relative to one another are so accurate that the Bahamas, Cuba, Jamaica, Haiti and Puerto Rico can be easily recognized, as well as the Leeward and Windward Islands as far as Trinidad. The gold-spangled banner of the king of Castile flies everywhere. Doubtless the cartographer had been able to obtain the new working drawings brought back by the Spaniards, in particular those of Nicolas de Ovando, who sailed around Cuba in 1508, and of Juan de Solís, who made a partial reconnaissance of the Gulf of Mexico in the same year. It must have been the latter who was responsible for the excellent representation of the coasts of what are today eastern Yucatán, Honduras and Nicaragua. The Gulf of Darien is still missing and the southern sea unknown—the news of Balboa's discovery (1513) had not yet reached Lisbon.

Above the equator, on *Terra Firme* in South America, the outline of the coast as far as the latitude of the mouth of the Amazon remains without place-names: only the islands on the edge of the continent are mentioned. Beneath a purple banner bearing the inscription *Ante Yllas*, the miniaturist has painted a delightful scene depicting several Negroes: 'one is drawing a bow; another, armed with a sort of hoe, is digging in the earth on the instructions of a third and turning up nuggets. They wear gold bracelets on their arms and legs, and the miniature is so detailed that we can see rings of the same metal dangling from their ears. A fourth person, crouching with a stick in his hand, watches them' (G. Marcel). Beneath the painting a short inscription reads: 'in this region belonging to the king of Castile gold is found'. The presence of these Negroes before the official organization of the American slave trade shows that the Spaniards had imported a black work force to Hispaniola (Haiti) by the beginning of the sixteenth century, in order to compensate for the rapid disappearance of the Indian population, weakened by epidemics and by working the placer mines.

Finally, out in the Atlantic, we see numerous Spanish and Portuguese vessels of the high seas cruising, linking the two shores of this enormous stretch of water and adding a perfect finishing touch to this magnificent work of art of the Portuguese Renaissance.

35-36

'KITAB-I-BAHRIYE'
by Piri Re'īs (1525-1526)
224 vellum leaves, illuminated ms, 350 × 460 mm

35 Leaf 76: *Coast of Asia Minor from the Gulf of Candarli to the Island of Bozcaada (Tenedos)*
36 Leaf 413: *Crete*
Paris, B.N.: Ms turc Supplément 956

These two illuminated documents are taken from the famous book of nautical instructions that the Turkish admiral, Piri Re'īs, dedicated to his sovereign, Soliman the Magnificent, in the year 1526.

Known as the *Kitab-i-bahriye*, this sea book contains both written and pictorial information, and is a vital document in the history of Mediterranean nautical cartography. Despite the existence of Western portolans such as the *Compasso da navigare* and the abundant production of portolan charts by Italian, Catalan and Portuguese draughtsmen, and even despite the appearance during the fourteenth century of books dealing particularly with the islands of the Archipelago (*isolari*), until the *Kitab* came on the scene no marine document described the entire range of coasts, ports and islands of the Mediterranean in such detail. This Turkish book contains no less than 848 pages of which 215 are individual sea charts, drawn and painted by hand. Combining text and image, the *Kitab* provided the Ottoman sailor (for whom it was intended) with the necessary information for sailing around the whole of the Mediterranean basin, from the Dardanelles to Gibraltar, and from Ceuta to the Sea of Marmara, including the islands and archipelagos scattered over the immense inland sea. It is a compendium of historical, geographical and nautical information. In the preface to his book, Piri Re'īs informs Soliman of the goal he had set himself: 'I do not believe that anyone has ever produced a more complete work... on Mediterranean navigation; it includes all the coasts, the islands, whether populated or deserted, the rivers, the rocks level with the surface of the water or beneath it, and the sand banks. I have clearly indicated the locations of all ports of this sea and suitable places on the Christian coasts for raids; finally, I have omitted nothing which could [help] guide a pilot....'

The two charts chosen show: first (No. 35) the islands of Lesbos (*Mytilene*) and Tenedos (*Bozcaada*); second (No. 36), what is already a very good outline of Crete. The charts are drawn on rhumb-lines without visible compass roses, and there is only an arrow in black ink to indicate the direction of north. They are polychrome, and a gold hatching emphasizes the contours of the coasts. Together with other information, the accompanying text gives practical advice on how to enter the 'new port of Mytilene' (Lesbos) and the port of Canea on the northern coast of Crete.

37

PLANISPHERE
by Diogo Ribeiro (1529)

1 vellum chart, illuminated ms, 850 × 2045 mm
Vatican, Biblioteca Apostolica Vaticana, Borgiano III

Derived from the *padrón real*, which was drawn up in secret in Seville and constantly revised, Diogo Ribeiro's nautical planisphere gives the outlines of the coasts known in 1529 and illustrates the tremendous progress made in the discovery of the world in less than forty years. Its title, inscribed at the top and bottom of the chart, defines the nature of the document: 'A universal chart containing everything that has been discovered in the world up to now. Diogo Ribeiro made it in the year 1529 in Seville. It is divided into two parts, according to the treaty agreed between the Catholic kings of Spain and King John [II] of Portugal at Tordesillas in the year 1494'. Above the scroll indicating the South Pole (*Polus Mundi Atarcticus*), two oriflammes—Spanish and Portuguese; one turned to the west, the other to the east—symbolize the division of the world into equal shares. They can also be found (reversed) at the lower right of the chart, above the illustration of an astrolabe. Diogo Ribeiro thereby draws the navigator's attention to the fact that the Moluccas archipelago (situated at the frontier between the two zones) is, according to him, clearly in the Spanish zone, just beyond the antimeridian.

This planisphere, often considered to be the finest example of marine cartography, was the work of a Portuguese deserter who had entered the service of Charles V in 1519 and was to serve him to his last breath (1533). The talents of this former companion of Vasco da Gama and Albuquerque on their eastern voyages rapidly gained recognition in Spain. Diogo Ribeiro was one of the group of scholars in Seville who planned Magellan's voyage, and he was named 'cosmographer and master of charts and navigational instruments to the hydrographic service of the Casa de Contratación' in 1523. By virtue of this appointment, he succeeded Sebastian Cabot in the office of 'pilot major': his two mappae mundi of 1529 (the other one is in Weimar) bear eloquent witness to his skills. The present chart, often called the 'Borgia Chart', is now preserved at the Vatican in the collections of the Sacred Congregation for the Propagation of the Faith, where it was deposited in 1830; but it is only 'Borgian' because it was formerly housed in the museum of Cardinal Stefano Borgia at Velletri. The arms of the Rovere and Chigi families, painted at the foot of the chart near the margin, presumably indicate a noble provenance. On the other hand, the presence of the arms of Pope Julius II, who died in 1513, between the two escutcheons remains a mystery.

Following the fundamental principles of the *padrón*, this planisphere only shows coastlines actually sighted by mariners, and no concessions are made to the imagination. Henceforth, the delineation of the eastern seaboard of America, from the Straits of Magellan to Labrador, was to be continuous. In North America, the cartographer notes the many European expeditions in search of a hypothetical Northwest Passage, which was believed to lie between Florida and Newfoundland; joining the Atlantic to the Pacific, it would have permitted quicker voyages to the fabulous Spice Islands than the route around the Cape of Good Hope or even through the Straits of Magellan. Thus the chart successively illustrates the explorations of John Cabot (1497-1498), who sailed from Bristol; the Corte Reals (1500-1503), who set out from Lisbon; Estevan Gómez (1524-1525), who sailed from Corunna; and of Vasquez de Ayllon (1520-1526) and Francisco de Garay (1521), who embarked from San Domingo and Jamaica respectively. The only explorer missing from the list is the Italian Giovanni da Verrazano (1523), sent out by Francis I on the same mission. Of course these explorations did not achieve their goal, but they enabled Europe to form a much clearer impression of the extent and diversity of the American coast from Labrador to South Carolina. In South America, the cartographer indicates the progress made by Francisco Pizarro on the Peruvian coast (1527), as well as the discovery in 1515-1516 of the River Plate (*Tiera de Solís*) and Magellan's discovery in 1519 (*Tiera de Patagones*). In the Far East, while the East Indies to the east of Sumatra (*Camatra*) still remain a mystery, the coast of China is delineated for the first time up to and beyond Canton (*Camtam*), today Guangzhou, illustrating the reconnaissances undertaken by the Portuguese fleet on the shores of the Celestial Empire since 1515-1516.

Diogo Ribeiro certainly deserved his title of 'Cosmographer Royal'; his planisphere teems with information of a cosmographic nature. It is, firstly, one of the earliest charts to show a longitude scale on the equator, the first graduated representation of the earth's circumference since its sphericity had been proved experimentally by the return to Spain of Magellan's last pilot, Del Cano (1522). This measurement was still approximate; in fact it was only to become completely accurate in the second third of the eighteenth century, when the use of the chronometer allowed space and time to be measured simultaneously. Until then, as long as mariners were obliged to rely on the log and the hourglass to estimate distances travelled, whether to the east or the west, the calculation of longitude at sea would remain inaccurate. On our chart, the error made in the location of the Moluccas (*Gilolo*), wrongly sited in the Spanish zone, when they rightfully belonged to Portugal, clearly illustrates this problem. At the foot of the chart appear a quadrant and an astrolabe, with an inscription explaining how to use them in order to obtain latitudes.

Finally, in the Pacific, a circular declination table is given, with a calendar, the signs of the zodiac and, in the middle, a compass rose. Here again the cosmographer explains how it should be used with the compass rhumb to discover the value of a degree expressed in leagues. Even more remarkable is the explanation he gives for the axis of the Mediterranean, whose torsion has been corrected: for the first time on a nautical document, the 36th parallel passes, as it should, through the Straits of Gibraltar, the north of Cyprus and the south of Asia Minor; whereas, on all earlier charts, it had been falsified by magnetic variation and had linked Gibraltar with the mouth of the Nile. The cartographer points out that he used some isolated latitudes that had come to his notice; therefore, this is not a survey based on astronomical navigation, which was not practised in the Mediterranean before the seventeenth century.

As on any chart for royalty, the decoration is sumptuous. In the four corners, the winds are symbolized by cherubs' heads. The interiors of the continents, particularly America and Africa, are adorned with a varied flora and fauna, often very accurately drawn birds and mammals, although sometimes they are extremely strange. As on all large-scale nautical planispheres, the compass roses illuminate the vellum with their vivid colours: here they add emphasis to a double network of rhumb-lines, one covering the western hemisphere; the other the eastern hemisphere. The names of the seas are inscribed on elegant scrolls on the immense expanse of ocean revealed by Magellan's circumnavigation. Twenty ships, with archaic rigging and all sails set, are either bound for the Moluccas or returning from them.

That fabulous and remote archipelago, from which only one of Magellan's five ships, the 'Vitoria', was to return safely (in 1522) with an enormous cargo of spices, was to haunt the imagination of western mariners. The whole of Ribeiro's chart reflects this obsession at the very moment, when Charles V, strangely enough, was handing over to Portugal all his rights over that immensely rich archipelago (Treaty of Saragossa, 1529).

38

ATLANTIC CHART
by Gaspar Viegas (1534)
1 vellum leaf, illuminated ms, 700 × 960 mm
Paris, B.N.: Cartes et Plans, Rés. Ge B 1132

Intended for Portuguese pilots, this nautical chart is extremely bare, containing only the details essential for navigation: outlines, rhumbs, compass roses, distance scales, a latitude scale and place-names along the coasts. On both sides of the Atlantic, Portuguese flags recall the fact that these shores were first sighted by Portuguese shipping. The orientation of the Brazilian coast is an improvement on previous surveys, and the ports are sited in nearly the correct latitude. The cartographer Gaspar Viegas has taken advantage of information provided by Admiral Martim Afonso da Sousa, who had returned to Lisbon the previous year after

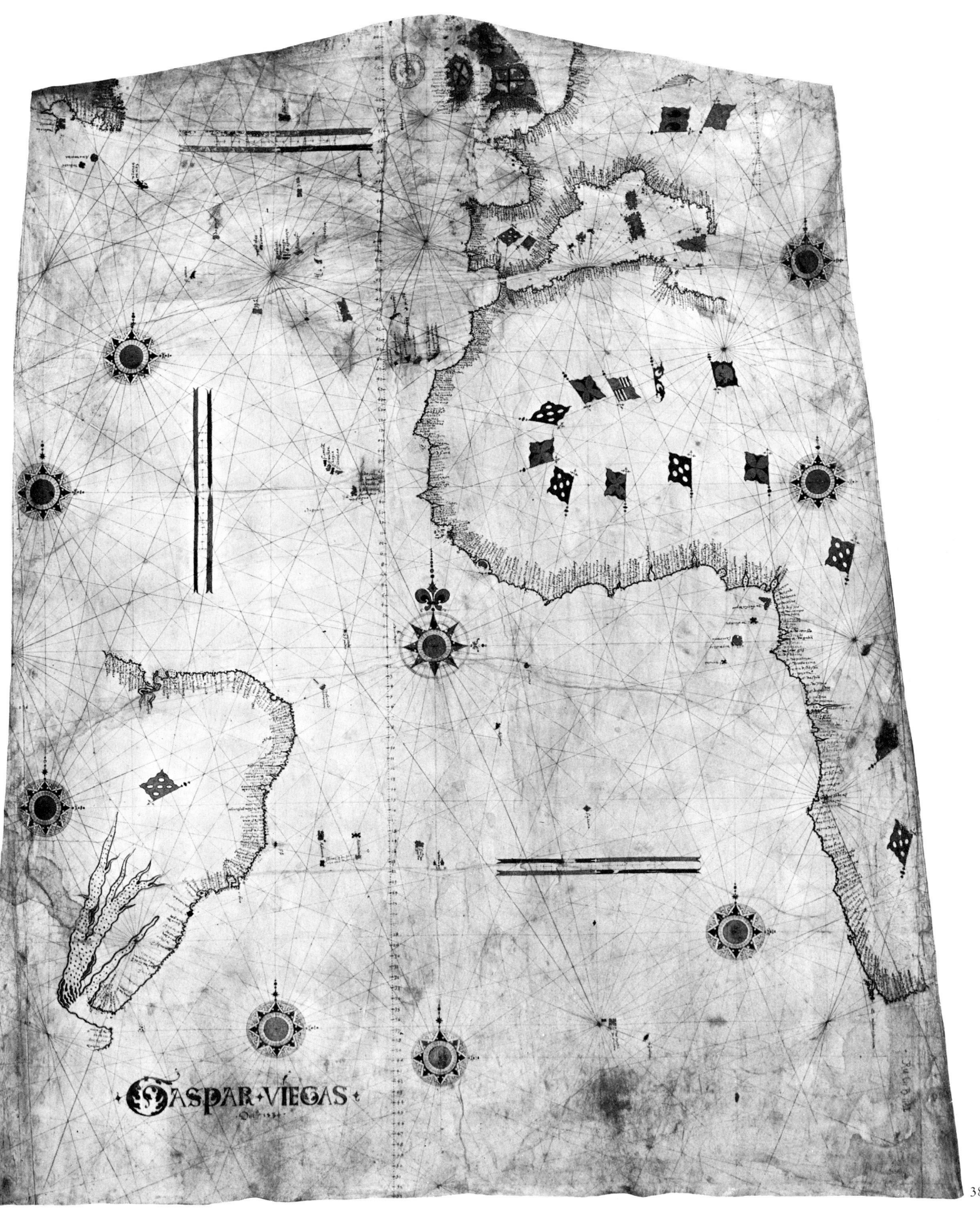

two years of exploration along the coasts of Brazil, where he had gone to expel French traffickers illegally established in the Pernambuco region.

He also had a scientific mission, consisting of an exploration of the River Plate. Several names coined during his voyage appear on the chart: for example, on the north coast, the bay of *Diogo Leite* and on the south coast, the port of São Pedro (*Sam p.o.*) and the Martim Afonso da Sousa River (*rio de m̄ti a de Sousa*). The chart also shows very clearly a certain number of sea lanes, particularly the one linking Rio Bay with the island of Tristan da Cunha, which allowed navigators to reach the Indian Ocean while avoiding the currents around the Cape of Good Hope.

The signature and the date—*Gaspar Viegas out⁰ 1534*—are in the bottom left-hand corner of the document. This is the only work definitely attributable to this excellent cartographer about whom nothing else is known.

39-40

'BOKE OF IDROGRAPHY'
by Jean Rotz (1542)
16 vellum leaves, illuminated ms, 595 × 770 mm
39 Leaf 9ᵛ-10ʳ: *The East Indies*
40 Leaf 21ᵛ-22ʳ: *The Atlantic Ocean*
London, British Library, Royal Ms 20 E IX

The first known cartographer from Dieppe, Jean Rotz (often called Roze in French official documents), had a singular career. Born at the beginning of the sixteenth century, the son of a Scottish nobleman in business in Dieppe, Rotz was soon involved in the maritime world. His father, probably an associate of Ango, allowed him to go to sea and possibly—although no proof exists—to take part in the Parmentier brothers' adventurous expedition to Sumatra in 1529. In any case he affirms that, 'through our experience of long-distance navigation', he was soon exposed to the newly discovered world. As his father's business partner, Jean Rotz visited Guinea and Brazil between 1530 and 1539. Then, curious to understand the connections between these new territories, he seems to have gone to Paris to study science for two years. It was at this time that he must have begun compiling the *Boke of Idrography*, intending at first to present it to Francis I, 'his sovereign and natural lord'. Then, suddenly, we find him in London with a wife and children, the *Boke of Idrography* now dedicated to Henry VIII. Like many other hydrographers of quality, Rotz became a 'servant to Henry VIII', and remained so from 1542 to 1546. In 1547, he was back in France again as a 'merchant residing in Dieppe', where he was also a captain in the navy.

The *Boke of Idrography* is an atlas consisting of eleven regional charts and a mappa mundi. They are preceded by a dedication containing a learned explanatory text on how to locate geographical positions. The regional charts, all painted to the same scale on the recto of the vellum, could be laid out flat and assembled into a large-size general chart (3,965 × 2,135 mm), affording the royal patron an overall view of the known world.

Oriented with north at the bottom, these portolan charts constructed on rhumb-lines are all plane charts with constant degrees of latitude; no mention is made of longitude. The distance scales are arranged in the borders adorned with foliated scrolls. The script and delineation are carefully done, but no more than that. Rotz strives to adhere to reality without regard for the aesthetic or imaginary considerations familiar to his contemporaries. His inspiration is Portuguese: the sumptuous compass roses, crowned with a fleur-de-lis, are redolent of Portuguese influence, and the nomenclature is Portuguese to a fault. French names such as Saint Nazaire appear as *Senazer*; English names like Southampton or the New Forest become *Antonha* and *a bosco*. Nevertheless, Rotz's personal contribution makes him the precursor of the Dieppe hydrographic school of the classical period (situated between 1540 and 1556), when a group of hydrographers with totally original concepts flourished. The charts of the East Indies (No. 39) and the Atlantic Ocean (No. 40) enable us to compare the treatment of two very different worlds and illustrate the originality of the author.

Jean Rotz is the first Frenchman to represent the East Indies, delineating their outline from India to southern China, and although the coasts of Asia and the East Indies, as well as the nomenclature, are of Portuguese inspiration, not everything is exclusively Portuguese. For example, there is a mysterious land situated south of Java, surrounded by islands such as *Flores* and *Timor*, two of the present-day Sunda Islands. This land does not appear on any Portuguese chart, whereas it is shown with various dimensions on nearly all the Dieppe charts of the sixteenth century. Le Testu (No. 51) calls it 'Java Major'; Jean Rotz leaves it nameless, simply covering it with nondescript tall trees and rocks but, like his compatriots, showing it to be of an enormous size.

From the eighteenth century onwards, geographers like the Englishman Dalrymple in 1786 and the Frenchman Barbié du Bocage in 1807 gave this Dieppe 'invention' the credit for the discovery of Australia two centuries before Cook. The scholars of today are still uncertain whether the men of Dieppe could have had access to a partial survey of the fifth continent.

The originality of this document also lies in a curiously accurate illustration of recently visited lands, which seems directly inspired by the *Discours de la Navigation* by Crignon, historiographer of the voyage of the Parmentier brothers (1529). Thus, the inhabitants of *Trapobane* (Sumatra) are dressed in short blue tunics and armed with what seems to be a scimitar, but even more curious is the procession covering the northern part of the Indochinese peninsula. Inhabitants are advancing, armed with long lances, scimitars and broad shields. A figure on foot, dressed in a brown tunic and a turban, precedes a mounted noble horseman, protected by a servant with a parasol; the horseman carries a flaming torch. At the end of the procession a servant is beating on a gong. There is nothing imaginary about this vivid scene: Crignon's *Discours* had described thus the arrival of the Parmentier brothers' expedition in the village of Ticou, on the west coast of Sumatra. Likewise, the dwelling painted in the north of Malaysia is a house on stilts typical of traditional Indonesian building techniques. Thus we find in this portolan chart, alongside the daring representation of what may be a foreshadowing of Australia, the portrayal of new information on native life which bears witness to the researches of the Humanists of Dieppe under Francis I.

The Atlantic Ocean chart is more austere in appearance. Framing the ocean are the coasts of Europe and America, shown with north at the bottom: thus Labrador and Iceland appear at the foot of the leaf. A great ship—a carrack—plunges towards the coast of Portugal. Seven vignettes with fortifications of various designs possibly symbolize the states of Europe. Labrador, a primitive land, is inhabited by figures wearing skins and armed with bows; a bear accompanies them. The two latitude scales shown on either side of the chart introduce us straightaway to Rotz's solution to the cartographic problem of the variation of the magnetic needle: near the coasts of Europe, the latitudes stretch from 33° to 78°N; whereas, along the American shores, they stretch from 29° to 74°N. This difference of 4° between east and west is the cartographer's way of expressing his understanding of magnetic variation. He indicates thereby that an east-west crossing of the Atlantic entails a considerable compass variation towards the west. Renaissance mariners were to learn—often to their cost—that it was even greater when sailing in regions bordering on the magnetic North Pole.

In America, two points are worth noting. Newfoundland is still shown in the traditional but imaginary way as an archipelago, in the south of which, however, appear three real bays: Saint Mary, Placentia and Fortune. The double dotted line drawn off-shore is one of the first indications of the cod-fishing grounds of the Grand Banks.

The second original feature of this chart is the long peninsula bordered by the *Cost of Labrador*. It is probable that this immense territory, pointing east and taking up the whole of the foot of the leaf, represents Labrador joined on to Greenland; this is sometimes called pseudo-Labrador or French Labrador. It is found in almost all sixteenth-century Dieppe cartography. In any case, it poses a problem: was it the result of a misinterpretation by the first navigators (Cabot, the Corte Reals), who may have mistaken the Davis Strait—and even the Hudson Strait—for a gulf; or is its NW-SE inclination influenced by a knowledge of the very strong magnetic variation in these regions? These questions have not yet received a definite answer.

These two charts are none the less representative of the talents of a very great hydrographer—Jean Rotz is always down to earth, drawing what he knows and thereby encouraging Henry VIII to commission further expeditions to the 'new lands' and beyond.

41

MAPPA MUNDI
by Battista Agnese (1543)
1 vellum leaf, coloured ms, 195 × 295 mm
Paris, B.N.: Cartes et Plans, Rés. Ge FF 14410

Surrounded by twelve cherubs' faces symbolizing the winds, this coloured oval mappa mundi appears in a nautical atlas executed in Venice by the Genoese cartographer Battista Agnese. It provides an expressive overall view of the distribution of the continental landmasses (coloured green) and oceanic expanses known in the first half of the sixteenth century. The persistence of 'Ptolemaic' concepts is demonstrated by the absence of the Indian peninsula from the depiction of Asia. In America, on the other hand, there is a tentative sketch of a Northwest Passage.

Addressing himself to the ship-owners and rich merchants of the 'Serenissima' Republic, the author draws their attention to the existence of two new maritime routes. The first is the spice route opened up by Magellan (1519-1521), drawn in black. It goes right round the world; in the China Sea there is a note: *Esta mar dale Malucho* ('here is the Molucca Sea') from which came cloves, ginger, pepper, nutmeg and cinnamon. In actual fact, this extremely long route, which was difficult to navigate, was practically abandoned for nearly two and a half centuries. The second sea route, indicated by a pale gold line, is the gold route, which regularly linked Seville and Peru after the fall of the Inca Empire (1532): chests and bales of gaudy material, glass beads and showy lace imported from Spain, were unloaded at Nombre de Dios and transported across the Isthmus of Panama on mule-back before re-embarking for the port of Callao in Peru, following in reverse the maritime axis taken by the fabulous consignments of Peruvian gold. This treasure would be unloaded on the quays of Sanlúcar de Barrameda, Seville or Cadiz, under the inquisitorial gaze of the employees of the Casa de Contratación.

Battista Agnese was one of the greatest cartographic popularizers of his day: no less than seventy-one of his marine atlases of the same type remain, all constructed in Venice between 1536 and 1564.

42

PLANISPHERE
by Guillaume Brouscon (1543)
1 vellum leaf, coloured ms, 650 × 450 mm
San Marino, California, Henry E. Huntingdon Library and Art Gallery

This planisphere is contained in a little xylographic nautical guide that for a long time was attributed to a Siennese author. Dr. Dujardin, an eminent Breton scholar, identified it as being the work of Guillaume Brouscon, a cartographer at Le Conquet, near Brest.

The port of Le Conquet, a dependency of the Abbey of Saint-Mathieu situated at the furthest extremity of the region of Léon, was a bustling centre of trade and coastal traffic for all the ports of the West. 'Chart makers' were recruited from among certain families, like the Brouscons in the sixteenth century and the Troadecs in the seventeenth.

The dangers of navigation along these coasts provided the 'chart makers' with a wide and regular clientele. The trade in charts, together with that of calendars and nautical guides, flourished for two centuries, in particular because reproduction from wood engravings (xylography) enabled production of copies to keep pace with demand.

This planisphere is surrounded by a trompe-l'oeil frame in which the date '1543' and the signature 'G.B.', so long a puzzle, appear twice. Opposite the signature appears the quartered escutcheon of Artus de Cossé, Marshal of France, and one of the most famous warriors of his day (1512-1582). Intended for a noble patron, the chart is very carefully made.

The New World, whose outline can be compared with that of Desliens in 1566 (No. 58), bears eleven flags indicating ownership: Canada is under the French flag, and a standard bearing the quartered arms of the Dauphin and Brittany recalls that the future Henry II had been Dauphin and Duke of Brittany since 1536 through his grandmother Anne of Brittany. The Dauphin was especially interested in the discovery of new territories.

It is in America that the most original features are to be found. Newfoundland appears as an island and not as an archipelago. Even more original is the fact that the triangular island is oriented normally, with its base in the south, whereas Desliens, the only Dieppois not to depict Newfoundland as an archipelago, shows it upside down (No. 58). The correct outline would not appear until the second generation of Dieppe cartographers, and Guillaume Levasseur (No. 67). The Breton cartographer is particularly well informed about this island, which his compatriots, in search of cod, had been visiting for half a century.

Indications of the Canadian territories discovered by Jacques Cartier (1534-1542) are found in the place-names: *Ochelaga* (later Montreal) and *Sagane* (Saguenay).

The south of the American continent is curiously sophisticated in comparison with other contemporary outlines. The 'land of Magellan' (*Magaillan*) generally resembles the southern territory of the Harleian Mappa Mundi, but if we examine the islands, on the chart from east to west, we can recognize Staten Island (*terre de Leri*), the extremity of Tierra del Fuego (*Fogos*), and the islands situated south of the Strait of Magellan (*cab de Lopes* and *Travisa*).

According to R. Hervé, the outline of the 'island of Magellan' seems to be drawn to a larger scale than the continent and contains a sketch of what was later to be known as the Lemaire Strait, dotted with numerous islands and situated between Staten Island and Cape Horn, itself an island. This would imply an accurate knowledge of a passage officially navigated by the Dutch explorers Lemaire and Schouten seventy-five years later (1616).

The austral continent, untiringly sought by navigators, appears on this planisphere to the south of Asia. Named in a baroque cartouche, the *TERRE OSTRALE* is drawn to the south of *Taprobane* (Sumatra), increasing in width as it descends towards the Antarctic. No identification with the coastline of Australia is possible. The austral myth had exerted the same influence on this Breton cartographer as on Le Testu and Desceliers.

Knowledge and intuition in this cartography go far beyond the traditional interests of Breton mariners: coastal trade and cod fishing.

43-44

PILOT'S MANUAL FOR THE USE OF BRETON SAILORS
by Guillaume Brouscon (1548)
26 vellum pages, illuminated ms, foliated 4 to 29, 175 × 140 mm
43 *Atlantic Chart*, folding plate, 275 × 310 mm
44 Folio 25[r]: *Tide Table* and folio 25[v]: *Chart from Le Havre to Muros*
Paris, B.N., Ms français 25374

Reduced to pocket size and bound in leather, this guide is noteworthy both for the nautical information it contains and for the simple yet eloquent graphic forms by which the information is conveyed.

The text consists of five chapters covering twelve pages, in a familiar but concise style, explaining how to make the astronomical calculations that are essential in high-seas navigation: how to find the latitude of a point at sea by measuring the altitude of the stars, the sun and the 'North Star', and how to transpose a degree in latitude into the distance to be followed 'on a particular rhumb-line', along which the ship's course was set. This simplified explanation is followed by a declination table and a perpetual Julian calendar of moveable feasts. The remainder is all pictorial: sketches of boats, compass roses, tide tables and charts.

43 Atlantic Chart

Folded at the head of the manual, this large chart covers the coasts of the Atlantic from the Baltic islands to North Africa. The signature, 'G. BROVSCON', is inscribed on a scroll and the date, '1548', in a cartouche on the frame.

As on the planisphere of 1543, eleven banners indicate the countries; over *BORDEO* (Bordeaux) flies the fleur-de-lis standard of the Dauphin and future King Henry II. Towers bar the entrance to the Sound near *Copeneuen* (Copenhagen); others indicate a narrow passage in the Hebrides archipelago. The copious nomenclature is French, even in the case of English ports like Plymouth, which becomes *plemu*, or Portsmouth, alias *porsmu*. Despite the inaccuracy of the outlines—especially in the Cotentin—and the relative inexactitude of certain latitudes (Saint Mathieu Point, for example, is at 49°N instead of 48°3'N), the area charted, one with which Breton sailors had to be familiar, and the presence of a latitude scale in the Atlantic from 34° to 59°N, show that, unlike the other charts in this guide, this is an actual navigational chart and reference work, enlightening its owner as to his position and serving as an introduction to those western ports which were active at the time.

44 Tide Table and Chart from Le Havre to Muros

Navigation in the Atlantic, the Channel and the North Sea, and arrivals and departures in the ports in this area were entirely dependent on the regular rhythm of the tides. From the Middle Ages, the west had known that they were caused by the moon: in the eighth century, the Venerable Bede described the interconnection between the phases of the moon and the monthly tide cycle, and in the fourteenth century the Catalan Atlas (No. 8) took account of the daily correlation between high tide and the moon's crossing of the meridian by drawing on a compass dial the 'establishment' of fourteen ports. The 'establishment' is a somewhat unsuitable term indicating 'the moment of high water in a port' on the days of the new moon and the full moon. Until late into the nineteenth century this information was given by showing the position of the moon on the horizon at that moment, which amounted to using the compass rose as a clock, each of its thirty-two points being equivalent to three quarters of an hour ($32 \times 3/4 = 24$ hours).

The method used by Brouscon to 'establish' the ports of the west is a model of ingenuity: it consists of drawing on a little chart (whose rhumb-line network has vanished) a sinuous line that meets a compass rose at the appropriate point. On the chart of Le Havre to Muros in Spain, where bird's-eye views and banners indicate Rouen (*ROUAN*), *Nantes*, *Libourne* and Bordeaux (*bourdeos*), two compass roses, whose centres are marked with the first letters of the author's name (*G. BR.*—the remainder is given on the three compass roses of the next chart: *OU. S. CON*), are placed perpendicularly to one another—one has its north in the south, the other in the west!—obviously indicating that they are not there to orientate the document. For example, if we follow the line leaving Le Conquet (*cōquest*), Brouscon's home port, we arrive at the SW of the rose. This means that, when the tide is high at Le Conquet on the first and the fifteenth of the month, the moon will be shining in the SW. The procedure can be repeated for any port, especially as the lines are of different colours according to which of the points of the rose they intersect.

But for the convenience of the user, this information has to be provided on an hourly basis and, if possible, should show the times of the ebb and flow for any other day of the month, taking into account the fact that the interval between the first high tide and the moon's crossing of the meridian increases regularly by forty-five minutes a day, except on the eleventh and the eighteenth of the month, when it jumps to ninety minutes. This is the purpose of the tide table on folio 25 (No. 44, left).

The calendar-rose on it is so devised that a simple reading suffices in the case of an 'established' port like Le Conquet. But an artful addition extends its use *pour toutes mares, depuis suest jusques a oest nor oest* ('for all tides, from SE to WNW') that is, for any port whose 'establishment', read on the charts, is included between these two points on the compass rose. The rose has six concentric circles. From the periphery towards the centre we find successively:

— the day of the moon, in thirty divisions numbered in Arabic figures from 1 to 30;
— the four phases of the moon, on the first, eighth, fifteenth and twenty-second days, with spring tides (symbolized by waves) on the third and seventeenth days and neap tides (illustrated by uncovered rocks) on the ninth and twenty-fourth days. The longer interval of ninety minutes on the eleventh and eighteenth days is indicated in the appropriate divisions;
— the third circle gives the times of high tides, and the fourth the times of low tides; dashes and dots are joined to the Arabic figures giving the hours: a dash is equivalent to a quarter of an hour, a dot to half an hour;
— the fifth arranges the points of the compass starting from SW: from 1 to 8 on the right and from 1 to 6 on the left; the points with which the diagram is not concerned (from NW to ESE) are obliterated with stars;

— the sixth circle belongs to the compass rose, in whose centre we again see the initials 'G.B.'

As long as the day of the moon is known, a glance will suffice to discover the times of high and low tide in an 'established' port in the SW: on the twentieth day, for example, flow is at 7:30 (a.m. and p.m.) and ebb is at 1:30 (a.m. and p.m.). For an 'established' port on any of the fourteen other possible points—Saint-Brieuc (*s briec*) for example, 'established' in the west—the corrections to be made are indicated in the fifth circle, where west bears the number 4, indicating that it is four compass points after SW. It is therefore necessary to subtract 3/4 hour $\times$ 4 = 3 hours from the times given for SW. Conversely, for a port established in the SE, say Caen (*Can*), since SE is eight points of the compass before SW, it is necessary to add 3/4 hour $\times$ 8 = 6 hours to the times given for SW.

Brouscon's nautical guide responded to a persistent need of navigators on western seas, and it is not surprising that several copies, manuscript or engraved, exist in libraries in England and France. At an unknown date, John Marshall even made a copy of it in English, now in the British Library (Royal Mss 17 A 11). Quoting successively from E.G.R. Taylor and H.D. Howse, 'this [is a] very remarkable contribution to the navigation of northwest Europe', not only because of the quality of its information but also because its graphic and cartographic representations, far from limiting its use to Breton sailors, made it a comprehensible instrument for any western sailor—even if he were illiterate and whatever his native tongue.

45

ATLANTIC CHART
(after 1549)
1 vellum leaf, illuminated ms, 880 × 630 mm
Paris, B.N.: Cartes et Plans, Rés. Ge B 1148

A new feature can be observed in the construction of this anonymous Portuguese document. In addition to

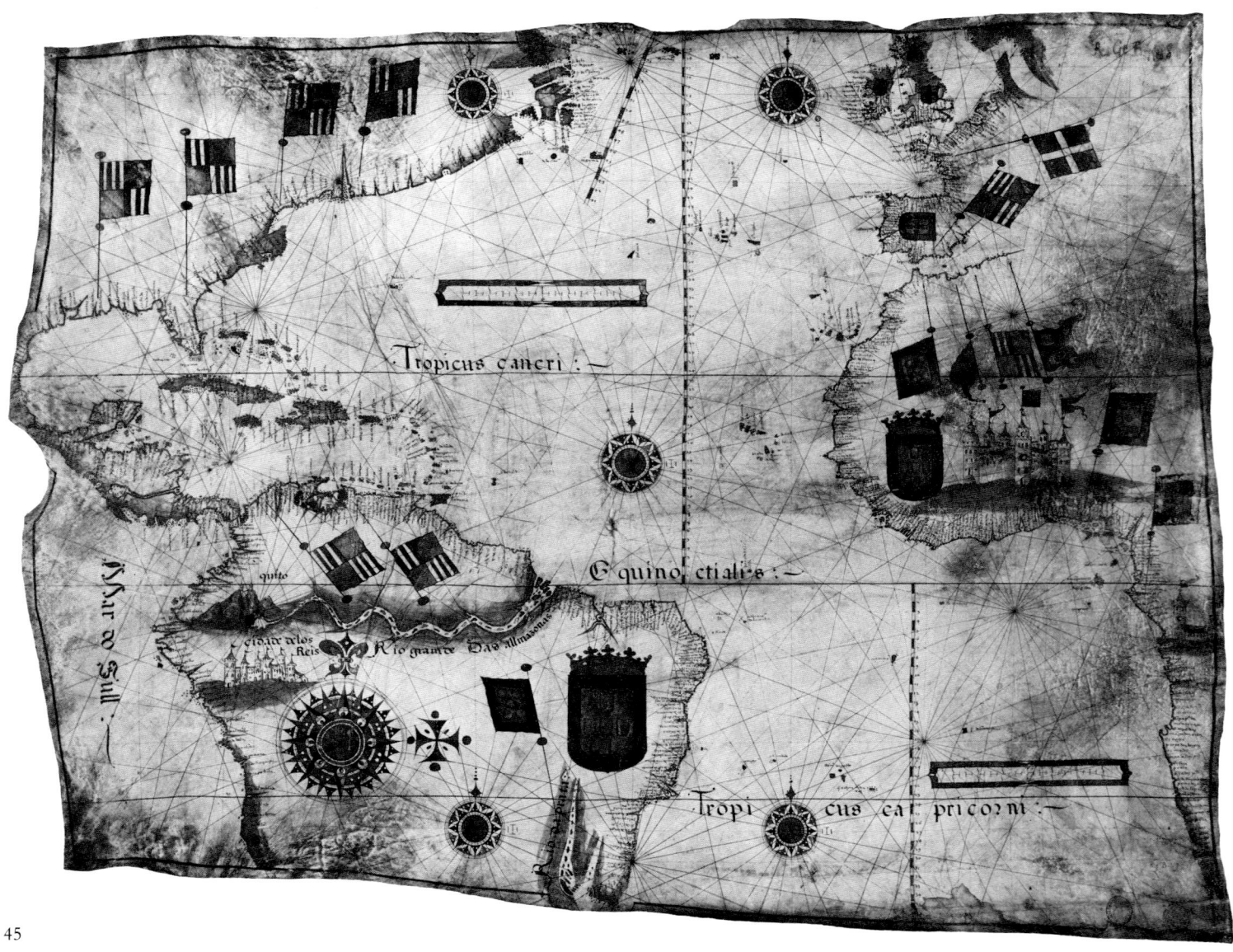

45

the normal latitude scales, drawn in the northern and southern hemispheres, a second latitude scale appears in the Newfoundland area, inclined SSW-NNE. This scale indicates the degree of magnetic variation in this region, which is particularly affected by terrestrial magnetism. Indeed 'magnetic variation continued to increase when travelling westwards; mariners sailing by dead-reckoning would unwittingly follow a course more and more inclined to the west the further they sailed from Europe and would arrive on the American coast at much lower real latitudes than they expected' (Gernez). Faced with this difficulty, some unknown pilot of the beginning of the sixteenth century must have made astronomical observations in that region from which the real latitudes were deduced. For similar reasons an auxiliary scale was placed in the Newfoundland area, inclined to a degree equivalent to that of the magnetic variation: its graduation differs by 3° or 4° from the general scale, which still shows estimated latitudes. The Portuguese scholar Pedro Reinel is credited with encouraging the use of this device at the beginning of the sixteenth century.

In South America, the *Rio gramde Das allmazonas* appears. Its still schematic outline symbolizes the foolhardy adventure of Orellana, a former shipmate of Gonzalo Pizarro, in his search for Eldorado. In just seven months in 1542, in a modest brigantine, he managed to sail more than 4,000 kilometres down the Amazon without a guide, compass, gun-powder or any food other than what could be obtained from the often hostile inhabitants of the riverbanks. Orellana even claimed to have discovered a town exclusively populated by female warriors, real 'Amazons' with fair skins and long hair, who greeted him with a hail of arrows. The greatest river in America owes its name to this astonishing adventure.

The harmony and accuracy of the decoration are admirable: six compass roses typical of the Portuguese school, with fleurs-de-lis in the north and the cross of the Order of Christ in the east, emphasize a network of rhumb-lines with sixteen secondary centres. Portuguese and Castilian coats of arms, escutcheons and banners indicate political allegiances: urban centres are shown in illuminated bird's-eye views. In South America a beautiful painting, more imaginary than realistic, shows the Spanish town of Lima, heart of Spanish power in Peru, which was founded in 1535 by Francisco Pizarro, who named it *Cidade de los Reis*. Another painting draws attention to the important Indian city of *Quito*, one of the great cities of the Inca Empire, situated at an altitude of more than 2,800 metres on the slopes of the Pichincha volcano and occupied in 1534 by one of Pizarro's lieutenants. In Africa, the Portuguese trading-post of São Jorge da Mina (Elmina), with its imposing fortifications, towers above the Gulf of Guinea, and a simple church at the mouth of the Congo indicates the trading-post founded by Diogo Cão sixty years before.

Some writers have used a comparison of the script to base their attribution of this anonymous nautical document to Jorge Reinel; others have attributed it to Sebastião Lopes or Bartholomeu Velho because of similarities in the delineation. It can be dated to the middle of the sixteenth century and must in any case be later than 1549, as it shows the *Cidade de Salvador* (now Bahia), founded by the Portuguese in that year in Todos os Santos Bay in Brazil.

46

ATLANTIC OCEAN CHART
by Diego Gutierrez (1550)
2 vellum leaves, illuminated ms assembled into a chart, 1318 × 885 mm
Paris, B.N.: Cartes et Plans, S.H. Archives no. 2

On their crossings of the Atlantic, it was some time before the Spaniards and Portuguese distinguished true bearings from magnetic bearings, despite the Rule of the North Star. In the Newfoundland area the instability of the compass needle was such that it proved necessary, from the beginning of the sixteenth century, to take astronomical bearings, as is shown on this chart by the presence of a special scale (inclined SSW-NNE) relating exclusively to the Grand Banks. However, the whole sea lane was influenced by magnetic variation, and the cosmographers of the Casa de Contratación thought that pilots ought to be notified of this by a correction of the nautical charts. They indicated two graduations of latitudes differing from each other by two or three degrees, and this double graduation inevitably involved the representation of two equators and four tropics.

This chart by Diego Gutierrez is a typical example of this apparently ingenious but totally unworkable theory. A first scale of latitudes (oriented N-S, and graduated 63°N by 13°S) passes between Faial and Flores in the Azores, while a second (also oriented N-S and graduated 60°N by 16°S) passes between Trinidad (*La Tranidad*) and the mouths of the Amazon (*Rº grande de las amazonas*). Each degree on this second scale is 2°30' further north than the corresponding degree on the first scale. A single network of rhumb-lines, with fourteen compass roses and five distance scales completes this curious nautical document.

In 1520 Ferdinand Columbus, son of the discoverer of America, (in *Coloquio sobre las dos graduaciones diferentes que las cartas de Indias tienens*) and, in 1542, the Norman pilot Jean Rotz denounced the 'absurdity' of such charts, insisting on the confusion caused to mariners by this double graduation: they did not know on which one to rely. In 1544, Sebastian Cabot, 'pilot major' of the Casa de Contratación in Seville, forbade Diego Gutierrez to construct such charts which, he said, were prejudicial to navigation. The cartographer obviously took no notice of this. His chart of 1550 bears his signature and official title in the top left-hand corner: *Diego Gutierrez cosmographo de Su mag.^{d} me fizo en sevilla Año de 1550.*

47

PLANISPHERE
by Pierre Desceliers (1550)
4 vellum leaves, illuminated ms assembled into a chart, 1350 × 2150 mm
London, British Library, Add. Ms 24065

This magnificent planisphere, the masterpiece of the 'father of French hydrography', Pierre Desceliers of Dieppe, has both an historical and a geographical interest. The authenticating signature and date appear in red, in capital letters in part, in a cartouche: *Faicte a Arques par Pierres Desceliers pbre [presbytre] lan: 1550.*

It is a plane chart constructed on a network of rhumb-lines. Along the left-hand border, from the equator to the poles, appear the twelve climates inherited from Ptolemy, and latitudes are given in keeping with the length of the days of the year. Three escutcheons dedicate it to Henry II, king of France; Grand Constable de Montmorency and Admiral Claude d'Annebaut. Although nautical, it is not a navigational chart; rather it is a princely chart intended to enlighten the court on the state of the known world in 1550. The delicacy of the execution and the beauty of the colouring may give the impression that this is less a scientific document than a piece of visionary art; however, although the twenty-four notes often contain extrapolated information, generally this chart is of a high scientific quality.

The delineation and nomenclature are of Portuguese inspiration and, in particular, can be compared with the chart by Reinel (1516) and Cabot's planisphere (1544). However nearly all the names are gallicized.

Eastern America has the same features as on the portolan charts of the Dieppe school. Newfoundland is depicted as an archipelago, and the Saint Lawrence is drawn up to a point that is roughly at the junction of that great river and the Ottawa (*jusques icy a este Mons. De Roberval*, 'Monsieur De Roberval has been as far as here'). In the west beyond, a battle between pygmies and cranes is shown; this legend went back to Homer and was situated in Africa. The Middle Ages transplanted it to Tartary in Asia. Jacques Cartier considered Canada to be the 'extremity of Asia', and Desceliers who, like all the Dieppe school, benefited from Cartier's contribution to cartography, in his turn located this myth, which had traditionally been sited in Tartary, near Ottawa. Before achieving recognition as an unexplored territory, the American west was regarded as a dependency of Asia. This provides an example of how conceptual connections can be more complex than they seem at first sight.

The outline of Africa is uneven: Prester John is depicted near the marshy sources (*paluds*) of the Nile, level with the south of Ethiopia.

In Asia, references are made to Marco Polo (*marc paul vénicien*), and the Great Khan is shown. Japan (*Zipangü*) is represented as a much simplified parallelogram situated near the continent.

In the south the Spice Islands, the Moluccas, are charted with varying degrees of accuracy. But, most importantly, there appears to the south of the Sunda archipelago a land shown by nearly all the Dieppe cartographers: *Jave*, which Le Testu called Java Major. This mysterious, cultivated and inhabited land covers a vast continent occupying the whole of the south of the planisphere. It is the 'austral land' (*Terre Australle*), or 'totally undiscovered land' (*terre non du tout descouverte*), which is found on nearly all sixteenth-century charts from Dieppe, before disappearing in the seventeenth century.

Pierre Desceliers signed four other planispheres dedicated to important noblemen, but this one is the most carefully drawn and richly illustrated. No doubt the reference to the king explains the perfection of its execution.

Its author is not totally unknown to us, unlike many other Dieppe cartographers. He was not only a cartographer but also a geographer, whose writings, which have now disappeared, shaped the second generation of the Dieppe school. A brass seal with a double impression, preserved in the Dieppe museum and bearing his initials, is believed to be the seal used to countersign royal diplomas awarded to pilots. He appears to have been the first hydrographer commissioned to teach nautical science in a French port.

Desceliers was a priest, living in Arques, a village 7 kilometres from Dieppe. Unlike other Dieppe hydrographers such as Le Testu or Jean Rotz, he does not appear to have ever gone to sea. Desceliers was of noble birth; his father and brothers were military men attached to the defence of the castle of Arques, where it seems that Desceliers lived and died. Nothing more is known of him.

48-51

'UNIVERSAL COSMOGRAPHY'
by Guillaume Le Testu (1556)
58 paper plates, illuminated ms, 370 × 530 mm
48 Folio 53: *Florida*
49 Folio 57: *New France*
50 Folio 58: *Newfoundland*
51 Folio 33: *Java Major*
Château of Vincennes: Bibliothèque du Service historique de l'Armée de terre, D.L.Z. 14

These four charts are included in one of the most beautiful Norman atlases of the sixteenth century, which contains 50 sea charts, painted and illuminated on paper. This *Cosmographie Universelle, selon les navigateurs, tant anciens que modernes, par Guillaume Le Testu, pillotte en la Mer du ponant de la ville Francoyse de Grace* ('Universal Cosmography, according to navigators both ancient and modern, by Guillaume Le Testu, pilot in the western sea, from the French town of [Havre de] Grace'), is dated 5 August 1556 and dedicated to Coligny, admiral of France. It is a prized possession of the Ministère de la Guerre ('Defense Department') in Paris. Preceded by six representations of the universe in projection, the atlas illustrates the scientific interests of this pilot who sailed for the king but died a pirate.

Le Testu was a curious figure, very typical of his period. A Protestant, he was probably born around 1512 at Le Havre, became a pilot at Dieppe and was then appointed pilot royal at Le Havre in 1556. He took part in several expeditions of exploration or colonization, like Villegagnon's voyage to Brazil, made the same year as this atlas. What links were there between this atlas, the expedition to Brazil commissioned by Coligny and the appointment of Le Testu as the king's pilot for Le Havre? Probably more than one. His friend the monk Thevet describes him as being 'valiant, cunning and skilful'. He did not scorn trafficking or even piracy, and his knowledge of the sea won him the friendship of the boldest mariners. In 1572, Philippe Strozzi gave Le Testu the command of a vessel to make for Nombre de Dios 'with the sole intention of reconnoitring the approaches and elevation of the said coast': the coast in question being that of southern Mexico, where the Spaniards took on board the gold from Peru. On his arrival, the inhabitants fleeing the Spaniards informed him of the arrival of a convoy 'of more than three million in gold', and offered him their help in seizing it. Mindful of his duty, Le Testu hesitated before agreeing to take part in this adventure in league with his friend Francis Drake. The Spanish convoy appeared, and after hamstringing the mules, the men shared the fabulous booty of 'gold plates like the seals of the Grand Chancellery of France'. But behind the convoy followed the soldiers of the Spanish king; a struggle ensued, and Le Testu was killed by an arquebus shot, while his accomplice Drake managed to escape with the loot. 'My heart bleeds', wrote Thevet, 'when my mind's eye recalls the piteous disaster which befell this good captain, my good friend and one of the most expert pilots of our age'. These four charts illustrate the scholarship, skilled draughtsmanship and imagination of this man of the Renaissance.

48 *Florida*
From north to south, this chart (No. 48) deals with part of the stock-fish or dried cod region (*bacailaux*), 'Neuve Espaigne' (Florida) and the region of 'Nombre de Dios' (southern Mexico). Thatched huts, naked inhabitants and deer crossing the dense forest recall a part of the New World in America, sighted in 1512 by the Spaniard Ponce de León. The Spaniards laid claim to Florida—so called because it was sighted on Palm Sunday, often called Florid Easter. But they were unable to establish themselves there, being constantly repulsed by the natives.

The French nomenclature of the east coast of Florida recalls Verrazano's voyage of 1524, and the deep river *Anoroegua* can be compared to the Aranbega appearing on Verrazano's chart. By corruption, this name became that of a vast imaginary country, Norumbega, which was to achieve great fame and be the goal of several expeditions until Champlain destroyed the myth by a meticulous exploration in 1613.

49 *New France*
The next two charts (Nos. 49-50) are a good illustration of the confusion created in even the cleverest minds between the traditional image of North America, inherited from the Portuguese and Verrazano, and Jacques Cartier's discovery of the Saint Lawrence and Canada.

Chart No. 49 portrays the coast of North America, from Florida (where the Spanish flag flies) to Canada, indicated by the French colours. The abundant Portuguese nomenclature bears witness to the amount of traffic on this coast *dicte bacaillaux*, where cod was plentiful and which had been discovered and surveyed by the Corte Reals in 1500; but it also illustrates the exploration of the Saint Lawrence by Cartier and Roberval.

There is a contradiction between the two charts; the representation of Newfoundland as an archipelago is followed on the next leaf (No. 50) by an outline of a massive island, joined to the continent. Jacques Cartier had discovered that Newfoundland was an island at the end of his second voyage (1535-1536), but the Portuguese portolan charts used as prototypes by the Dieppe school were divided on this point, and Le Testu is undecided.

On the other hand, along the Saint Lawrence, the stages of Cartier's second voyage are clearly indicated: *sept Iles, Rivière de Saguené, l'Ille d'Orléans, Ochelassa, Grande Goulemme*. This landscape-chart is probably the most faithful illustration of the image that Cartier's contemporaries had formed of this promising discovery.

50 *Newfoundland*
Covering latitudes 41° to 68°, this chart, with a distance scale duplicating the previous one, depicts Newfoundland joined to Canada, like the Portuguese charts.

Thus the author shows Newfoundland in its new and then its old configuration—as an island or an archipelago—and portrays the Saint Lawrence on one chart as a river and on the other as a bay. The Norman cartographer remained deeply attached to the Portuguese school, despite his respect for the discoveries of Cartier of Saint-Malo.

The many natives portrayed are a reflection of ancient myths. Men with dogs' heads struggle with fabulous beasts; in Labrador, naked savages fight among themselves with spears. Mediaeval travellers' tales abound with descriptions of these monstrous creatures inspired by the fables of the ancient world (Pliny, Solinus). Le Testu transposes these fictitious beings to the New World where Cartier had given them a new lease on life.

At sea, on the contrary, the ships of the ocean fleet are the exact image of those which Le Testu had commanded as king's pilot at Le Havre, and one of them appears to be the most accurate representation available of the 'Grande Hermine', Jacques Cartier's ship.

51 *Java Major*
The chart of *Grande Jave* and *Petite Jave* (No. 51) is one of the most vivid and beautiful examples of the portrayal of a mysterious and unknown, or largely misunderstood, land that would remain so until the end of the eighteenth century and the definitive discovery of Australia by Captain Cook.

This land-mass, which could be an island or a peninsula, is situated southwest of *Timor* and the archipelago of the *Moluques*. To the northwest appears the southern part of *Taprobane*, or Sumatra. Situated between the Moluccas and the Sunda Islands, this land is washed by the Pacific Ocean and portrayed as a land-mass inhabited by savages living from hunting and gathering. Java Major also has centres of population and cultivated land. Nutmeg and spices are loaded on to ships bound for the Moluccas, the centre of the spice trade. The boat is identical to the one sailing in the Molucca Sea (folio 31). The inhabitants either wear feathers or are dressed like the inhabitants of India.

This land is joined in the south to the vast mass of 'austral lands': the drum-shaped Antichthone of Aristotle, extending around the globe to the north of the South Pole (folio 6).

The nomenclature is Portuguese, with some French names.

Situated between the Moluccas and the South Pole, at 5 degrees from the equator, what is this inhabited land called Java? Seen next to a modern map, only Australia compares with this representation in overall shape and location, but the Moluccas are erroneously located to the east, and although it is correctly situated to the west, Sumatra is too close. It would seem that realism and imagination have both had a hand in this representation. In another note Le Testu defines this island as 'unknown land'; and in yet another he says that he shows it but *n'y voulant adjouter Foy* ('without wishing to give it credence').

Thus the confusion here is even greater than in the case of Newfoundland. The fact that Australia was an island continent was not established until 1642-1644. Many of the expeditions sent to this area are unknown to us, but we do know that the Parmentier brothers reached Sumatra in 1529 and met their deaths there. The Dieppe school had some inkling of the Moluccas and neighbouring territories from Portuguese deserters and also from privateers or sailors from their own country.

This chart also reproduces errors made by the Portuguese. One of these was deliberate: in order to locate this largely unknown land within their zone—demarcated in 1494 by the Treaty of Tordesillas—they moved it several degrees west; Le Testu does likewise. The northwest coast, the best known, is more accurate. We may therefore assume that he transposed here what he knew of the Moluccas, endowing the unknown territory with the luxuriant vegetation, population, economy and shipping of the known area. Was this invention purely imaginary to please the eye, or was he trying to suggest to Coligny what might be done with this land if it were occupied?

This work in which the artist's imagination was given free rein should be compared with the atlas by J. Rotz (No. 40).

Whereas Le Testu represents Java Major to the 35°S latitude (i.e., almost all of Australia is visible), Rotz depicts nothing beyond 19°S (less than a quarter of the continent); however, the general shape of the coasts in both works is comparable.

Le Testu's and Rotz's works are not illustrated in the same manner: Rotz's depiction of nature is simplist; Le Testu's detailed and refined. Rotz appears to be less well informed or less imaginative, but probably more realistic.

With an artist's intuition, Le Testu foreshadowed an Australia with an acceptable configuration, inhabited by a civilization borrowed from the Humanist vision of Fertile Arabia.

52-54

ATLAS
by Diogo Homem (1559)
8 vellum leaves, illuminated ms, 440 × 586 mm
52 Leaf 1: *Western Europe*
53 Leaf 2: *Eastern Atlantic and Western Mediterranean*
54 Leaf 5: *Black Sea*
Paris, B.N.: Cartes et Plans, Rés. Ge DD 2003

Like Andreas (No. 55), Diogo Homem was the son of Lopo Homem, official cartographer to the king of Portugal; and like his brother, he left Lisbon and went into exile. After 1545 he lived in London for some time, then moved to Venice where he lived almost permanently until 1576. He seems to have been the most prolific Portuguese cartographer of the sixteenth century. More works by Diogo Homem are known today than by any other cartographer of the period: no less than twelve universal or Mediterranean atlases and eleven great charts have survived.

The atlas of 1559, from which the three charts reproduced here are taken, covers western Europe, the Mediterranean and the Black Sea. Eight leaves of superbly illuminated vellum are preserved in a contemporary binding bearing on the recto of the upper board the name of a Ravenna family, *Domenico di Rossi*, for whom the atlas was presumably intended. Its luxurious format, with a trompe-l'oeil frame on every leaf, scales inserted in ornate cartouches picked out in gold and cardinal points inscribed on coloured scrolls, should not detract from its specifically maritime interest. On each chart several compass roses (one or two of which have thirty-two branches) with their profusion of vividly coloured rhumb-lines (yellow, red or green) allow the navigator to plan and steer his course with greater ease. The hinterland is generally devoid of geographical data; only an occasional bird's-eye view is given of some mountains such as the Pyrenees or the Atlas chain. In contrast, coats of arms, armorial shields and banners—often large in size and richly painted—indicate to the sailor which coast he is skirting or in which country he is landing. At the mouth of the Tagus, the watercolour view of Lisbon (No. 53) probably recalls the nationality of the cartographer, a fairly frequent practice at the time. On the shores of the Black Sea (No. 54), beside the Turkish flags, the Genoese oriflamme still flies on the Crimean peninsula. Was Diogo Homem really unaware of the fact that all the Genoese trading-posts there had fallen into Ottoman hands eighty years before (1475)?

Nevertheless, it is to him that we owe the best executed and most decorative sixteenth-century nautical charts of the Mediterranean basin.

55

UNIVERSA AC NAVIGABILIS TOTIUS
TERRARUM ORBIS DESCRIPTIO...
by Andreas Homem (1559)
10 vellum leaves, illuminated ms assembled into a chart, 1500 × 2940 mm
Paris, B.N.: Cartes et Plans, Rés. Ge CC 2719

This is the largest Portuguese nautical planisphere of the Renaissance; it is also the only work known by this son of Lopo Homem, Andreas Homem, who went to Paris from Antwerp in 1560, apparently with the intention of obtaining a post as cosmographer to the king from Admiral de Coligny. His chart has been preserved in the French archives ever since.

Illustrating once again the division of the world into two equal parts, the cartographer draws the demarcation line (*Linea Divisionis*) of the Treaty of Tordesillas. At the top of the document is another reminder of that treaty, superb armorial shields drawn side by side: Spanish to the west, Portuguese to the east. The network of rhumb-lines is centred on the intersection of the equator and the demarcation line: fifteen full or half compass roses highlight its outline. The tropics of Cancer and Capricorn and polar circles are indicated, and there is a latitude scale in both hemispheres, graduated from 0° to 90°. In the four corners of the document, the league scales (*Tabvla levcarvm*) are inscribed in decorative baroque cartouches. Above and below each of them are discs containing solar declination tables (latitudes) borrowed from the Portuguese pilot Francesco Faleiro, author of an important treatise on navigation published in 1535 for the use of Spanish sailors (*Tratado del Esphera y del arte del marear*).

Andreas Homem has broken away entirely from 'Ptolemaic authority'. His elaborate planisphere is solely based on nautical experience and bears witness to the knowledge of the coasts of the world held by mid-sixteenth-century navigators. The outlines stretch from the California peninsula in the west to the Ryukyu Islands (*Insulae que dicuntur lequios*) off the coast of China to the east. Only Japan (*Insula Siampagu*) still retains its fantastic mediaeval shape, despite having been visited annually by the Portuguese for more than fifteen years.

Working in Antwerp, where the most recent data could reach him, the cartographer is conspicuously well informed on northern Europe, where he not only outlines the Gulfs of Bothnia and Finland but also draws the Scandinavian and Arctic coasts up to the point reached by Chancellor in 1553; an inscription in the Arctic Ocean gives the name of its 'inventor'. We must admire the honesty of the cartographer, who confesses his ignorance by preferring to leave a gap in the outline of the Chilean coast south of Santiago rather than invent it. He could not yet have known that, in the very year in which he drew his planisphere, the Spaniards had finally mastered the redoubtable Araucanian Indians and had succeeded in establishing themselves throughout the territory of southern Chile. In fact, by 1559, all the coasts of the South American continent—apart from those of Brazil that remained the domain of the Portuguese—had been sighted and occupied by the subjects of the king of Spain.

Above all, this nautical chart shows that since 1434, when Gil Eanes sailed past Cape Bojador, 'the Portuguese sailors had surveyed all the coasts of Africa, including Madagascar, a large extent of the coasts of Asia and the islands of Malaya, the coasts of Brazil, and all in a relatively accurate way.... This hydrographic survey... of more than 60,000 kilometres of coastline... constituted a tremendous task which, because of the difficulties of all kinds encountered: fragile ships, crews too often sick and always ill-nourished... the clumsiness of the observational instruments employed... is genuinely unique... and deserves our unstinted admiration' (Gernez).

56

ATLANTIC AND MEDITERRANEAN
by Giacomo de Maggiolo (1563)
2 vellum leaves, illuminated ms, assembled into a chart, 1023 × 850 mm
Paris, B.N.: Société de Géographie, Rés. S.G. Y 1704

Prince Roland Bonaparte bequeathed to the Société de Géographie in Paris one of the finest examples of Genoese cartography of the sixteenth century. It is a fairly large document consisting of two juxtaposed vellum leaves. It tends to be admired first as a picture, because of its copious yet harmonious decoration, whose principal features are unity in the choice of colours (predominantly violet and blue) and refinement if not preciosity of drawing—whether we consider the strings of hillocks indicating the relief, the multitude of vignettes for towns occupying the hinterland or the fleet of ships and galleons with billowing sails that cruise among the Atlantic archipelagos from the Canary Islands to Norway, flying the flags of Genoa, Portugal and Spain.

The regal figures the artist has arranged all over the chart occupy the largest amount of space; he contrasts a great number of African and Asian sovereigns, solemnly posing in front of sumptuously coloured tents (especially the Grand Turk [*Lo Gran Turco*]) with the smaller figures of the kings of Europe, dressed in classical style and gracefully seated in very affected postures: *RE DE SPANIA, RE DE FRANIA, LO INPERATOR, RE DE POLONIA, VELACHIA, RE DE ROSSIA, RE DE MOSCHOVIA*. Among the standards floating over the towns, we note the multiple presence of the Islamic crescent over the whole African and eastern area between the River Senegal (*rio de Senaga*), *Fiome* (Fiume, now Rijeka) on the Adriatic and the regions of central Europe to the north of Walachia.

On the margins of the chart, in the north and south, are two gilded friezes with geometrical motifs, two distance scales adorned with scrolls and three very discreet compass roses. In the west there is a latitude scale graduated from 12° to 71°N and a Virgin and Child on a throne, indicating at one and the same time, in a tradition going back to Becharius, both the head of the chart and the central axis of the rhumb-line network. The signature is at the Virgin's feet: *Iacobus de maiolo composuit hanc cartam in ianua anno domini 1563 die XX may in lospitaleto*.

Giacomo de Maggiolo was one of the most skilful artists in a family in which the profession of cartographer was handed down for several generations from the beginning of the sixteenth century to around 1650. His father, Vesconte de Maggiolo, was also an expert in this field and bore the official title of *magister cartarum pro navigando*, 'master of navigational charts'. Vesconte had been granted a large pension by the Genoese Senate to exercize his talents in that city, which he did from 1519 onwards. A partner in his father's work from an early age, Giacomo obtained the same privilege in 1544, subject to the same condition. All his production, which spans the period 1551 to 1573, was therefore signed in Genoa, where he must have died in 1606 or 1607, passing on the torch to his nephews.

The interest of this chart 'composed' in 1563 lies principally in the configuration given to northern Europe. For more than two centuries, the dominant prototype was one created at the beginning of the fourteenth century, either in Genoa or Majorca, and reproduced unaltered by the whole Catalan school. That this image remained unchanged for so long is a reflection of the primacy enjoyed by Mediterranean cartographers: their commercial interests did not extend beyond Flanders, and the Hanseatics jealously guarded their domain from foreign exploration.

However, geographic curiosity at the time of the great discoveries brought about a fundamental change in approach: Maggiolo's knowledge of northern Europe is idiosyncratic, rather good at some times and quite bad at others, and drawing on several sources that we must try to identify. An indication of the leads to follow is provided by the astonishing presence in the North Atlantic of two islands, each of which may represent Iceland. One of them, bearing the name *IXLANDA*, is schematic, better situated than the other in latitude and is borrowed from scholarly geography. The other, the mysterious island of *FIXDANDA*, had already appeared on Catalan nautical charts of the second half of the fifteenth century: its general outline and the two deep bays on its west coast suggest that it originated in sketches made by sailors.

Thus Maggiolo is working from two types of documentation. For Denmark and Scandinavia, he draws on some edition of Ptolemy's *Geography* in the 1468 version, which contains several modern charts (*tabulae modernae*) by the German monk and cartographer Nicolaus Germanus and in which Norway is found with the same regional divisions (*SUECIA, GOTIA, DACIA*), suspended from the narrow *VERMELANT* peninsula and joined by it to a Greenland (*ENGRONELANT*) curiously situated just to the north, beyond a vast anonymous bay. The Ptolemaic place-names extend as far as Finland (*PILLA PELLANT, GOTIA ORIENTALIS*), whose outline, however, does not correspond to reality. Jutland has taken on a concave shape that is very backward in comparison with the Catalan prototype of the fourteenth century.

This rejuvenated version of Ptolemy is neither the earliest nor the most successful. The Dane Claudius Clavus had preceded Germanus by some forty years and had drawn Greenland as a long peninsula encircling Iceland far to the west and with less flagrant inaccuracy. The erroneous interpretation on Maggiolo's chart was nevertheless perpetuated for decades and printed many times from 1501 onwards. Vesconte de Maggiolo, together with Francesco Rosselli, may have been one of the first to introduce it to nautical cartography, thereby illustrating the esteem in which the great Alexandrian geographer was then held in Europe.

However when it came to delineating the Baltic, the early sixteenth-century portolan charts, especially the Portuguese ones, also made use of less theoretical sources: nautical charts or sailing instructions. Giacomo de Maggiolo also does this; but in 1563 the available surveys no longer only dealt with the southern shore of this sea. The gulfs of Bothnia and Finland, first individualized by Jacob Ziegler in an engraved chart of 1532, are outlined here with great precision and the correct orientation. The anonymous islands strewn over them are meticulously drawn and placed, and the nomenclature, which is thin on the Swedish coast south of Lake Malar (*melor*), is very abundant from Lübeck (*Lo bique*) as far as Vyborg (*Vurgura*). In the Gulf of Bothnia, which is not closed off in the north, no less than twenty-six toponyms appear, of which five are inscribed in red ink (*Lemos, mor tisara, Retnaval, Gestria, estrogotia*). With a few rare exceptions, these are the same as the names in the *Carta marina* drawn up in 1539 by the Swede Olaus Magnus, who is known to have used nautical charts among many other documentary sources.

Navigators in these regions must, therefore, have surveyed the coasts with the aid of a compass, as had been the practice in the Mediterranean since the thirteenth century. The introduction of this instrument to the Baltic Sea seems to have been belated, since in 1460, in the mappa mundi which he constructed that year for the king of Portugal, the Venetian Fra Mauro still expressly declares that the mariners on 'that sea' did not use it and navigated by soundings: *per questo mare non se navega cum carta ni bossola ma cum scandaso*. It is certain, however, that nautical instructions for this region had long been compiled and collected and that charts of it had existed from the fifteenth century onwards, even if they are now lost. The earliest nautical charts to survive, made by the Dutch, date from the first half of the sixteenth century. As for the sea books (*Seebuch*), they were not widely popular until they appeared in print in 1532, and then in 1540-1541.

This was the time when navigation in the Baltic reached the peak of its expansion, stimulated by the discovery of the Northeast Passage in 1553 and the irresistible advance of the Dutch in the face of the stubborn opposition of Lübeck and the Hanseatics. There was a strong demand in the west for Scandinavian products, and the modern states that were forming on these shores at the expense of the mediaeval feudal domains (the Teutonic Order) clashed in a violent struggle to control this trade. Thus, in the 1560's, Denmark, Sweden, Russia and Poland came into conflict with each other. At the same time, the Hanseatic navigators, who had been sailing to the coasts of the Atlantic from the fifteenth century onwards, also ventured into the Mediterranean, putting into Marseilles, Leghorn and Genoa.

In short, the integration of northern Europe into Italian and Portuguese cartography coincided with its access to new trading relationships set up during the sixteenth century. It remained for cartographers to abandon the Ptolemaic prototypes, which had so often had a regressive influence, and to put their trust in information provided by seafarers. But even in Venice and Lisbon, where nautical cartographers were well acquainted with Scandinavia from around 1550 (as can be observed in the last atlases of Battista Agnese, or the works of the Homems), compromise charts like those by Maggiolo can still be found quite late.

The delineation of the north would not be seriously undertaken until the end of the century, and then it was the work of the Dutch.

57

MEDITERRANEAN BASIN
by Georgio Sideri, called Calapoda (1565)
1 vellum leaf, illuminated ms, 290 × 430 mm
Paris, B.N.: Cartes et Plans, Rés. Ge D 4497

Little is known of Georgio Sideri, called Calapoda, apart from his nine works that were constructed between 1537 and 1590. The earliest was drawn in Candia, his native town, and signed simply 'Callapodha'; the name of Sideri does not appear in conjunction with it until 1560. For ten years prior to that date his signature ceases to mention the place where his charts were composed, but always stresses his Cretan origin. In the northeast corner of the 1565 chart, the colophon above the *monti Tartarum* (Urals) is no more informative: *Georgio Sideri dicto Calapoda Cretensis fecit nel anno domini: 1565: die... lugiai.*

It is possible that Calapoda had emigrated to Venice, then the parent state of Crete. In any case his clientele belonged to the Venetian nobility, and on three of his works appear the arms of the Calbo, Emo and Michiel families.

In support of the opposing thesis, which claims that he continued to work in Candia, the only archival documents found concerning him relate that in 1568 'Master Menegis Theotocopoulos', that is, El Greco (also born in Candia, in 1541), sent drawings from Venice to Sideri in Crete by an unreliable third party who did not pass them on to him.

Sideri appears to have needed these drawings urgently, since he took legal action to reclaim them. Furthermore, Sideri may have had connections with the Cretan branch of the Monastery of Saint Catherine of Mount Sinai, as he includes a large vignette of it with a long inscription in a composition that otherwise has no particular religious theme. This *metoichon* had a school through which passed several Greek scholars of the period. On the other hand, this vignette, like the other illustrations on the chart, may simply be based on a Catalan prototype.

The influence of prototypes on this hydrographic school is immediately noticeable in the decoration, which returns to the classic themes of Majorcan cartography, but in a detailed personal interpretation, evident in the depiction of mountain chains, for example, where serried peaks spring from a green mass, their summits outlined in thick black curves, seemingly illuminated from the west.

It also appears in the choice of certain geographical outlines which are flagrantly archaic for the period and in comparison with other works by Sideri: Madeira and the Azores appear under their ancient title of *Insule Fortunate Sancti Brandani*, with a southerly orientation and too near the coast—errors dating back to the Catalan Atlas (No. 8). The British Isles, with Ireland shown far too large, are based on prototypes popularized by Beninstasa. The Baltic Sea is depicted as extending too far from west to east, as it had appeared in Majorcan cartography since the fourteenth century; whereas in 1550, in a planisphere preserved in the Biblioteca del Civico Museo Correr in Venice, Sideri had accurately delineated the gulfs of Bothnia and Finland and part of the Norwegian coast. This regression could have been the result of an express wish on the part of the client, who may have stipulated certain outlines. Unfortunately, the dedication in fine capitals on a gold background, inscribed in the frame on the left, has become partly illegible (*NOBILIS...OPERA*), and the name is undecipherable.

In other respects, the author is anxious to be up to date: in Morocco (*marocho*), above a compass rose and next to the pole of a standard planted on the coast, an inscription in red ink indicates the site of an event of the previous year that had caused a great stir in the west: *Lisola pignō de Veles che preso... filipo: nel 1564...* ('the island of Peñón de Velez, taken... by Philip: in 1564...'). Peñón de Velez was a nest of redoubtable pirates a short distance from the Spanish coast, which formed an ideal base for preying on its inhabitants and disrupting Seville-based shipping. For four years Philip II, and with him the whole of Christendom, had been waiting for an attack by the Turkish fleet. The latter's troops had broken through at the siege of Djerba in 1560, thereby ensuring their domination over the central Mediterranean. In order to halt their progress, the king of Spain, supported by the Pope among others, had raised a powerful fleet under the command of Don García de Toledo, Captain-General of the Sea. When the expected adversary did not materialize, the Spanish fleet profited from the respite by undertaking a training mission against the Barbary pirates. Besieged by an imposing fleet of more than ninety galleys, without counting the other ships, Peñón de Velez surrendered after a few days, on 6 September.

In Venice it was whispered that this was a useless and costly demonstration of strength, but it bore witness to the development of the situation in Spain's favour, after the difficulties of the previous years. Although he worked in a Venetian environment, the cartographer thought it worth mentioning.

58

PLANISPHERE
by Nicolas Desliens (1566)
1 vellum leaf, coloured ms, 270 × 450 mm
Paris, B.N.: Cartes et Plans, Rés. Ge D 7895

This planisphere is by Nicolas Desliens, a Dieppe hydrographer about whose life nothing is known. This beautiful and finely drawn work belongs to the family of plane charts based on the compass rose and provided with a latitude scale. The orientation with north at the foot of the chart, while singular in our eyes, would not have seemed so to Renaissance mariners.

It contains a synthesis of the scientific knowledge of the very well-informed Dieppe school of hydrography in the second half of the sixteenth century. Henceforth, eastern America is known from Labrador to Tierra del Fuego. Newfoundland is no longer subdivided: it is represented as an island and not an archipelago, but the orientation of the triangular island is inaccurate, unlike the earlier planisphere (1543) by Brouscon (No. 42). The Saint Lawrence River as far as Quebec city is one vast gulf; Florida and the Spanish West Indies are demarcated. Peru, Brazil and the River Plate are well outlined; and the arc formed by North America defines the limits of known territory.

Africa, Europe and Asia also display uncertainties and some remarkable intuitions. South of the Moluccas appears Java Major, which is shown on nearly all Dieppe portolan charts. But here, in contrast with Le Testu (No. 51) and Desceliers (No. 47) this vast continent is not joined on to the Antarctic. Ten years have passed since Le Testu's atlas, and this planisphere shows a *Mer Australle incongneue* ('unknown Southern Sea') in its correct place. Moreover, at the same date, Le

Testu showed neither Java Major nor any austral land on his planisphere. Balancing this unknown austral sea, there appears in the north a *Mer Septentrionalle incongneue*, both in Asia and America: one of the versions of the Northwest and Northeast Passages to Asia.

In addition, this planisphere gives an indication of the political allegiances of these lands. The fleur-de-lis flag of France floats over *R. May* in North America, at the latitude of Bermuda, recalling the unfortunate expedition of Ribaut to Florida, and over the *Terre du Laborador* and Canada, discovered by the French and annexed in 1535.

In South America, a French standard floats level with the *R. de Plate*, whereas a Portuguese flag is perched on Cape St Augustine in memory of Villegagnon's settlement of 1555 to 1560.

The extent of the Portuguese presence in Africa and Asia is emphasized by the number of Portuguese banners: Java and Taprobane (Sumatra) are Portuguese, suggesting that some Dieppe cartographers did not contest their claim to these possessions. Likewise, Spain is present along the whole of the Pacific seaboard of South America and in the West Indies, *toutes Espaignolle* ('wholly Spanish').

Two replicas of this chart are preserved in the National Maritime Museum in Greenwich: one dated 1567, the other dated 1568 and signed by Pierre Hamon.

59

ATLAS
by Fernão Vaz Dourado (1571)
18 vellum leaves, illuminated ms, 540 × 405 mm
Leaf 7: *East Indies and Japan*
Lisbon, Arquivo Nacional da Torre do Tombo: Casa Forte, no. 70

Born in Goa around 1520, the son of a high Portuguese official and an Indian mother, Fernão Vaz Dourado is considered one of the greatest Portuguese cartographers of the second half of the sixteenth century. Having decided on an army career, he took part in the siege of Diu in 1545, then sailed as far as Bengal in about 1547, under the command of Vasco da Cunha, who mentions him in his account of the voyage as 'cosmographer in this part of the Indies'. Six of Vaz Dourado's marine atlases constructed between the years 1568 and 1580 have fortunately survived, allowing us to appreciate their fresh and vivid illumination, evidence of his talent as a draughtsman and painter.

This nautical chart of the coasts of Southeast Asia is the seventh leaf of an atlas now preserved in Lisbon but made in Goa in 1571. The presence of the da Costa arms at the beginning of the work would seem to indicate that it was intended for Francisco da Costa, who was appointed governor of Malacca early in 1571. The title of the document is inscribed around the margins between two red and blue lines: 'On this sheet is drawn [the coast] from Cape Comorin to Japan and the Moluccas with all the land as far as the north'. Vaz Dourado's cartographic sketch of Japan is already close to the actual configuration; the islands of Kyushu and Honshu—the largest in the archipelago—are drawn like a crescent around the island of Shikoku; the greater part of Honshu and the whole of Hokkaido are still missing. This stage in the European mapping of the coasts of Japan, carried out exclusively by Portuguese navigators over a period of less than thirty years, was to serve as a prototype until late into the seventeenth century. On land, finely drawn pagodas with golden roofs are inserted in Burma (*Aracam*), Siam, the Indochinese peninsula and China (*Reinos da China*), wherever Buddhism was practised. On the other hand, in Bengal (*Bemgala*), a shield and two Muslim banners indicate an Islamic kingdom, the forerunner of present-day Bangladesh. Over Ceylon, Malacca, the *Costa de Moro* of Halmahera (*Gilolo*) and over Japan float Portuguese flags, bearing witness to the Portuguese presence in these regions.

Both a navigational instrument and a reflection of contemporary reality, Vaz Dourado's chart accurately illustrates Portuguese commercial presence and its vitality. In the Chinese maritime provinces, red capitals are used to indicate the cities of *Camtam* (Canton), today Guangzhou, *Ochimche* (Quanzhou) and *Liampo* (Hangzhou), near which the Portuguese would choose deserted and isolated coastal islands on which to set up temporary commercial fairs from July to November every year. During these summer months they lived in straw huts, awaiting visits from junks attracted by the lure of novel or rare commodities, among which pepper played an important role. In the Gulf of Canton (whose size is exaggerated on the chart) at the mouth of the Pearl (Zhu) River, is the first mention of the town of *Macao*, the first permanent post to be created by the Portuguese, founded in 1557 on an unpromising location at the furthest point of the small, rocky and uninhabited island of Goa-Xan. A few years later (1563), this mercantile town already numbered 900 permanent Portuguese residents and a greater number of Malays, Indians and slaves. On the arrival of the Jesuits, it was raised to the rank of a bishopric, with jurisdiction over China and Japan (1568); ten years after its foundation, Macao had already become an important city.

In the China Sea, to the left of the compass rose and near a sprinkling of islands, a long inscription in red cursive script indicates: 'The coast of Luzon and adjacent islands, Pedro Fidalgo passed by here on his way from Borneo aboard a Chinese junk. Swept by a gale, he skirted the island and headed for Lamao'. Lamao can probably be identified as the island of Nanao Dao, at the entrance to the great bay where the port of Swatow, or Shantou, now stands. It was from there that a large part of the trade was carried out between China and the great islands of the East Indies, especially Borneo. The Portuguese pilot must have used dead-reckoning to map the chain of the Palawan Islands, unduly extending them in a northeasterly direction, since neither Formosa nor Luzon had yet been properly surveyed.

Finally, a Portuguese flag over Japan recalls the opening of the port of Nagasaki to foreigners the previous year (1570). From now onwards the starting point of the trade with Japan was transferred from Goa to Macao. Rich galleons carrying silks and other Chinese goods on the outward voyage would return from Japan with cargoes of silver ingots. These fruitful exchanges continued almost every year until 1639, when a draconian decree ordering that all Catholics be put to death closed the doors of the Japan archipelago to the subjects of the king of Portugal for several centuries.

With its rhumb-lines, latitude scales, a distance scale in the top left-hand corner in a fine baroque cartouche and its warnings of sand banks and reefs, the chart of Fernão Vaz Dourado enables the navigator to take a bearing and plot his course. The latter would also have had at his disposal detailed rutters similar to the *Grand Routier de Chine* by the Dutchman Jan Huyghen Van Linschoten (1596), who says he received his information from a Portuguese pilot named Pero da Cunha. Van Linschoten's rutter, printed in many editions, spread Portuguese maritime knowledge of these Far Eastern regions throughout Europe.

60

BRAZIL
by Jacques de Vau de Claye (1579)
1 leaf, illuminated ms, 590 × 450 mm
Paris, B.N.: Cartes et Plans, Rés. Ge D 13871

Brazil was not always dominated by the Portuguese. Discovered in 1500 and claimed for the king of Portugal by Cabral, it seems to have been the goal of French expeditions before that date. In 1503, Paulmier de Gonneville of Honfleur, in a report on his voyage to the admiralty of Rouen, relates that 'for several years back, sailors from Dieppe and Saint-Malo have been [there] to fetch red dye-wood, cotton, monkeys, parrots and other commodities'. Verrazano (1528) and Le Testu (1551) visited and surveyed this coast, drew it and traded with the Indians. Wood was the main commodity traded, and since the royal edict of 1549, Rouen was the centre of this lumber trade. Relations between the French traders and the Indians were excellent.

In 1555, with Coligny's approval and partly subsidized by the French king, an expedition was mounted to colonize a point on the Brazilian coast. At the head of six hundred men, Durand de Villegagnon, a knight of Malta, landed in Ganabara (Rio) Bay and built a fort on an island—Fort Coligny. Protestant reinforcements were sent out later, but the Portuguese took the fort and destroyed it in 1569.

Nevertheless, the French continued to trade on the north coast of Brazil. In 1581 the queen of France decided to take advantage of the vacant throne of Portugal and entrusted her cousin Philippe Strozzi with the command of a fleet encharged with the seizure of Brazil, of which he was to become viceroy. Halted in the Azores by a Spanish fleet, the expedition was destroyed and Strozzi killed. Philip II became master of Brazil, but Norman ships did not cease trading with the Indians until the middle of the seventeenth century.

This chart, like the following one, was made in Dieppe in 1579. Nothing is known about Vau de Claye, and only these two charts by him are known to exist. The outlines are inspired by Portuguese charts, but the nomenclature is French. Inscriptions are there to assist the reader at every point. This is a nautical chart, indicating shoals, reefs and bays, and an economic chart with inscriptions commenting on the products of the country: gold, ambergris, brazil-wood, sugar and cotton. It is also a sort of ethnographic chart, showing the Indian tribes and their villages and explaining their cannibalistic propensities; the Amazons near the Marañon are also described. Finally, it is a natural-history chart, indicating the presence of monkeys and birds sought for their plumage.

The real function of this chart, however, is probably quite different: a semi-circle, drawn from *St Domingue* to the river *do pracel*, marks the territory of ten thousand *saulvages pour fere la guerre aux portugais* ('savages to make war on the Portuguese'). Thus it would seem that this chart had a military purpose, indicated by the way the banner with the Strozzi arms appears to dominate the chart, and that it shows a plan of campaign for the conquest of the Brazilian coast between the Amazon and the São Francisco River (Bahia). So this beautiful chart would have formed part of the preparations for carrying out a plan of conquest conceived by Catherine de' Medici; however, thwarted by Strozzi's death in the Azores, it came to nothing.

61

RIO DE JANEIRO BAY
by Jacques de Vau de Claye (1579)
1 vellum leaf, coloured ms, 310 × 670 mm
Paris, B.N.: Cartes et Plans, Rés. Ge C 5007

If the previous chart of Brazil (No. 60) is presumed to be a military chart, the present one is even more enlightening. *Le vrai pourtraict de Geneure et du Cap de Frie* is a portolan chart reduced to one compass rose, whose north is on the right of the leaf. The name

Geneure stands for Janeiro, as one of the colonists on the Villegagnon expedition, the Protestant pastor Jean de Léry, explains: 'the sound and salt-water river is named Ganabara by the savages and Geneure by the Portuguese because, as they say, they discovered it on the first day of January'.

After 1559, the French had to give up their possessions in Brazil, and Villegagnon abandoned his French Island in Rio Bay. From 1565 the town of Rio expanded, and Fort Coligny (taken in 1569) was razed to the ground.

The idea of retaking this possession, which had been in French hands for fourteen years, is revealed by the inscriptions on this plan. To the north of the town, one in particular specifies, *ici est le côté pour prendre Geneure* ('here is the side from which to take Janeiro'). We know that three years after the construction of these two charts, Strozzi was entrusted with retaking Rio Bay, but the naval disaster of the Azores put an end to this plan of conquest.

The chart is also informative on the development of the sugar-cane industry. Sugar cane had been imported to Brazil from Madeira by Martim da Sousa in 1531. After fourteen years of colonization, the Portuguese had expanded this industry, which was taking over from the lumber trade in the south, especially where the *matta*, or coastal forest, no longer existed.

The talent for organization of the Portuguese soon led them to exploit the hinterland; Villegagnon's plan had been quite different. Starting with a fortified island modelled on Malta, he wanted to found a settlement that would provide a refuge for Protestants (Coligny sent out three hundred Calvinists) and, with the aid of the Indians, break the Iberian monopoly in America. However, theological disputes undermined the infant colony, and it fell an easy prey to the Portuguese.

This chart, constructed ten years after the fall of Fort Coligny (the island is now called Villegaignon), was intended to help in the reconquest of the finest site in Brazil.

62

ATLAS
by Joan Martines (1583)
7 vellum leaves, illuminated ms, 405 × 590 mm
Leaf 3: *South America*
Paris, B.N.: Cartes et Plans, Rés. Ge DD 682

After its brilliant Majorcan period, the next flowering of the Catalan cartographic school took place in Sicily in the sixteenth and seventeenth centuries, probably as a result of the Jews migrating from one Aragonese possession to the other.

Incorporated into Spain with the status of a viceroyalty, the island of Sicily served as an advanced post in Spain's struggle against the Turks. The Christian fleets opposing the Turkish advance gathered in Messina, an important port of call, easily supplied and 'lying in ambush on its corridor of water' (Braudel). It was there that the cartographers usually resided also.

Joan Martines was one of these cartographers. Despite a considerable production over a long period of time—more than thirty atlases and charts between 1550 and 1591—all we know of him is what is stated in the colophons of his last atlases, when he had become cosmographer royal (*cosmographo del Rey nro segnor*) in Naples. Until then, all his works had been signed in Messina, invariably using the formula that we can read in a fine black script on the first leaf of this atlas: *Joan Martines En Messina Añy 1583*.

Beginning with an oval mappa mundi inspired by Ortelius, without rhumbs but framed by eight puffing, curly-headed cherubs symbolizing the winds, this atlas (formerly in the Santarem Collection) contains six nautical charts, three of which are devoted to the New World.

South America, bounded by the 'seas', *MARE DEL SVR* (Pacific Ocean) and *MARE OCEANO* (Atlantic Ocean), has its latitudes indicated by two reversed scales on either side of the equator (*CIRCVLVS AEQVINOCTIALIS*). Extending about 10 degrees beyond the tropic of Capricorn (*TROPICVS CAPRICORNI*), it goes no further than Concepción Bay in Chile (*Chilli*) and the vast mouth of the *rio de la Platta* in the south. What the cartographer has sought to represent is not 'discovery', but rather the recent extension of the sovereignty of Philip II—who had become Philip I of Portugal in 1580—to cover the whole of South America. Portuguese and Spanish territories are still distinguished by different coloured borders, pink for the coast of Brazil—whose outline is interpreted in a restrictive way from the mouth of the Amazon (*RIO DE ORIGLIANA* and *RIO MARAGNON*) to the *rio acaravellas* at only 19°S—and gold for the rest of the chart. But only the flag of Castile flies over the twenty-one vignettes of towns that occupy the hinterland, recalling that, by the terms of the bull *Inter Coetera*, the 'Indies' had been the personal property of the Castilian crown before becoming Spanish.

The arrangement of the vignettes reflects the two different systems of colonization. They are almost absent in Brazil, where only two anonymous towns are depicted—the vast estates of the captains-donatory had as yet only been exploited along a narrow coastal belt. They are numerous, on the other hand, in the area that the Spaniards had explored in every direction between 1530 and 1550, and whose *adelantado*—conquistador and governor at the same time, and invested directly by royal authority—had founded towns complete with an administration everywhere. Some of these, situated in the Andean provinces and studding the banks of the great rivers and their tributaries from *S. Anna* to *Giurumata*, seem to illustrate the route opened up by Irala in 1540, which joined the regions of the River

Plate to the great lakes Poopó and Titicaca, identifiable here by their outlines.

The inland nomenclature is directly borrowed from the engraved atlases of Ortelius. The toponyms have not all been reproduced, but they are identical. The mountain chains are arranged in the same style, and the strictly identical outline of the major hydrographic basins is very accurate in comparison with that of contemporary nautical cartography. Ortelius was no doubt beholden to information provided by the Jesuits who, with the Mercedarians and other religious orders, had helped to open up the Spanish Amazon and the Plate regions during the second half of the sixteenth century. The cartographer probably drew on other, more accurate sources for the coasts such as the *padrones* of the Casa de Contratación; on the coasts he has meticulously indicated the sand banks (at the mouths of rivers on the northern coast of Brazil), reefs and approaches strewn with dangerous archipelagos (red, encircled with black).

These multiple borrowings are a hallmark of the Catalan tradition, of which Joan Martines is obviously a part, although he has been called Spanish, Portuguese and even Genoese. The Catalan origin of this cartographer, who expresses himself in Spanish and serves the king of Spain, is suggested by the form of his forename and the ending of his surname as well as by his style, decorative interpretation of geographical data and the splendid execution of his compass roses.

63

PORTUGUESE PLANISPHERE
(ca. 1585)
4 vellum leaves, coloured ms assembled into a chart, 1145 × 2180 mm
Paris, B.N.: Cartes et Plans, S.H. Archives no. 38

This Portuguese nautical planisphere, preserved in the archives of the French navy since 1665 as a note on the verso of the document confirms, is unfortunately neither signed nor dated. French specialists have attributed it to Pedro de Lemos, but specialists in Portuguese cartography believe it to be by Sebastião Lopes, who may have constructed it in Lisbon around 1585.

Two land-masses are clearly defined on it: on one side the American continent; on the other the tripartite world of Europe, Africa and Asia, where the Philippine archipelago makes its first appearance in its entirety, having been named in honour of Philip II *(Filippinas)*. Each hemisphere has its individual network of rhumblines. In the Arctic, towering over the inhabited regions, is a continental land-mass of enormous proportions—a sort of roof of the world—divided into four great polar islands separated by narrow sounds. Like Mercator in his chart of 1569 dedicated to navigators *(Nova et aucta orbis terrae descriptio ad usum navigantium emendate accommodata)*, the author of this planisphere still relies on the mediaeval Scandinavian idea of the Arctic regions, propagated in Renaissance scientific circles by the circulation of a manuscript dating from 1364, the 'Inventio Fortunata' (The Fortunate Discovery) by an erudite Oxford astronomer, Nicholas of Lynn. This 'fortunate discovery' revealed that 'at the Arctic Pole, there is a highly magnetic rock 33 German miles in circumference; an angry, eddying sea surrounds this rock ... and there are islands around it, two of which are inhabited'. Thus the existence of magnetic north was known by the middle of the fourteenth century. We now know that it is located far in the Canadian north in the Queen Elizabeth archipelago and that the Arctic actually consists of an expanse of frozen sea extending over 1,400,000 square kilometres. Despite the maritime discoveries of the English and Dutch in the course of their searches for the Northwest and Northeast Passages after 1590, the representation of a mythical northern continent continued to reappear sporadically in western cartography for nearly another century.

The vividly coloured illumination has both a nautical and a political significance: twenty compass roses, eleven shields and forty banners give the chart a particularly arresting pictorial quality, recalling once again the division of the world between the Spaniards and the Portuguese. In America everything is Spanish, apart from Newfoundland and Brazil. In Africa and the East Indies, including China and Japan, Portuguese influence predominates despite Arab expansionism. In Europe each country is marked with its own coat of arms. The only illustrations are three gold crosses, marking the site of Golgotha in Jerusalem and symbolizing Christ's sacrifice, and two paintings in Africa depicting the trading-posts of Elmina and the Congo.

How did this magnificent maritime document reach France? Was it brought there by some Portuguese pilot in exile, or was it stolen from a Portuguese carrack? This still remains one of history's many secrets. In any case, in its day it had a great influence on Dutch cartography. The world map, published in Amsterdam in 1592 by the Flemish cartographer and theologian Petrus Plancius, shows many similarities to this Portuguese planisphere, which provided northern European pilots with the outline of an eastern world as yet unknown to them.

64-65

ATLAS
by Joan Martines (1587)
21 parchment leaves, illuminated ms bound in one volume, 580 × 800 mm

64 Leaf 8: *Island of Cyprus*
65 Leaf 10: *Southeast Asia*
Madrid, Biblioteca Nacional, Vit. 4-20

The number and volume of works by Joan Martines is impressive. Most of his atlases contain five to seven leaves; four of them have more than ten. However, by far the most imposing one, inherited from the Royal Palace library, is preserved in the Biblioteca Nacional in Madrid. It consists of a collection of nineteen charts, generously drawn on a double folio; the first recto and last verso form the end-papers of a sumptuous red-leather binding with gold-tooled boards, embossed in the centre with a crowned shield bearing the arms of the various realms of Philip II.

These arms and the provenance of the document encourage the belief that it was intended for the king himself, who may have commissioned it when he was preparing the expedition of the 'Invincible Armada' against England. This hypothesis is supported, not only by the fact that another atlas by Martines fell into the hands of the English when they overcame the armada, along with the ship carrying it, but also by the date of its construction and the composition of the work, the first part of which concentrates on some of the islands of Europe with Ireland *(IRLANDIA)*, Scotland *(ISCOTIA)* and England *(INGLATERA)*.

The second part of the atlas charts the world from east to west, by continent or region. Both sections are introduced by representations of the globe borrowed from engraved atlases: one in the form of two bracketed hemispheres on an orthographic projection, the other being an oval mappa mundi imitated from Ortelius. Laconic as usual, the signature is at the foot of the first leaf: *Joan Martines En Messina Añy 1587*.

Cyprus (No. 64), sixth and last of the islands dealt with in this work, has been drawn to a large scale that shows up the coastal indentations. It seems surrounded by the names of its promontories—the Greeks called it 'the island of capes'—inscribed in capital letters that fan out around it. Some of these originated in legends: *CAPO DI LI GATE*, or Cape of the Cats refers to the place near the shore where cats were bred by Basilian monks to kill snakes. To the west, at *CAPO SANCTO EPIPHANIO*, (Cape Arnauti), the intervention of Saint Helen, the mother of Emperor Constantine, is said to have calmed the storms that raged 'between Christmas and Epiphany'. Inland, the blue shape of *Mons Olÿmus* (Mount Olympus), now the Troodos range, stands out clearly from within a rather confused general effect. We can also see Famagusta *(Famagosta)* and *Nicosia*, girded by rivers.

The outlines, orientation and nomenclature, together with the title—*CYPRVS INSVLA*—are all reproduced from the *Theatrum Orbis Terrarum* by Ortelius, in the Latin edition of 1570, which was a faithful copy of Venetian prototypes of the middle of the century. Ortelius had been content to add (as Martines also does) the names of the four districts of the Hellenistic and Roman periods given by Ptolemy: *SALAMINIA, LAPATHIA* for Lapethia, *AMATUSIA* and *PAPHIA*.

Beyond the unnamed sea, following a tradition dating from the *Tabulae Modernae* of Ptolemy's *Geography*, Martines has delineated the continent surrounding the island to stress its proximity both to Syria *(SVRIA)*, where Mount Lebanon *(Monte Libano)* looms, and especially to Anatolia *(NATOLIA)*, whose southernmost point is only a few leagues from Cape *CORNACHITI* (Kormakiti). An inscription in red ink close to the coast near the port of *Slelimur* (a corruption of Anamur) declares, *porto novamente facto dal Gran Turcho*: borrowed from Italian cartography that reproduced it tirelessly after its first mention in May 1570, the inscription recalls the Turkish fortification of Karamania *(CARAMANIA)*, with a view to launching a campaign against Venetian-held Cyprus.

Apart from the mappae mundi, none of the charts up to the tenth leaf is graduated in latitude. Southeast Asia (No. 65), on the other hand, which is shown on the tenth leaf of the atlas, is spanned by the two red lines of the tropic of Cancer *(TROPICVS CANCRI)* and the equator *(CIRCVLVS AEQVINOCTIALIS)*, while in the west a scale, alternately yellow and blue, goes from 45°N to 17°S. Since it is on the same size parchment as the previous chart and the area represented is much larger, this chart is drawn to a quarter of the scale of the others.

Here again Martines has been inspired by contemporary engraved cartography: his principal source for Asia seems to have been the great chart of the world constructed in 1569 by Gerard Mercator, who was himself indebted to Gastaldi. The Pacific archipelagos are strictly identical to Mercator's, and the prototype of Japan *(IAPAN)*, for example, is very backward in comparison with the outlines of it appearing at the same time on certain Portuguese nautical charts. Mercator had tried to harmonize new geographical information with classical and mediaeval toponymy; Martines does not reproduce the explanatory inscriptions of his prototype, but archaisms crop up in several places, for example in Sumatra, given its Ptolemaic name of *TAPROBANA*, or at *QUINZAI*, Marco Polo's name for the Chinese port of Hangzhou.

The general title *Archipelago di San Lazaro* had been used since Magellan for the Mariana Islands *(Restinga de Ladrones*: Thieves' Reef) and for the Philippines *(PHILIPPINAS)*. Their representation and that of the other Pacific islands owes much to the Spanish expeditions, competing with the Portuguese to establish themselves there. The Caroline Islands *(Illa de Arecifes, Illa di Matalotes* or *los Iardines)* were almost all discovered in 1543 by Villalobos, who was attempting to establish himself in Mindanao *(MINDANA)* after the conference of Badajoz had ousted Spain from *Tidore*. Wishing to consolidate their positions in the Philippines by creating a maritime link to the east between Luzon

(CAILON) and Mexico, the Spaniards, on rounding the north of the Marianas, also discovered *Malabrigo, Los dos ermanos, Los volcanes* and *la Farfana*, now the Japanese Bonin Islands. But the chart drawn up in 1565 by Urdaneta, the originator of this route, remained a secret for a long time, and the positions of all these islands are only approximate.

There is considerable approximation also in the southern part of the chart, where Java *(IAVA MAIOR)* and New Guinea *(NOVA GVINEA)*, only surveyed on their northern coasts, are too extended in latitude. It was undecided—Mercator expressed the problem in an inscription—whether New Guinea was an island or an outcrop of the 'austral continent'.

Out of the nineteen charts in this atlas, fifteen are borrowed, like these, from Ortelius or Mercator and only four are genuine portolan charts. This beautiful work is, in short, no more than a manuscript version of the engraved atlases recently made popular in the Low Countries by Dutch cartographers, who were also subjects of the king of Spain.

66

THE MEDITERRANEAN
by Nicolaos Vourdopolos (early seventeenth century)
1 parchment leaf, coloured ms, 505 × 590 mm
Paris, B.N. Ms supplément grec 1094

The earliest rutters, or sea books, in demotic Greek appeared in the first half of the sixteenth century. Their content illustrates the influence exerted by Venice on her colonial sailors; one of the manuscripts is even accompanied by a μαρτελόγιον *(martelogion)* as an appendix, closely copied from Venetian navigational tables. Even the language in which the Greek rutters are written shows traces of the *lingua franca* in its vocabulary, style and toponymy.

This imitativeness is detectible in this chart by Nicolaos Vourdopolos, one of the few examples known from this period in which the nomenclature is in Greek. A quarter of it is in red ink and the remainder in two different black inks. The toponyms reveal an uncertainty in spelling (σμηρνη instead of σμυρνη) and frequent borrowings from Venetian vocabulary. The area covered is confined to the Black Sea and Mediterranean basin, for although the outline of the Atlantic coasts from Morocco to Portugal is given, there are no place-names beyond Gibraltar.

Constructed on a network of rhumb-lines with thirty-two points centred on Sicily, the chart is oriented towards the west, where the neck of the parchment is adorned with a Calvary and a monogram invoking the victorious Christ: $\frac{IC \mid XC}{N \mid K}$ *(Iesous Christos Nika).* A west-east rhumb-line passes through this monogram and serves as a symmetrical axis for the arrangement of extremely beautiful half and full compass roses that decorate seven of the sixteen secondary centres of the *marteloio* in the Portuguese manner. The remaining illumination, consisting of bird's-eye views of mountains, animals and palm-trees in Africa and vignettes of towns, is rather reminiscent of the Catalan school as Sideri interpreted it (No. 57). Genoa, and above all Venice, are especially well illustrated and true to life. The signature appears in the northwest corner: πιυμα Νικολάου άναγνόστου βουρδοπολου, άπό τὴν Πάτμων *(piuma Nicolaou anagnostou Bourdopolou, apo ten Patmon)*. Apart from his name, the signature informs us that the author of the chart was born on Patmos, that he was a 'reader'—a monastic occupation—and that he was nevertheless comparatively uneducated, since there are spelling mistakes even here. No date is given.

This Vourdopolos may well be the same man as the author of another chart, described in 1897 by the Italian scholar Magnaghi, which was preserved then and today still in private archives in Volterra. Also in Greek, the latter is signed: Ἔργον Χειρός Νικολάου βουρδοπολου ἐκ νέσου Πάτμω ἐν ἔτει 1608 *(ergon cheiros Nicolaou Bourdopolou / ek nesou Patmo en etei 1608*, 'manuscript work by Nicolaos Bourdopolos of the island of Patmos, in the year 1608').

In the following year—1609—one Nicolaos Vourdopolos was the last signatory of an act in the archives of the Monastery of Saint John the Theologian in which several inhabitants of the island, clergy and laity, agreed to demolish some houses too near to the said monastery the better to ensure its defence against the piratical 'sons of Agar' (Egyptians).

While a comparison of handwriting would only be possible if we could consult the chart examined by Magnaghi, the circumstantial evidence of name, place and convergent dates suggests that these three individuals were one and the same, and that the document in Paris dates from the early years of the seventeenth century.

67

ATLANTIC OCEAN
by Guillaume Levasseur (1601)
1 vellum leaf, illuminated ms, 744 × 990 mm
Paris, B.N.: Cartes et Plans, S.H. Archives no. 5

This is an original work: a portolan chart adopting the system of waxing latitude initiated by Mercator in his mappa mundi of 1569 and which Edward Wright explained in 1599. Before Mercator, portolan charts were plane charts, that is, nautical charts based on equally measured degrees of latitude and longitude.

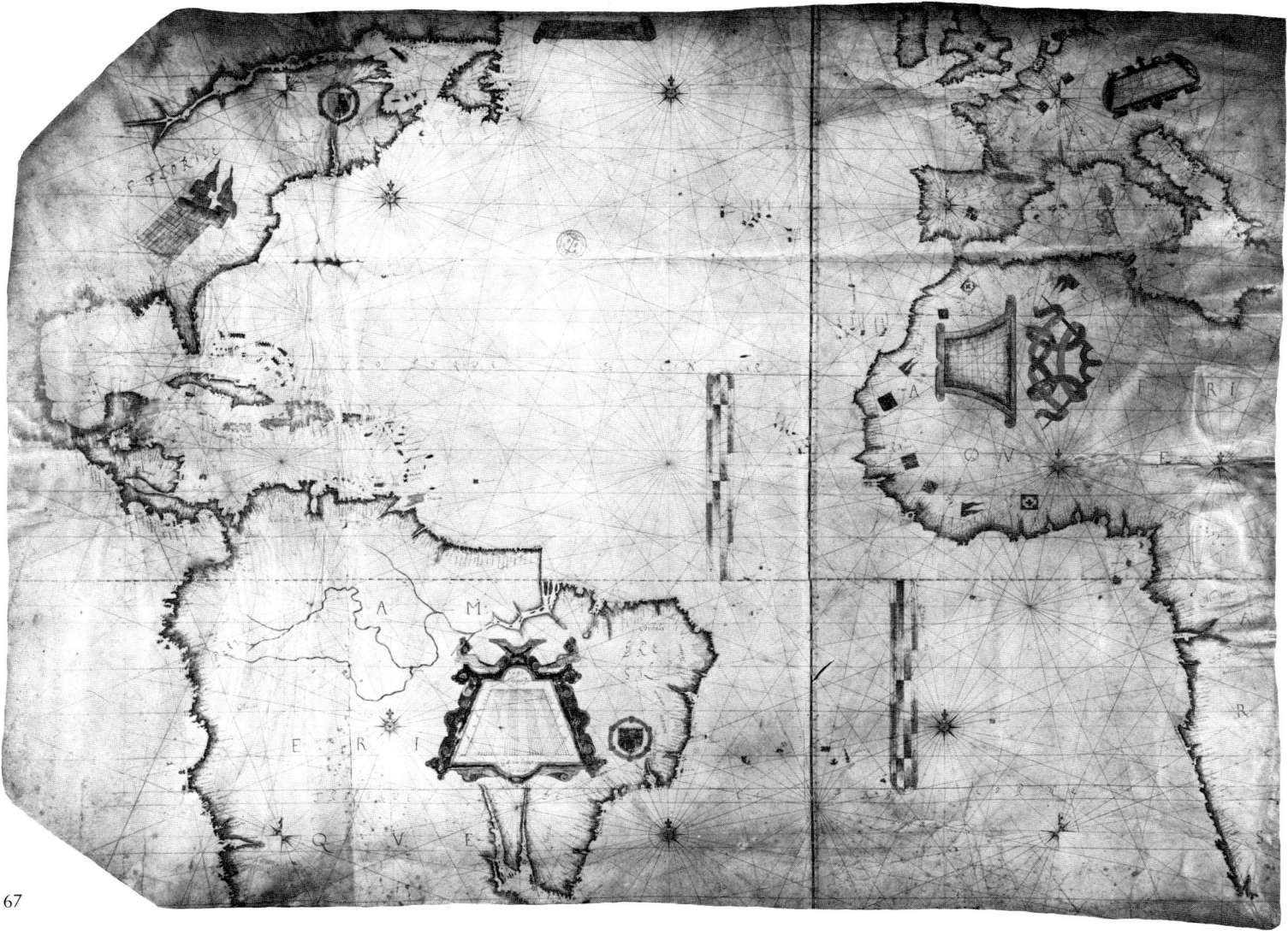

But as Mercator stated, 'the degrees of latitude should be enlarged little by little, and moved upwards towards the north, so that the latitude scale there becomes variable'—this is 'Mercator's variable'.

On this chart, a classic latitude scale of constant degrees is given along a prime meridian located, as on most of the Dieppe charts, near the Cape Verde Islands. But at the foot of the leaf, in an ornamental cartouche, a waxing-latitude scale from 0° to 60° appears in perspective. Thus if his ship followed the same rhumbline, a navigator could calculate the value of the different meridians he had crossed, in relation to the equator.

On the scroll, wound round the compass of which the Dieppe school was fond, appears the dedication: *Faict pour Ignas Paulmier par G. Lev. Z. 1601*. Little is known of this cartographer. Born in Dieppe in the second half of the sixteenth century, he died at Rouen before 1643. This is the only portolan chart we know of by him. A former weaver in Dieppe, Levasseur studied nautical science through the writings of Desceliers. In 1629 he was commissioned to survey the coasts of France and was appointed a paid pilot in 1635 at Dieppe. Levasseur was a mathematician. In the Bibliothèque Nationale in Paris there are eight manuscripts by him dealing with the art of navigation and, in particular, the *Géodrographie*, in which he explains how reduction is achieved: 'on sea charts the parallels have to be left equal so that the meridians also remain parallel, especially as the said meridians cannot approach each other in order to shorten their parallels as they do naturally on the globe; it is necessary for the degrees of latitude to increase by an amount equal to that by which the parallels should decrease, and this enlargement is proportionate to the reduction or narrowing of the respective parallels'. This was the theory of charts with waxing latitude, known as 'reduced charts'. They were later printed on vellum by the Dutch and sold in the Atlantic ports. However they came into general use slowly, and many plane charts were still constructed during the seventeenth century.

Apart from the waxing-latitude scale, at the top of the chart level with America, there are two scales graduated from 0° to 40° and from 40° to 55°. These may be auxiliary scales enabling navigators to calculate the inclination of the magnetic needle. This oblique meridian appears intermittently in nautical cartography, since it is still to be found on Basque charts of the end of the seventeenth century (Nos. 91, 97).

The abundant nomenclature is part French, part Portuguese. According to Mr Ganong, it is on this chart that the name of Quebec makes its first appearance. Moreover he states that, although twenty-eight of the names along the Saint Lawrence come from Jacques Cartier, seven new names that still survive make their appearance. The source of this original nomenclature is unknown, but we may assume that it was given to Levasseur by a navigator who had gone to Canada between 1580 and 1600, possibly Pont Gravé, a pilot in Canada before 1600 and later a companion of Champlain's.

This is the most valuable chart for Canadian toponymy before Champlain. With this sober, yet richly informative vellum we finally take a still uncertain step away from the traditionally flat depiction of vast expanses and towards the representation of latitudes on a variable projection.

68

ATLANTIC, MEDITERRANEAN SEA, BLACK SEA
by Francesco Oliva (1603)
1 vellum leaf, coloured ms, 540 × 900 mm
Paris, B.N.: Cartes et Plans, Rés. Ge C 5093

As in the case of the Maggiolos—and the history of the period provides several other examples—cartography was a family art among the Olivas who originated in Majorca but emigrated to Spanish Italy, where the earliest members of the family, Bartolomeo and Jaume, practised their craft in the second half of the sixteenth century. Their descendants to the third generation bore the name of Oliva, alternating it with the surname Riczo. Later members in the seventeenth century signed themselves Oliva or Caloiro Oliva, some living in Messina, one at Leghorn and others in Marseilles, a city with which the family seems very early to have had occasional links and where several of them established themselves, the last of whom called himself Ollive in the French style.

We know of ten artists in all, of differing talent, who used variants of this name and whose identified production spans the period from 1538 to 1664. Their kinship is not always clearly defined, but that is not so in the case of Francesco Oliva—grandson of Jaume, son of Domenico and brother of Joan Oliva, all three of whom had worked in Naples, where they must have taken turns in the same workshop. Joan and Francesco collaborated on several occasions, and their styles are very similar. But while Joan was a prolific cartographer and moved around readily from Messina to Naples and Marseilles, Francesco has only left about ten, possibly thirteen works, all executed in Messina between 1562 and 1615.

The chart of 1603 is carefully composed with all its decoration oriented towards the west where, marked off at the base by a latitude scale, Saint Anne and the Virgin and Child appear enthroned in the animal's neck and, at their feet, the signature: *Franciscus Oliva fecit in nobile urbe messane anno 1603*.

The work is tripartite, has banners indicating *AFRICA*, *ASIA* and *EVROPA* and is organized in relation to the principal west-east line of the rhumb network. All the secondary centres have been decorated with compass roses or sometimes, for lack of space, with just the initials of the winds set out in a star.

The illustration is chiefly political, portraying the armoured sovereigns of Europe bearing shields and brandishing swords, (*re de Spania, re de Fransa, Imperatori, re de Ongaria* [King of Hungary]), and the Muslim sovereigns dressed in long robes and armed with scimitars with the crescent of Islam on their shields *(re de Cacco*[?]*, Re de Fesse* [Fez]*, re de Alger, re de Tunisi, re de Tripoli, Grasorda de Babilonia* [Grand Sultan of Cairo]*, gran turco)*. A monotonous and deadly war was then being waged on the Hungarian front, between the Holy Roman Empire and the Turks. Begun in 1593, it would last until 1606.

There are also views of towns in perspective: stereotyped and difficult to identify in Islamic territory (which contains six), and more individual in Europe where, apart from the classic portrayals of Venice and Genoa, Ragusa *(Raqusa)* can be recognized. Its astonishing power in the sixteenth century derived from its position at the crossroads between the land routes to the Balkans and the sea, and sailors were familiar with all of Ragusa's ports. Likewise Barcelona *(Barsalona)* which, after a long decline, was beginning to reawaken and prosper, trading actively in the western Mediterranean and sometimes as far as Alexandria. Finally there is Marseilles *(Marsella)*, established in the markets of the Levant since the Capitulations of 1536 and having increased her influence there thanks to the war between Venice, Spain and the Turks (1570-1571). Marseilles was going through a period of relative opulence despite her difficulties—the plague, pirates and civil war. The cartographer gives a very vivid image of this city of some 30,000 inhabitants tightly packed on the north side of the port around the three hills of Saint-Laurent, Moulins and Carmes; on the high ground, he depicts a row of little mills with vibrant sails, which could no doubt be seen from afar by navigators.

This meticulous decoration is superimposed on outlines that contain no borrowings from theoretical geography but, on the contrary, are based on observed data. In the North Sea, for example, the sand and pebble shoals are accurately charted, and the dotted arc stretching from the English coast to the German Bight probably represents the Dogger Bank, an extensive shoal at a depth of less than 20 metres. There are inaccuracies however; for example, in the Red Sea region which has lost the Sinai Peninsula and on the shores of the Atlantic where the cartographer has over-accentuated the indentations of the estuaries, especially those of the Gironde and the Bristol Channel. Finally, and most importantly, the introduction of a latitude scale has not led to any of the corrections of orientation that might be expected at such a late date; the chart is still based on magnetic north and retains the torsion of the Mediterranean to the northwest, making Beirut *(Barut)* appear on the 40th parallel, whereas it is really just below 34°N.

Such persistent errors show the Mediterranean sailors' lack of interest in the measurement of latitudes in a sea so narrow from north to south. The scale indicated probably only concerned the coasts of the Atlantic, although the author has not troubled to specify it. This was almost always the case in contemporary manuscript cartography.

69

DESCRIPTION OF NEW FRANCE
by Sieur de Champlain (1607)
1 vellum leaf, coloured ms, 370 × 545 mm
Washington, D.C., Library of Congress

This chart, devoid of ornamentation, is an original work that leads abruptly into a new dimension of representation.

This is Champlain's first cartographic work, executed at Port Royal (Annapolis Royal) in Acadia after a sojourn, he says, 'of three and a half years when I have been in Acadia'. In the course of four voyages made in a pinnace, Champlain explored 3,600 kilometres of coastline with the intention of surveying the American coast.

The chart delineates the coast of New France and present-day New England. The title, signature and date appear in the baroque cartouche at the bottom right-hand corner of the chart: *Description des costs, pts, rades, illes de la nouvele france faict selon son vray méridien Avec la déclinaison de lement de plusieurs endroits selon que le sieur de Castes le franc le démontre en son livre de la mécométrie de l'emmt faict et observé par le sieur de Champlain—1607* ('Description of the coasts, points, roads, islands of New France made according to the true meridian. With the magnetic variation of several places according to how the Sieur de Castes Le Franc demonstrates it in his book on magnetic measurement; made and observed by the Sieur de Champlain—1607'). A dotted line leading in an easterly direction from Port Royal probably marks the track of vessels bound for France.

In order to comprehend the full significance of this vital chart in the history of cartography, it would be as well to read the work published by Champlain in 1613, *Les Voyages du Sieur de Champlain, Saintongeois...*, a detailed journal of his stay in Acadia from 1604 to 1607, with all the places located in latitude.

After his first voyage of exploration along the Saint Lawrence in 1603, Champlain reembarked from Le Havre on 7 March 1604 with the expedition commanded by Pierre du Gua de Monts, entrusted with exploring and mapping the region situated between latitudes 40° and 46°N. King Henry IV had appointed Champlain geographer to the expedition. Arriving on 8 May at Cape La Hève, he was instructed to examine the coast stretching to the south in order to find a port capable of accommodating the ships and their colonists.

After a terrible winter spent at *Sainte Croix* on the river of the same name, where thirty-five out of his seventy-five men died of scurvy, the colonists abandoned the settlement in favour of *Port Royal* near the *baye Françoise* (Bay of Fundy). It was there that this chart was executed during the summer of 1606 at the request of de Monts.

This document contains two original features for the period: localities are determined in both longitude and latitude. In order to determine the longitude, Champlain relied on the declination of the magnetic needle. In his title to this chart, he refers to the method of Guillaume le Nautonier, Sieur de Castelfranc, who had published a work in 1603 in which he establishes the position of a place in longitude by combining a calculation of the magnetic variation with the latitude. Le Nautonier had compiled tables of variations to which Champlain referred. The chart was constructed from a prime meridian located at Port Royal. Champlain later broke away from this method of calculation, writing in 1632, 'God has not bestowed on man the use of longitude'. After several observations, it was noticed that the magnetic lines did not encircle the globe in a regular pattern; moreover, in 1633, Henry Gellibrand discovered that magnetic variations altered every year. It is now known that the calculation of longitude can only be carried out scientifically after the construction of stable ship's chronometers.

This chart also makes Champlain the first ethnographer of North America. The coast is shown up to an average of 50 kilometres inland. Dense forests cover this territory, indicated by Champlain as being composed of tall trees of various species: oaks, birches, aspens, spruces and pines forming the primeval forest, now vanished for ever. Settlements are shown, some are French: *Sainte Croix*, *Port Royal*; others are Indian. According to Champlain the Souriquois, Micmacs from Novia Scotia, are nomads and meet to the north of the River Norumbega; the Etchemins, Indians from Massachusetts, grow maize and vegetables. The chart locates their settlements and compares them to those of the Iroquois, sedentary like them, and which Champlain had visited in 1603. For the first time he defines the boundary between nomadic and sedentary Indians of that time.

Some of the names he gave to these islands and rivers still survive, for example: *île des Monts-déserts*, and *île haute* at the entrance to the *Penobscot*. Sailing up the River Norumbega, Champlain gave the lie to the earlier belief, dating from Verrazano to Le Testu (No. 49), in the existence of a rich, fortified and densely populated city. Champlain declares that he saw nothing of the sort. This chart is rich, therefore, in invention and instruction, unattached to any tradition: the locations and descriptions are entirely the product of Champlain's genius.

This chart was incorporated practically in its entirety in the engraved chart of 1612. Later, without copying it, Hudson's chart of 1609 followed it, as did Smith's chart of 1614 as regards the coast of New England. It provides an accurate description of New France at the moment of its foundation and of New England before the arrival of the English colonists of the future Massachusetts, and it introduces what will be the new conception of geography, henceforth based solely on the objective observation of localities and their measurements.

70

ATLANTIC OCEAN (N.E.), MEDITERRANEAN SEA AND WESTERN BLACK SEA
by Harmen and Marten Jansz (ca. 1610)
1 vellum leaf, coloured ms, 850 × 710 mm
Paris, B.N.: Cartes et Plans, Rés. Ge B 1129

As the inscription in black cursive script appearing in North Africa under *Barbaria* indicates, this Dutch sea chart was drawn in the port of Edam by two brothers, Harmen and Marten Jansz, who state their profession as 'writers of charts' *(caertschrijvers)*: in other words, they did not actually construct charts but produced copies of existing prototypes for outward-bound navigators. Drawn on rhumb-lines, with a latitude scale in constant degrees graduated from 27° to 74°N and with its two distance scales (one positioned on the continent of Europe; the other, in Dutch miles, along the latitude scale), this is still a plane chart, but it is also a nautical chart in the full sense of the word because of its characteristic bareness, on which the only salient features are the sea lanes and the outline of the coasts with their abundant toponymy. Particularly prominent are the routes that sailors from the Zuider Zee would have to take in order to reach the waters of the North Atlantic and the Arctic Ocean. The shores are shaded in various colours—yellow, green or violet—indicating to the navigator when he is about to cross a frontier. Inland the names of the countries (usually inscribed in capital letters) tell him which coast he is skirting or in which country he is about to land. Only the illumination of the three compass roses and the baroque cartouche containing the distance scale bring a touch of colour to this document, which was intended solely for setting a course and following the correct route.

What is most striking, at the very first glance, is the fantastic progress made in the delineation of the coastline of northern Europe in comparison with previous charts, whether Italian, Majorcan or even Portuguese.

Before 1580 or thereabouts, the outline of the Dutch, German, Danish, Norwegian and Swedish coasts on western nautical charts remained very incomplete. The obstacles the Hanseatic League placed in the way of free movement along the coasts of the North Sea up to the end of the fifteenth century were certainly partly to blame for this state of affairs; it seems, moreover, that mariners who sailed the North Sea and the Baltic Sea at this time relied above all on their local knowledge, assisted by rutters, or sea books. The earliest known rutter is the German *Seebuch* dating from the middle of the fourteenth century and preserved today in the Commerzbibliothek in Hamburg. Now extremely rare, some twenty of these 'sea books' appeared in Amsterdam, Antwerp, Copenhagen, Lubeck, London and Leiden during the sixteenth century. Detailed large-scale charts drawn by Scandinavian cartographers had indeed been devoted to the Scandinavian countries in the first half of the sixteenth century, like the *Carta marina et descriptio septentrionalium terrarum*, by Olaus Magnus, published in Venice in 1539, or the *Caerte van Oostland*, by the pilot Cornelis Anthonisz, published in Amsterdam in 1543 and best known now through the Italian chart of Francisco Camocio (1562). However these charts, more topographical than hydrographical in content, had little influence on contemporary nautical cartography, which remained a predominantly southern craft until the last quarter of the sixteenth century.

The great turning point in Dutch marine cartography occurred in 1584-1585, with the publication in Leiden of the *Spielghel der Seevaerdt*, compiled by a pilot from Enkhuizen, Lucas Janszoon Waghenaer. This collection of forty-four nautical charts of the European shores of the Atlantic and the Baltic—drawn to a scale of 1:370,000 and accompanied by profiles of coasts and precise instructions—testifies to the efforts made by the inhabitants of northern Europe to construct charts of their coasts for themselves and to stop using charts drawn by Mediterranean or Portuguese cartographers. This chart by the Jansz brothers is an example of this tendency.

In addition, the chart gives an account of Dutch voyages to the freezing waters of the Arctic (1594-1596) in search of a Northeast Passage, which they hoped would allow them to reach the China coast by a faster route than the one taken via the Cape of Good Hope by the Portuguese and Spaniards. The Dutch were under the delusion that these northern waters would be free of the ice and icebergs that finally overcame the resistance of Barentsz on his third voyage, exhausted by an involuntary ten months' wintering at latitude 76°7′N. Only the southwest coast of Novaya Zemlya, sighted by Barentsz and his companions, is shown here: the vellum comes to an end at 74°N, which prevents it from representing all the results of the voyage (Bear Island, Spitsbergen, the anchorage at Ice Haven) that can be seen on Barentsz's posthumous chart *(Delineatio cartae navigationum per Batavos)*, which appeared in Huygen Van Linschoten's reprint of the *Itinerario* (The Hague, 1598). Judging by the partial nomenclature of Novaya Zemlya and the outline of Iceland, the Jansz brothers were probably inspired by it. Their chart is thus later than 1598 and may be datable to circa 1610 like the planisphere *Nova orbis terrarum geographica ac hydrographica*, which they constructed at Edam in the same year. Moreover, this chart bears many resemblances in its geographical limits and outlines to the chart of the coasts of Europe drawn by another Edam cartographer, Corneliz Doetsz, dated 1610 and now preserved in the Bibliothèque Royale in Brussels.

Marten and Harmen Jansz's chart of the coasts of Europe was revised by Abraham Goos in 1620 and published in 1621, thereby gaining a wide public.

71

ATLANTIC OCEAN
by Pierre de Vaulx (1613)
1 vellum leaf, illuminated ms, 681 × 958 mm
Paris, B.N.: Cartes et Plans, S.H. Archives no. 6

This nautical chart by Pierre de Vaulx looks like a miniature painting and was very probably made for the edification of a prince, but an informed knowledge of the regions of incipient colonization in America has provided it with several original features.

The Atlantic Ocean *(La R. Occeane)* is named in gold letters, now partly effaced, to the south of the West Indies and Cape Verde Islands. This was the trade-winds route followed since the beginning of the seventeenth century by Spanish galleons, Portuguese vessels and French and English privateers.

Although we are now into the seventeenth century, this is still a plane chart. The network of rhumb-lines has eight roses, seven of which have human faces. A very large one, deep blue and gold, situated in Peru opposite Lima *(Lyme Citté des Roys)*, may well symbolize the sun of the Incas.

The allegiances of the newly discovered lands are indicated by beautiful escutcheons: the shield of France appears in North America *(Nouvelle France)* and in Brazil *(La France Antarticque)*. The shield of Castile, surmounted by a helmet and encircled by a rich baroque medallion, is located in the centre of South America with another Spanish shield above it in *Noeufves Espaignes*. There is no sign of the Portuguese colours.

The abundant nomenclature in America is French. In Acadia settlements are indicated: *Port de Monsieur du Mont* (1603), after Champlain's companion; *le fort des français* (1612); *port Rossignol* and *port mouton* and the *cap de la Hève*,—all visited by Champlain and de Monts in 1604—were to become the focal points for the colonization of Acadia under Razilly, around 1630. They had existed before their annexation by the crown, being visited by fishermen and fur traders, acting as agents for the trading companies. The outlines of Newfoundland are accurate for the period, and the names on the east coast are thickly distributed: this was the coast visited by fishermen from Saint Malo fishing for cod to dry—*la côte malouine*. The Gulf of Mexico is accurately recorded; the iconography is traditional.

Pierre de Vaulx belonged to a family related to some of the leading citizens of Le Havre. It seems that his father (a native of Pont-Audemer) established himself in Havre de Grâce (Le Havre), attracted by the privileges bestowed on the inhabitants of this new town. He was probably the man who obtained permission from Francis I to build 'a ship of 500 or 600 livres'. Pierre's elder brother Jacques was a cosmographer and pilot before him, employed in the king's name at Le Havre. A manuscript by Jacques, dated 1583, is preserved in the Bibliothèque Nationale; *Les Premières Oeuvres* is a scholarly summary of contemporary nautical science, illustrated with beautiful miniature charts. The younger brother Pierre seems to have been less of a scholar; he employed a rudimentary method of projection for this chart. Pierre de Vaulx's empirical knowledge, however, bears witness to an extensive acquaintance with the shores of the 'ocean river', based on experience.

72

JAPANESE CHART OF THE INDIAN OCEAN
(ca. 1613)
1 vellum leaf, illuminated ms, 965 × 630 mm
Tokyo National Museum, Division I, no. 784

77

JAPANESE CHART OF THE NIPPONESE
ARCHIPELAGO
(ca. 1625)
1 leaf vellum ms, 915 × 690 mm
Tokyo National Museum, Division I, no. 783

The Portuguese first visited the coasts of Japan around 1541-1543, when Antonio da Mota, Francisco Zeimoto and Antonio Peixoto landed on the little island of Tanegashima to the south of Kyushu. This marked the beginning of Luso-Japanese commercial relations that were to last for almost a century (1543-1636) until the archipelago finally closed its doors to all foreign incursions and retreated into an almost total national isolation that was to last for more than two centuries: only the Dutch and the Chinese would still be tolerated at Nagasaki. The Portuguese mercantile marine had sprung into action immediately, since eighty ships managed to reach the Japanese archipelago in less than fifty years (between 1543 and 1590).

The Japanese were neither indifferent nor in the least passive in the face of western penetration. In 1587 Shogun Hideyoshi invited merchants from Kyoto, Sakai and Nagasaki to obtain a licence to trade with overseas countries: South China, Tonkin, Annam, Cochin China, Cambodia, Siam, Malacca, Formosa, the Philippines, Borneo and the Moluccas. The ships designated for this officially sponsored trade were called *go-shuinsen* and sported a magnificent vermilion jib as their emblem. Thus, in the first third of the seventeenth century, more than three hundred of these licensed ships sailed the waters of Southeast Asia, and Japanese quarters grew up in Manila, Tourane, Haiphong, Phnom Penh and Ayuthia. The birth of the Japanese portolan chart dates from this period and was to last as long as Japan remained open to the outside world—until 1636. Only twenty-one examples of this priceless nautical cartography appear to be extant today (see also no. 77).

There do not seem to have been any truly Japanese sea charts before the end of the sixteenth century; a few rutters of the portolano variety, but devoid of charts, were apparently sufficient for coastal trade within the archipelago from island to island. On long-distance commercial sea lanes, however, the need for a chart became more pressing. Although it was forbidden, sometimes on pain of death, it was not unusual for the *go-shuin* ships to take Portuguese pilots on board, since their superior maritime skills had not escaped the attention of those in charge of the new trade. Through them the Japanese mariner familiarized himself with the use of the compass, the astrolabe and the rhumb-line chart, and thanks to the prodigious capacity for assimilation of the Japanese, it was not long before these merchant ships were carrying on board Japanese versions of the Portuguese portolan chart. The best example of this collaboration is provided by an inhabitant of Nagasaki, Ikeda Yoyemon, who said that he had learnt his astronomical navigation from the Portuguese pilot Manoel Gonzalo, in whose company he had made two crossings to the Philippines. His rutter provides many details on the maritime knowledge of the period.

Two types of Japanese charts were born during this brief period. The first was a chart of the Indian Ocean and Southeast Asia absolutely similar to the corresponding Portuguese chart except for an improvement in the outline of Korea, Formosa and Japan: the chart of 1613 reproduced here is a striking example of this type; the style of its cartouches for the scales and the illuminated compass roses are indeed completely Portuguese.

The second type of chart is concerned with Japan proper. These portolan charts are no longer copies but original works executed by the Japanese themselves. The second chart (no. 77) from the Tokyo National Museum—a large-scale delineation of the outline of the Nipponese archipelago, whose latitudes are nearly correct—shows that the Japanese had acquired a skilful command of astronomical navigation before 1625.

This curious Luso-Japanese cartography seems to have been forgotten in Japan itself, however; and its influence only remains visible on a few later Portuguese charts (for instance No. 86) that may have benefited from the astronomical surveys carried out during this collaboration.

73

ATLANTIC CHART
by Domingos Sanches (1618)
1 vellum leaf, illuminated ms, 950 × 840 mm
Paris, B.N.: Cartes et Plans, Rés. Ge AA 568

Drawn on vellum, with the signature *Dominguos Sanches a fes em Lisboa anno 1618* inscribed on and below a pink and gold scroll in the bottom right-hand corner, this Atlantic chart by Domingos Sanches is the only known work by this cartographer. The extensive decoration on the chart probably justifies the assumption that it was never used on board ship. The many delicately coloured miniatures on both land and sea make this marine document a harmonious mural painting that recalls the extent of the maritime and colonial power of Spain and Portugal at the beginning of the seventeenth century, when they were united under the sceptre of Philip III of Spain, the grandson of Charles V. Twelve Spanish and Portuguese shields or escutcheons indicate political allegiances, and six ships and caravels flying Iberian flags sail the oceans, while a Mediterranean galley is shown off Alexandria in Egypt. The towns occupied by the Spaniards in South America: *Potochi*, Lima *(Ciudad de los Reys)*, *Quito* or the Portuguese trading-posts on the African coast at *Anguola*, the *Congo*, Elmina *(Mina)* and *Quiloa* are depicted in somewhat fanciful bird's-eye views. The author has filled the geographical void of the interior of the African continent with scenes of native life: in Guinea two women are pounding millet, in Monomotapa a Bantu warrior is shooting with a bow and arrow. Nor is local fauna omitted—the continent is decorated with illustrations of an ostrich, camels, elephants and monkeys.

However, the most surprising thing about the decoration is the tinted drawings of various patron saints.

In the American northwest, the Virgin and Child appear in a frame adorned with flowers. In the top right-hand corner. *S. Barbora* stands near her tower, a palm frond in her hand. To the south, on the ocean, six other figures are painted, among whom we can recognize Saint Benedict *(S. Beto)*, Saint Joseph *(S. Josep)* and the Infant Jesus, Saint Stephen *(S. Estevão)* and Saint Leonard *(S. Lionardo)*. A. Cortesão believes that the beginning of the decline in Portuguese sea power, which especially at that time was suffering from numerous shipwrecks and almost continously in conflict with Dutch competitors, may have favoured a renewal of religious fervour among mariners that was reflected in cartography by the representation of such a large number of intercessors.

In this respect, this chart by Domingos Sanches—a sort of geographical votive offering—can be compared with the works of Antonio Sanches and Pascal Roiz and forms with them a highly individual school in Portuguese cartography of the first decades of the seventeenth century.

74

ATLAS OF THE MEDITERRANEAN
by Charlat Ambrosin (1620)
5 vellum leaves, illuminated ms in a Lavallière morocco binding, 470 × 670 mm
Leaf 4: *Sicily, Malta, Gulf of Tunis, Southern Sardinia*
Paris, B.N.: Cartes et Plans, Rés. Ge DD 2018

The first specimens of Marseilles hydrography are contemporary with the commercial expansion of that port in the direction of the ports of the Levant in the sixteenth century. The few examples of this period to survive seem to have been inspired by Venetian prototypes and although the Catalan tradition imported from Messina and Naples by the Olivas also had an influence, we still find charts by a Marseilles cartographer being signed in Venice until the 1660's.

It may be to these influences that the only surviving atlas by Charlat Ambrosin owes its Italian nomenclature, delicate script and the style of its decoration. The author did, however, sign it in French on the last leaf *(A Marseille, par Charlat Ambrosin, l'an 1620)* and dedicated it to the young King Louis XIII, whose royal arms, crowned initial and emblem of lilies are stamped on the binding. In a subtly coloured frame—successively blue, violet, sea-green, red and almond-green—the five charts of the atlas are bordered by a frieze, in which lilies, trophies and helmets alternate with the monogram of Louis de Bourbon *(LDB)*.

The atlas begins and ends with a 'normal portolano': the first one is classically constructed on a network of rhumb-lines; the second, more unusually, is on a square grid. In between, three larger scale charts show, successively, the Atlantic and western Mediterranean—where a vignette of Marseilles occupies a large space—the *ARCHIPELAGO* and part of the eastern Mediterranean and finally the central Mediterranean or, more precisely, the strategic area between the two basins of the Mediterranean from Tunisia to southern Italy: the fortified frontier between Christianity and Islam, but also a necessary passage for east-west trade. In short this chart provides the point of departure, destination and principal ports of call for the polaccas, tartanes and other Provençal ships then sailing to the Levant.

After ships of heavy tonnage had had their day, small sailing ships (about 45 tons on average) had their turn in the Mediterranean. Marseilles specialized in such ships, where everything was sacrificed to speed. One of these galleons or vessels—the latter visited the great Levantine ports, whereas 'barks' covered the route to Candia, the Archipelago and Morea—can be seen sailing between Sardinia *(I. de Sardaigne)* and the Maghreb coast *(Barbaria)*. According to Deshayes de Courmenin, who made the trip in 1621, the voyage from Marseilles cost about 12 crowns and, with a favourable wind and no attack by pirates, took fifteen to twenty days to Constantinople and less than a month to Syria. Two routes were possible after leaving Cagliari *(Calari)*: one passing north of Sicily, and calling at Palermo and Messina; and another one, longer but more frequented, calling at Trapani and Malta. The cartographer, who located these ports on the chart fairly accurately, indicating good moorings in Malta, the bays of *Marsa Muset* and *Marza Sirocho* and the upper and lower towns of Trapani *(Trapano Monte* and *Trapano)* together with the dangerous approach to the Aegadian Islands, thought it necessary to go further into detail and provided perspective views of them in a cartouche at the head of the document. The orientation of the town views is shown by a little compass (-S [Sirocho] at *Palerme In Sicilia*, P [Ponente] at *Messina in Sicilia*, ⊕ [Levante] at *Trapani In Sicilia*, P [Ponente] again at Malta *[Malta Isula])* and emphasizes the situation of each port. The increased scale has enabled some names to be added: the islands outside *Trapano Novo* are all named; in Malta the little fort of *St Elme* is shown commanding the access to the two bays, as well as the quarters of the old town (Borgo) protected by the forts of *St Micael* and *St Angelo*.

Knowledgeable as he is about the coasts, the author has not neglected the hinterland, where rivers and market towns are indicated together with conventional drawings of hills for the relief—only Mount Etna, spitting fire, is clearly identified as *Monte Albano*.

The nomenclature in the hinterland and the nature of the outlines suggest that the source was contemporary engraved charts: indeed, from its layout to the choice of the framed views of ports, this leaf of the atlas closely resembles a chart of Sicily in the first printed atlas of the Mediterranean, *Caerboeck van de Midlantsche zee*, published by Willem Barentsz in Amsterdam in 1595. Ambrosin may either have used the same—predominantly Italian—sources, or more probably, used Barentsz's atlas directly, for it was published in French in 1599.

75

THE PACIFIC
by Hessel Gerritsz (1622)
2 vellum leaves, illuminated ms assembled into a chart, 1070 × 1410 mm
Paris, B.N.: Cartes et Plans, S.H. Archives no. 30

The author of this decorative chart was born in 1580 at Assum, a small village in northern Holland. Beginning as an apprentice engraver to Willem Janszoon Blaeu, Hessel Gerritsz set up on his own account in Amsterdam, where he rapidly acquired a great reputation as a cartographer. In 1617, he was appointed to the post (which he kept until his death in 1633) of cartographer to the Dutch East India Company *(Vereenigde Oost Indische Compagnie)*, usually known by its initials, V.O.C. Being responsible for an official hydrographic service, Gerritsz followed the progress of maritime discovery carefully, constantly anxious to keep the nautical charts for outward bound navigators up to date. Since the charts were supposed to remain secret, they were left in manuscript.

This chart of the Pacific, now preserved in the archives of the French navy in Paris, is one of the finest pieces Gerritsz produced. The richness of its appearance does not detract from the accuracy of its information. All the coasts and islands shown are those sighted during the sixteenth century by the Portuguese and Spaniards and, more recently, by the Dutch and English. To the west the coasts of Korea *(Coray)*, China *(Sina)* as far as Guangzhou (Canton) and western Borneo are located with an astonishing overall precision. Out to sea, going from north to south, the chart indicates Japan *(Iapan)*, with a still uncertain outline, as well as the two archipelagos of the Philippines *(I. Filipinas)* and the Marianas *(I. de las velas o de los Ladrones)*, which were jointly baptized the *Archipelago de S. Lazaro* by Magellan in 1521. Further south, Celebes, the Moluccas, eastern Indonesia and the northern coast of New Guinea appear in their positions. To the east, opposite the coast of Asia, the western coast of America is delineated from the province of *Quibira* (discovered by Coronado in 1540) in the north of *California*, down to Tierra del Fuego. Between the two shores, the titles *Mar del Sur, Mar Pacifico* are inscribed in large gold-leaf capitals. The fleets of the Dutch East India Company depicted off the coast of Peru and north of the tropic of Cancer may perhaps refer to those of Olivier Van Noort (1601-1604) or Joris van Spilberghen (1617), the first Dutchmen to sail around the world. The position of the ships probably indicates, although still only approximately, the course to follow when sailing from the American coast to the Asiatic archipelagos. At the foot of the document, a tempest scene recalls the terrible gales which beset the fleets of Loaysa (1526), Drake (1576), Hawkins (1594) and Mahu de Cordes (1598-1600) when they entered the Pacific, the account of which still makes terrifying reading. These evocative illustrations fill the immense stretch of water which, in 1622, is far from having revealed all its secrets.

Australia is the largest piece missing, and yet an inscription on the left near the tropic of Capricorn mentions the voyage of a certain Captain Willem Janszoon. In 1605 he set sail in the 'Duifken', or 'Little Dove', bound for New Guinea. He sailed along its southern coast, then continuing on a SSE course, came upon an unknown land between latitudes 9° and 14°S, which he did not suspect of being one of the shores of a new continent (present-day Cape York in fact), where he put in. This constitutes the first authenticated landing of a European ship in Australia. On this chart by Hessel Gerritsz, the newly discovered land, through a pardonable confusion in view of the period, bears the name of *Nueva Guinea*.

Across the ocean, we can also follow the itinerary of a voyage made by Lemaire and Schouten, whose course is outlined by the cartographer. They were the first to round Cape 'Hoorn', which they named after the town of Schouten's birth; they rested at *Juan Fernández* Island, then crossed the Pacific in a northwesterly direction, passing through the Tuamotus, Samoa, Tonga and the *Salomon* Islands (near which, on the chart, we can see Polynesian pirogues). Then they skirted the northern coast of New Guinea, which they called *Custe van de Papuas*, before reaching the Moluccas and then Batavia. To assist the navigator, a network of rhumb-lines centred on the equator covers the ocean: the central compass rose and other secondary roses emphasize its outlines. On the margins of the chart a latitude scale in constant degrees is graduated from 60°N to 60°S; the longitudes, on the other hand, are not indicated—the cartographer remains uncertain of the exact dimensions of this oceanic hemisphere.

Up-to-date with the latest discoveries, Hessel Gerritsz's chart is also particularly ornate. In the top right-hand corner are painted the portraits of the discoverers of the Pacific: *Núñez de Balboa*, the first European to see the Southern Sea with his own eyes (1513); *Fernão de Magellan*, who after a hazardous voyage lasting thirteen months, sailed out into a great ocean that, by way of contrast with the dangers he had just endured, he called the 'Pacific' (28 November 1520) and *Jacob Lemaire*, who rounded Tierra del Fuego in 1616. In the centre there is a small planisphere, whose projection and outlines differ from those of the main chart: it is constructed on waxing latitude. California is represented on it as an island, and a maritime passage across North America joins the two oceans. These errors of outline had been current in Europe since the publication in London in 1625 of Henry Brigg's book, *A Treatise of the Northwest Passage to the South Sea*.

Finally, on the left, a baroque cartouche contains the scales, and at the bottom, allegorical figures encircle the signature and date. The latter may have been retouched in 1634 by Willem Janszoon Blaeu, successor to Hessel Gerritsz in the post of cartographer to the Dutch East India Company; he may also have been the author of the planisphere. A gilded trompe-l'oeil frame, on which the four cardinal points are inscribed, completes this famous marine instrument of the Dutch cartographic school.

A similar chart was presented in the following year to what was termed the Nassau fleet, which was setting out on the same route under the command of Jacques l'Hermitte and Geen Huyghen Schapenham. On their return, Gerritsz published the account of their crossing (1625-1626).

76

AEGEAN SEA
by Alvise Gramolin (1624)
1 leaf, illuminated ms, 1070 × 650 mm
Paris, B.N.: Cartes et Plans, Rés. Ge B 550

The Archipelago, or Aegean Sea, constitutes a distinct maritime unit, the chief islands of which were held by Genoa and Venice in the Middle Ages. Since the very first atlases it has been given an individual treatment in nautical cartography, often being drawn to a larger scale than the other Mediterranean basins.

Alvise di Nicolo Gramolin, a little known artist of the first half of the seventeenth century—his catalogued works span the years between 1612 and 1630—seems to have taken a particular interest in reproducing it. He has done so without originality but with meticulous care and a well-tried aptitude for decoration, of which this chart (formerly in the collection of Santarem and then of the orientalist Miller) is a fine example.

It has been signed twice: in Roman characters at the top near the Turkish tents is inscribed: *1624 IO ALVISE GRAMOLIN FECI LANO*; in the lower left-hand corner, under the oblique scroll bearing a distance scale, in small letters, the author has specified his Venetian origin: *Io Alvise Gramolin da Venetia feci lano 1624*.

Gramolin has assembled on this document information gathered from several sources. From the portolan chart that provided the coastal nomenclature he has also borrowed an ancient convention, confined to the Archipelago, of circumscribing it between the names of the four cardinal points, written on the margins —*SEPTENTRIO, ORIENS, MERIDIES, OCCIDENS*—and organizing it along the north-south axis of a network of rhumb-lines that defines the centre. This time, therefore, the top of the chart coincides with north, where the magnificent thirty-two-point compass rose is surmounted by an elegant fleur-de-lis.

The delineation of the two largest islands of the Archipelago, Crete *(ISOLA DE CANDIA)* and Euboea (anonymous), whose scale and orientation are only approximately compatible with the rest of the chart, is more in keeping with the tradition of the *isolari* or chorographic charts. The relief is painted in elevation, accurately so in the case of Crete, still in Venetian hands. Between the green and maroon hillocks of the mountain chains, the artist has found space for plains (painted yellow and streaked with red) traversed by rivers. No toponyms are given, but it is easy to recognize, among others, the Messara, stretching from east to west at the foot of Mount Ida, with a circular symbol that is present in all cartography of the island from the fifteenth century and recalls the labyrinthine lair and the legend of the Minotaur. Euboea, on the other hand, is too vast and its relief poorly located. Some red belfries indicate towns, among them *Negroponte*, joined by a bridge *(Lo ponte)* to the continent.

Finally, the author has borrowed from engraved cartography (possibly from Ortelius where they appear in an identical form) the names of the gulfs and the few towns depicted inland in vignettes in vivid shades of blue, orange and violet. Apart from ancient Troy *(TROGIA)*, penned in a different script, these are probably the final stages on the routes of the caravans that supplied Levantine towns, and they are slightly magnified in the drawing. In Anatolia, *burnoa* (Aydin, in the valley of the Maeander?) and *securio* (Bursa?) near the Sea of Marmara are named. In Macedonia and Thrace, we see *Sistrocopista*, *Asera* (Serrai in the valley of the Struma?) and *Caragusa*.

At this time, the Archipelago had long since become the crossroads of Turkish power: tents, oriflammes and shields proclaim their sovereignty as far as *MOREA*. Venice had made many concessions in order to preserve this market and deserved being called 'concubine of the Turk' by the Spaniards. Now, in the first quarter of the seventeenth century, Venice was in a fair way to losing control of the Aegean to her western rivals: the French and, above all, the Dutch and English. The two latter were flooding the Archipelago with their 'mahout' and 'londrin' cloth, submerging Venetian drapery in its traditional markets of Smyrna *(Lesmire)* and *Constantinople (COSTANTINPOLI)*. Worse still, Dutch and English ships equipped with powerful artillery had invaded the eastern Mediterranean, and the Venetians themselves had begun to charter them, judging the foreign ships more capable than their own of keeping the Barbary corsairs at arm's length.

As its cartography indicates, at a difficult moment in its history, Venice was still able to shine, but could no longer innovate.

77

JAPANESE CHART OF THE NIPPONESE ARCHIPELAGO (ca. 1625)
See: No. 72

78

HYDROGRAPHIC DESCRIPTION OF FRANCE
by Jean Guérard (1627)
2 vellum leaves, coloured ms assembled into a chart, 1205 × 810 mm
Paris, B.N.: Cartes et Plans, S.H. Archives no. 12

Like many of his colleagues, Jean Guérard was both pilot and hydrographer. His voyages took him from Dieppe to Brazil, where he led expeditions in the northeast of the country and to the island of Maranhão, when La Ravardière and Razilly organized their expedition in 1612. Later Guérard sailed to the Red Sea and studied magnetic variation there. As early as 1615, he was entrusted with teaching hydrography at Dieppe and examining pilots, as Desceliers had done fifty years before. In 1627, Guérard appears on pay sheets together with other experienced pilots who have been instructed to 'describe the coasts and elevations of the islands of France'. This famous Dieppe hydrographer has left us seven charts on vellum and a manuscript describing the coasts of France from Calais to Saint Jean de Luz.

This chart of the coasts of France is a very beautiful parchment, with the arms of President de Lozon, counseller to the Paris Parlement and later president of the

Grand Council. A streamer bears the signature and date, as well as an enigmatic inscription *(Tempora navali fulgent rostrata corona 1627)* borrowed from Virgil's *Aeneid* (VIII, 684): 'His forehead gleams, wreathed with the naval crown'. The date may be a reference to Richelieu's campaign against Protestants, which culminated in Razilly's victory over the English at the Ile de Ré in October, 1627. Another streamer declares: *Ergo Maria invia Gallis*, that is to say, the sea is closed to the French, or Gauls. These statements remain something of a mystery.

However, the interest of this portolan chart lies elsewhere: soundings are given in greater numbers than on Waghenaer's first nautical atlas, translated into French in 1600 *Le nouveau miroir* ('The Mariner's Mirrour'), in which the coasts of the west are preceded by soundings. That nautical rutter may have inspired Guérard. But here the soundings are complemented by a curious representation of the undercurrents explained in an inscription on the right of the folio: twelve lines of shoals looking like rivers are indicated by the letters *A* to *M*. From St George's Channel to the Gironde, they stand out individually: for example, *L* shows the current penetrating from the sea to the mouth of the Loire; the sea bed was composed, according to the inscription, of 'coarse coral sand on shore'. South of the Isle of Ushant *(Ile d'Ouessant)* the sea bed is composed of 'coarse red gravel, pebbles and mud'. This analytical precision is novel for its period.

The collection of twenty-three charts in Waghenaer's atlas (a basic tool for European sailors until the appearance of the *Neptune françois* in 1693) gives different soundings from the ones shown here. It is reasonable to assume that the description of the sea bed is more accurate than the figures given for the soundings: it was easier to gather samples of the sea bed from a boat than to measure the depth of the sea with a hand-held lead and line—that rudimentary system was far too prone to error.

Another chart similar to this one and dated the same year contains an inscription describing the 'ports, harbours and roadsteads of the kingdom of France'. There is an interesting reference to Dieppe: 'In the said Dieppe, there is a good harbour and a very good roadstead for anchoring ships; ships of 400 tons can enter there at high tide for the space of three or four days, from the thirteenth to the eighteenth days of the lunar month, and from the first to the fourth; a number of great ships go from there on all sorts of voyages.... There are also thirty to forty ships, each of which go on two voyages fishing for herring off the coasts of Scotland and England. There are several little boats that go fishing for fresh fish. It is a very good place to station ships to protect the coasts from pirates because of its good roadstead.'

This quotation provides a comprehensive picture of the volume of trade out of Dieppe at the beginning of the seventeenth century. Although the analysis covers all the ports of Normandy from Le Tréport to Pontorson, no other port is shown to such advantage as Dieppe.

This detailed description of the coasts of France may be considered the first serious comparative study of the ports of Normandy.

79

ATLANTIC OCEAN (NORTH)
by Hessel Gerritsz (ca. 1628)
1 vellum leaf, coloured ms, 1120 × 870 mm
Paris, B.N.: Cartes et Plans, Rés. Ge DD 2987 (no. 9648)

This is already a modern chart, as its title makes plain: *Carte nautique des bords de Mer du Nort, et Norouest, mis en longitude, latitude et en leur route, selon les rins de vent* ('nautical chart of the shores of the North and Northwest seas, showing their longitude, latitude and direction, according to the points of the compass'). It is constructed on Mercator's projection, which is still of such practical usefulness today that it is employed by all modern naval services. At the time of this chart, Mercator's projection was not yet widely used, and it is indeed rather surprising that it took mariners nearly half a century to recognize the advantages afforded them by this method of projection. The longitude scale, graduated from 305° to 70°E, appears at the top and bottom of the document. In the centre, on the prime meridian that passes through Corvo (Azores), the waxing-latitude scale is graduated from 30° to 80°N. The ocean is covered with loxodromic lines along which a course could be steered. To the west of the meridian the chart shows western Greenland and the coast of America from Baffin Bay to Virginia. To the east of the meridian, apart from eastern Greenland, appear Spitsbergen, Iceland, Great Britain and the coast of Europe from *Finmarck* to Gibraltar. As on all charts constructed on waxing latitude, the area of the northern regions is exaggerated in comparison with the southern regions, which explains, at least in part, the enormous size attributed to Greenland.

The author, Hessel Gerritsz, who was cartographer to the Dutch East India Company, was also cartographer to the Dutch West India Company from its creation in 1621. In this capacity he was kept informed, and took due note of, the maritime expeditions at the end of the sixteenth century and the beginning of the seventeenth that sought to discover a Northwest Passage. Explorers set out from Denmark, England and Holland to find a way through a supposedly ice-free Arctic and reach Japan, China and the Spice Islands more directly than by following the southern routes via the Straits of Magellan or the Cape of Good Hope. The outlines and nomenclature of the chart by Gerritsz faithfully reflect the still recent voyages of Martin

Frobisher (1576-1578), John Davis (1583-1587), George Waymouth (1602), James Hall (1605-1607), Henry Hudson (1607-1610), Thomas Button (1612), William Baffin (1615-1616) and William Hawkeridge (1625). It is astounding to see Frobisher Bay *(M. Frobishers Straith)* appear in southeast Greenland, when in actual fact the explorer had reached Baffin Island and discovered a gulf situated a little to the north of the Hudson Strait, later named *Meta Incognita* (Unknown Goal) by the queen of England. Frobisher had taken Mercator's chart along with him and so interpreted his landfall in accordance with the delineation it gave of the North Atlantic.

The completely fictitious concepts of this representation had been borrowed by Mercator from a chart published in Venice in 1558 to illustrate a hypothetical voyage made by the two Zeno brothers around 1380. This erroneous location was to be perpetuated in cartography for nearly two centuries; the presence of the island of *Frislandt*, situated to the southwest of Iceland on the chart, was also the result of mediaeval fantasies.

The fact that Baffin Land was an island was still not known; on the other hand, in the bay of the same name, Gerritsz already indicates the possible existence of passages *(Sir James Lancasters Sound, Alderman Jones Sound, Thomas Smiths Sound)* without suspecting that this route would be adopted by Roald Amundsen on the first navigation of the Northwest Passage three centuries later (1903–1906). The outline of Hudson Bay is still incomplete; it did not achieve its definitive form until the explorations of Captains Luke Fox and Thomas James (1631-1632), which combined Button's and Hudson's discoveries and definitely proved that there was no possible western outlet from Hudson's Bay. Hessel Gerritsz's chart was made before these two voyages. The fact that its title is in French suggests that this chart may have been made for the French historiographer Théodore Godefroy, with whom the Flemish cartographer corresponded. In any case, it has been in France since the eighteenth century and comes from the collection of the geographer Bourguigon d'Anville. The few paintings—warships, Eskimo kayaks and a fair number of whales, especially near Spitsbergen where hunters found them in abundance—provide a sober illustration for the mapping of these marine expeditions that were always difficult and sometimes fraught with danger. As well as prodigious riches (the immense shoals of fish, thousands of whales, seals, walruses and billions of birds), voyages in these northern seas had other revelations in store: 'The seamen who attempted them discovered by bitter experience the unpredicted difficulties of navigation in high latitudes—the immense power of pressure ice, the great rise and fall of tides, the enormous range of compass variation' (cf. Cumming, Skelton, Quinn).

Hessel Gerritsz's chart was revised by Jacob Aertz Colom and Dirck Rembrandt van Nierop, who published it in the second half of the seventeenth century.

80

NORTHERN OCEAN
by Jean Guérard (1628)
Vellum leaves, coloured ms assembled into a chart, 860 × 1280 mm
Paris, B.N.: Cartes et Plans, S.H. Archives no. 39

This chart by Jean Guérard shows a particular interest in the coasts of northern Europe. Contemporary with the chart by Hessel Gerritsz (No. 79), it provides new information from the French explorers of these cold waters. It can also be compared with a beautiful planisphere constructed by Guérard three years earlier in 1625.

It is a plane chart: its fine outlines, often half-effaced, are derived from important work by English and Dutch cartographers. Although the delineation was inspired by various sources, the nomenclature of the newly discovered lands is French. Points of French settlement are located, and the seven cartouches at the top and bottom of the chart, together with the outline of the coasts of the White Sea and the Arctic Sea, all indicate a deep curiosity about this region.

First of all comes Spitsbergen, called *Nievland*. As on Blaeu's chart (1629), only the southern part of the island is shown, but with gallicized names. The *P. des gars* preceded by an anchorage was a place frequented by Basque harpooners, as was the *R. De Kloeck*.

Having traditionally hunted whales in the Bay of Biscay, from the twelfth century (see Nos. 92, 97) the Basques followed them to Labrador and Spitsbergen. They served as auxiliaries to the Dutch: on Flemish ships, the head fisherman or *speksynder* took command when approaching Arctic waters; by tradition he was a Basque. One of them is known by name: Vrolicq of Saint Jean de Luz, a burgher of Le Havre by adoption. He fished off Spitsbergen as early as 1618 and inspired a chart of *France arctique* very similar to this one. Novaya Zemlya is partly indicated; to the east, where the rounded shape of the island is sketched, appears the *lieu ou hiverna les hollandais* ('the place where the Dutch wintered'). It was there that Barentsz, who had discovered Spitsbergen, spent the winter with seventeen of his companions in 1596. Following the coast in the south, the *ysles de l'admirauté* appear and the *baie de Dieppe*, which is present on many Dutch charts and indicates the establishment of fisherman from Dieppe on this great island.

The outline goes as far east as the sketch of the Yamal Peninsula, indicating a special interest in the coasts of Russia and Lapland. Moreover, the cartouches arranged at the top and bottom of the chart provide information on this sea lane that Guérard wanted to make better known. They depict anchorages, all situated between the North Cape of Norway and the furthest point of the White Sea gulf: the coast bordering what he calls *Murmanskoy More* and the *Mer Blanche* is now in Russian Lapland. Apart from the outlines of coasts and islands, the seven cartouches show anchorages that can be located on Guérard's main chart and on a modern chart. From north to south they are *Wardous*, now the Varanger Peninsula, the Cape of *Kegro*, the Isle of *Kildyn* and the entrance to the *Kola* River (the present site of the port of Murmansk), *Sueteno* (Bay of Sviatoi Nos), where salmon was fished, *Lombascoura* (Bay of Lumbovsk), the Archangel River with the town of the same name that was called *Saint Michel Archange* —the centre of trade between Russia and the west for a very long time.

Thus the chart marks the anchorages sighted along the coast, one of which—with its opportunities for salmon fishing—would provide some variety in the monotonous diet of these long-distance expeditions. But the charted territory does not stop here: it continues eastward to the region called *Bajda*, inspired, so it seems, by the chart of Russia engraved by Gerritsz in 1613, although the nomenclature is often gallicized and Guérard's own.

Beyond the strait of *Nassau* (Vaïgach) there is a good sketch of the Yamal Peninsula, although the mouth of the Ob is wrongly located. The name *Molgomzaja* is that of a new town, founded by the Russians in 1601, on the site of a former fur trading-post. Coastal navigation between Archangel and the Ob was practised by Russian seal and whale hunters and by fur trappers.

The English were the first to penetrate as far as the Kola coast in 1553, in search of a passage to China. The French also looked for the Northeast Passage, and some historians have credited Verrazano, who sailed from Dieppe in 1523, with reaching 'the confines of Norway which are at 71°'. In 1626 Richelieu was appointed governor of Le Havre, and a memorandum was submitted to him on the possibility of trading with Russia. In 1629 a commercial treaty was signed between the king of France and the tsar of Russia.

We can well imagine that Guérard, a famous Dieppe hydrographer appointed 'pilot' in 1635, would be anxious to participate in any plans for the expansion of Norman trade with Russia. He would then have combined his scholarly knowledge with the information supplied by Norman pilots who had visited the coast of Lapland and constructed as comprehensive a chart as possible on the route to follow to the furthest known reaches of the Arctic coast of Russia.

This well-used portolan chart bears witness to little-known activities of the Normans in the Arctic Ocean. At first glance the extent of the coastal survey on the document and the stress placed on the coasts of Russia and Lapland are striking. The sources are various, both foreign and Norman, but the undoubted effort involved in synthesizing them leads us to think that Guérard contributed to the expansion of the sea routes used by French pilots probing the obscure far north of the Russian Empire.

81-82

THE 'DUCHESS DE BERRY' ATLAS
(ca. 1628)
20 vellum leaves, illuminated ms, 270 × 380 mm
81   Leaf 1: *Planisphere*
82   Leaf 18: *Coast of Peru*
Paris, B.N.: Cartes et Plans, Rés. Ge FF 14409

These two leaves are taken from a collection of twenty charts, named the 'Duchess de Berry' Atlas after its former owner. The Bibliothèque Royale in Paris had the good fortune to acquire it in 1838 at the Château de Rosny sale. This is a nautical atlas in every sense of the term; only the coasts are shown and little attention is paid to the decoration. A comparison of similarities in the script and outline with an atlas of Brazil also preserved in Paris (Ms portugais no. 6), has led experts to attribute the 'Duchess de Berry' Atlas to the cartographer João Teixeira Albernas I, who described himself in 1627 as 'page of the bedchamber to His Majesty and his cosmographer for the kingdom of Portugal'.

81 *The Planisphere*
In its oval frame, with the title *TYPVS ORBIS TERRARVM* inscribed in gold letters on a purple band, the planisphere appears at the head of nineteen detailed nautical charts. The overall view of known coastlines is sandwiched between two continental land-masses of gigantic proportions: in the north the *Terra Incognita Septentrional*, already seen on the great Portuguese nautical planisphere of 1585 (No. 63), and in the south the *Terra Incognita Avstral*.

This fantastic representation is an eloquent illustration of the hypothesis concerning the Antipodes that was widespread in scientific circles at the beginning of the seventeenth century, and which had been widely popularized by the Flemish cosmographers Gerard Mercator and Abraham Ortelius. The austral continent was considered at the time to be a necessary counter-balance to the other terrestrial land-masses; even men of letters (not the least of them Montaigne) were party to this obsession, and the existence of this continent was so generally believed that some authors, like La Popelinière in his book *Les Trois Mondes*, suggested that expeditions should be sent there!

At the foot of South America, the outline of Tierra del Fuego and an *Estreito novo* ('new strait'), allow the atlas to be dated to around 1628. Several years after the two Dutchmen Lemaire and Schouten returned to Europe in 1621, Portuguese navigators went to verify the existence of the 'new' maritime passage depicted here.

82 *The Coast of Peru*
On the eighteenth leaf of the atlas, the chart of the

coasts of Peru offers a slightly stylized representation of what are now Ecuador and Peru. Out to sea Cocos Island (*J: de Coqos*) and the *Galapagos* archipelago are located with approximate longitudinal accuracy. This is a nautical chart reduced to the bare essentials: outlines, rhumbs, compass roses, scales and place-names along the coast—no mention is made of the Andes chain that no mariner could fail to observe from the sea. Inland, the only vignette in the whole atlas draws our attention to the site of Potosí *(Potossy)*, famous for its many silver mines discovered around 1540 by one of Francisco Pizarro's officers. A legend even claims that when an Indian made a fire, his hearth-stones melted! Potosí, one of the highest cities in the world (at an elevation of nearly 4,200 metres below the Cerro Rico) was, in the first third of the seventeenth century, the greatest city on the American continent. Charles V had conferred on it the title of Imperial City, and it had no less than 160,000 inhabitants at that time. The exhausting work in the mines was carried out by forced labour, or *mita*, with Indian conscripts, while at the Casa de la Moneda in the city itself a wretched workforce minted silver coin for the king of Spain. It is estimated that nearly seven million kilograms of silver crossed the Atlantic in just forty years (1560-1600). Today the former mining centre is simply a town in Bolivia, with just a quarter of the population it had three centuries ago and only a few fine monuments to recall its glorious past.

83

PROVENÇAL ATLAS OF THE MEDITERRANEAN
by Augustin Roussin (1633)
3 vellum leaves, illuminated ms, 277 × 394 mm
Leaf 3: *France, Spain, Maghreb*
Paris, B.N., Ms français 20122

Once he had persuaded Montmorency to relinquish his post of Admiral of France, Richelieu, who was created 'grand master, chief and superintendent of navigation and trade' in October 1626, instituted inquiries into the state of the coasts. The reports concerning the coast of Provence—of great strategic value in the struggle against Spain—soon multiplied. The reports of Brèves in 1626, Vitry in 1628 and 1631 and, above all, of Seguiran in 1633, all denounced the distressing vulnerability of this coastline. Against the Barbary pirates and the insolence of Spain, there were no fortified defences or war fleet: the whole Levant squadron consisted of three vessels, and the corsairs of Algiers were accustomed to visit Martigues to lay in supplies of slaves, while Spanish galleys on their way to Italy called in at Tour de Bouc with impunity. The merchant marine, which nevertheless continued its traffic with the commercial ports of the Levant, suffered greatly from this insecurity.

Spurred on by the Spanish menace, but prevented from acting until 1631 on account of the conflict between himself and the Duke de Guise who was governor of Próvence, Richelieu replaced the Duke by the Marshal de Vitry, accelerated the process of equipping the province and despatched several of his agents to work on the spot. Contemporary accounts describe them working on charts or having them made in order to determine the places to be fortified and the ports to which the forty-five warships, whose construction had been ordered in a *règlement* of 1628, should be attached.

It was no doubt in connection with this somewhat feverish activity displayed on the coasts of Provence between 1631 and 1634 that this chart was constructed by Augustin Roussin and dedicated to Cardinal Richelieu. This document, drafted in Provençal, is still preserved in its original red morocco binding with finely decorated boards and with, in its upper part, the dedication engraved in gold letters: *Pour: MONSEIGNG. R. Le .CARD. L.* Nearby, a note in cursive script, in black ink, indicates: *carte marine du détroit et mer du Levant* ('sea chart of the strait and sea of the Levant'). The atlas consists of three leaves of the same format, but the scale and orientation of the charts are different. The overall organization has not been left to chance. Proceeding from east to west—it begins with a chart of the Archipelago—the atlas also increases in size, and the author has taken special pains over the last leaf, on which he has placed his signature in the bottom right-hand corner: *Augustinus Roussinus me fecit Masailiae anno Domini 1633*. Above it are the arms of his patron: a gold coronet, cardinal's hat, three chevrons gules and a marine anchor.

The chart, constructed on a semi-network of rhumbs with only seven secondary centres, delineates the western basin of the Mediterranean from Toulon and Bougie *(Bugia)* as well as the shores of the Atlantic from Groningen *(Groninge)* to Cape Bojador *(c. Buxador)*. An infinite variety of colours—pink, blue, orange, red, yellow, white, gold, green—is employed to illuminate three great compass roses with imposing fleurs-de-lis and three distance scales inscribed in cartouches. On their respective territories, attractive figurines depict the three protagonists in the political situation that preoccupied Richelieu. The Cardinal was contemplating signing a treaty with the Dey of Algiers in order to put an end to privateering; the Dey wears a sabre at his side and is aiming his bow and arrow at the coasts of Europe. At his feet is a shield of gules with argent crescent. In Spain, King Philip IV holds a sceptre and is accompanied by a wild eagle. Finally, a crowned Louis XIII, wearing the collar of the Order of the Holy Spirit, stands near an azure shield from which the lilies of France are missing.

No archival document has yet revealed what Augustin Roussin's office was. The delicacy of execution and the importance of the client suggest, however, that he must have been a hydrographer of established reputation, possibly attached to the admiralty of Provence. At least one other atlas is known by Augustin Roussin; it is signed in French and bears the arms of the Duke of Savoy, who was governor of Provence and admiral of the Levantine seas in the sixteenth century.

84

UNIVERSAL HYDROGRAPHIC CHART
by Jean Guérard (1634)
1 vellum leaf, illuminated ms, 369 × 479 mm
Paris, B.N.: Cartes et Plans, S.H. Archives no. 15

This document bearing the arms of Richelieu appears to be a research document rather than a navigational instrument. Devoid of rhumbs but with an abundant nomenclature, it is more geographical than nautical.

Above all, it is scholarly: every means of measurement has been included, except for a distance scale. The waxing-latitude scale appears on the lateral borders and along the prime meridian, which is situated west of the Canary Islands. This variable scale makes this document a reduced-projection chart. Longitude is measured along the northern and southern margins and along the equatorial line from 180° to 360° and from 0° to 180°.

The climates and zones, notions inherited from antiquity, are arranged on either side of the equator, also in the margins. In addition, two spheres enable several problems of nautical astronomy to be solved. The sphere on the left is a calendar: from the periphery to the centre, the concentric circles represent the months, days, signs of the zodiac, phases of the moon and seasons. In its centre, starting from an individual central point, arcs of a circle illustrate the 23½° declination of the sun. On the right a sphere illustrates the known concepts of the terrestrial globe: meridian, equator, ecliptic, tropics and polar circles.

Even the frame of this planisphere contains a large quantity of physical and other scientific information, and the representation of the world refers to both recent discoveries and ancient beliefs. A few examples will show how this mental approach was innovatory and conservative at the same time. Thus Europe provides information on newly occupied lands: Novaya Zemlya and Spitsbergen are almost completely outlined, whereas the chart of 1628 (No. 80) only showed the west coast. In Spitsbergen, called *Terre Verte* ('Green Land'), is the 'French refuge or Port St Louis' *(refuge aux Français ou Port St Louis)*: the Basque and Norman fishermen under the direction of Vrolicq of Le Havre had obtained a monopoly of the whale-fishing in this area in 1632 but had been expelled by the Dutch and only retained a *refuge* named Saint Louis, in honour of Louis XIII. Later, in 1647, a Basque from Ciboure invented a technique for melting whale-oil on board ship; henceforth the huts and furnaces in these seasonal harbours were only used occasionally. Although the king of Denmark officially claimed possession of Spitsbergen, the Compagnie du Nord sent its whalers to this region until the end of the seventeenth century.

Off Ireland, two islets *(brasil* and *maidan)* are imaginary islands that many sixteenth-century portolan charts had placed there.

In Asia, although the Great Wall of China is well drawn, Marco Polo's name of Cathay *(Cathaya)* still appears in the north. Japan is foreshortened and oriented east-west, whereas the Philippines, the Sunda Islands and New Guinea are accurate on the whole. By contrast, the *terre australe incognve* ('unknown austral land') stretches the whole way along the bottom of the chart. Thus the belief in a southern continent merging in South America with Tierra del Fuego was still held in the middle of the seventeenth century and would last until Cook's circumnavigation of the globe in 1772-1775.

In North America, the French settlements of *Québec*, *Tadoussac* and *Port-Royal* are indicated, as well as the *habitation des hollandais* ('Dutch settlement') in the north of Virginia—this was to become the future New York, founded in 1612 by the Dutch as Nieuw Amsterdam. The latest English discoveries in Labrador, Hudson Bay, Button Bay and the Davis Strait are mentioned. On the other hand, an inscription placed level with the Great Lakes and to the north of California (shown here as an island) notes: *Lon croit qu'il y a passage de là au Japon* ('it is believed that there is a passage thence to Japan'). Sharing this belief, Champlain had advocated sailing up the Saint Lawrence to the Great Lakes, then down a river flowing out of a lake and 'in the south into the Vermejo or California Sea'. The passage was not found on the voyage of 1612; nevertheless, twenty years afterwards, Guérard still held tenaciously to the idea of a possible passage.

In South America, the Orinoco, still poorly known and rarely drawn, appears here with a fairly convincing outline. *Le c. de nord* indicates the attempt by some Rouen merchants to found a colony in Guiana from 1626 onwards.

Guérard shows himself to be receptive to the flow of discoveries, both French and foreign, as well as to modern forms of representation, while still remaining attached to earlier concepts.

85

INDIAN OCEAN
by João Teixeira Albernas I (1649)
1 vellum leaf, coloured ms, 845 × 705 mm
Paris, B.N.: Cartes et Plans, S.H. Portefeuille 213, div. 3 pièce 2

86

PACIFIC OCEAN
by João Teixeira Albernas I (1649)
1 vellum leaf, coloured ms, 890 × 740 mm
Paris, B.N.: Cartes et Plans, S.H. Portefeuille 177, div. 2 pièce 1

In 1644 a French scholar and collector of travellers' tales, Melchisédech Thévenot, published in Volume II of his *Relations de divers voyages curieux*, devoted to the East Indies, two engraved sea charts covering the coasts from the Cape of Good Hope to Japan. Only the first one bears the signature: 'João Teixeira, cosmographer to His Majesty made in Lisbon in the year 1649', but the two leaves—drawn to the same scale and of similar draughtsmanship—are clearly by the same hand. Thévenot boasted of having had them engraved from Portuguese manuscript charts brought back by a Frenchman, Monsieur de la Grand Maison, who had captured them from one of the king of Portugal's carracks. The charts reproduced here are the same two Portuguese originals brought back to Paris by Monsieur de la Grand Maison and preserved in the collections of the Service hydrographique of the French navy ever since.

They are the very same type of charts that were given to ships bound for the East Indies from Lisbon and following the route known as the 'carreira da India' from the time of Vasco da Gama to the age of the steamship. This route was appallingly dangerous: the number of shipwrecks in those days was staggering; around 1650 only one ship in three returned from the Indies. On the outward journey they were often overloaded with men, especially soldiers due to disembark at strongholds along the way. On the return journey they were weighed down with cargoes of spices, precious wood, furniture, indigo, bales of silk, lengths of cotton, cases of porcelain. The ships often set out too late: the carracks had to leave Lisbon at the very beginning of spring and round the Cape of Good Hope before the end of July, otherwise they would miss the westerly monsoon and have to winter on Mozambique Island, where malaria and yellow fever were endemic; sailors and passengers died there like flies. On the return journey, if the ships left Goa too late in the winter, they were caught by cyclones and dashed on to the East African coast. These were dangerous voyages, requiring the use of up-to-date sailing directions and the most accurate hydrographic charts available.

The charts shown here are the work of João Teixeira, a member of a cartographic family that had been established in Lisbon for several generations. The charts give careful outlines for following the spice route: the first chart extends from south of the Cape of Good Hope to the Sunda Strait, the second represents the coasts of Asia from Bengal to an imaginary strait, named the Strait of Anian *(Estreito de Anian)*, which foreshadows the one sighted a century later (1741) during the great expedition led by Vitus Bering and his lieutenant, Chirikov. The still mythical concept of a maritime passage separating the Asiatic and American continents crystallized in the imagination of Renaissance Humanists on reading the geographers of antiquity (Strabo, Pliny and Ptolemy) and the travels of Marco Polo and on comparing them with the accounts of recent Spanish and Portuguese discoveries, in particular those of Columbus, Balboa and Magellan. In a little book, *La Universale Descritione del mondo*, published in Venice in 1562 and now unfortunately lost, the cosmographer Giacomo Gastaldi voiced the opinion that this passage existed, and the cartographer Zaltieri introduced it to commercial cartography in 1566 ('Il Disegno del discoperto della Nova Franza', in *Atlas Lafreri*).

The insets on the margins of the two charts by Teixeira show the care taken in the depiction of trading-posts and ports of call: Sofala, Mozambique and Mombasa on the east coast of Africa; the island of Socotra at the entrance to the Red Sea; Muscat and Hormuz, the keys to the Persian Gulf; Diu and Goa on the west coast of India; Bengal and Chittagong on the Ganges delta, and Arakan and Pegu on the coast of Burma. Drawn to a larger scale than the charts themselves, these insets gave pilots accurate information on the depth of water, anchorages, rocks, reefs and sandbanks to avoid.

The Pacific chart (No. 86) shows considerable improvements over the one by Vaz Dourado (No. 59). Japan *(ilhas de Japão)* appears in the correct latitudes; only the contours of *Yezo* (Hokkaido) are still inaccurate. The cartographer must have benefited from the astronomical surveys carried out before the closing of the archipelago. Korea, Taiwan, the Philippines and the Marianas *(ilhas das Velas)* now appear. The presence of the north coast of New Guinea *(Nova Guinea)*, along which Schouten had sailed in 1616, and a very tentative sketch of the west coast of Australia, surveyed by Captain Nuytz and Captain de Witt in 1627-1628, bear witness to Lisbon's awareness of the explorations made by the ships of the Dutch East India Company, which was becoming an increasingly dangerous rival of the Portuguese.

Despite all this, errors and uncertainties remain: to the east of New Guinea an inscription mentions 'the land discovered by Pedro Fernandes de Queirós', who, on landing at Espiritu Santo in the New Hebrides in 1605-1606, thought he was taking possession of the austral continent. At the top of the chart, another inscription refers to a 'land sighted by João da Gama on his way from China to New Spain', which may have been Hokkaido. In 1591 João de Gama was Captain Major of Malacca and was doubtless entrusted with the command of one of the rich galleons that regularly sailed from Guangzhou (Canton) to Manila and on to

Acapulco and which, on leaving China, had to reach latitude 42°N in order to catch the right wind.

The bird's-eye view of the Great Wall of China, the coats of arms indicating nations or political allegiances and the vividly coloured compass roses contribute a beautiful decorative effect to these otherwise austere charts whose sole purpose remains the indication of sea lanes, trading-posts and port of call. Although comparatively late, João Teixeira's charts, like nearly all Portuguese sea charts, do not employ waxing latitude; they remain 'plane charts', which explains why the northern coasts of Asia appear to be squashed.

87

INDIAN OCEAN
by Pieter Goos (1660)
1 engraved and coloured vellum leaf, 715 × 890 mm
Paris, B.N.: Cartes et Plans, S.H. Portefeuille 213, div. 3 pièce 12

This sumptuous cartographic depiction on vellum of the coasts and sea lanes of the Indian Ocean and the western Pacific was engraved in Amsterdam in about 1660 by the Flemish cartographer Pieter Goos. Inspired by the works of the Blaeus, it recalls with accuracy and elegance the extent of the dominions of the Dutch East India *(Oost Indien)* Company at its zenith. Constructed on Mercator's projection, it has a waxing-latitude scale and gives the outline of the coasts of Africa and Asia from the Cape of Good Hope *(C. de Bona Esperança)*, where the Dutch fleet regularly called, to the south of Yeso, or Hokkaido *(t'landt Van Eso)*, which the explorer Martin Gerritszoon had reached in June 1643 after his reconnaissance of the eastern shore of Hondo. In Japan *(Iapan)*, the Dutch had taken advantage of the expulsion of the Portuguese and occupied in their place the artificial island of Deshima in Nagasaki Bay. For more than two centuries (1640-1854), they were the only Europeans to trade with the Japanese archipelago and were thus instrumental in maintaining contact between the civilizations of the west and the Land of the Rising Sun.

From its foundation in 1602, everywhere on the shores of Southeast Asia and the East Indies, the Dutch East India Company pursued a policy of hounding the Portuguese out of their strongholds, obtaining a monopoly of the spice trade from local sultans and establishing powerful trading-posts where they could concentrate all the riches of the Orient that were so coveted in Europe: pepper, cloves, nutmeg, mace, cinnamon, saltpetre, cotton cloth and sails *(calicot)*, silks, exotic woods, precious stones and porcelain. It is estimated that more than twelve million pieces of porcelain were shipped to Holland between 1607 and 1682.

After they arrived in the Far East (1595), the main priority of the Dutch was to achieve mastery of the peninsula and straits of Malacca, which commanded the spice route and the route leading to China and Japan. They expelled the Portuguese from Malacca in 1641, occupied *Achem* (Kutaradja) and *Iambi* (Jambi) in Sumatra in 1616 and were on the northwest coast of Java by 1595. Henceforth the spice route was not only open to them but also well guarded, and they went on systematically eliminating any Portuguese presence they still encountered. This period of conquest lasted from 1624 (capture of *Banda* and *Amboine*) until 1667-1669 (capture of *Timor*, *Ternate*, *Ceram* and *Macassar*). At the same time, Batavian merchants were establishing trading-posts in the Yemen *(Moha)*, on the shores of the Persian Gulf and on the Indian peninsula in *Bengala*. The Dutch took *Ceylon* in 1656, occupied *Formosa* from 1622 to 1662 and had settlements in Persia, *Siam*, *Cambodja*, *Conchinchina* and on the island of *Aynam* and to the southwest of Borneo. Space does not permit us to list here the hundred or so trading-posts the Dutch possessed in the East Indies in the second half of the seventeenth century, but it is worth noting that they did not yet have any in East Africa, on the Philippines or on the coast of China. In Java the town of *Batavia* (Jakarta), founded in 1619 where no previous settlement existed, was the headquarters and storehouse of this formidable Dutch trading empire. A governor-general appointed in Amsterdam by the seventeen members of the governing board or 'Collegium of 17', lived permanently in Batavia and decided which cargoes to send to Holland, imposing strict limits on the consignments in order to maintain maximum prices in Europe.

The Dutch East India Company contributed greatly to overseas discoveries. Its most important contribution to the history of discovery was the voyage undertaken by Abel Janszoon Tasman and his shipmate Franchoys Jacob Vissher (1642-1643) on the orders of Governor-General Anthony Van Diemen. These two competent pilots sailed part of the way round Australia *(Hollandia Nova)* a journey that was not to be completed until a hundred and twenty-five years later (by Cook, 1768-1771). To the southeast of this new continent, they sighted the southern coast of a territory they named *Anthoni van Diemens Landt* (Tasmania), although they were uncertain whether it was an integral part of the continent or an island. The two navigators also skirted the east coast of New Zealand and discovered the islands of Tonga and Fiji which there was not room to show on this chart. In 1644 Tasman was sent back alone to discover whether there was a navigable passage between New Guinea and Australia: he did not find the strait that had in fact already been navigated in 1606 by Luis Váez de Torres. As far as Tasman was concerned, New Guinea was joined to Australia. On the other hand, he surveyed the northern coast of New Holland and the west coast of the

Cape York peninsula *(Carpentaria)*, sighted by Willem Janszoon at the beginning of the century (No. 75). Pieter Goos takes the results of the two voyages by Abel Tasman into account; he also mentions various other chance landings made by Dutch vessels on the Australian coast. Since it was impossible at the time to determine longitude at sea accurately, these ships bound for Java had failed to go about soon enough and had made quite fortuitous discoveries of new territory to which they gave their name or that of their commander: *t'Landt de Eendracht* (1616), *Edels Landt* (1619), *t'Landt Leeuwin* (1622), *t'Landt van P. Nuyts* (1627), *G.F. de Wits Landt* (1628); for a great deal of the discovery of Australia was left to chance.

In the second half of the seventeenth century, Dutch cartographers had acquired a mastery of the projection which Mercator had established a century earlier. The sea lanes, indicated on this chart by a network of accurately drawn loxodromes, stand out quite clearly. In the southern Indian Ocean, for example, we can follow the route taken by the Dutch East India Company's ships on voyages to and from Batavia. On leaving Cape Town, in July at the latest, the fleet headed due south in order to catch the westerly trade winds in latitudes 39° or 40°S, which would allow them to cross the ocean. At the longitude of Java, pushed by south-easterly winds, the fleet would steer north and head towards the Sunda Strait, through which it passed to reach Batavia. Under the most favourable conditions, this crossing took no more than two months. The return journey was by the same route, but in order to catch a favourable wind the departure had to be timed for the end of December. On this chart by Pieter Goos, six of the ships shown are located at points along this route: three are heading for the Sunda Strait, and three are returning from it. Off Australia, near Tasmania, a warship, apparently dressed over all with flags, probably alludes to the expedition of Tasman and Visscher. In the northwest of the document, off Cape *Gardafui*, an eighth ship of the Dutch East India Company seems to be bound for India or Ceylon.

This nautical chart is illustrated with evocative paintings: at the bottom of the chart around the title *Oost Indien* ('East Indies'), a large composition recalls the contacts between Dutch traders and the masses of Asia; at the top, encircled by the army of the Grand Mogul, a large caravan is crossing Central Asia and heading for the Middle East. The miniaturist has used the geographically unexplored spaces of Africa to complete his painting. However the rich paintings adorning this chart should not in any way obscure the practical nature of the document: the chart under examination has obviously seen service aboard ship; preserved in the collections of the Service hydrographique of the French navy, it bears the pencilled outline of several tracks, which confirm its use at sea—one links Ceylon and Mauritius; another leaves Saint Augustine Bay in southwest Madagascar, goes up the Mozambique Channel and heads for Surat; others link the Cape to the Sunda Strait.

Nautical charts were beginning to lose their confidentiality, at least when they were of a general nature like this one. In Holland at this time, a commercialization of universal marine atlases was under way (A. Colom, 1659; H. Doncker, 1659; P. Goos, 1660). On this chart, below the cartouche placed in southern Africa, is a note indicating that it can be obtained from Johannes Van Keulen. After the death of Pieter Goos (1675), Van Keulen took over the copper engraving plate of the 'East Indies' on his own behalf.

88

MACASSAR ROADSTEAD
by Fred Woldemar (1660)
1 vellum leaf, coloured ms, 705 × 900 mm
Paris, B.N. Société de Géographie, Rés. Bon. Y 832

This seascape recalls an episode in the Spice War illustrating the hostility that prevailed in Celebes not only between the Portuguese and the Dutch, but also between the Dutch and the sultans of Macassar.

On 8 June 1660, two Dutch vessels had gained a dazzling victory over six Portuguese ships at anchor in the roads of Macassar, a possession of Sultan Hassanudin. The heroes of this exploit were the chiefs of the Dutch squadron, Johan Van Dam and Johan Truytman, who had set out in the van on the flagships 'Mars' and 'Breukel', theoretically in order to discuss peace terms with the sultan. In the inscription in the top right-hand corner of the document, Woldemar mentions this feat of valour of 8 June, while the painting itself gives an absolutely accurate representation of the battle fought four days later, on 12 June 1660, when the two admirals returned in force with the full Dutch squadron.

The accounts of two eye witnesses, confirmed by Woldemar's painting, enable us to follow the course of events. A Dutchman, Wouter Schouten, who had signed on as surgeon aboard the 'Hasselt', took part in the whole campaign. And William Mainstone, an agent of the English trading-post in Macassar, was present at the arrival of the two Dutch admirals and during their exploit of 8 June. As for Woldemar, the author of this prestigious painting doubtless executed for the Dutch East India Company, he gives such accurate details that we are entitled to assume that he must have witnessed these events at first hand. Thanks to this seascape and its accompanying numeration, we can follow the events of 12 June almost as if we were there. On that day, the full Dutch squadron appeared in the roads. On land and sea the belligerents hoist the red flag as a token of war. Only the English trading-post *(E. Engelse Logie)*, by virtue of a treaty, maintains neutrality and simply flies its national flag, white with a red cross. The Portuguese ship *(33. Do Prijs Madre dios de los Remedios)* taken by the admirals on 8 June takes part in the battle and, like all vanquished ships, trails its flag of origin at the stern. On the left of the painting, we can see the hulk of the ship of Francisco Vieira, a Portuguese adviser to the sultan, as well as the wrecks of two ships burnt on 8 June. *(F. 'tgesprongen schip van Fransisse Fiera en 2 wracken op strant)*. Following the tactic adopted by the admirals, the large ships of the Dutch squadron (distributed to the right and left of the bay) are concentrating their fire on Samboupo, the sultan's palace *(K. Het Royaele Casteel Sampoppe)*. Near the fortress of Panakoke, the little boats in which Van Dam, Truytman and most of the troops were hidden are pretending to be unable to manoeuvre. Samboupo, assisted by the Portuguese, is replying vigorously to the attack; other Portuguese who have remained in their quarters *(C. Portuguees quartier)* are also bombarding the Dutch ships. The Dutch squadron intensifies its fire. From all sides men fly to Hassanudin's rescue, especially the four thousand men from the fort of Panakoke. This was the mistake that the two Flemish strategists were waiting for: immediately they land their troops, take the fortress and, as we can see on the document, the Macassarese defenders take flight *(R. Het geconqest voor de Casteel Pannacoca* and *S. Maccassaerse troppen vluchten)*.

Peace was signed in December 1660, and the Portuguese were expelled for good in 1661; nevertheless, hostilities resumed in 1666 and 1667. It was not until 1669 that Admiral Speelman finally forced the kingdom of Macassar to surrender.

89

MEDITERRANEAN
by François Ollive (1662)
2 vellum leaves, illuminated ms assembled into a chart, 680 × 975 mm
Paris, B.N.: Cartes et Plans, S.H. Archives no. 43

François Ollive, several of whose works are signed in Latin (Francescus Oliva), has often been confused with an earlier relative of the same name who worked in Messina at the end of the sixteenth century and the beginning of the seventeenth (No. 68). Apart from having to assume that the Messina cartographer lived for over a hundred years, nothing in the style of their respective charts allows us to suppose that they were one and the same person. Whereas the earlier author is classical in his composition and sombre in his choice of colours, François Ollive uses, on the contrary, a very vivid palette with emphasis on green and orange, and his charts are profusely illustrated in a rather Baroque style. Ollive seems to have always worked in Marseilles, where he took over from another Oliva—a miserable cartographer christened Salvatori—possibly in 1643. His production spans some twenty years, up to 1664.

This chart preserved in Paris by the Service hydrographique of the French navy is thus one of Ollive's last works. In the top right-hand corner, a rococo cartouche adorned with lions' heads and supported by two sea monsters bears a long title in French: *CARTE PARTICULLÊRE DE LA MER MEDITERRANEE FAICTE PAR MOY FRANÇOIS OLLIVE A MARSEILLE 1662* ('special chart of the Mediterranean Sea made by me, François Ollive, in Marseilles 1662'). This is echoed in the bottom left-hand corner, where an *ESCHELLE DE MILLES* ('scale of miles') is brandished by a lion (already a traditional symbol in Marseilles cartography), which is found again in the centre of a fleur-de-lis in the southernmost of the nine compass roses. Crowned armorial shields complete the decoration of the terrestrial regions: in *AFRICA* those of Egypt and the Barbary states—*MARROC, FES, TERMISEN* (Tlemcen), *ARGER, TVNIS, TRIPOLI*; in Europe *(EVROPA)* the shields of Spain, *FRANCE*, Savoy, Austria-Hungary and the Ottoman Empire; in *ASIA* a single vignette at Jerusalem *(IERUSALEM)* features an *Ecce Homo*.

At the head of the document, the author has given a special place to the depiction in perspective of four great western Mediterranean ports, with the Provençal ports of Marseilles and Toulon framing Genoa and Naples *(NAPOLI)*. These portraits are charming and up to date; on the south bank of Marseilles, for example, looms the fort of Saint Nicolas, built in 1660 and giving physical expression to the recent royal annexation of the city. On another chart of the same year, very similar in every respect and even larger, François Ollive had shown Marseilles and Toulon on the one hand and the ports of the African coast (Algiers, Tunis, Tripoli and Alexandria) on the other. These could be part of a series attempting to illustrate, region by region, the Mediterranean ports with which the ports of Provence were in continuous contact.

Notwithstanding the inaccuracy of its outlines, especially of the Atlantic coasts, which leaves a lot to be desired, this chart is constructed on geographical north and generally corrects the orientation of the Mediterranean basin. The great number of toponyms inscribed in Roman characters are signs of its late date. The toponyms are mostly in French but superimposed on a coastal nomenclature that is amost entirely Italian, except in France, and in North Africa the *Bastion de France*: situated between Bône *(Bona)* and *Tabarca*, this concession, a sixteenth-century creation of Marseilles, had been placed under royal protection by command of Richelieu. In return for a fee to the dey of Algiers, some twenty ships fished there for coral, which was bartered in the Levantine ports for spices and indigo. Between 1635 and 1658 the Bastion was also one of the chief anchorages for Marseilles trade with Barbary, a trade that was frequently interrupted by war. Dormant for almost half a century, conflict had just broken out again with the Barbary states after an incident provoked by the governor of the *BASTION* in 1660. By tying up the Grand Turk's allies, the French squadrons blockading Tripoli and Algiers that year indirectly assisted the Venetians in their interminable war over Candia, begun in 1645.

These clashes in the eastern Mediterranean are symbolically illustrated here by scenes of naval battles that pit the two principal warships of the period against each other. To the north of Syrtis Major (Gulf of Sidra), two ships armed with lateral batteries are fighting close alongside; off Egypt two galleys with sails furled are in head-on combat, using their artillery placed in the bows. The identification of the flags is not easy, but it appears that the battles are between Genoa and Tripoli on the one hand, and the Grand Turk and the Order of Malta on the other. It was from that Order, 'a nursery of officers for the fleets of Catholic countries', that the most illustrious figures from Marseilles came to be engaged in these combats: Chevalier Paul and Bailiff Jean-Baptiste de Valbelle.

One or other of them may have ordered this chart. In the absence of a dedication and archival research, it is not known for whom the chart was intended; but this genre was fashionable in the second half of the seventeenth century, and 'specialized charts' with scenes of naval battles were numerous. Their mainly pictorial character is emphasized by the trompe-l'oeil frame that transforms this chart into a painting. Supplanted in common use by engraved cartography, the Mediterranean portolan chart—often reactionary in its geographical content—had become no more than a decorative object.

90

INDIAN OCEAN
by John Burston (1665)
1 vellum chart, coloured ms, 780 × 945 mm
Paris, B.N.: Cartes et Plans, S.H. Portefeuille 213, div. 3 pièce 4

In the closing years of the sixteenth century, a number of shops were established in the hamlets near the Tower of London (Ratcliff, Saint Katherine, the Minories) where seafarers could buy the manuscript sailing charts they needed. Similarities in the style of these documents and in the compass roses, scale scrolls and choice of colours encourage the belief that there was a community of craftsmen who influenced each other's cartography. Doubtless because they were too few in number to found their own guild, several of them affiliated themselves to the Drapers' Company thereby gaining access to a structured institution and an organized apprenticeship system. The archives of this corporation enable us to reconstruct more than a hundred years (1590-1719) of the history of the master and apprentice cartographers known today as the Thames school.

John Burston was one of these craftsmen; he served his apprenticeship under Nicolas Comberford (1628-1637) and then produced charts on his own account between 1638 and 1665. This chart dealing with navigation in the east was drawn in the year of his death (1665).

John Burston's chart covers the Indian Ocean and its coasts from Saldanha *(Saldania Bay)* near the Cape of Good Hope *(c. de Boena Esperanca)* to Malaysia *(Malaia)*, with parts of the Gulf of *Siam*, *Sumatra* and western *Java*, where the English East India Company had maintained a powerful trading-post in the port of Bantam since the beginning of the seventeenth century. In the bottom right-hand corner of the black and white document here appears a tentative sketch of the west coast of Australia *(y landt van Eendracht)*, sighted by a Dutch ship thanks to a chance favourable wind (1616). The author's signature: *Made by John Burston... Anno Domini 1665* is inscribed at the foot of the chart; it informs us that the cartographer's shop is in the ward of *Ratcliff*. The work is particularly well finished, and the script is clear and elegant. Despite being an extremely austere nautical instrument, this chart achieves a beautiful decorative effect with the two baroque cartouches framing the scales, the happy choice of the colours emphasizing the outlines and the originality of its compass roses whose centres have different floral motifs. However, the technique of this chart is backward for its time: it is still constructed as a plane chart. Since it was intended for the Indiamen (the merchant ships of the East India Company) whose trade at the time was mostly conducted with the trading-posts of *Suratt*, Madras *(Maddrasapatam)*, *Massulipatam* and *Bantam*; the distance scales are given in English leagues *(This Scale Containeth Two Hundred English Leagues)*. The cartographer also includes one or two notes in his own language. To the east of Madagascar *(St Lorenso)* off the island of Mauritius *(Mauritios)*, we read: *The Meridian of the Highest traration*, which may be an allusion to the magnetic force in this part of the southern hemisphere. Another note, situated near a cluster of reefs north of the Australian coast—*Rocks where the Trial was cast away*—obviously refers to the wreck of a British ship in this area.

However, it appears that the work of the author of this portolan chart is not truly original. There is little doubt that he based at least the African part of it on a Portuguese prototype: the outline of Africa and its nomenclature are very similar to those found on an atlas of the same period by Teixeira Albernas II (No. 94). In the seventeenth century, English mapping of the East Indies still remained largely derivative of the cartography of the two great maritime powers trading in Southeast Asia—Portugal and, above all, Holland.

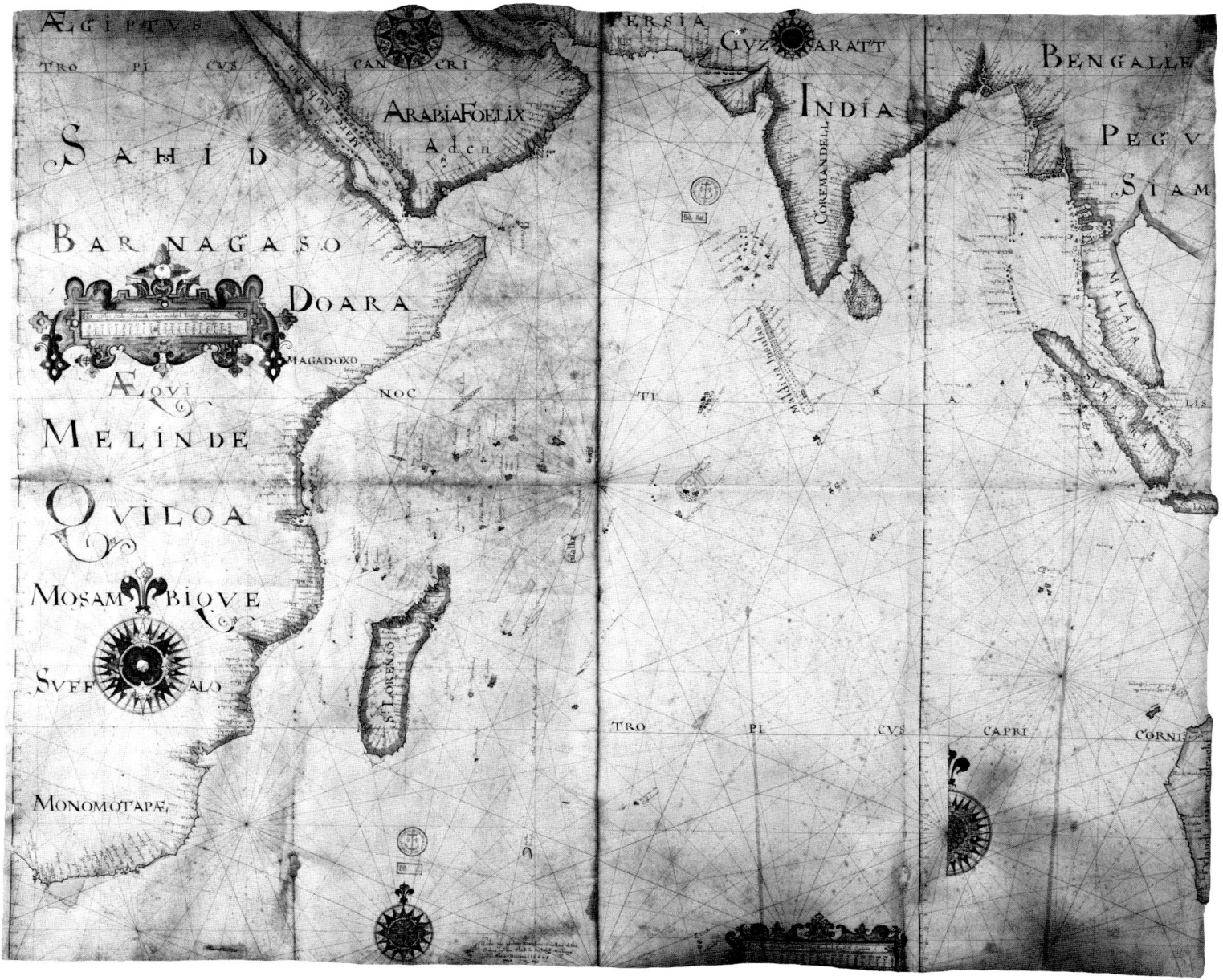

90

Nevertheless, John Burston's chart made an impression, and it reappeared in an enhanced form in the work of his apprentice John Thornton. Indeed the chart John Thornton made of the Indian Ocean in 1682 is generally considered as marking the zenith of the Thames school; it reproduces his master's chart in part. When the former apprentice became official cartographer to the East India Company, he mostly corrected the outline and nomenclature of Siam and Malaysia, which had appeared in a very archaic form on Burston's chart.

91

NORTH ATLANTIC
by Denis de Rotis (1674)
1 vellum leaf, coloured ms, 880 × 435 mm
Paris, B.N.: Cartes et Plans, S.H. Archives no. 21

The Basques, neighbours of the Portuguese, had a long acquaintance with the Atlantic: from about the tenth century onwards they hunted whales in the Bay of Biscay and traded in whale products. Archaeological evidence seems to indicate that, from the twelfth century onwards, they took the route towards Newfoundland later followed by the Corte Real brothers, where whales were found in greater numbers than in the Bay of Biscay. From 1560 to 1570, the largest share of this harpoon fishery was in their hands. It has been estimated that two thousand Spanish Basques came annually to the Labrador coast to work in the whale industry. In Red Bay (then known as les Buttes), piles of whalebone and rounded tiles, the remains of the furnaces used for rendering whale fat into oil, have been found. A busy trade in whale oil was established with Flanders and England, but the hunted whales decreased in numbers. By the beginning of the seventeenth century, it seems that the fleet of Spanish

265

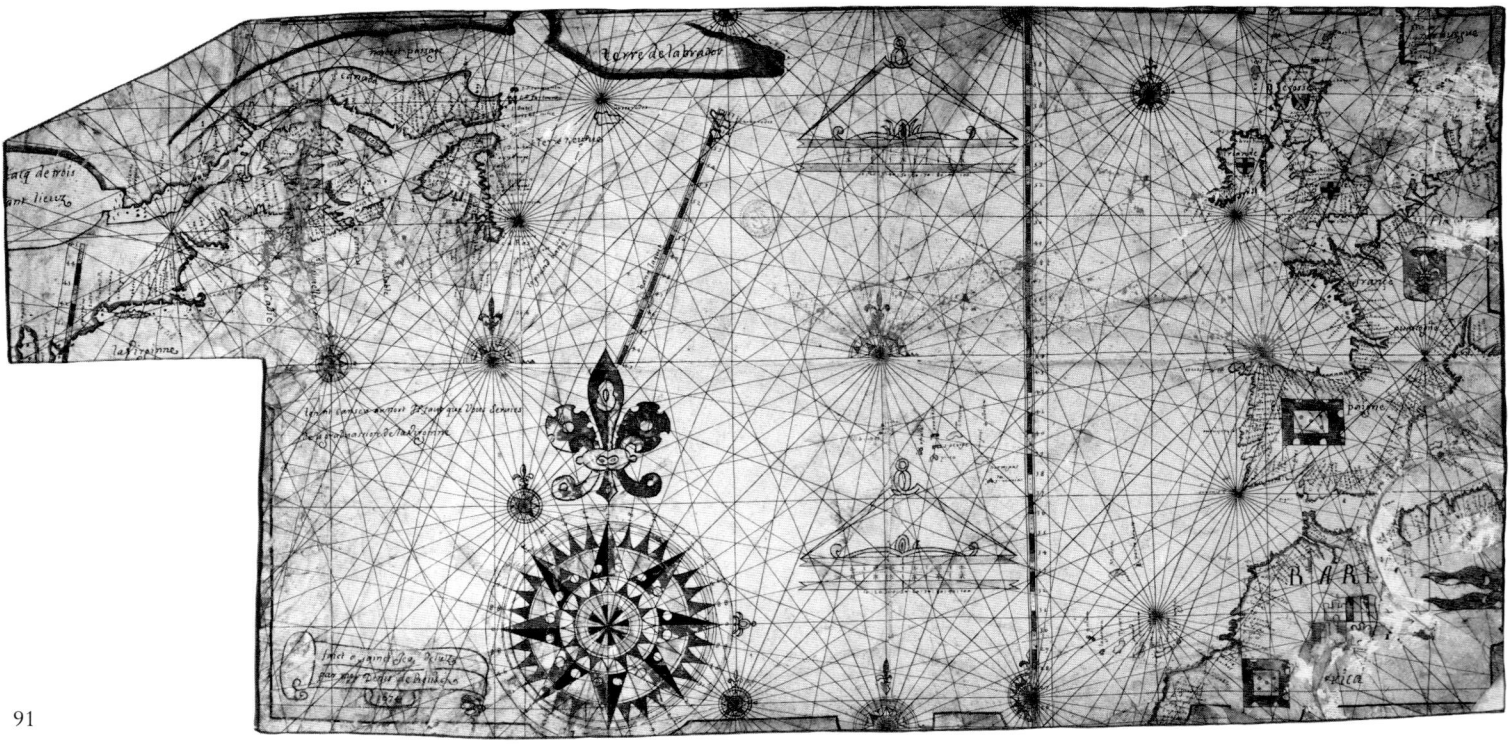

91

Basque vessels in Labrador had diminished. On the other hand, cod-fishing intensified, and French Basques came in groups from the Labrador region and established themselves to a certain extent on the west coast of Newfoundland, also hunting whales and rendering their fat into oil with the help of the Micmac Indians.

This portolan chart, *faict à Sainct Jea[n] de Luz par moy Denis de Rotis 1674* ('made at Saint Jean de Luz by me, Denys de Rotis 1674'), is a fine illustration of the activities of these French Basques in the eighteenth century. In 1635, there were thirty-nine 300-ton whalers and twenty cod-fishing boats in the Labrador region. The almost total monopoly of 'whale-killing' which the Basques held until the eighteenth century, conferred a testy autonomy on them.

Magnetic variation is emphasized by two short latitude scales, inclined NNE-SSW, one to the east of Newfoundland *(terre neuve)* and the other along the American coast. An inscription *(tennt canseu au nort Il faut que Vous Servies de la graduassion de la Virginne)* indicates that the mariner, when he observes his compass is perturbed, should not rely on the general latitude scale but rather on the scale situated on the coast of Virginia. This is still the oblique meridian inherited from Pedro Reinel.

Canada is confined to a narrow strip of land, bordered to the north by the *noroest passage*: the famous Northwest Passage to China sought by Cartier, Champlain and La Vérendrye, as well as by Portuguese, English and Dutch explorers, but which was not discovered until the beginning of the twentieth century. This passage is closed off to the north by Labrador *(terre de labrador)*, whose configuration recalls that of Labrador joined to Greenland as it appeared, a century earlier, on some portolan charts from Dieppe.

This portolan chart is therefore a blend of verified scientific fact and anachronic borrowings. Despite its late date, it is still constructed like a Portuguese nautical chart of the beginning of the sixteenth century.

92

ISLE OF BREHAT
by Pierre Collin (1666)
1 vellum leaf, illuminated ms, 750 × 960 mm
Paris, B.N.: Cartes et Plans, S.H. Portefeuille 45, div. 2 pièce 2

This chart, *Le Plan de l'isle de brehat auecque Tous et chacun les Rochers, Bancqs et Escueils à deux lieux aux Enuirons de laditte isle...* ('Plan of the Isle of Bréhat, with each and every rock, bank and reef for 2 leagues around the said island...') is a rarity for its day, consisting of a large scale cartographic survey (approximately 1:30,000) that provides very accurate information on dangerous passages. At the head of the chart a large painting of the arms of France and Navarre appears, with the insignia of the Order of Saint Michael and the Order of the Holy Spirit. The initials 'L.B.' (probably standing for Louis de Bourbon) below the escutcheons suggest that the chart was executed in homage to Louis XIV, who was, briefly at that time, the owner of the isle of Bréhat (1657?-1665). The naval combat depicted offshore to the right artistically represents the rivalry between the great maritime powers, Holland and England, who were at war, while Louis XIV pursued a wait-and-see policy for the next few months. One solitary ship at the bottom is in difficulties: its mainsail yard is down, and no identifying national flag can be seen; only the red flags signifying belligerency still flutter in the wind.

This map by Pierre Collin was probably used to illustrate Charles Colbert's political and economic report, since the information provided by the cartographic outline closely resembles that of the written report. Charles Colbert, the future Marquis de Croissy and brother of the man known as the great Colbert, had been commissioned in 1665 to inspect the coast of Brittany. His itinerary took him from Vitré to Vannes; Bréhat was one of the important stops on his journey owing to its strategic position opposite the Channel Islands. Among the officials accompanying him, Colbert mentions La Villejegu and Collin by name, the latter no doubt the author of this exceptionally interesing historical document.

93

HUDSON STRAIT AND DAVIS STRAIT
(before 1677)
1 vellum leaf, coloured ms, 406 × 570 mm
Paris, B.N.: Cartes et Plans, S.H. Portefeuille 123, div. 6 pièce 1

This chart depicts the entrance to the Hudson Strait *(Hudsons Straigts)*, the ESE coast of Baffin Island and the west coast of Greenland *(Groinland)*, which encircle the northern Atlantic Ocean at the edge of the Arctic Circle and were the scene, at the end of the sixteenth century and in the first third of the seventeenth, of the maritime explorations in search of a Northwest Passage. On Labrador *(Lborador)*, the eloquent inscription New Britain *(Nova Brittania)* recalls the history of these explorations, carried out mainly by English mariners whose daring deserves all our admiration. Embarked on frail craft, they came upon hostile and unknown elements, currents that were often contrary, immense masses of floating ice and a bewildering fauna. The name *Nova Brittania* had already appeared on the chart *The North part of America*, which had circulated in 1625 to illustrate the two tracts that Henry Briggs devoted to the probable existence of a Northwest Passage.

This anonymous chart shows all the characteristics of a work of the Thames school: a latitude scale in constant degrees, a single illuminated compass rose, coasts picked out in vivid colours, clear script, a distance scale in English leagues *(A Scale of 60 Eng Leagues)* and a yellow trompe-l'oeil frame. Its whole interest lies in the nomenclature that recalls the expeditions to these northern shores by Martin Frobisher (1576 and 1578), John Davis (1585-1586-1587), Henry Hudson (1610–1611), Thomas Button (1612-1613) and William Baffin (1615-1616). The chart bears many signs of their passage. South of Baffin Island, for example *C. Elizabeths*, Resolution Isle *(C. Resulution)* and *Queene Anns Fore Land* were named by Frobisher. On the west coast of Greenland on the island now known as Nunarssuit, John Davis sighted Cape Desolation *(C. Disolation)* in 1585. During his third voyage in 1587, Davis sailed up the west coast of Greenland from *C. Farewell* as far as latitude 72°12′N. On *London Coast* he noted a compass variation of 28° to the west; then crossing the strait which now bears his name, he skirted Baffin Island, sighted *Cape Bedford* and *C. Wallsingham*, christened Cape Mercy *(C. of Gods Mercey)*, noted for its bluff 460 metres high and turbulent currents, which is the northernmost promontory of the extremely deep *Cumberlands Baÿ*. Here Davis hoped he had found the Northwest Passage, but he soon realized that it was nothing more than an immense gulf dotted with a large number of islands. Again he noted the compass reading, which here showed a variation of 30° to the west. On the east coast of Baffin Island he also named *Lumbs Inlett* and *Warwicks Foreland*, where he noted the great number of cascades. At the entrance to Hudson Strait, beyond Cape Chidley *(C. Cheddley)* and *Buttons Iland* and east of *Cape Charles* is the outline of the large indentation of Ungava Bay, surveyed by Henry Hudson in 1610, when he was sailing unwittingly toward his tragic fate: a few months later Hudson was abandoned by his companions and cast off with his son on a bark canoe in the middle of the bay that now bears his name. On our chart Ungava Bay is not named, but it is sketched in, albeit imperfectly.

This anonymous English chart still contains many geographical errors: Frobisher Bay is totally absent, the size of the islands of southern Greenland is exaggerated and the orientation of the coast of Labrador, which should have had a SSE inclination after Cape Chidley, is inaccurate.

This manuscript document appears to have been one of the sources of the chart by John Thornton, John Seller, William Fisher, James Atkinson and John Colson, engraved in London and entitled *A Chart of ye North part of America. For Hudsons Bay comonly called ye North West Passage*, which J.D. Black and C. Verner have dated to around 1677-1678. It is included in an atlas compiled at the end of the seventeenth century by Blathwayt, one of the leading figures in the Plantation Office, which was responsible for maintaining a completely up-to-date graphic documentation on the British overseas settlements; the outlines and nomenclature of this manuscript are absolutely the same as those of the engraved chart. They are to be found again on the chart by John Thornton in *The English Pilot: The fourth book*, printed in London in 1689 and republished in 1698. Nevertheless, the manuscript chart bears many more soundings than the two engraved charts.

Were they deliberately concealed on publication? The English may well have hesitated to divulge all the details of this sea lane at the moment when, at the suggestion of two French deserters (Groseillers and Radisson), the Hudson's Bay Company was being founded in England. The two Frenchmen had learnt from the Indians that it was easier to reach Hudson's Bay by sea than over land, and the charter granted to the company by King Charles II on 2 May 1670 gave it: 'the monopoly of trade on all seas, straits, bays, rivers, gulfs, creeks, lakes, also with all the lands and territories bordering these shores and belonging to no one'. The company intended to trade in skins, particularly beaver; was it keeping the secrets of the route to itself?

94

EMPIRE OF MONOMOTAPA
by João Teixeira Albernas II (1677)
1 vellum leaf, coloured ms, 615 × 500 mm
Paris, B.N.: Société de Géographie, Rés. Og 21

From the fifteenth century to the beginning of the nineteenth, the black empire of Monomotapa *(Inperio do Motapa)*, the birth-place of Southern Rhodesia, now Zimbabwe, occupied the plateau situated at an altitude of 1,000 metres between the Zambezi and the Limpopo. A sort of inland island, it was isolated to the north and south by the valleys of those two great rivers, bounded to the west by the Kalahari desert and to the east by the Inyanga mountain chain. The only practical means of access was to sail up the Zambezi. Arriving after the Arabs, the Portuguese were attracted by the riches of the subsoil, founding trading-posts on the river at *Sena* and *Tene* from the beginning of the sixteenth century. There African gold was exchanged for loin-cloths and glass beads imported from Lisbon or Goa. This chart by João Teixeira Albernas shows the location of the trading-posts along the river, and the gold mines on the plateau *(M. de Ouro)* are represented by coloured hills seen in perspective. On the left, a long inscription gives details of the navigability of the river, 'feasible for the first 640 kilometres or thereabouts, after which a long portage was necessary as far as Zumbo' (Randles).

This late Portuguese document has both a nautical and a political significance: it is intended to facilitate navigation in the waters of the western Indian Ocean, and it also illustrates a stage in the Portuguese colonization of southern Africa. The title is explicit: 'Chart from the Cape of Good Hope to Mombasa with the demonstration of the Zambezi River where the fleet commanded by the Prince of Portugal was sent in this year of 1677, made by João Teixeira Albernas in Lisbon'. The prince in question was then the Regent, the future King Pedro II, who had prepared a plan for the colonization of the Zambezi and despatched four ships with instructions to carry it out. The gold trade was at that time in the hands of independent Portuguese traders who had private armies and recognized no authority whether Portuguese or African. The royal expedition was unable to re-establish order however, and in 1683 the black chiefs of Monomotapa decided to close the mines and, a few years later (1693), to expel all the colonists from their country.

This cartographer, grandson and disciple of João Teixeira Albernas I (Nos. 85-86) owes his fame to the execution of a manuscript atlas of the coasts of Africa (dated 1665), which was commissioned by a French diplomat who had been posted to Lisbon, Jean Frémont d'Ablancourt. (The atlas is preserved in the Archives Nationales, Paris, shelf-mark N.N. 20 Afrique No. 1). A work published in Amsterdam in 1700, entitled *Suite du Neptune François ou Atlas nouveau des cartes marines...*, used engravings of all these African charts by João Teixeira Albernas, thereby ensuring their survival.

95

MOCHA
by Augustine Fitzhugh (1683)
1 vellum leaf, coloured ms, 325 × 385 mm
Paris, B.N.: Cartes et Plans, S.H. Portefeuille 211, div. 3 pièce 1

The little harbour town of Mocha *(Moha)*, the most important in Fertile Arabia *(Arabia Felix)* according to our cartographer, lies on the shores of the Red Sea, some 60 kilometres from the Bab-el-Mandeb Strait. It took on a considerable economic and commercial importance in the seventeenth century, as it had become a major trade port for Yemeni coffee and an important transit centre for the India trade. Apart from coffee, it also acted as a trade centre for various other products from India, black Africa and the Mediterranean. The existence of coffee, both as a plant and as a drink, was not known in Europe until the end of the sixteenth century, but it quite rapidly became a sought-after commodity, obtained at first from the Surat and Bombay markets, until the two great Dutch and English Companies—the V.O.C. and the East India Company—established their own trading-posts in Mocha. The English trading-post opened there in 1682 and lasted until 1726.

This depiction of Mocha dates, therefore, from the year after the opening of the British trading-post. The cartographer's signature *(Made by Augustine Fitzhugh at the Corner of the Minnories... 1683)* is inscribed along the coastline on the right of the document. As the compass rose indicates, the chart is oriented with north on the left so that the port appears full on. The scale (*A Scale of three Miles*, 102 mm or 1:50,000 approximately) is large enough for us to appreciate the accuracy of the description made of it at the beginning of the eighteenth century by the Chevalier de La Roque: the port consists of two tongues of land bent in the shape of a bow and thus forming a perfect half-moon.... The town is surrounded by walls in the old style: half stone, half beaten earth and straw'. On Fitzhugh's plan a dotted line surrounding the principal monuments allows us to reconstruct the form of the archaic enclosure. Above the outline of the coast and the drawing of the harbour, two bird's-eye views are painted, made from a ship moored 3½ miles from the coast. The view appearing at the top of the document is painted in fair weather (*the wether Being Cleare...*); Mocha then appears as a little white fortified town, over which a vast range of high mountains towers, while on either side of the town a low coast fringed with palm-trees extends as far as the eye can see. The second view shows what can be seen on a cloudy day (*... if the wether be hazey...*). The Red Sea mist veils the tall peaks but makes the town itself seem nearer, as if it had been drawn to a larger scale. This mirage effect is admirably conveyed. Below, two inscriptions explain the picture. On the left appears a list of the monuments (houses, mosques) and most notable parts of the town (*A Table of the moste Remarckable and principall places About*), which refers both to the chart and the panoramic views. On the right a long list of instructions deals particularly with the precautions to be taken when navigating the Mocha roadstead. Its approaches were made hazardous by the presence of large sand banks: the largest and most dangerous one was in the north and is indicated on the chart by numerous soundings. Vessels with a heavy tonnage are recommended to moor 2½ miles offshore in at least 9, 8 or 7 fathoms of water. Ships with a lesser tonnage could go in further, and a special mark inscribed at 3½ fathoms shows how far they could go: this was where the ships coming from India would cast anchor. Also indicated is the fact that the most violent winds blow from the NNE. The cartographer speaks of them as if he had personally been present on the voyage during which the chart was made.

With its pictorial and visual qualities this document artistically illustrates the prestigious past of a port that is no more than a large village today. Its author, Augustine Fitzhugh, was an artisan of the Thames school. He began his apprenticeship under John Thornton in 1675 and set up on his own account in 1683: Fitzhugh produced charts on his own during the years 1683 to 1697.

96

NORTHWEST COAST OF JAVA
by Joan Blaeu (1688)

1 vellum leaf, coloured ms, 415 × 1030 mm
Paris, B.N.: Cartes et Plans, S.H. Portefeuille 192, div. 3 pièce 4

This chart was constructed by Joan Blaeu, who remained cartographer to the Dutch East India Company until his death in 1705. Drawn to a large scale (approximately 1:250,000), the chart shows the outline of the northwest coast of Java as seen from the sea (north is at the foot of the document), with the roadstead and a plan of the two ports: *Bantam* and *Batavia* (Jakarta). The chart clearly indicates shallows, a sprinkling of islands and wide stretches of sand banks. Today, alluvial deposits have caused certain parts of the coast to advance by more than 2 kilometres: the ancient city of Bantam is no longer by the sea and the port of Batavia, so heavily used in the seventeenth and eighteenth centuries, has had to be replaced by the new port of Tanjungpriok, 10 kilometres north of the old one.

The port of *Bantam* is shown in perspective; at the end of the sixteenth century it was a prosperous trading centre where all the eastern fleets met. Chinese junks also visited it regularly, and when the Dutch (Cornelis Van Houtman in 1595) and the English (Sir James Lancaster in 1602) first landed there, Bantam was the most flourishing market on the northern coast of Java where pepper, cloves, cinnamon, nutmegs and all sorts of spices coming from elsewhere (Sumatra, Borneo, the Banda and the Molucca Islands) could be obtained. The English East India Company was the first to establish a trading-post there (1603) and was to be the only one to remain there in the seventeenth century until, in 1684, following the signing of a treaty between the local sultan and the governor-general of the Dutch East India Company, Bantam became a protectorate of that company and the English were forced to withdraw. On the chart, the English trading-post is still indicated, while behind it the tricolour flags of the Dutch East India Company float over their own establishments.

The city of Batavia, on the other hand, is represented by a plane illustration. Founded in 1619 by Jan Pieterszoon Coen on the ruins of Jakarta, it was built on an unhealthy marsh on either side of the Chiliwong River. Designed somewhat in the image of Amsterdam, to serve as headquarters of the Dutch East India Company in the Far East, Batavia, with its wooden houses and tree-lined canals, was a little fortified city protected by a strong citadel whose tall tower, crowned with a weathercock, acted as a landmark for shipping. Landings were made in a welcoming harbour, equipped with two long jetties where many ships could be moored; on this plan the canals, encircling walls, fortress and two jetties are all plainly visible.

This chart is a typical example of the progress made by Dutch marine cartography, which improved and became more accurate during the second half of the seventeenth century. Many large-scale surveys had combined to complete the portrayal of the great ocean spaces revealed by long-distance navigation and first charted by the Portuguese.

97

CHART OF THE ISLE OF NEWFOUNDLAND
by Pierre Detcheverry (1689)
1 vellum leaf, coloured ms, 315 × 570 mm
Paris, B.N.: Cartes et Plans, S.H. Portefeuille 125, div. 1 pièce 2

This second Basque chart has several interesting features. Dated 1689, fifteen years later than the portolan chart by Denis de Rotis (No. 91), it depicts the coasts predominantly frequented by the Basques. It was executed at Placentia, the French capital of Newfoundland founded in 1660 on the south coast to defend the French fishermen from incursions by the English fishermen based at Saint John's. In the title, the dedication mentions Sieur Parat, appointed governor in 1685, who had become notorious for his dissolute morals, greed and lack of courage in dealing with English privateers. In 1690 he had to flee to France.

This chart was probably made at Parat's request as part of his defence at Court against the criticisms of his administration. He commissioned it from a Basque because the port was almost exclusively used by Basque fishermen; in 1690 they instigated a mutiny, which their numbers made extremely serious.

Not only does this document enable us to visualize contemporary life in Placentia *(Plaicance)* but its nautical qualities are such that it was reproduced in the eighteenth century and even in the nineteenth: in 1828 Admiral Halgan made a copy of it in his own hand adding notes of several soundings. This chart can therefore be described as a prototype.

The nomenclature is Basque, especially that of the west coast, known in the eighteenth century as the 'Basque coast'. The meaning of most of the names is given in a memorandum of 1710, compiled by traders from Saint Jean de Luz and Ciboure to prove how long they had occupied this coast. Some of the names are evocative: *Ophorportu:* milk-jug; *ulycillho*: fly-hole; *Miariz*: Biarritz—these names are also found on the chart by de Rotis. The isle of *Miquelon* next to the isle of *St Pierre* makes one of its first cartographic appearances.

The prototype status of the chart and its Basque nomenclature are both explained when we learn more about Pierre Detcheverry, known as Dorre, a nickname still used in the Basque country that distinguished him from other men with the same surname. Descended from an old shipowning family of Saint Jean de Luz, in 1677 Detcheverry published a Basque translation of the most famous sea book, or rutter, on Newfoundland, which had been previously published in French in 1579 by a Basque, Martin de Hoyarsabal, and republished several times in various French Atlantic ports. This rutter, much prized by cod-fishermen, was not supplanted until the end of the eighteenth century when Cook published his. Detcheverry did the Basque translation for his compatriots and added a rutter of the west coast of the island that was not included in the other editions. Thus this chart by a competent cartographer marks an epoch in the knowledge of Newfoundland.

98

THE BANDA ISLANDS
(End of the seventeenth century)
1 vellum leaf, coloured ms, 355 × 540 mm
Paris, B.N.: Cartes et Plans, S.H. Portefeuille 186, div. 14 pièce 16

This large-scale English chart (approximately 1:60,000) shows the Banda Islands at the end of the seventeenth century. Consisting of a group of mountainous islands of volcanic origin, they are part of the Moluccas province and are situated 70 miles south of the eastern extremity of Ceram. The three largest—*Banda Island* (Banda Besar or Great Banda), *Nero Island* (Naira) and *Gunape I* (Goeneng Api)—are grouped around an inner sea that shelters ships during the monsoon and provides an access to Banda Naira, the port for the archipelago. On the chart it is represented by the fortress towering over the broad bay situated on the southern coast of *Nero Island*. Sickle-shaped Great Banda, bordered in the south by a coral rock, a volcano *(Burning Island)*, and Naira island form, without doubt, the edge of a vast crater. The narrow sound separating the volcano from its neighbour Naira is navigable by boats of small tonnage. To the northwest, west and southeast other, smaller islands dot the ocean: *Port Sanguÿ I* (Soenanggi), *Port Waÿ I* (Aï), *Port Roon I* (Roen), and *Rossingem Island* (Rozengain), of which only the northernmost tip can be seen at the bottom of the chart. All the islands are fringed with reefs.

The rhumbs of the solitary compass rose and the scale *(A Scale of foure miles)* allow the relative locations of the islands to be determined and the distances separating them to be calculated. Many widely disseminated soundings are also present. The rows of trees along the coast or around the castles symbolize the plantations of nutmeg-trees that grow wild in the eastern Banda Islands and whose fruit, a dark brown nut, is a favourite spice among Europeans. To this day the islands supply three-quarters of the world consumption of nutmeg.

The Banda Islands were discovered by the Portuguese in 1512 (Antonio d'Abreu); they were supplanted there in the seventeenth century by the Dutch who were anxious to appropriate the monopoly of the nutmeg and mace trade for the benefit of the Dutch East India Company. The English also attempted to establish a commercial presence on Pulo Run (1616), but Dutch intransigence was such that the English company soon withdrew from its trading-posts in the Molucca and Banda islands (1624). The East India Company preferred to centralize its trade at Bantam and import its spices from Macassar and Sumatra.

Alexander Hamilton, who sailed among the East Indies for thirty-five years (1688-1723), still speaks of Banda in his day in the following terms: 'I'll...direct my Course to the Islands of Banda, where Cloves, Nutmegs, and Mace grow but are now all engrossed by the Dutch who allow one of them called Pullo-wey [Aï], to belong to the English, after they had been at 40 Years Pains to cut down all the Clove and Nutmeg Trees that grew on it and have made it Death for the Natives ever to plant any on it'. The systematic practice of such methods allowed the Dutch to retain their dominance over the market.

This chart of the Banda Islands forms part of the production of the Thames school in the last third of the seventeenth century, when traditional ocean charts of the great voyages of exploration were replaced by a multiplicity of charts dealing with smaller areas and constructed to a much larger scale. Several hundred have survived from this period, many of which refer to the East Indies. They mark a transition in the evolution of nautical cartography from the manuscript chart to the engraved chart, frequently providing the sources or prototypes of the plates of marine atlases published in the eighteenth century.

99

PERSIAN GULF
by John Thornton (1699)
1 vellum leaf, coloured ms, 635 × 745 mm
Paris, B.N.: Cartes et Plans, S.H. Portefeuille 209, div. 2 pièce 5

John Thornton, a former apprentice of John Burston under whom he learnt his trade from 1656 to 1664, is considered to be one of the masters of the Thames school. The Hudson's Bay Company and the East India Company chose him as their hydrographer and commissioned him to provide the navigational charts required by their pilots on embarkation. His production covers the years 1667 to 1701: thirty-three signed manuscript examples of his specialized work still remain; no less than twenty-seven deal with navigation in the Orient, and twenty-two of these date from the years 1699 and 1701 alone. Parallel to his career as cartographer to the great companies, Thornton also produced engravings of considerable commercial significance: the nautical atlas *The English Pilot: The third book, describing the sea coasts...in the Oriental navigation* made him famous. This precious collection of thirty-five sea charts accompanied by nautical instructions appeared for the first time in London in 1703 and, together with its numerous reprints, was an enormous success. It is a sort of *Neptune oriental*, which preceded the analagous French and Dutch publications (Jean-Baptiste d'Après de Mannevillette, 1745 and J. Van Keulen II, 1753) by more than half a century.

The chart of the Persian Gulf (*Sinus Persicus*) is one of a series of individual charts that the captain of an Indiaman would have taken with him on embarking: it gives the outline of the coasts from Muscat (*Muscatt*) on the Gulf of Oman to beyond Jask (*Cape Jasques*) on the southern Iranian shore. One of the most heavily used sea lanes in the world today, owing to the oil fields that have enriched the countries on its banks, the Persian Gulf was only very imperfectly known at the end of the seventeenth century. There is an evident disparity in the extent of geographical knowledge of the two shores.

The outline of the Arabian peninsula (*Arabia Felix*) beyond the Strait of Hormuz is still very inaccurate. The Qatar peninsula and the island of Bahrain are totally absent, unless the rather shapeless drawing of the two islands named *Samaka* and *Debragu* is meant to be a tentative representation of them. On the other hand, the cartographer does not forget to show the immense bank in the south, taking up nearly a third of the area of the gulf, where from April to October hundreds of fishing smacks and several thousand men fish the pearl oysters that lie scattered in its shoals.

By contrast, the outline of the Iranian coast is already accurate; the numerous islands, for example Lark (*Larack*), Hormuz (*Ormuse*) and especially the two largest, Qeshm (*I. Chisme*) and Kharg (*Carack I*), are in exactly the right place; and the presence of numerous soundings, reefs and sand banks along the coast bears witness to visits by western navigators. The fishing village of Kong (*Cong*) is surmounted by a banner that may be Indian, for according to the traveller Alexander Hamilton: 'most of the Pearl that are caught at Bareen ... are brought hither for a Market, and many fine horses are sent thence to India'. Over the two ports of the Persian Gulf shown from above, Bandar Abbas (*Gombaroon*) at its entrance and Basra (*Buzaroe*) at its end, floats the flag of the English East India Company. At Bandar Abbas it coexists with that of the Dutch East India Company.

In *Persia*, to the right of the degrees of latitude and painted to a larger scale than the chart, are two views in perspective of the island of Kharg (*Carack*). The first (*Carack lies 5 miles*) gives a general profile of the island as seen from a ship 8 kilometres off shore; the other is drawn from nearer, from the very spot to the southeast of the island where it is advised to cast anchor. The inscription near the compass rose specifies that this should be done at a depth of 10 fathoms, 1 mile from the coast. This near to the coast, we can see the houses and vegetation of a cultivated plain stretched out at the foot of wooded hills. Moreover, according to the cartographer, it is the same view that he had on his departure from the island. Kharg was an important port of call for gulf traffic; not only did it provide—as the cartographer indicates—drinking water and fresh food (onions and grapes), but it was also there that ships were obliged to take on board a pilot to navigate them to the town of Basra *(Buzaroe)* at the northern extremity of a gulf, which was encumbered with alluvial deposits and sand banks that made navigation extremely tricky. The town of Basra is situated 70 miles from the sea and shown in bird's-eye view on the chart on both banks of the Shatt al 'Arab, the river formed by the confluence of the Tigris and the Euphrates.

Although of a late period, this is still a plane chart constructed on rhumbs with a latitude scale composed of constant degrees. The distance scale marked in English leagues *(A Scale of Fifty English Leagues)* is in the bottom left-hand corner of the document above the signature of the author: *Made by John Thornton at the Signe of the Platt in the Minories Anno: 1699.* Although it is by the hand of the hydrographer to the East India Company, the chart does not appear to have been surveyed by an English pilot. The persistence in the nomenclature of forms such as Buza-*roe*, Gomba-*roon* would seem to indicate the use of a Dutch source, probably derived from the first surveys carried out during Cornelis Cornelisz Roobaker's maritime expedition to the Persian Gulf in 1645. This was a common practice: time and again it seems that the hydrographer to the East India Company based his charts on the work of the hydrographer to the Dutch East India Company. On the other hand, the harmonious construction of this English chart, the elegance of its single compass rose, the colours chosen to highlight its outlines together with the careful script, the austere framing of the scale and the trompe-l'oeil frame with its simple yellow border remain the essential characteristics of the work of this cartographer of the Thames school.

100

AMOY BAY
by John Thornton (1699)
1 vellum leaf, coloured ms, 780 × 605 mm
Paris, B.N.: Cartes et Plans, S.H. Portefeuille 179, div. 15 pièce 5

Situated opposite the island of Formosa (Taiwan), the port of Amoy (Xiamen) is in the southeast of Fujian Province on a large bay into which the River Jiulong *(R. Chinchin)* flows. Its deep-water anchorage is well protected from late-summer typhoons, and its hinterland of hills together with the great mountainous Island of *Amoy* towering over the roadstead and the Island of Quemoy (Chimen Tao) protecting its eastern approaches provide some of the finest scenery in this province of southern China.

After 1670 the English merchants of the East India Company, anxious to sell English goods, especially woollens, were tempted to establish themselves on the coast of the Celestial Empire, which until then had been totally barred to Europeans, who were often called 'southern barbarians'. Only the Portuguese had managed to keep the door ajar by settling in Macao. With no legal right of entry, the Dutch and English had engaged in furtive trading with the coastal city of Amoy. In 1676 the English company even succeeded in establishing a trading-post there, but relations remained delicate. In 1680, when the Manchu armies captured Amoy, they forced the English to suspend their operations and await the decision of Emperor Kangxi before resuming them. In 1684, the emperor authorized foreigners to enter the China Sea and trade there on a limited basis. Encouraged by this news, the directors of the English company wasted no time: in May 1685 the 'China Merchant' was sent to Amoy to re-open the trading-post. The ship was cordially received and a warehouse was offered at a reasonable price. The 'China Merchant' was the forerunner of a large fleet of Indiamen linking China and England, and its arrival also marked the opening of the tea route. On the chart, the trading-post *(English Fictory)* is indicated on Amoy Island, between the town *(Towne of Amoy)* and the royal palace *(Kings Palace)*.

With its solitary compass rose and shaded coastlines, this austere hydrographic sketch, which is already drawn to a large scale (about 1:110,000), is obviously intended to serve a purely nautical role. There is no depiction of the region's rugged terrain apart from two hills surmounted by a pagoda *(Chinchin hill Pagode)* and *East Point* which are included solely as useful landmarks. In the southeast near the yellow margin at about latitude 24°, *The hole in ye Wall or Chappell Iland* is indicated; according to Alexander Hamilton, it was christened thus because 'there is a large Hole that passes quite through it, being undermined by the Sea below. It appears like the Arch of a great Bridge. About seven Leagues within it, is the inner harbour of Amoy'. From Chapel Island onwards, by following the line of soundings, it would appear possible to avoid sand banks, reefs and rocks level with the surface of the water, all indicated on the chart. The little island of Gulang Yu *(I. Colomsem)* together with *Amoy* Island formed the inner harbour, where ships were perfectly secure. The best anchorage would seem to be south of Kulangsü, and the channel bordering it to the west permits easy access to the inner harbour itself.

As the signature *(Made by John Thornton ... Anno 1699)* confirms, this chart was made by the hydrographer to the East India Company. In contrast with the previous chart, it is based on original English surveys made on the spot during the first English expeditions to the coast of China: one survey was made in the very year that the English trading-post was founded (1676); the other is included in the journal of a voyage made by Captain J. Kempthorne in the years 1686 to 1688. The two manuscripts are preserved in the British Library in London. In the collections of the Service hydrographique of the French navy in Paris, there is another plan of Amoy Bay drawn by John Thornton two years later (1701), which contains some useful corrections: the Jiulong Jiang (*Chinchin* River) is now located south rather than north of *Rad Point*, and Chapel Island has been moved 5 minutes further south. The number of voyages made these constant updatings possible and help us to understand the techniques employed in those days by cartographers to a great company.

Appendices

Glossary

Astrolabe
The nautical version is a circular or semi-circular instrument graduated in degrees. In use it is suspended from a ring in the meridian plane while a sight-bar, or alidade, is rotated to measure the height of a star above the horizon. (Discovered at the end of the fourteenth century)

Auxiliary-Latitude Scale (or Oblique Meridian)
A small latitude scale (some 15° at the most) parallel or oblique to the general latitude scale (*q.v.*) and conflicting with it in the graduation and value assigned to a degree. Such scales appear on some thirty charts between 1504 and the end of the seventeenth century; they were intended to correct errors in estimated latitude due to magnetic variation (*q.v.*).

Compass
A direction-finding instrument, consisting of a mobile magnetic needle pivoting on an axis above a compass rose (*q.v.*); the point of the needle indicates magnetic north. From the thirteenth century, the compass was encloses in a 'little box', whence its Italian name (*bossola*), from which the French term *boussole* is derived.

Compass Rose
A star with 8, 16 or 32 divisions—all or some of which are decorated—dividing the horizon into cardinal and collateral points. It appears on compass dials and on nautical charts from the Catalan Atlas (No. 8) onwards, i.e. from *c.* 1375.

For the sake of clarity, this term should be confined to this decorative feature. By extension it is also used for the circle of the horizon, divided by 8, 16 or 32 straight lines: the marine compass.

Distance Scale
A scale indicating the ratio by which real distances are reduced when represented on a given chart. On portolan charts it appears in graphic form as divisions whose value, in miles or leagues, was rarely provided before the sixteenth century.

Geographical Coordinates
The position of a point on the globe, defined by its latitude (the distance in degrees separating it from the equator) and its longitude (the distance in degrees separating it from a chosen prime meridian).

Latitude Scale
A line graduated in constant degrees, running north-south and most often bi-coloured, which appeared on Portuguese nautical charts around 1500 in the transitional period separating navigation by dead reckoning from astronomical navigation. The latitude scale is often accompanied by a drawing of the equator and of the two tropics of Cancer and Capricorn, and later of the polar circles.

Longitude Scale
A scale that appeared on Portuguese nautical charts in 1529 as an equator graduated in degrees. The longitude scale assumes that the value for a degree of longitude remains constant whatever its latitude. While this is not the case on a sphere, it is true on a nautical chart drawn according to Mercator's projection (*q.v.*).

Loxodrome
The curved portion of a spiralling line that cuts all the meridians at the same angle and heads towards the poles without ever reaching them. The Portuguese mathematician Pedro Nunes gave the same definition for the rhumb (*q.v.*) in 1537. On charts drawn on Mercator's projection (*q.v.* under projection), a loxodrome is shown as a straight line.

Magnetic Variation
At a given time and place, the angle between the direction of geographic north and that of magnetic north.

Marteloio (or *Martelogio*)
An Italian term of debatable origin and etymology found in the expression *toleta de marteloio* ('*marteloio* tables'). On its own the word *marteloio* indicates the visible framework of the portolan charts—a complex network of lines radiating both from the centre and the periphery of one or more circles that were delineated at first, but later assumed. These lines, called rhumb-lines (*q.v.* under rhumb) correspond to the directions, or winds, of the compass rose (*q.v.*): the black lines being the eight principal winds, the green lines the half-winds and the red lines the quarter-winds.

Marteloio tables are tables that accompany nautical atlases and charts from at least as early as the fourteenth century. By triangulation, using the triangles formed by the rhumb-lines (*q.v.*) of the framework, a sailor who had gone off course could reckon his position and correct his course.

Mercator's Projection: *See* under projection

'Mercator's Variable'
Another name for the waxing-latitude scale (*q.v.*).

Oblique Meridian
Another name for the auxiliary-latitude scale (*q.v.*).

Oikoumenê ('Inhabited Land')
A term used by the scholars of antiquity to describe the explored portion of the Temperate Zone, beyond which were the Torrid and Glacial Zones, supposedly devoid of human life.

Perpetual Calendar
A calendar placed at the head of atlases and nautical guides from the end of the fourteenth century, which classifies years by their 'golden number', i.e., by their position in the nineteen-year cycle of the phases of the moon. A simple scan provides the user with the dates of the new moon (which determine the tides) and those of the moveable religious feasts.

Portolan
Strictly speaking, a collection of written nautical instructions (*portolano*). By extension, the term is also used to designate the chart used in association with them: a sort of register of the ports along coasts, located by direction and distance. To avoid confusion the latter has been systematically called a portolan chart throughout this book.

Projection
A mathematical technique for representing all or part of a curved surface on a plane. It necessarily involves the distortion of one or several elements of the curved surface—length, angle or area. An equivalent projection is one in which the area is accurate; a conformal projection is one that retains accurate angles. Therefore nautical charts are preferably drawn on a conformal projection.

A portolan chart (*q.v.* under portolan) is a chart without an explicit projection, but its manner of construction by 'routes and distance' (see pp. 11–12) relates it to the conformal-projection chart.

A plane chart is a chart on a cylindrical projection. Meridians and parallels are shown by straight lines, perpendicular and equidistant to each other, the degrees of longitude and latitude having a constant value.

A 'reduced chart' is a chart on Mercator's projection: meridians and parallels are represented by perpendicular straight lines but, towards the poles, the value of a degree of latitude increases in order to maintain, at every point of intersection, the correct ratio between a degree of latitude and a degree of longitude — although the value of a degree of latitude actually diminishes as one approaches the poles.

Quadrant
An instrument serving the same purpose as the astrolabe (*q.v.*) but lighter and handier. It consists of a quadrant of a circle, whose convex part, or limb, is graduated into 90 degrees. The sights are attached on one side. At the top of the right angle formed by the two sides of the quadrant is fixed a plumb-line; in use the latter hangs free and indicates the height above the horizon of the star being sighted.

Rhumb
The angle (11°15′) equivalent to one of the 32 points of the compass; the term is also applied to the rhumb-lines that separate the compass points from each other. These lines are the main element of the *marteloio* (*q.v.*) and show directions.

The name rhumb network is given to the sum of the rhumb-lines contained within one of the circles of the *marteloio*.

Sounding
A measurement of the depth of water calculated in fathoms (= 6 feet) and shown on nautical charts from the end of the sixteenth century.

Terrestrial Magnetism
A field of force created on the surface of the earth by the movement of fluids at its core and acting like a magnet on the compass needle. This field varies in intensity and direction depending on where it is measured on the earth's surface (from the sixteenth century onwards, nautical charts occasionally point this out), and its distribution alters with time (the irregularities drift west by 1° of longitude every five years). Comparative measurements of this drift can sometimes be used to date anonymous documents.

Tide Table
A circular diagram that indicates, or enables the user to calculate, the times of the tides in a given port on every day of the lunar month, by indicating the position of the moon on the horizon at particular times. The first attested example of a tide table is found on the Catalan Atlas of *c.* 1375 (No. 8).

Waxing-Latitude Scale (or 'Mercator's Variable')
A latitude scale (*q.v.*) graduated in degrees of unequal value that increase progressively in length towards the poles so that the projection (*q.v.*) of the chart conforms to the sphericity of the earth. Constructed empirically by Mercator in 1569, the mathematical formula, or 'Mercator's variable', was expounded by Edward Wright in 1599.

Winds
From the times of ancient Greece, the winds have been used to personify the directions into which the horizon is divided. The names of the eight principal winds, inscribed on their corresponding rhumb-lines (*q.v.*) are shown on nautical charts on the periphery of the *marteloio* (*q.v.*). These winds are sometimes depicted as puffing faces and arranged in the same manner.

Zodiac
The area of the heavens in which the sun seems to move when viewed from the earth. From ancient times the zodiac was divided into twelve zones bearing the names of the nearest constellations, which are represented by signs. These signs of the zodiac, which divide the year into twelve months, appear on the calendars placed at the head of nautical atlases.

Genealogy of the Hydrographic Schools *by* Roger Hervé

(Rev. Hist. écon. soc., XLV, 1967)

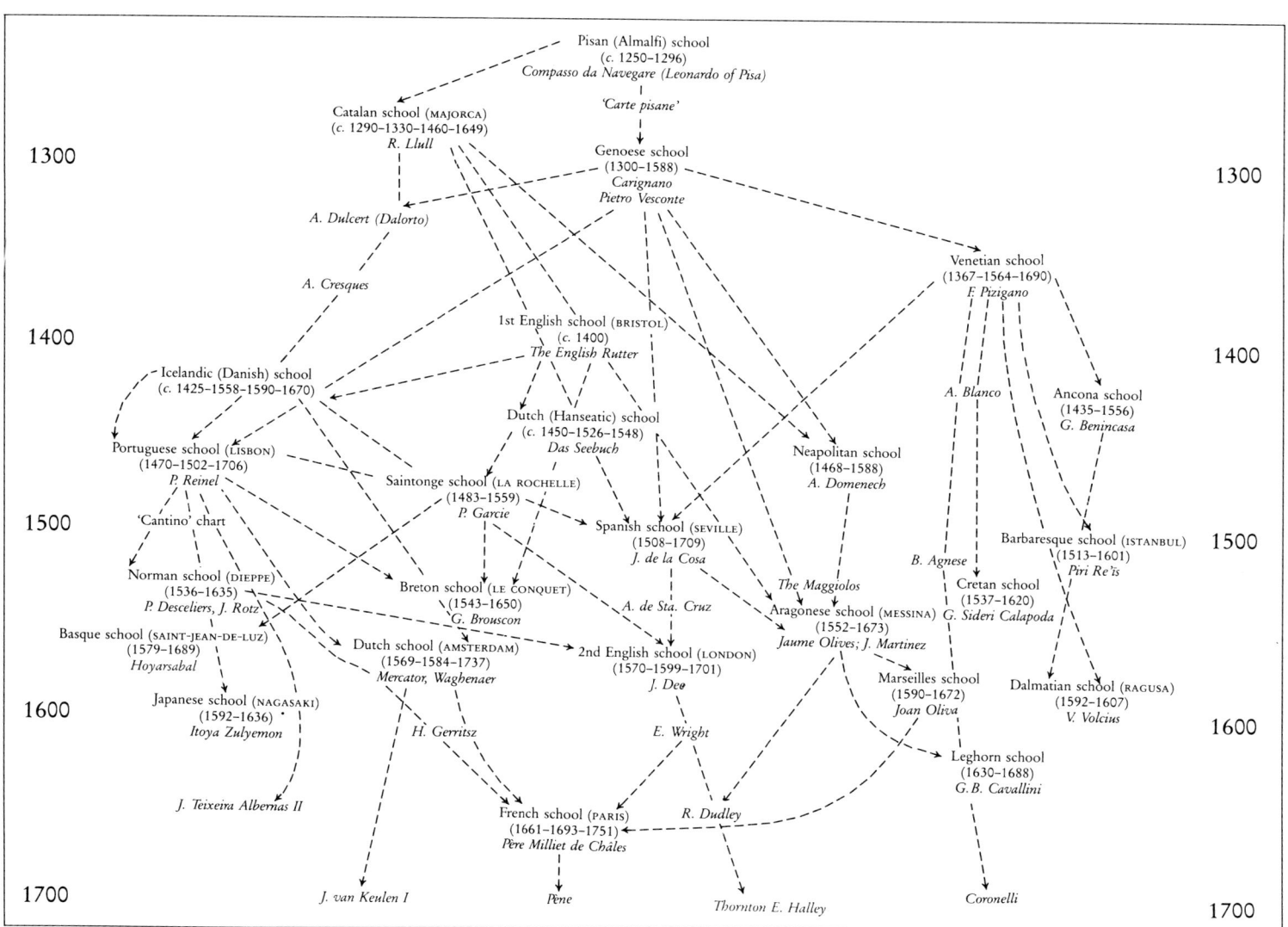

Classification of the Portolan Charts by Hydrographic Schools

Barbaresque school: 28, 35, 36
Basque school: 91, 97
Breton school: 42, 43, 44
Catalan school: 7, 8, 9, 12, 16, 17, 62, 64, 65, 68
Dutch school: 70, 75, 79, 87, 88, 96
English (Thames) school: 90, 93, 95, 98, 99, 100
French school (after 1660): 92
Genoese school: 1, 2-4, 5, 6, 21, 23, 24, 26, 41, 56
Greek (and Cretan) school: 57, 66
isolario: 13, 14
Japanese school: 72, 77
Marseilles school: 74, 83, 89
Norman school: 39, 40, 47, 48-51, 58, 60, 61, 67, 71, 78, 80, 84
Portuguese school: 25, 27, 29-34, 37, 38, 45, 52-54, 55, 59, 63, 73, 81, 82, 85, 86, 94
Saintonge school: 69
Spanish school: 22, 46
Venetian school: 10, 11, 15, 18, 19, 76

Acknowledgments

B.N. = Bibliothèque Nationale, Paris
I.R.H.T. = Institut de Recherche et d'Histoire des Textes
C.N.R.S. = Centre national de recherches scientifiques

The authors wish to thank the following people:

C. Astruc, curator-in-chief, Manuscript Department, B.N., Paris;
G. Astruc, I.R.H.T., Paris;
F. Avril, curator at the Manuscript Department, B.N., Paris;
L. Casanova, curator at the Biblioteca Correr, Venice;
C. Florentis, Monastery of Saint John the Evangelist, Patmos;
B. Flusin, I.R.H.T., Paris;
F. Garnier, I.R.H.T., Orléans;
P. Gras, honorary curator at the Public Library, Dijon;
R. Hervé, honorary curator at the B.N., Paris;
J. Irigoin, member of the Institute, professor at the Sorbonne (Paris IV);
A.D. Kominis, director of the University of Athens;
L. Lagarde, curator at the Department of Maps and Plans, B.N., Paris;
S. Lambert, assistant curator at the Musée de la Marine, Marseilles;
F. Lapadu-Hargues, curator at the Department of Maps and Plans, B.N., Paris;
M. Lassithiotakis, formerly of the Manuscript Department, B.N., Paris;
M. Manoussacas, director of the Istituto Ellenico di Studi Bizantini, Venice;
G. Parguez, curator-in-chief of the Municipal Library, Lyons;
M. Pastoureau, curator at the Department of Maps and Plans, B.N., Paris;
M. Pelletier, curator-in-chief of the Department of Maps and Plans, B.N., Paris;
A. Pierre, curator at the Department of Maps and Plans, B.N., Paris;
A. Ratti; Venice;
G. Romanelli, director of the Biblioteca Correr Venice;
M.F. Tiepolo, director of the Archivio di Stato, Venice;
C. Villain-Gandossi, *chargée de recherche* at the C.N.R.S.

Bibliography

Abbreviations

N.B. Only nouns are capitalized.

I.S.O. Standard International Abbreviations:

Act. geogr.	*Acta geographica*, Amsterdam
Act. Coloq. Hist. marit.	*Actes du ... Colloque international d'histoire maritime*, Paris
Act. Congr. nat. Soc. sav.	*Actes du ... Congrès national des Sociétés Savantes*, Paris
Amer. hist. Rev.	*American Historical Review (The)*
Amis Bibl. Lyon	*Amis de la Bibliothèque de Lyon*, Lyons
Ann. Econ. Soc. Civ.	*Annales. Economies. Sociétés. Civilisations*, Paris
Ann. Géogr.	*Annales de Géographie*, Paris
Arch. int. Hist. Sci.	*Archives internationales d'histoire des Sciences*, Paris
Arch. stor. per Dalmazia	*Archivio storico per la Dalmazia*, Rome
Atti Accad. naz. Lincei	*Atti della Accademia nazionale dei Lincei*, Rome
Atti Soc. ligure Stor. patria	*Atti della Societa ligure di storia patria*, Genoa
Bibliogr. Soc. amer. Papers	*Bibliographical Society of America Papers*
Bibl. Ec. Chartes	*Bibliothèque de l'Ecole des Chartes*, Paris
Bol. Soc. Geogr. Lisboa	*Boletim da Sociedad de geografia de Lisboa*, Lisbon
Bol. geral Col.	*Boletim geral des Colonias*, Lisbon
Boll. Mus. civic. veneziani	*Bolletino dei musei civici veneziani*, Venice
Boll. civic. It. colombiano	*Bolletino civico Istituto colombiano*, Genoa
Boll. reale Soc. geogr. ital.	*Bolletino della Reale Societa geografica italiana*, Rome
Bull. Géogr. hist. descript.	*Bulletin de géographie historique et descriptive*, Paris
Bull. Inst. hist. belge Rome	*Bulletin de l'Institut historique belge de Rome*, Rome
Bull. Sect. Géogr.	*Bulletin de la Section de Géographie*, Paris
Bull. Soc. archéol. Finistère	*Bulletin de la Société archéologique du Finistère*
Bull. Soc. Géogr.	*Bulletin de la Société de géographie*, Paris
Bull. hisp.	*Bulletin hispanique*
Cah. Inst. hautes Et. Amér. lat.	*Cahiers de l'Institut des hautes études de l'Amérique latine*, Paris
Can. Cartogr.	*Canadian Cartographer (The)*, Ottawa
Can. hist. Rev.	*Canadian Historical Review (The)*, Toronto
Centr. for East Asia cult. Stud.	*Center for East Asia Cultural Studies (The)*
Comm. Acad. Mar. Belgique	*Communications de l'Académie de Marine de Belgique*, Antwerp
C.R. Conf. African Ouest	*Compte rendu ... de la Conférence des Africanistes de l'Ouest*
C.R. Séanc. Soc. Géog.	*Comptes rendus des séances de la Société de Géographie*, Paris
Congr. Bibl. nord.	*Congrès des bibliothèques nordiques*, Rome
Congr. int. Sci. hist.	*Congrès international des sciences historiques*
Econ. Stor.	*Economia e storia*, Rome
Geog. J.	*Geographical Journal (The)*, London
I. M.	*Imago Mundi*, London
Mar. Mirror	*Mariner's Mirror*, London
Mém. Soc. royale Géogr. Egypte	*Mémoires de la Société royale de géographie d'Egypte*, Cairo
Pac. hist. Rev.	*Pacific Historical Review*
Rev. afr.	*Revue africaine*, Algiers
Rev. belge Philol. Hist.	*Revue belge de philologie et d'histoire*, Brussels

Rev. Hist. Col.	*Revue d'histoire des colonies*, Paris
Rev. Hist. écon. soc.	*Revue d'histoire économique et sociale*, Paris
Rev. Et. islam.	*Revue des études islamiques*
Rev. hist.	*Revue historique*, Paris
Riv. geogr. ital.	*Rivista geografica italiana*, Florence
Riv. maritt.	*Rivista marittima*, Rome
Scottish geogr. Mag.	*Scottish Geographical Magazine (The)*, Edinburgh

Other Abbreviations used in the Bibliography:

Agrup. Est. Cartogr. antiga	*Agrupamento de Estudios de Cartografia antiga*
Akad. Mar. Belgie Mededeelingen	Akademie der Marine van Belgie. Mededeelingen
Ann. Facolt. Lett. Filosof.	*Annali della Facolta di Lettere e Filosofia della Università di Cagliari*
Atti reale Accad. Peloritana	*Atti della reale Accademia Peloritana*
Berichte über die Verhandl. der Sachs. Akad. der Wiss. phil. histor. Klasse	*Berichte über die Verhandlungen der Sächsischen Akademie der Wissenschaft, philosophisch-historische Klasse*
Bijdrag. Taal. land. Volk.	*Bijdragen voor Taal-landen Volkenkunde*
Com. Trav. hist. sci.	Comité des Travaux Historiques et Scientifiques (C.T.H.S.)
Act. Congr. intern. Hist. Descobrim.	*Congresso internacional de Historia dos descobrimentos. Actas.*
Fac. Philos.	Faculté de philosphie et lettres
Quart. Journ. Current Acquis.	*Library of Congress: Quarterly Journal of Current Acquisitions*
Minist. Educ. y Ciencia	Ministerio de Education y Ciencia
Proc. Roy. Hist. Soc.	*Proceedings of the Royal Historical Society of Sydney*
Publ. of the Hispanic Soc. of America	Publications of the Hispanic Society of America
Rendic. Acc. naz. Lincei. Sci. mor. stor. filolog.	*Rendiconti della [reale] Accademia Nazionale dei Lincei. Classe di'Scienze morale storiche e filologiche*
Tijdschr. kon. Nederl. AardrK. Genoots.	*Tijdschrift van het Koninklijk Nederlandsch Aardrijkskundig Genootschap*
Union geog. intern. Commiss. Bibliogr. Cartes anc.	Union géographique internationale, Commission pour la Bibliographie des cartes anciennes
Verhand. Kon. Inst. Taal. land. Volk.	*Verhandelingen van het Koninklijk Instituut voor Taal-land-en Volkenkunde*
Zeitschr. Gesells. Erdk.	*Zeitschrift der Gesellschaft für Erdkunde zu Berlin*

Portolan Charts: General Works

Ailly, P. d'. *Imago Mundi*. 3 vols. Ed. by E. Buron. Paris, 1930. [Latin text with Fr. trans.].

'A la découverte de la Terre: Dix siècles de cartographie, Trésors du département des Cartes et Plans'. Exhibition Cat. Paris: Bibliothèque Nationale, 1979.

Alba, Duke of, ed. *Mapas espanoles de America siglos XV-XVII*. Madrid, 1951.

Almagia, R. 'Quelques questions au sujet des cartes nautiques et des portulans d'après des recherches récentes'. In *Arch. int. Hist. Sci.*, no. 1 (1947): 237–46.

–. 'Intorno ad alcune carte nautiche italiane conservate negli Stati Uniti'. In *Atti Accad. naz. Lincei* VII, nos 7–12 (1952).

–. *Monumenta Cartographica Vaticana*. Rome, 1944. [fol.].

Andrews, M.C. 'The British Isles in the Nautical Charts of the 14th and 15th Centuries'. In *Geogr. J.* LXVIII, 6 (London, 1926): 474–81.

–. 'Scotland in the Portolan Charts'. In *Scottish Geogr. Mag.* XLII (1926): 129–53; 193–213; 293–366.

Anthiaume, Abbé A. 'Les Cartes géographiques et principalement les cartes marines dans l'Antiquité et au Moyen Age'. In *Bull. géogr. hist. descript.* XXVI (Paris, 1912): 355–443.

Bägrow, L. and Skelton, R.A. *History of Cartography*. Cambridge, 1964.

Bellio, V. 'Alcune Osservazioni sulla cartografia medieval del mar Baltico'. In *Riv. geogr. ital.* XIV (1907): 449–75.

Björnbo, A. and Petersen, C.S. *Anecdota Cartographica Septentrionalis*, Haunia, 1908.

Björnbo, A. 'Cartographia Groenlandica'. In *Meddelelser öm Grønland* XLVIII (Copenhagen, 1912).

Broc, N. *La Géographie de la Renaissance (1420–1620)*. Paris, 1980.

Campbell, T. 'The Toponymy of Early Portolan Charts—A Neglected Key to their Understanding'. In *10th Conference on the History of Cartography*. Dublin, August, 1983.

'Cartes et figures de la Terre'. Exhibition cat. Paris: Centre Pompidou, C.C.I., 1980. [4°].

Catalogo de plantas e mapas da Cidada do Rio de Janeiro. Mapoteca, 1966.

Catalogue of the Manuscript Maps, Charts and Plans and the Topographical Drawings in the British Museum. Vol. III. London, 1861.

Casanova, L. 'Inventario dei Portolani e delle Carte nautiche del Museo Correr'. In *Boll. Mus. civic. veneziani* 3–4 (1957).

Champlain, S. de. *Voyages*. Paris 1613.

Clos-Arceduc, A. 'L'Enigme des portulans. Etude sur la projection et le mode de construction des cartes à rumbs du XIVe et du XVe s'. In *Bull. Sect. Géogr.* LXIX (Paris, 1956): 215–31.

Crone, G.R. 'Globe de Behaim'. In *Mappemondes A.D. 1200–1500*. Amsterdam, 1964 [With a detailed bibliography].

Davies, A. 'Behaim, Martellus and Colomb'. In *Geogr. J.* (London, 1977): 451–9.

Faleiro, F. *Tratado del esphera y del arte del marear, con el regimiento de las alturas...* Munich, 1915.

Fite, E. and Freeman, A. *A Book of Old Maps Delineating American History from the Earliest Days Down to the Close of the Revolutionary War...* New York, 1926–69 [fol.].

Foncin, M.; Destombes, M. and M. de. La Roncière. *Catalogue des cartes nautiques sur vélin conservées au Département des Cartes et Plans*. Paris: Bibliothèque Nationale, 1963.

Fournier, Père S.J., *Hydrographie*. Paris, 1643 and 1667. New ed. Grenoble, 1973.

Frabetti, P. *Carte nautiche italiane dal XIV al XVII secolo conservate in Emilia-Romagna*. Florence, 1978 [8°].

Ganong, W.E. *Crucial Maps in the Early Cartography and Place Nomenclature of the Atlantic Coast of Canada*. Toronto, 1964.

Gernez, D. 'Les Cartes avec échelles de latitude auxiliaire pour la région de Terre-Neuve'. In *Comm. Acad. Mar. Belgique* (Antwerp, 1952): 93–117.

–. 'Les Indications relatives aus marées dans les anciens livres de mer'. In *Arch. int. Hist. Sci.* 7 (Paris, 1949): 671–91.

Guillen y Tato, J.F. *Monumenta Cartographica Indiana*. 2 vols. Madrid. 1942.

Hamy, E.T. *Etudes historiques et géographiques*. Paris, 1896.

Hapgood, C.H. *Les Cartes des anciens rois des mers*. Monaco, 1981. [1st Eng. ed., 1966].

Harrisse, H. *Découverte et évolution cartographique de Terre-Neuve et des pays circonvoisins, 1497–1769*. Paris, 1900.

–. *The Discovery of North America, a Critical Documentary and Historic Investigation with an Essay on the Early Cartography of the New World*. Paris, 1892. [4°].

Hervé, R. 'Filiation des écoles hydrographiques'. In *Rev. Hist. écon. soc.* XLV, no. 1 (Paris, 1967). [With 1 inset table].

Hobbs, W.H. 'Zeno and the Cartography of Greenland'. In *I.M.* VI (1949): 15–19.

Howse, H.D. and Sanderson, M. *The Sea Chart*. Newton Abbot, 1973.

Howse, H.D., 'Some Early Tidal Diagrams'. In *4th International Reunion for the History of Nautical Science and Hydrography*. Sagres-Lagos, 4–7 July 1983.

Kamal, Y. *Monumenta Cartographica Africae et Aegypti*. 5 parts in 16 vols. Cairo, 1926–51. [See esp. Part IV: *Epoque des portulans et des déscouvertes*; large-fol.].

Kelley Jr., J.E. 'Non-Mediterranean Influences that Shaped the Atlantic in the Early Portolan Charts'. In *I.M.*, no. 31 (1979).

Kimble, G.H.T. *Geography in the Middle Ages*. London, 1938.

Kisch, G. *La Carte: Image des civilisations*. Paris, 1980. [Translated from Eng.]

Klemp, E. *America in Maps Dating from 1500 to 1856*. New York – London, 1976.

Koeman, C. 'The Chart Trade in Europe from its Origin to Modern Times'. In *Terrae Incognitae*, no. 12 (1980): 49–64.

Kretschmer, K. *Die italienischen Portolane des Mittelalters: Ein Beitrag zur Geschichte der Kartographie und Nautik*. Berlin, 1909. [4°].

Laguardia-Trias, R.A. *Estudio de Cartologia*. Madrid 1981. [leaflet, 8°].

Lane, F.C. 'The Economic Meaning of the Invention of the Compass'. In *Amer. hist. Rev.* LXVIII, no. 3 (1963).

La Roncière, C. de. 'Les Portulans de la Bibliothèque de Lyon'. In *Amis Bibl. Lyon* (1929). [4°].

–. *La Découverte de l'Afrique au Moyen Age: Cartographes et explorateurs*. 3 vols. In *Mém. Soc. royale Géogr. Egypte* V, VI and XIII. Cairo, 1925-7. [fol.]

–. 'Un inventaire de bord en 1294 et les origines de la navigation hauturière'. In *Bibl. Ec. Chartes* LVIII (1897): 1–16.

La Roncière, M. de. 'Les cartes marines de l'époque des Grandes Découvertes'. In *Rev. Hist. écon. soc.* XLV, no. 1 (Paris, 1967): 15–28.

Lynam. E. *The Carta Marina of Claus Magnus*. Jenkintown, 1949.

Marcel, G. *Choix de cartes et mappemondes des XIVe et XVe siècles*. Paris, 1896. [fol.].

–. *Récentes Acquisitions de cartes par la section géographique de la B.N.* Paris, 1897.

–. *Recueil de portulans*. Paris, 1886. [fol.].

–. *Reproductions de cartes et de globes relatifs à la découverte de l'Amérique du XVIe au XVIIIe siècle*. Paris, 1893. [in-fol.].

Mollat du Jourdin, M. and Habert, J. *Giovanni et Girolamo Verrazano, navigateurs de François Ier*. Paris, 1982. [Coll. 'Voyages et Découvertes'].

Nordenskiöld, A.E. *Periplus, An Essay on the Early History of Charts and Sailing Directions*... Stockholm, 1897. [fol.].

Nunn, G.E. *Origin of the Strait of Anian Concept*. Philadelphia, n.d.

Randles, W.G.L. *De la terre plate au globe terrestre: Une mutation épistémologique rapide 1480–1520*. Paris, 1980.

Ratti, A. 'La Carte geografiche di Candia del Museo civico Correr'. In *Boll. Mus. civic. veneziani* XXIV (1979): 89–91.

Raynaud-Nguyen, I. 'Découverte et représentation cartographique: le cas de l'Afrique de l'ouest aux XIIIe et XIVe siècles'. Sorbonne, Paris: Master's thesis, 1971.

Reparaz, G. de. 'Les Sciences géographiques et astronomiques au XIVe siècle dans le nord-est de la péninsule ibérique et leur origine. In *Arch. int. Hist. Sci.*, no. 3 (1948).

Ristow, W.W. and Skelton, R.A. *Nautical Charts on Vellum in the Library of Congress*. Washington, D.C., 1975.

Ritchie, G.S. *500 Years of Graphical and Symbolical Representation on Marine Charts*. Internal Hydrographic Organisation, 1975.

Rohr, H. *Die Entwicklung des Kartenbildes zwischen Kanal und Mittelmeer von den ältesten Weltkarten bis Mercator*. Leipzig, 1939.

Ruelens, C. *Les Monuments de la géographie des bibliothèques de Belgique*. Brussels, 1887.

Schück, A. *Der Kompass*. Part I: *46 Tafeln und Verzeichnis derselben*. Hamburg, 1911.

Sigurdsson, E.H. *Kortasaga Islands*. Reyjavik, 1971. [fol.].

Skelton, R.A., *Explorer's Maps*... London, 1958.

–; Marston, T.E. and G.D. Painter. *The Vinland Map and the Tartar Relation*. New Haven, 1965.

Spekke, A. 'A Brief Cartographic—Iconographic View of the Eastern Baltic Coast up to the 15th Century'. In *I.M.* V (1949).

Stevenson, E.L. *Portolan Charts. Their Origin and Characteristics with a Descriptive List of Those Belonging to the Hispanic Society of America*. New York, 1911.

Stylianou, A. *The Map of Crete and Cyprus in the 'Theatrum Orbis Terrarum' of Abraham Ortelius (1570): A Review of the Cartography of Crete up to this Time*. Athens, 1974.

Stylianou, A. and J. *The History of the Cartography of Cyprus*. Nicosia, 1980.

Taylor, E.G.R. *The Haven-Finding Art, a History of Navigation from Odysseus to Captain Cook*. 2nd ed. London, 1971.

–. *Mathematical Practitioners of Tudor and Stuart England Times*. London, 1954.

Teixeira da Mota, A. 'L'Art de naviguer en Méditerranée du XIIIe au XVIIe siècle et la création de la navigation astronomique dans les océans'. In *Act. IIe Colloq. Hist. marit.* (Paris, 1957/58): 127–56.

Teleki, P. *Atlas zur Geschichte der Kartographie der Japanischen Inseln*... Budapest-Leipzig, 1909. [large folio].

Vögel, W. 'Die Einführung des Kompasses in die nordwesteuropäische Nautik'. In *Acta Cartographica* XXIV (Amsterdam, 1976).

Washburn, W.E. 'Japan on Early European Maps'. In *Pac. hist. Rev.* XXI, no. 3 (1952): 221-36.

Waters, D.W. *The Art of Navigation in England in Elizabethan and Early Stuart Times.* London, 1958.

–. *The Rutters of the Sea. The Sailing Directions of Pierre Garcie: A Study of the 1st English and French Printed Sailing Directions.* New Haven-London, 1967.

Winter, H. 'The Changing Face of Scandinavia and the Baltic in Cartography up to 1532'. In *I.M.* XII (1955): 45-54.

–. 'The Origin of the Sea Chart'. In *I.M.* XIII (1956): 39-44.

–. 'The Pseudo-Labrador and the Oblique Meridian'. In *I.M.* II (1937): 61-73.

Hydrographic Schools

Mediterranean Cartographers

Afetinan, Dr. *Life and Works of the Turkish Admiral Piri Re'īs: The Oldest Map of America Drawn by Piri Re'īs.* Ankara, 1975, X-80 pp.

Akçura, Y. 'Carte de Piri Re'īs'. In *Turk Tariki Arastirma Kurumu Yayinlarinden*, no. 1 (Istanbul, 1935). [Text in Turkish, German, English, French].

Almagia, R. 'La Carta nautiche di Gabriel de Vallsecha (1489)'. in *Riv. maritt.* XLI (Rome, 1908): 93.

–. 'Il Mappamondo di Albertin da Virga'. In *Riv. geogr. ital.* XXI (Florence, 1914): 92-6.

Astruc, C. and Concasty, M.L. *Catalogue des manuscrits grecs de la Bibliothèque nationale.* Part 3: Vol. III. Paris, 1960.

Atlas catalan de Cresque Abraham (El): Primera edicion completa. Barcelona, 1975.

Atlas de Joan Martines 1587. Facsimile ed. Madrid: Ministry of Education and Science, 1973. [fol].

Braunlich, E. 'Zwei türkische Weltkarten aus dem Zeitalter der großen Entdeckungen'. In *Berichte über die Verhandl. der Sachs. Akad. Wiss. phil. histor. Klass.* LXXXIX, no. 1 (Leipzig, 1949), 29 pp.

Bruzzo, G. 'Di Grazioso Benincasa e del suo portolano (une lettera inedita)'. In *Riv. geogr. ital.* IV (Rome, 1897): 443-8.

Campana, A. 'Da Codici del Buondelmonte'. In *Studi Bizantini e Nevellenici* (Rome, 1957): 32-52.

Caraci, G. 'An Unknown Nautical Chart of Grazioso Benincasa 1468'. In *I.M.* VII (1950): 18-31.

–. 'Il Cartografo messinese Joan Martines e l'opera sua'. In *Atti della reale Accademia Peloritana.* (Messina, 1936).

–. 'Un altra carta di Albertin da Virga'. In *Boll. reale Soc. geogr. ital.* III, nos 10-11 (Rome, 1926): 781-6.

Cardonne. *Le Flambeau de la mer Méditerranée de Piri Re'īs.* Paris, 1765. [Transl. into French, B.N., Ms. français 22972].

Crino, S. 'Notizia sopra una carta da navigare di Vesconte Maggiolo che si conserva nella Bibliotheca Federiciana di Fano'. In *Boll. reale Soc. geogr. ital.* XLI (Rome, 1907).

Degenhart, B. and Schmitt, A. 'Marino Sanudo und Paolino Veneto'. In *Corpus der italienischen Zeichnungen 1300-1450.* Vol. II. Berlin, 1980.

Delatte, A. *Les Portulans grecs.* Liège: Fac. Philos., 1947.

Destombes, M. 'François Ollive et l'hydrographie marseillaise au XVIIe siècle'. In *Neptunia* (Paris, 1955): 1-4.

–. 'Cartes catalanes du XIVe siècle'. In *Union geog. intern. Commiss. Bibliogr. Cartes anc.* I (1952).

Emiliani, M. 'L'Arcipelago Dalmata nel portolano di Grazioso Benincasa (sec. XV)'. In *Arch. stor. per Dalmazia* XXII, no. 131 (Rome, 1937): 402-22.

–. Carta nautiche dei Benincasa—Cartografi anconitani. In *Boll. reale Soc. geogr. ital.* I (Rome, 1936).

Fall, Y.K. *L'Afrique à la naissance de la cartographie moderne (XIVe-XVe siècles: les cartes majorquines).* Paris, 1982.

Ferreto, A. 'I Cartografi Maggiolo oriundi di Rapallo'. In *Atti Soc. ligure Stor. patria* LII (1925): 53-83.

Friesleben, H.C. *Der katalanische Weltatlas vom Jahre 1375.* Stuttgart, 1977. [fol.]

Garand, M.C. 'La Tradition manuscrite du *Liber Archipelagi Insularum* à la Bibliothèque nationale'. In *Scriptorium* XXIX (1975): 69-76.

Grosjean, G. *Mapamundi: Der katalanische Weltatlas vom Jahre 1375.* Zürich, 1977. [fol.].

Guarnieri, G.G. *La Scuola Livornese di cartografia nautica.* Pisa, 1965.

Heawood, E. 'An Unplaced Atlas of Augustin Roussin'. In *Geogr. J.* LXVII, no. 1 (1931).

–. 'The Roussins as Chartmakers'. In *Geogr. J.* LXVII, no. 4 (1931).

Kahle, P. *Piri Re'īs, Bahrije...* 2 vols. Berlin, 1926.

Kimble, G.H. *The Catalan World Map of the Biblioteca Estense at Modena.* London: Royal Geographical Society, 1934.

Kretschmer, K.C.H. 'Die Atlanten des Battista Agnese'. In *Zeitschr. Gesells. Erdk.* XXXI (Berlin, 1896): 362-8.

Legrand, E. *Description des îles de l'Archipel par C. Buondelmonte...* Greek version. Paris, 1897. [large 8°].

–. *Bibliographie hellénique ou description raisonnée des ouvrages publiés en grec par des Grecs aux XVe, XVIe et XVIIe s.* n.p., 1885–6.

Macrymichalos, S.I. *Hellenes cartographoi to 16 ai (Greek Cartographers of the 16th Century).* Athens, 1964.

–. 'Ellenikoi Portolanoi tou 16 ou, 17 ou kai 18 ou aionos (Greek Portolans of the 16th, 17th and 18th Centuries)'. In *O eranistes,* nos 3–4; no. 5 (Athens, 1963): 127–55; 211 ff.

Magnaghi, A. 'Carte nautiche esistenti a Volterra'. In *Riv. geogr. ital.* IV, no. 1 (Florence, 1897): 34 ff.

Marcel, G. Note sur une carte catalane de Dulcert de 1339. In *C.R. Séanc. Soc. Géogr.* (Paris, 1887): 28–35.

Martin, L. 'A Manuscript Atlas by Battista Agnese'. In *Quart. Journ. Current Acquis.* I, no. 2 (Washington, D.C., 1944). Reprint 1972.

Motzo, B.R. 'Il Compasso da navigare, opera italiana della metà del secolo XIII'. In *Ann. Facolt. Lett. Filosof.* VII (Cagliari: University, 1947).

Oldham, R.D. 'Francesco Oliva the Younger'. In *Geog. J.* LXXVII (1931).

Oz, T. 'Turkish Maps in the Topkapu Saray Museum'. In *I.M.* VII (1949): 92.

Reparaz, G. de. 'L'Activité maritime et commerciale du royaume d'Aragon au XIIIe s. et son influence sur le développement de l'école cartographique de Majorque'. In *Bull. hisp.* XLIX (1947): 421–51.

Rey Pastor, J. and Garcia Camarero, E. *La Cartografia Mallorquina.* Madrid, 1960. [12°].

Skelton, R.A. 'The Cartographical Work of Grazioso Benincasa'. In *Geogr. J.* LXXXIX (1937): 291–2.

Soucek, S. 'A propos du livre d'instruction nautique de Piri Re'īs'. In *Rev. Et. islam.* 41 (1973): 241–55.

Stevenson, E.L. *Portolan atlas Joan Martines en Messina any 1582.* Publications of the Hispanic Society of America, No. 88.

Vogel-Gardthausen, *Die griechischen Schreiber des Mittelalters und der Renaissance.* Leipzig, 1909.

Wagner, H.R. 'Additions to the Manuscript Atlases of Battista Agnese'. In *I.M.* IV (1947): 28–30.

–. 'The Manuscript Atlases of Battista Agnese'. In *Bibliogr. Soc. amer. Papers* 25 (1931): 1–110.

Winter, H. 'Catalan Portolan Maps and their Place in the Total View of Cartographic Development'. In *I.M.* XII (1954): 1–13.

–. 'Petrus Roselli'. In *I.M.* IX (1952): 1–11.

–. 'A Late Portolan Chart at Madrid and Late Portolan Charts in General'. In *I.M.* VII (1950): 37–46.

Western Cartographers

Almagia, R. 'Una carta attributa a Cristofo Colombo'. In *Rendic. Accad. naz. Lincei Sci. morale stor. filolog.* I (Rome, 1925): 749–73, 6th series.

Anthiaume, A. *Evolution et enseignement de la science nautique en France et principalement chez les Normands.* 2 vols. Paris, 1920.

–. *Cartes marines, constructions navales, voyages de découvertes chez les Normands 1500–1650.* 2 vols., Paris, 1916.

–. 'Un pilote havrais au XVIe s., Guillaume Le Testu'. In *Bull. Géogr. hist. descript.,* nos 1–2 (Paris, 1911), 70 pp.

Black, J.D. *The Blathwayt Atlas.* Vol. 1: *Atlas;* Vol. II: *Commentary.* Providence, 1970–5.

Bourdon, L. 'André Homem, cartographe portugais en France'. In *Agrup. Est. Cartog. antiga* 79 (Coimbra, 1973).

Campbell, T. 'The Drapers' Company and its School of 17th-Century Chart-Makers'. In *My Head Is a Map: Essays and Memoirs in Honour of R. V. Tooley.* London, 1973, pp. 81–106.

Cootes, C.H. *Autotype Facsimiles of 3 Mappemondes of Desceliers with Introduction.* 1898.

Cortesão, A. *History of Portuguese Cartography.* Coimbra, 1969.

–. *The Nautical Chart of 1424 and the Early Discovery and Cartographical Representation of America...* Coimbra, 1954. [fol.].

–. *Cartografia e cartografos Portugueses dos seculos XV-XVI.* 2 vols., Lisbon, 1935. [4°].

–. and Teixeira da Mota, A. *Portugaliae Monumenta Cartographica.* 5 vols. Lisbon, 1960. [large folio and 1 vol. of tables, 4°].

Davies, A. 'The Date of Juan de la Cosa's World Map and its Implication for American Discovery'. In *Geogr. J.* III (1976): 111–16.

–. 'The "English Coats" on the Map of Juan de la Cosa'. In *I.M.* XIII (1956): 26–9.

Denucé, J. *Les Origines de la cartographie portugaise et les cartes des Reinel.* Gent. 1908.

Destombes, M. *Catalogue des cartes nautiques sur parchemin 1300–1700: Cartes hollandaises.* Saigon, 1941. [4°].

Deulin, G. 'La Cartographie portugaise à la Bibliothèque nationale de Paris'. In *Bol. geral. Col.* (Lisbon, 1939–40).

Dujardin, Dr. 'Guides nautiques et traités de navigation illustrés des "faiseurs" et "faiseuses" de cartes marines du Conquet au XVIe s'. In *Act. 87e Congr. nat. Soc. sav.* (Paris, 1968).

Dujardin-Troadec, L. *Les Cartographes bretons du Conquet, la navigation en images 1543–1650.* Brest, 1966.

Gaffarel, P. *Etude sur un portulan inédit de la Bibliothèque de Dijon*. 1876.

Gallois, L. 'La Cartographie du Moyen Age et la carte attribuée à Christophe Colomb'. In *Rev. hist.* CLIII (1926): 40–51.

–. 'Une nouvelle carte marine du XVIᵉ s., le portulan de Nicolas de Caverio'. In *Bull. Soc. Géogr.* (Lyons, 1890): 4 ff.

Gernez, D. 'Importance de l'oeuvre hydrographique et de l'oeuvre cartographique des Portuguais au XVᵉ et au XVIᵉ s'. In *Congresso Mundo Português*. Memorias III. Lisbon, 1940.

–. 'L'Influence portugaise sur la cartographie nautique néerlandaise du XVIᵉ s.'. In *Ann. Géogr.* 259 (1937): 1–9.

–. 'Quel procédé Mercator employa pour tracer le canevas de sa carte de 1569 à l'usage des marins'. In *Akad. Mar. Belgie Mededeelingen* I n.d., pp. 1–26.

Heidenreich, C.F. 'Exploration and Mapping of S. de Champlain 1603–1632'. In *Cartographica*, no. 17 (1976).

Hervé, R. *Découverte fortuite de l'Australie et de la Nouvelle-Zélande par des navigateurs portugais et espagnols entre 1521 et 1528*. Paris, 1982.

–. 'Le Résultat de la critique des cartes dieppoises et documents apparentés'. In *C.T.H.S.* (Paris, 1982). [See Appendix no. 1: 'Le planisphère de Brouscon 1543'].

–. 'Australia in French Geographical Documents of the Renaissance'. In *Proc. Roy. Hist. Soc.* (Sydney, 1955): 23–38.

Hotz, A. 'Cornelis Cornelisz Roobacker's sheepjournaal Gamron-Basra (1645)'. In *Tijdschr. kon. Nederl. AardrK. Genoots.* II, series XXIV (1907).

Kammerer, A. 'La Découverte de Madagascar par les Portugais et la cartographie de l'île'. In *Bol. Soc. Geogr. Lisboa* 67, nos 9–10 (1949).

–. 'La Découverte de la Chine par les Portugais au XVIᵉ s. et la cartographie des portulans'. In *T'oung Pao*, Suppl. to XXXIX (Leyden, 1944). [Large 8°].

–. 'La mer Rouge, l'Abyssinie et l'Arabie depuis l'Antiquité… au XVIIᵉs.' In *Mém. Soc. royale Géogr. Égypte* XV, XVI, XVII (Cairo, 1929–52). [In 7 vols., fol.].

Keuning, J. '16th Century Cartography in the Netherlands'. In *I.M.* IX (1952): 57 ff.

–. 'Hessel Gerritsz'. In *I.M.* IV (1947): 49–66.

Koeman, C. *Atlantes Neerlandici*. Vol. 4: *Celestial and Maritime Atlases*. Amsterdam, 1970.

–. *Lucas Janszoon Waghenauer, sa vie et son Spieghel der Zeevaerdt*. Lausanne, 1964. [4°].

–. [ed.] and Barents, W. *The Caertboek van de Midlandtsche Zee 1595*. Amsterdam, 1970.

Lang, A.W. *Seekarten der südlichen Nord- und Ostsee*. Hamburg, 1968.

–. 'Traces of Lost North European Sea Charts of the 15th Century'. In *I.M.* XII (1955): 31–44.

La Roncière, C. de. *La Carte de Christophe Colomb*. Paris, 1924.

–. 'Le Premier routier-pilote de Terre-Neuve 1579'. In *Bibl. Ec. Chartes* LXV (1904): 167–72.

La Roncière, M. de. 'Un document inédit de la V.O.C.: Une représentation cartographique de l'île de Ceylan en 1666'. In *Act. VIIIᵉ Colloq. Hist. marit.* (Beirut, 1966; Paris, 1970): 583–9.

–. 'Manuscript Charts by John Thornton Hydrographer of the East India Company (1699–1701)'. In *I.M.* XIX (1965): 44–50.

Marcel, G. 'Atlas Miller'. In *C.R. Séanc. Soc. Géogr.* (Paris, 1897): 384 ff.

Nunn, E. *The La Cosa Map and the Cabot Voyage*. Jenkintown, 1941.

–. *The Mappamonde of Juan de la Cosa: A Critical Investigation of its Date*. Jenkintown, 1934.

Piersantelli, G. 'La Pittura nella "Charte del navigare" del Cantino'. In *Boll. civi. Ist. colombiano* I, no. 2 (Genua, 1953).

Piot-Chape, R. 'Le Calcul des marées par les cartographes du Conquet aux XVIᵉ et XVIIᵉ s.' In *Bull. Soc. archéol. Finistère* CIII (1975): 121–5.

Revelli, P. 'Un cartografo genovese amico a Cristoforo Colombo: Nicolo Caveri (Nicolaus de Caverio)'. In *Rendic. Acc. naz. Lincei. Sci. mor. stor. filolog.* VIII (Rome, 1947): 449–58.

Robinson, A.H.W. *Marine Cartography in Britain*. Leicester, 1962. [4°].

Roukema, E. 'Some Remarks on the La Cosa Map'. In *I.M.* XVI (1959): 38–54.

Santarem, Viscount of 'A cerca da carta maritima dos Archivos de Dijon'. In *Estudios de Cartografia antiga* II (Lisbon, 1919): 118.

Schilder, G. 'Development and Achievements of Dutch Northern and Arctic Cartography in the 16th and 17th Centuries'. In *VIIᵉ Congr. Bibl. nord.* (1981).

–. 'The North Holland Cartographic School'. In *3rd International Reunion for the History of Nautical Science and Hydrography*. Greenwich, 1979.

–. *Australia Unveiled*. Amsterdam, 1976.

–. 'Organization and Evolution of the Dutch East India Company's Hydrographic Office in the 17th Century'. In *I.M.* 28 (1976): 72 ff.

Skelton, R.A. 'English Knowledge of the Portuguese Discoveries in the 15th Century: A New Document'. In *Act. Congr. intern. Hist. Descobrim.* II (1961): 365–74.

Smith, T.R. 'Manuscript and Printed Sea Charts in 17th-century London: The Case of the Thames School'. In Thrower, N.J.W. [Ed.]. *The Compleat*

Plattmaker: Essays on Chart, Map and Globe Making in England in the 17th and 18th Centuries. Berkeley, 1978, pp. 45–100. [4°].

Stevenson, E.L. *Marine World Chart of N. de Caverio, 1502.* New York, 1908.

Teixeira da Mota, A. 'Influence de la cartographie portugaise sur la cartographie européenne à l'époque des découvertes'. In *Act. Ve Colloq. Hist. marit.* (Lisbon, 1960; Paris, 1966): 223–48.

Vannereau, M.A. *Un épisode de la rivalité hollando-portugaise dans les Indes orientales: Macassar 1660.* Paris, [forthcoming].

Verner, C. and Skelton, R.A. *The English Pilot.* Amsterdam, 1967–73. [fol.] [Reprint of vols. 3–5 by Fischer, J. and W.; Thornton, J; Seller, J. and C. Price, n.p., 1689, 1701].

Vigneras, L.A. 'The Cartographer Diogo Ribeiro'. In *I.M.* XVI (1962): 76–83.

Wallis, H. *The Maps and Text of the* Boke of Idrography *presented by Jean Rotz to Henry VIII 1542.* Oxford, 1982.

Wieder, F.C. *Monumenta cartographica.* 5 vols. The Hague, 1925–33. [fol.]

–. *The Dutch Discovery and Mapping of Spitsbergen 1596–1829.* Amsterdam, 1919.

Japanese Cartographers

Nakamura, H. [ed.] *Monumenta Cartographica Japonica.* 2 vols. Tokyo, 1972.

–. 'The Japanese Portolanos of Portuguese Origin (16th–17th Century)'. In *I.M.* XVIII (1964): 24–44.

–. *East Asia in Old Maps.* Yokohama, 1962. [Résumé of the Japanese *History of the Mapping of Eastern Asia*].

–. 'Les Cartes du Japon qui servaient de modèle aux cartographes européens au début des relations de l'Occident avec le Japon'. *Monumenta Nipponica* II, no. 1 (1939).

General History

Albuquerque, L. de. 'O Tratado de Tordesillas e as difficuldades tecnicas da sua aplicação rigorosa'. In *Agrup. Est. Cartogr. antiga* LXXXIII (Coimbra, 1973).

Armstrong, T. 'In Search of a Sea-Route to Siberia 1553–1619'. In *VIIe Congr. Bibl. nord.* (Rome, 1981).

Aspetti e cause della decadenzia de Venezia nell secolo XVII. Venice and Rome, 1961.

Balard, M. *Gênes et l'Outre-Mer.* Vol. I: *Les actes de Caffa du notaire Lamberto di Sambuceto (1289–1290).* Paris and The Hague, 1973.

Barkham, S. 'The Basque Whaling Establishment in Labrador 1536–1603'. In *VIIe Congr. Bibl. nord.* (Rome, 1981).

–. 'The Identification of Labrador Ports in Spanish 16th Century Documents'. In *Can. Cartogr.* XIV (Ottowa, 1977).

Bevilacqua, F. *Storia della cultura veneta.* Vol. III: *Geografi e cosmografi.* Venice, 1980.

Boxer, C.R. *Jan Compagnie in War and Peace (1602–1799).* Hong Kong, 1979.

–. 'The Carreira da India, 1650–1750'. In *Mar. Mirror* (London, 1960): 35–55.

–. 'Francisco Vieira de Figueiredo, a Portuguese Merchant Adventurer in South-East Asia, 1624–1667'. In *Verhand. Kon. Inst. Taal. land. Volk.* 52 (1952). [In Dutch].

Braudel, F. *La Méditerranée et le monde méditerrané à l'époque de Philippe II.* 4th ed. Paris, 1979.

–. 'Les Espagnols et l'Afrique du Nord de 1492 à 1577'. In *Rev. afr.* (Algiers, 1928): 184–233; 351–428.

Chaudhuri, K.N. *The Trading World of Asia and the English East India Co. 1660–1760.* Cambridge, 1978.

Chaunu, P. *Les Amériques XVIe, XVIIe, XVIIIe s.* Paris, 1976.

–. *L'Expansion européenne du XIIIe au XVe s.* Paris, 1969.

Colomb [Columbus], Christopher. *Oeuvres.* Edited by A. Cioranescu. Paris, 1961.

Constantoudaki, M. 'Domenicos Theotocopoulos (El Greco) de Candie à Venise: Documents inédits (1566-1568)'. In *Thesaurismata* 12 (1975): 292–308.

Coolhaas, W.P. 'Outre-Mer néerlandais, chronique de l'histoire coloniale'. in *Rev. Hist. Col.* (Paris, 1957): 310–87.

Cornelius, F. *Creta Sacra sive de episcopis utriusque ritus graeci et latini in insula Cretae.* 2 vols. Venice, 1755.

Cumming, W.C.; Skelton, R.A. and Quinn, D.B. *La Découverte de l'Amérique du Nord.* Paris, 1972. [Trans. from English].

Dainville, F. De. *La Géographie des humanistes.* Paris, 1940; new ed. Geneva, 1964.

Dapper, O. *Description exacte des îles de l'Archipel.* Amsterdam, 1703.

Deshayes de Courmenin, L. *Voiage de Levant fait . . . en l'année 1621.* Paris, 1624.

Devisse, J. 'Commerce africain médiéval'. In *Rev. Hist. écon. soc.* (Paris, 1972).

Dufourcq, C.E. *L'Espagne catalane et le Maghreb aux XIIIe et XIVe s. (1212–1331).* Paris, 1966.

Grossi-Bianchi, L. and E. Poleggi. *Una Città portuale del Medioevo, Genova nei secoli X–XVI.* Genua, 1979.

Hamilton, A. *A New Account of the East Indies.* Edinburgh, 1727.

Julien, C.A. *Les Français en Amérique au XVIIe s.* Paris, 1976-7.

Klerck, E.S. de. *History of the Netherlands East Indies.* Rotterdam, 1938.

Koeman, C. [ed.] *Land- und Seekarten im Mittelalter und in der frühen Neuzeit.* Munich, 1980.

La Bretagne en 1665, d'après le rapport de Colbert de Croissy . . . J. Berenger, Jean Meyer . . . Brest: Centre de recherche bretonne et celtique, 1978.

Les Grandes Escales. Brussels, 1974.

Laguardia-Trias, R.A. 'El Predescubrimiento del Rio de la Plata'. In *Agrup. Est. Cartogr. antiga* 13 (Lisbon, 1973).

La Morandière, C. de. *Histoire de la pêche française de la morue dans l'Amérique septentrionale.* 3 vols. Paris, 1962-6.

La Roncière, C. de. *Histoire de la Marine française.* 6 vols. Paris, 1909-32.

Laroque, J. de. *Voyage de l'Arabie heureuse. . . .* Paris, 1715.

Léry, J. de. *Voyage fait en la terre de Brésil.* Ed. by P. Gaffarel. Paris, 1880; R. Mayeux. Paris, 1957; S. Delpech. Paris, 1980.

Lussagnet, S. *Les Français en Amérique pendant la 2e moitié du XVIe siècle.* Vol. I: *Le Brésil et les Brésiliens: Choix de textes et notes.* Vol. II: *La Floride. . . .* Paris, 1953-7.

Manuscrits enluminés d'origine espagnole VIIe-XVIIe s . . . Paris: Bibliothèque Nationale, 1982. [Under the direction of F. Avril].

Masson, P. *Histoire des établissements et du commerce français dans l'Afrique barbaresque 1560-1792.* Paris, 1903.

–. *Histoire du commerce français dans le Levant au XVIIe s.* Paris, 1896.

Mauny, R. *Tableau géographique de l'Ouest africain du Moyen Age. . . .* Dakar, 1961.

–. *Les Navigations médiévales sur les côtes sahariennes antérieures à la découverte portugaise.* Lisbon, 1960.

Mauro, F. *Le Brésil du XVe à la fin du XVIIIe s.* Paris, 1977.

–. *L'Expansion européenne (1600-1870).* Paris, 1967.

Methivier, H. 'Richelieu et le front de mer de Provence'. In *Rev. hist.* LXXXV (Paris, 1939).

Morison, S.E. *The European Discovery of America.* 2 vols. New York, 1971-3.

Needham, J. *Science and Civilisation in Ancient China.* 8 vols. [published]. Cambridge, 1954-76. Vol. III: *Mathematical and the Sciences of the Heaven and the Earth.* Cambridge, 1959.

Noiret, H. *Documents inédits pour servir à l'histoire de la Crète sous la domination vénitienne.* Paris, 1892.

Nystazopoulou Pelekidis, M. *Venise et la mer Noire du XIe au XVe s. Venezia e il levante fino al secolo XV.* Ed. by A. Pertusi. Vol. 1, part 2. Florence, 1973, pp. 541-82.

Papadopoulos, S.A. [ed] *The Greek Merchant Marine: 1453-1850.* Athens, 1972.

Picard, R.; Kerneis, J.P. and Bruneau, Y. *Les Compagnies des Indes, route de la porcelaine.* Paris, 1966.

Pulido Rubio, J. *El Piloto mayor de la Casa de la Contratación de Sevilla.* Seville, 1950.

Quinn, D.B. *America from Concept to Discovery: Early Exploration of North America.* 5 vols. London, 1979. [4°].

Rainaud, A. *Le Continent austral, hypothèse et découvertes.* Paris, 1893.

Randles, W.G.L. *L'Empire du Monomotapa du XVe au XIXe s.* Paris and The Hague, 1975.

Rich, E.E. *Hudson's Bay Co. (1670-1870).* Toronto, 1960.

Schouten, G. *Voyage de Gautier Schouten aux Indes orientales (1658-1665).* Rouen, 1775.

Thevet, A. *Les Singularitez de la France antarctique.* Ed. by P. Gaffarel. Paris, 1878; new ed. Paris, 1982.

Thiriet, F. *La Romanie vénitienne au Moyen Age.* Paris, 1972.

Van Dam Van Isselt, W.E. 'Maître Johann Van Dam et le châtiment de Makassar en 1660'. In *Bijdrag. Taal. land. Volk.* LX (1908): 1-44. [In Dutch].

Wright, J.K. *The Geographical Lore of the Time of the Crusades.* New York, 1925.

Photo Credits

Ingrid de Kalbermatten, working under the authors' instructions, was the photo documentalist for this book.

All the photographs reproduced in this book are the property of the Bibliothèque Nationale, Paris, with the exception of the following:

Dijon: Bibliothèque publique   Pl. 27 (photo: Minirel, Dijon)
Istanbul: Topkapi Sarayi   Pl. 28 (photo: Reha Günay, Istanbul)
Lisbon: Arquivo Nacional da Torre do Tombo   Pl. 59 (photo: Abilio Barata and Mario Soares, Lisbon)
London: British Library   Pls 39-40, 47
Lyons: Bibliothèque de la Ville   Pls 5-6, 10; page 12
Madrid: Biblioteca Nacional   Pls 64-5
–. Naval Musem   Pl. 22
Modena: Biblioteca Estense   Pl. 25; page 24 (photos: Roncaglia, Modena)
Nancy: Musée historique lorrain   page 22 (photo: Gilbert Mangin, Nancy)
San Marino, California: Henry E. Huntington Library and Art Gallery   Pl. 42
Tokyo: Tokyo National Museum   Pls 72, 77
Vatican: Biblioteca Apostolica Vaticana   Pl. 37; page 19
Venice: Biblioteca del Civico Museo Correr   page 14 (photo: Osvaldo Böhm, Venice)
Vincennes, Château of: Bibliothèque du Service historique de l'Armée de terre   Pls 48-51 (photos: Central Color, Paris)
Washington, D.C.: Library of Congress   Pl. 69

Index of Proper Names

Abreu, Antonio d'   221, 270
Adam, Guillaume   17
Adam, Canon   8
Agnese, Battista   28, 227, 237
Ailly, Pierre d' (Cardinal)   20, 21, 210, 211
Albuquerque, Alfonso d'   220, 221, 223
Alexander VI, Pope   20, 222
Alfonse de Saintonge: *see* Fonteneau, Jean
Alfonso V, King of Portugal   207
Alfonso X the Wise, King of Castile   13
Alfragan   210
Amazons   231, 240
Ambrosin, Charlat   26, 251, 252
Amundsen, Roald   256
Anaximander   8
Angiolo, Jacopo   20
Ango, Jean   30
Anne (Saint)   246
Annebaut, Claude d'   232
Anne of Brittany   228
Anthonisz, Cornelis   35, 248
Anville, Jean Baptiste Bourguignon d'   256
Araucanian Indians   235
Aristotle   234
Atkinson, James   267
Ayllon, Vasquez de   224

Bacon, Roger   16, 17
Baffin, William   256, 267
Balboa, Vasco Núñez de   253
Baldeia, Alfonso Gonzales   210
Bantus   220, 250
Barbara (Saint)   251
Barbié du Bocage, Jean-Denis   226
Barentsz, Willem   32, 249, 252, 256
Bar Sauma   17
Basques   256, 259, 265, 266, 270
Beatus de Liebana   9
Beccha (or Becaria): *see* Becharius
Becharius, Battista   208, 209
Becharius, Francesco   33, 209, 236
Bede, Venerable   8, 29
Behaim, Martin   23, 26, 210, 218
Bellandi, Simon d'Andrea   33
Benedict (Saint)   251
Benincasa, Grazioso   209, 210, 238
Bening, Alexandre   215

Bering, Vitus   260
Bernard de Chartres: *see* Silvestris, Bernard
Berry, Marie Caroline, Duchess de   257
Bianco, Andrea   210
Blaeu (family)   32, 261
Blaeu, John   269
Blaeu, Willem Janszoon   252, 253, 256, 262
Blathwayt   267
Bonifacio   200
Bordone, Benedetto   25
Borgia, Stefano (Cardinal)   223
Bouguereau, Maurice   35
Brendan (Saint)   205, 211
Briggs, Henry   253, 267
Brouscon, Guillaume   28, 228, 229, 230, 238
Bruni, Leonardo   21
Buondelmonte, Cristoforo   25, 206
Burston, John   264, 265, 271
Button, Thomas   256, 267

Cabot, John   31, 212, 224, 227
Cabot, Sebastian   27, 28, 223, 231, 232
Cabral, Pedro Álvares   215, 220, 221, 240
Cadamosto, Alvise da   210
Calbo (family)   237
Camden, William   31
Camocio, Francisco   248
Canistris, Opicinus de   18, 201
Cantino, Alberto   214
Cão, Diogo   211, 216, 231
Caribs   213
Carignano, Giovanni da   24, 25
Cartier, Jacques   28, 30, 228, 232, 233, 234, 246, 266
Casa da India   26, 32
Casa de Contratación   32, 223, 231, 242
Catherine de'Medicis   240
Caverio, Nicolaus de   28, 216, 217
Champlain, Samuel, Sieur de   30, 246, 247, 248, 249, 259, 266
Chancellor, Richard   235
Charles II, King of England   268
Charles V, King of France   34, 202, 205, 207

Charles V, King of Spain   223, 224, 250, 258
Chigi (family)   223
Christopher (Saint)   212
Chrysoloras, Emmanuel   20
Clavus, Claudius   23, 237
Coelho, Juan   220
Coen, Jan Pieterszoon   269
Colbert, Charles, Marquis de Croissy   267
Colbert, Jean-Baptiste   35
Coligny, Gaspard de (Admiral)   233, 234, 235, 240, 241
Collin, Pierre   266, 267
Colom, Arnold   262
Colom, Jacob Aertz   256
Colson, John   267
Columbus, Christopher   23, 26, 31, 210, 211, 212, 213, 215, 218, 219, 222
Columbus, Ferdinand   212, 231
Comberford, Nicolas   264
Comneno, Angelo   206
Cook, James   226, 234, 270
Cornaros (family)   203
Coronado, Francisco Vasquez de   253
Corte Real, Gaspard and Miguel   215, 216, 220, 222, 224, 227, 265
Cossé, Artus de, Marshal of France   228
Cossin, Jean   30
Costa, Francisco da   239
Cresques, Abraham   26, 202
Cresques, Jafuda   26
Crignon, Jean   226, 227
Cunha, Pero da   240
Cunha, Tristan de   220
Cunha, Vasco da   239

Dalorto, Angelino   201
Dalrymple, Alexander   226
Dam, Johan Van   262, 263
Datini, Francesco di Marco   33, 34
Davis, John   256, 267
Day, John   31, 212
Dee, John   31
Del Cano, Juan Sebastián   224
Desceliers, Pierre   30, 228, 232, 238, 235, 254
Deshayes de Courmenin, Louis   252

Desliens, Nicolas 28, 30, 228, 238
Detcheverry, Pierre 270
Dias, Bartolomeu 211, 216
Diaz de Solis, Juan 27
Diemen, Anthony Van 261
Doetsz, Cornelis 249
Domenico di Rossi (family) 235
Doncker, Hendrick 262
Drake, Francis 233, 253
Drapers' Company 31, 35, 264
Dulcert, Angelino 11, 15, 17, 25, 201, 205
Dürer, Albrecht 18

Eanes, Gil 210, 235
East India Company 255, 260, 264, 265, 268, 269, 271, 272, 273; see also Vereenigde Oost Indische Compagnie (V.O.C.)
Elisabeth I, Queen of England 31
Emo (family) 237
Eratosthenes 8
Este, Ercole d', Duke of Ferrara 214
Etchemins 247

Faleiro, Francesco 235
Ferdinand V the Catholic, King of Aragon and Castile 211, 215, 217
Fernandes, Valentim 220
Ferrer, Jacme 202, 205, 206
Fidalgo, Pedro 239
Fillastre, Guillaume 20, 21
Finé, Oronce 22
Fisher, William 267
Fitzhugh, Augustine 268, 269
Flamsteed, John 30
Fonteneau, Jean (called Alfonse de Saintonge) 30
Fournier, Père Georges 30
Fox, Luke 256
Francis I, King of France 26, 30, 219, 224, 226, 227, 249
Frémont d'Ablancourt, Jean de 268
Frobisher, Martin 255, 256, 267
Froes, Estevan 221

Gama, João da 260
Gama, Vasco da 216, 220, 223, 260
Garay, Francisco de 224
Garcie, Pierre (alias Ferrande) 30, 35
Gastaldi, Giacomo 243, 260
Gellibrand, Henry 247
Gerritsz, Hessel 32, 252, 253, 255, 256, 257
Gerritszoon, Martin 261
Gilbert, Sir Humphrey 31
Giroldis, Jacobus de 206, 207
Glockengiesser 210

Godefroy, Théodore 256
Gog 9
Gómez, Estevan 224
Gonçalves, Antão 210
Gonneville, Binot Paulmier de 30, 240
Gonzalo, Manoel 250
Goos, Abraham 249
Goos, Pieter 261, 262
Gossuin de Metz 10
Gramolin, Alvise di Nicolo 253, 254
Groseillers 268
Guérard, Jean 28, 30, 254, 255, 256, 257, 259
Guillaume de Conches 11
Guillaume de Nangis 16
Guise, Duke de 258
Gutierrez, Diego 231, 232

Hakluyt, Richard 31
Halgan, Admiral 270
Hall, James 256
Hamilton, Alexander 271, 272
Hamon, Pierre 239
Harley, Robert 30
Hassanudin, Sultan 262, 263
Hawkeridge, William 256
Hawkins, John 253
Henry of Mainz 11
Henry the Navigator 210, 219
Henry II, King of France 228, 229, 232
Henry IV, King of France 30, 247
Henry VII, King of England 212
Henry VIII, King of England 31, 226, 227
Herodotus 8
Hideyoshi, Shogun 250
Higden, Ranulph 18
Hojeda, Alonso de 213
Holzschuher, Georg 210
Homem, Andreas 32, 234, 235, 237
Homem, Diogo 234, 235, 237
Homem, Lopo 26, 28, 219, 234, 235, 237
Homer 232
Hondius, Jodocus 32
Honorius of Autun 11, 18
Houtman, Cornelis Van 269
Hoveden, Roger de 11
Hoyarsabal, Martin de 270
Hudson, Henry 32, 248, 256, 267
Hudson's Bay Company 268
Humboldt, Alexander von 213

Ibn Khaldūn 20
Idrīsī 205
Incas 227, 231, 249
Innocent III, Pope 9
Inter Coetera (bull) 241
Iroqois 247

Isabella of Castile 211
Isidore of Seville 8, 20, 202
James, Thomas 32, 256
Jansz, Harmen and Marten 32, 248, 249
Jews, Majorcan 205
John II, King of Portugal 26, 210, 223
John III, King of Portugal 27
Joseph (Saint) 251
Juan I, King of Portugal 202
Julius II, Pope

Kalperger 210
Kangxi, Emperor of China 227
Kempthorne, J. 273
Keulen, Johannes Van 262

La Cosa, Juan de 212, 213, 215
La Grand Maison, Monsieur de 260
Lambert de Saint Omer 11
Lancaster, Sir James 256
La Popelinière, Lancelot Voisin de 257
La Roque, Chevalier de 269
Las Casas, Bartolomeo de 212
Laurias (family) 207
La Vérendrye 266
La Villejegu 267
Lemaire, Jacob 228, 253, 257
Lemos, Pedro de 32, 242
Le Nautonier, Guillaume, Sieur de Castelfranc 247
Leonard (Saint) 251
Léry, Jean de 241
Le Testu, Guillaume 20, 30, 226, 228, 232, 233, 234, 238, 239, 240, 248
Levasseur, Guillaume 30, 228, 244, 245, 246
L'Hermitte, Jacques 253
Lily, George 31
Linschoten, Jan Huygen van 32, 240, 249
Lisboa, João de 221
Llull, Ramón 16, 25, 201
Loaysa 253
Lok, Michael 31
Lopes, Gregorio 219
Lopes, Sebastião 231, 242
Louis IX (Saint Louis), King of France 16, 198
Louis XIII, King of France 30, 252, 258, 259
Louis XIV, King of France 266, 267
Lozon, President de 254
Lynn, Nicholas de 242

Macrobius 8
Magellan, Fernão de 28, 210, 219, 223, 224, 227, 228, 243, 253

Maggiolo, Giacomo de 236, 237
Maggiolo, Vesconte de 236, 237, 246
Magnaghi 244
Magog 9
Mahu de Cordes 253
Mainstone, William 262
Malfante, Antonio 24
Manfred of Savoy 16
Manoel I, King of Portugal 27, 215, 219
Martellus Germanus, Henricus 210
Martines, Joan 241, 242, 243
Mason, John 32
Matilda, Empress 11
Mauro, Fra 17, 22, 26
Medina, Pedro de 35
Mela, Pomponius 8
Mercator, Gerard 21, 30, 31, 243, 244, 245, 255, 256, 257, 261, 262
Michiel (family) 237
Miller 219, 221, 222
Molineaux, Emeric 31
Montaigne, Michel Eyquem de 257
Montmorency, Grand Constable de 232
Montmorency, Henry II, Duke de 258
Monts, Pierre du Gua de 247, 249
More, Thomas 31
Mota, Antonio da 249
Münzer, Hieronymus 23

Navarro, Pedro 217
Niccoli 21
Nicolaï, Nicolas de 35
Nicolaus Germanus, Donnus 23, 236, 237
Nierop, Dirck Rembrandt Van 256
Noli, Antonio de 211
Noort, Olivier Van 253
Norden, John 31
Noronha, Fernando de 217
Nuytz, Peter 260

Olaus Magnus 237
Oliva/Oliva Riczo/Ollive (family) 26, 246, 252
Oliva, Bartolomeo 246
Oliva, Domenico 246
Oliva, Francesco 246
Oliva, Jaume 246
Oliva, Joan 246
Oliva, Salvatori 263
Ollive (family): see Oliva (family)
Ollive, François 26, 263
Order of Christ 219, 231
Order of San Stefano 16
Orellana, Francisco 231
Orosius, Paul 8

Orsini, Giordano (Cardinal) 25, 206
Ortelius, Abraham 32, 241, 242, 243, 244, 254, 257
Ovando, Nicolas de 222

Parat 270
Paris, Matthew 11
Parmentier, Jean and Raoul 226, 227, 234
Pasqualigo, Pietro 215
Paul de Saumur (Chevalier) 264
Pedreanes (called Le Français) 220
Pedro II, King of Portugal 268
Peixoto, Antonio 249
Pereira, Duarte Pacheco 26, 215
Pessagno 200
Philip I, King of Portugal 241
Philip II, King of Spain 32, 238, 240, 241, 242, 243
Philip III, King of Spain 250
Philip IV, King of Spain 258
Piccolomini 21
Pinzón, Vicente Yáñez 213, 215
Pius II, Pope 21
Pizarro, Francisco 224, 231, 258
Pizarro, Gonzalo 231
Pizigano, Zuane 25
Plancius, Petrus 242
Pliny 202, 234, 260
Polo, Marco 17, 210, 211, 232, 243, 259, 260
Ponce de León, Juan 222, 233
Pont Gravé 246
Ptolemy 8, 12, 13, 20, 21, 22, 209, 211, 217, 218, 219, 221, 227, 232, 235, 236, 237, 243, 260
Purchas, Samuel 32

Queirós, Pedro Fernandes de 260

Radisson 268
Raleigh, Sir Walter 31
Ravardière, Daniel de La Tousche, Sieur de 254
Ravasco, Laurenço 220
Razilly, Claude de 254, 255
Razilly, Francisco de 254, 255
Razilly, Isaac de 249
Reinel, Jorge 27, 219, 231
Reinel, Pedro 27, 28, 219, 231, 232, 266
Re'īs, Kemal 218
Re'īs, Piri 26, 218, 219, 222, 223
Ribault, Jean 239
Ribeiro, Diogo 27, 223, 224
Richard the Lion Heart, King of England 11
Richelieu, Cardinal Armand-Jean du Plessis, Duke de 26, 30, 35, 255, 257, 258, 259, 263
Roberval, Jean-François de la Rocque, Monsieur de 232, 233

Roiz, Pascal 251
Roobaker, Cornelis Cornelisz 272
Roselli, Petrus 208, 209
Rosselli, Francesco 237
Rotis, Denis de 265, 266, 270
Rotz (or Roze), Jean 30, 31, 226, 227, 231, 232, 234
Roussin, Augustin 26, 258, 259
Rovere (family) 223
Rubruek, William of 17

Sanches, Antonio 251
Sanches, Domingos 250, 251
Sand, George 207
Sanson, Nicolas 30, 35
Santa Cruz, Alonso de 13
Santarem, Viscount de 217, 218
Sanudo Torsello, Marino 24, 200
Savoy, Duke de 259
Saxon, Christopher 31
Schapenham, Geen Huyghen 253
Schedel, Hartmann 18
Schöner, Johann 23
Schouten, Willem Cornelisz 228, 253, 257, 260
Schouten, Wouter 262
Seller, John 267
Servet, Michel 21
Sideri, Georgio (called Calapoda) 237, 238, 244
Silvestris, Bernard 20
Smith, John 32, 248
Soleri, Guillemus 17, 202, 203
Soliman the Magnificent 223
Solinus, Caïus Julius 234
Solís, Juan de 221, 222
Soncino, Raimondo di 212
Sonetti, Bartolomeo 25
Souriquois 247
Sousa, Martim Afonso da 224, 241
Speed, John 31
Speelman, Admiral 263
Spilberghen, Joris Van 253
Stephen (Saint) 251
Strabo 8, 260
Strozzi, Philippe 21, 233, 240, 241
Sylvanus, Bernardus 23, 209

Tasman, Abel Janszoon 261, 262
Tatton, Gabriel 32
Teixeira Albernas I, João 257, 259, 260, 261, 268
Teixeira Albernas II, João 264, 268
Teutonic Order 237
Thales 8
Thévenot, Melchisédech 260
Thevet, André 233
Thornton, John 265, 267, 269, 271, 272, 273
Toledo, Don García de 238
Torres, Luis Váez de 261
Torsello, Marino Sanudo: see Sanudo Torsello, Marino

Toscanelli, Paolo   21, 210
Truytman, Johan   262, 263
Turco, Bartolomeo (alias Bartolomeo dalli Sonetti)   206

Unam sanctam (bull)   17
Urdaneta, Andrès de   244

Valbelle, Jean-Baptiste de   264
Vallard   30
Vallsecha, Gabriel de   207
Vau de Claye, Jacques de   30, 240
Vaulx, Jacques de   27, 249
Vaulx, Pierre de   30, 249
Vavassore, Giovanni Andrea di   35
Vaz Dourado, Fernão   239, 240
Velho, Bartholomeu   231
Vereenigde Oost Indische Compagnie (V.O.C.)   32, 252, 253, 261, 268; *see also* East India Company
Verrazano, Giovanni de   28, 30, 31, 224, 233, 240, 248, 257

Vesconte, Petrus   11, 12, 13, 15, 16, 24, 198, 199, 200, 201, 209
Vespucci, Amerigo   21, 22, 27, 213, 215, 217, 222
Viegas, Gaspar   224
Vieira, Francisco   263
Viladestes, Mecia de   17, 205
Vilanueva, Joaquin Lorenzo   205
Villalobos, Ruy López de   243
Villegagnon, Nicolas Durand de   240, 241
Vincent de Beauvais   17
Virga, Albertino de   204, 206
Virgil   15, 255
Vissher, Franchoys Jacob   261, 262
Vitry, Marshal de   258
Vivaldi, Ugolino and Vadino   17
Vourdopolos, Nicolas   244
Vrelant, Guillaume   215
Vrolicq   256, 259

Waghenaer, Lucas Janszoon   32, 248, 255

Waldseemüller, Martin   217
Waymouth, George   256
West Indische Compagnie (W.I.C.)   32, 255
White, John   31
Witt, G. F. de   260
Woldemar, Fred   262
Wolgemuth, Michael   18
Wright, Edward   31, 32, 244

Ximénez (Cardinal)   217

Yoyemon, Ikeda   250

Zaccaria, Benedetto   200
Zaltieri, Bolognino   260
Zeimoto, Francisco   249
Zeno, Antonio and Nicolo   256
Zhu Siben   17
Ziegler, Jacob   237

Geographic Index

Acadia   247, 249
Acre   11, 16, 198
Aden   220
Adige (river)   204
Adriatic Sea   20, 199, 207, 209, 236
Aegadian Islands   252
Aegean Sea   198, 199, 204, 213, 214, 253
Africa   18, 20, 24, 201, 202, 203, 205, 210, 211, 215, 216, 217, 218, 221, 224, 231, 232, 238, 242, 244, 246, 261
  North   248
Agadir   218
Agalega Islands   220
Aigues-Mortes   16, 198, 201, 207
Albania   213
Alexandria   207, 246, 250, 263
Algiers   263, 264
Alhucemas   217
Almeria   200, 204
Amazon (river)   221, 222, 240, 241, 242
Amboina   221
Ambre, Cape   220
America   20, 31, 203, 210, 212, 213, 214, 218, 223, 224, 227, 228, 231, 239, 242, 245, 249, 253, 255
  North   30, 32, 223, 233, 238, 239, 247, 249, 253, 259

  South   32, 224, 228, 231, 235, 239, 241, 249, 250, 257, 259
Amoy   272, 273
Amsterdam   32, 33, 35, 242, 248
  Nieuw: *see* New York
Anatolia   25, 217, 243, 254
Ancona   209
Andes (mountains)   258
Annam   250
Antarctic   228
Antillia (island)   210, 211, 218
Antikythera   213
Antilles   222; *see also* West Indies
Antipodes   257
Antongil Bay   220
Antwerp   31, 32, 207, 248
Aquileia   204
Arabia   202, 219, 220, 271
  Fertile   268
Aracan   260
Aragon (kingdom)   201, 202, 205, 207, 208
Ararat (Mount)   10
Archangel River   257
Arctic (region)   242
  Circle   267
  Ocean   32, 235, 248
  Sea   255, 256
Arnauti, Cape   243
Arques   28, 30, 232

Arquin   211
Ascension (island)   221
Asia   9, 20, 202, 205, 210, 212, 214, 217, 226, 227, 232, 238, 239, 242, 246, 253, 259, 260, 261
  Minor   214, 224
  Southeast   243, 250
Atlantic Ocean   13, 198, 199, 200, 201, 202, 203, 204, 206, 208, 209, 210, 211, 218, 219, 221, 222, 224, 226, 227, 229, 230, 231, 234, 236, 241, 244, 245, 246, 247, 248, 249, 250, 252, 255, 258, 267
  North   265
Atlas (mountains)   24, 201, 205, 214, 215, 235
Australia   33, 226, 227, 228, 234, 253, 260, 261, 262, 264
Austria-Hungary   263
Avignon   18, 201, 204, 208
Aynam   261
Ayuthia   250
Azores   202, 203, 211, 218, 219, 220, 231, 238, 240, 255
Azov, Sea of   199

Bab-el-Mandeb Strait   268
Babylon: *see* Cairo
Baffin Bay   255
Baffin Island   256, 267

Bahamas 222
Bahia 231, 240
Bahrein 220, 271
Balboa 222
Bali 221
Balkans 246
Baltic Sea 201, 205, 217, 237, 238, 248
Banda Islands 221, 269, 270, 271
Banda Naira 270
Bandar Abbas 271
Bangladesh 239
Bantam 264, 269, 271
Barcelona 25, 33, 34, 205, 246
Basle 21
Basra 272
Batavia 33, 253, 261, 262, 269
Bayonne 200
Beirut 247
Belle Ile 218
Bengal 239, 260, 261
   Bay of 219, 220
Benin 211
Bermuda 239
Biscay 209
   Bay of 256, 265
Black Sea 15, 198, 199, 204, 207, 208, 209, 211, 234, 235, 244, 246, 248
Blanc, Cape 210
Bojador, Cape 206, 210, 235, 258
Bolivia 258
Bologna 21
Bombay 216
Bon, Cape 15
Bonin Islands 244
Bordeaux 16, 229
Borgo 252
Borneo 240, 250, 253, 261, 269
Bosphorus 214
Bothnia, Gulf of 235, 237, 238
Bouda 205
Bougie 217, 258
Boulogne-sur-Mer 204
Bozcaada 223
Brabant 209
Brazil 30, 212, 213, 214, 215, 217, 218, 219, 221, 226, 231, 233, 235, 238, 240, 241, 242, 249, 254
Bréhat, Isle of 266, 267
Brenta (river) 204
Brest 228
Bristol 212, 224
   Channel 201, 247
Brittany 209, 267
Bruges 16, 198, 201
Burma 239, 260
Button Bay 259
Byzantium 208

Cadiz 212, 227
Caen 200, 230
Cagliari 252
Cairo 205, 207, 246
California 235, 253, 259
Callao 227
Cambodia 250, 261
Canada 228, 232, 233, 239, 246, 266
Canary Islands 201, 202, 203, 210, 218, 219, 236, 259
Canea 223
Cannanore 216
Canton: see Guangzhou
Cape of Good Hope 211, 212, 224, 248, 255, 260, 261, 264
Cape Horn 228
Cape Town 262
Cape Verde Islands 209, 210, 211, 212, 214, 218, 245, 249
Cape York (peninsula) 253, 262
Cardigan 209
Carolina, South 224
Caroline Islands 243
Cartagena 204
Casablanca 201
Caspian Sea 201
Castel Castre 16
Castile 214, 241
Cathay: see China
Cats, Cape of the 243
Celebes 253
Cephalonia 213
Ceram 221
Ceuta 201, 211, 217, 223
Ceylon 216, 220, 239, 261, 262
Chalcidice 214
Channel, English 229
Channel Islands 267
Chidley, Cape 267
Chile 235, 241
China 210, 220, 222, 224, 226, 235, 239, 240, 242, 248, 250, 253, 255, 259, 266, 272, 273
   Great Wall of 259, 261
   Sea 227, 239, 272
Chios 199, 206
Chittagong 260
Cipangu: see Japan
Cochin 250
Cocos Island 258
Cologne 208, 209, 211
Comorin, Cape 239
Comoro Islands 220
Concepción Bay 241
Conchinchina 261
Congo (region) 242, 250
   (river) 211, 231
Constantinople 199, 208, 214, 252
Copenhagen 229, 248
Corfu 206, 213
Corinth, Gulf of 214
Corsica 13
Corunna 224
Corvo 220

Crete 26, 198, 199, 214, 223, 238, 254
Crotone 199
Cuba 212, 213, 215, 222
Cyclades 206, 213
Cyprus 27, 224, 243

Damascus 207
Danube (river) 199, 207
Dardanelles 218, 223
Darien, Gulf of 222
Davis Strait 227, 259, 267
Denmark 200, 209, 236, 237, 255
Deshima 261
Desolation, Cape 267
Dieppe 28, 226, 232, 233, 240, 254, 255, 256
Dijon 26
Diogo, Bay of 226
Diu 260
Djerba 238
Dnieper (river) 199, 207
Don (river) 199
Dordrecht 200
Draa (valley) 205
Dresden 28

East Indies 219, 220, 221, 224, 226, 239, 240, 242, 271
Ebstorf 9, 10, 11
Ecuador 258
Edam 32
Egypt 205, 207, 218, 250, 263
Elbe (river) 209
Eldorado 231
Elmina 211, 212, 214, 215, 217, 231, 242
Enckhuysen 32, 248
England 198, 200, 201, 207, 209, 210, 211, 218, 230, 243, 255
   New 247, 248
Enkhuysen: see Enckhuysen
Epirus 206
Equator 212, 234, 241, 243
Ethiopia 232
Etna (Mount) 252
Euboea 199, 213, 254
Euphrates (river) 9, 272
Europe 18, 32, 200, 201, 202, 205, 206, 209, 210, 211, 214, 221, 222, 224, 227, 235, 236, 238, 242, 243, 246, 255, 256
   Western 234

Faial 220
Falkland Islands 34
Famagusta 243
Fernando de Noronha (island) 221
Ferrara 204
Fes 263
Fiji 261
Finistere, Cape 200

Finland 236
   Gulf of 235, 237, 238
Flanders 200, 201, 204, 207, 236
Florence 20, 21, 206
Flores 220, 226
Florida 210, 215, 221, 222, 224, 232, 233, 238, 239
Formigas Rocks 203
Formosa 240, 250, 260, 261, 272
Fort Coligny 240, 241
Fortune 227
France 17, 200, 202, 203, 204, 218, 226, 230, 254, 258, 263
   New 232, 233, 247, 248
Fréjus 204
Frisian Islands 209
Frobisher Bay 256, 267
Fuenterrabia 209
Fundy, Bay of 247

Gabes, Gulf of 207
Gaeta 199
Galapagos 258
Gallipoli 218
Ganabara: *see* Rio de Janeiro
Ganges (river) 9, 220, 260
Gardafui, Cape 220
Genoa 198, 199, 200, 204, 208, 211, 217, 218, 236, 237, 244, 246, 253, 263, 264
Gerakounia 199
Ghana 214
Gibraltar 16, 17, 18, 27, 198, 210, 223, 244, 255
   Strait of 224
Gironde (river) 204, 247, 255
Goa 239, 240, 260
'Golden Chersonesus' 22
Golgotha 242
Granada 208, 211, 212, 217
Grand Banks 227, 231
Great Lakes 259
Greece 204, 213, 214
Greenland 212, 215, 220, 227, 236, 237, 266, 267
Groningen 258
Guadalete (river) 212
Guadeloupe 213
Guangzhou 224, 239, 253
Guinea 211, 214, 215, 218, 226, 250
   Gulf of 211, 231
   New 253, 259, 260, 261
Guli-Guli 221
Guyana 213

Haiphong 250
Haiti 212, 213, 218, 222
Hangzhou 239, 243
Hanover 9
Hebrides 229
Heligoland 209
Hereford 11

Hokkaido 239, 260, 261
Holar 211
Holland 209, 255
   New 261
Hondo 261
Honduras 222
Honfleur 30, 240
Honshu 239
Hormuz 220, 260, 271
   Strait of 271
Hudson Bay 259, 268
Hudson Strait 227, 256, 267
Hull 200
Humber (river) 209
Hungary 246

Iceland 205, 211, 212, 227, 236, 237, 249, 255
IJssel (river) 209
India 32, 216, 219, 220, 226, 234, 260
Indian Ocean 10, 17, 22, 216, 218, 219, 220, 249, 250, 259, 261, 262, 264, 265
Indies 210, 214, 216, 260; *see also* East Indies, West Indies
Indonesia 253
Ionian Islands 206, 213
Ionian Sea 25
Ireland 200, 201, 209, 212, 220, 238, 243, 259
Istanbul 218
Italy 17, 199, 252

Jakarta: *see* Batavia
Jamaica 222, 224
Japan 33, 210, 216, 218, 222, 232, 235, 239, 240, 242, 243, 249, 250, 253, 254, 255, 259, 260, 261
Jask 271
Java 30, 221, 226, 232, 234, 238, 239, 244, 261, 262, 264
'Java Major': *see* Java
Jerusalem 8, 9, 10, 207, 217, 242, 263
Jiulong Jiang (river) 272, 273
Jutland 209, 236

Kanem 205
Karamania 243
Kea 213
Kegro, Cape of 257
Kharg 271, 272
Kildyn, Isle of 257
Kola River 257
Kong 271
Korea 250, 253, 260
Kyoto 250
Kythera 213
Kyushu 239, 250

Labrador 223, 224, 227, 234, 238, 256, 259, 265, 266, 267

Laccadive 220
La Hève, Cape 247
Lancaster 209
Land's End 200
Laplang 256, 257
Lark (island) 271
La Rochelle 16, 30
Lawrence, Isle of Saint 216, 220
Lebanon (Mount) 243
Le Conquet 28, 228, 229
Leeward Islands 222
Leghorn 237
Le Havre 35, 229, 233, 247
Leiden 248
Lek 209
Lemaire Strait 228
Lesbos 223
Le Tréport 255
Libourne 229
Lima 231, 249, 250
Limpapo 268
Lisbon 32, 200, 209, 210, 212, 214, 215, 217, 219, 224, 235, 260
Liverpool 209
Loire (river) 255
London 11, 16, 35, 201, 226, 248
   Tower of 264
Lopez, Cape 216
Lough Corrib 200, 207, 209
Louvain 211
Lübeck 237, 248
Lumborsk, Bay of 257
Luzon 239, 240, 243
Lyons 21

Macao 239, 240, 272
Macassar (kingdom) 262, 271
Macedonia 254
Madagascar 216, 219, 220, 235, 262, 264
Madeira 202, 203, 211, 218, 238, 241
Magellan, Strait of 223, 224, 228, 255
Maghreb 17, 25, 204, 205, 217, 252, 258
Majorca 24, 25, 201, 205, 207, 208, 209, 236
Major Sea 199, 204
Malacca 216, 220, 239, 250, 261
Malaga 209
Malaya 235
Malaysia 220, 227, 264, 265
Maldive Islands 220
Mali 201
Malta 241, 251, 252
Malvinas 34; *see also* Falkland Islands
Manfredonia 16
Manila 250
Maracaibo, Bay of 213
Maranhão 254
Mariana Islands 243, 244, 253, 260

Marmara, Sea of   15, 223, 254
Marrakech   208, 218
Marsdiep   209
Marseilles   11, 13, 237, 246, 251, 252, 263
Martim Afonso da Sousa River   222
Martinique   213
Martin Vaz (island)   221
Massachusetts   247, 248
Mastikhochoria   206
Mauritius   220, 262, 264
Mecca   10, 202, 217, 220
Mechlin   207
Medina   10
Mediterranean Sea   8, 13, 15, 16, 18, 20, 22, 25, 198, 199, 200, 201, 202, 203, 204, 206, 207, 208, 209, 211, 218, 219, 223, 234, 235, 236, 237, 244, 246, 248, 251, 252, 258, 263
Melinde   216
Melos   213
Meray, Cape   267
Mers el Kebir   204
Mesopotamia   201
Messina   34, 199, 252
Methoni   214
Mexico   233, 244
  Gulf of   221, 222, 249
Milford Haven   209
Mindanao   243
Mocha   268, 269
Mogadishu   220
Moldavia   207
Molucca Islands   219, 220, 221, 224, 232, 238, 239, 250, 253, 269, 270, 271
Molucca Sea   234
Mombasa   260
Monomotapa, Empire of   250, 268
Montreal   228
Morocco   217, 238, 244, 263
Moulouya   204
Mozambique   260, 262
Murmansk   257
Muros   229
Muscat   220, 260, 271
Mytilene   199, 223

Nagasaki   240, 250
  Bay   261
Nanao Dao   239
Nantes   16, 229
Naples   199, 252, 263
New Britain   267
New Forest   226
Newfoundland   30, 31, 214, 215, 221, 222, 224, 227, 228, 231, 232, 233, 234, 238, 242, 249, 265, 266, 270
New York   259
New Zealand   261

Nicaragua   222
Nicosia   243
Niger (river)   24, 205
Nile (river)   9, 24, 205, 207, 224
Nombre de Dios   227
Normandy   255
North Sea   200, 208, 209, 229, 246, 248
Northeast Passage   237, 239, 242, 248, 257
Northwest Passage   30, 31, 220, 224, 227, 239, 242, 253, 255, 256, 266, 267
Norumbega (river)   247, 248
Norway   201, 211, 222, 236, 238, 256
Nova Scotia   222
Novaya Zemlya   259
Nubia   205
Nunarssuit (island)   267
Nuremberg   210

Ob River   257
Ofran   206
Olympus (Mount)   243
Oman   220
  Gulf of   271
Oran   217
Orinoco (river)   259
Ottawa   232
Ottoman Empire   263
Otranto (canal)   199

Pacific Ocean   32, 210, 224, 234, 239, 241, 252, 253, 260, 261
Padua   204
Palawan Islands   240
Palermo   252
Palma   25
Panama, isthmus of   227
Paria, Gulf of   213
Paris   35, 211, 212, 226
Pearl Coast   213
Pearl River   239
Pegu   260
Peloponnese (peninsula)   213, 214
Persia   201, 261, 271
Persian Gulf   216, 218, 219, 220, 260, 261, 271
Peru   227, 231, 233, 238, 249, 253, 257, 258
Philippines   242, 243, 250, 253, 259, 260
Phnom Penh   250
Piave (river)   204
Pico   220
Pisa   16
Placentia   227, 270
Plate, River   224, 226, 238, 241, 242
Plymouth   229
Pointe de Grave   200, 209
Poland   207, 237

Pole:
  North   227
  South   223, 234
Pontorson   255
Poopó   242
Portovenere (bay)   199
Port Royal   247, 259
Portsmouth   229
Portugal   200, 201, 203, 209, 214, 216, 218, 221, 224, 227, 236, 244
Potosí   258
Principe   211
Puerto Rico   222
Pyrenees (mountains)   235

Qatar (peninsula)   271
Qeshm (island)   271
Quanzhou   239
Quebec   238, 246, 259
Quito   231, 250

Ragusa   246
Ravenna   204
Red Bay   265
Red Sea   24, 25, 201, 211, 212, 216, 217, 218, 247, 254, 260, 268, 269
Réunion   220
Rhine (river)   200, 209
Rhodes   199, 206, 214
Rhodesia   268
Rhone (river)   207, 208
Ribe   210
Rijeka   236
Rio de Janeiro   217, 240, 241
Rome   18, 20, 21, 209
Rouen   16, 229, 240
Roxo, Cape   210
Russia   237, 256, 257
Ryukyu Islands   235

Saguenay   228
Sahara   24, 205, 211
Saint Angelo, Castle of   206
Saint Augustine:
  Bay   262
  Cape   239
Saint-Brieuc   230
St. George's Channel   225
Saint Helena   221
Saint Lawrence (river)   232, 233, 234, 238, 246, 247, 259
Saint-Malo   200, 234, 240
Saint Mary   227
Saint-Mathieu, Abbey of   228
Saint Nazaire   200, 226
Saint-Sever   9
Saint Vincent, Cape   200
Sakai   250
Salerno   199
Salomon Islands   253
Samoa   253

Samson, Islands of: *see* Falkland Islands
San Domingo   224
Sandwich   201
Sanlucár de Barrameda   227
Santa Fe   211
Santa Maria   203, 212, 219
Santiago   235
Santiago de Compostela   208, 211
São Jorge   220
São Jorge da Mina   214; *see also* Elmina
São Miguel   220
São Pedro   226
Saragossa   224
Sardinia   13, 16, 251, 252
Savoy   263
Scandinavia   236
Scotland   200, 201, 209, 243, 255
Segorbe   205
Senegal   205
Senegambia   211
Seven Cities, Isles of the   31, 211; *see also* Antillia
Seville   32, 200, 204, 211, 223, 227, 231
Seychelles   220
Shantou: *see* Swatow
Shikoku   239
Siam   239, 250, 261, 265
   Gulf of   220
Sicily   11, 13, 15, 204, 205, 244, 251, 252
Sidjilmassa   205
Sidra, Gulf of   207, 264
Sierra Leone   215
Sierra Nevada   208
Sinai (Mount)   202, 208, 238
Singapur   221
Skagen, Cape   209
Skalholt   211
'Skerki Bank'   15
Socotra   17, 260
Sofala   260
Solway Firth (river)   209
Sousa, Martim Afonso da, River: *see* Martim Afonso da Sousa River
Southampton   16, 201, 226
Spain   200, 203, 207, 208, 209, 211, 214, 223, 227, 229, 236, 246, 258, 263
Spice Islands   224, 255
Spitsbergen   249, 255, 256, 259
Staten Island   228

Strasbourg   21
Sudan   205, 206
Sumatra   216, 219, 220, 221, 224, 226, 227, 228, 234, 239, 243, 261, 264, 269, 271
Sunda Islands   221, 226, 234, 259
   Strait   260, 262
Swatow   239
Sweden   237
Syria   202, 243, 252
Syrtes   13
Syrtes Major: *see* Sidra, Gulf of
Syrtes Minor: *see* Gabes, Gulf of

Tabelbalat   205
Tadoussac   259
Tafilalet   201
Tagus   235
Taiwan: *see* Formosa
Tamentit   205
Tana, Sea of   199, 207
Tanegashima   249, 250
Tartary   232
Tasmania   33, 261, 262
Tay (river)   201
Tenedos   223
Termisen   263
Terracina (bay)   199
Thessaly   213
Thames (river)   209
Thrace   254
Thule   212
Tierra del Fuego   228, 238, 253, 257, 259
Tigris (river)   9, 272
Timbuktu   205
Timor   226, 234
Titicaca, Lake   242
Tlemcen   207
Toledo   13
Tonga   253, 261
Tonkin   250
   Gulf of   221
Tordesillas   223
Touat   24
Toulon   258, 263
Tourane   250
Trapani   252
Trebizond   207
Treviso   204
Trinidad   221, 222, 231
Tripoli   263, 264
Troy   254
Tuamotus   253

Tunis   16, 198, 209, 263
   Gulf of   251
Tunisia   15, 252
Tyrrhenian Sea   16, 199

Ugento   199
Ulm   21
Ungava Bay   267
Ural (mountains)   237
Ursinio   206
Ushant, Isle of   204, 255
Üsküdar   214

Val de Cristo   205
Valencia   25, 204
Vannes   267
Varanger (peninsula)   257
Vecht   209
Velopoula   199
Venezuela   213
Venice   17, 23, 25, 28, 200, 203, 204, 207, 209, 210, 211, 214, 215, 217, 218, 227, 238, 244, 246, 252, 253, 254
Vicenza   21
Vicina   207
Vietnam   221
Virginia   210, 255, 266
Vitré   267
Vohemar   220
Volga (river)   201
Volos, Gulf of   213
Vyborg   237

Walachia   236
Warder   32
West Indies   212, 213, 215, 218, 221, 239, 249
White Sea   256
Windward Islands   222

Xiamen: *see* Amoy

Yamal (peninsula)   256
Yarmouth   218
Yemen   261
Yeso   261
Yucatán   222

Zambesi (river)   268
Zante   213
Zeeland   207, 209
Zimbabwe: *see* Rhodesia
Zuider Zee   209, 248

This book was printed in August 1984 by
Imprimeries Réunies S.A., Lausanne.
Setting: Typobauer Filmsatz GmbH, Scharnhausen,
   West Germany.
Photolithography (colour): Eurocrom 4, Treviso, Italy;
   (black and white): Atesa-Argraf S.A. Geneva.
Binding: Burkhardt AG, Zürich.
Editorial: Barbara Perroud-Benson.
Design and production: Franz Stadelmann.

Printed and bound in Switzerland

Blackwell's
Oxford
20 Oct 86
£38